THE CLERGY OF THE CHURCH OF IRELAND

The Clergy of the Church of Ireland

1000–2000

Messengers, Watchmen and Stewards

T.C. Barnard and W.G. Neely

EDITORS

FOUR COURTS PRESS

This book was set in 10.5 on 12.5 Ehrhardt for
FOUR COURTS PRESS LTD
7 Malpas Street, Dublin 8, Ireland
email: info@four-courts-press.ie
http://www.four-courts-press.ie
and in North America by
FOUR COURTS PRESS
c/o ISBS, 920 N.E. 58th Avenue, Suite 300, Portland, OR 97213.

ISBN (10-digit) 1–85182–994–6
ISBN (13-digit) 978–1–85182–994–1

A catalogue record for this title
is available from the British Library.

Printed in Great Britain
by MPG Books, Bodmin, Cornwall.

Contents

Abbreviations

Akenson, *Church of Ireland* D.H. Akenson, *The Church of Ireland: ecclesiastical reform and revolution, 1800–1885* (New Haven and London, 1971)

Alumni Dublinenses G.D. Burtchaell and T.U. Sadleir, *Alumni Dublinenses* (Dublin, 1935)

As by law established A. Ford, J.I. McGuire and K. Milne (eds), *As by law established: the Church of Ireland since the Reformation* (Dublin, 1995)

BL British Library, London

Cal. SP *Calendar of State Papers*

Cotton, *Fasti* H. Cotton, *Fasti Ecclesiae Hibernicae* (6 vols, Dublin, 1845–78)

Ford, *Reformation* A. Ford, *The Protestant Reformation in Ireland, 1590–1641* (2nd edn, Dublin, 1997)

Gillespie, *Devoted people* R. Gillespie, *Devoted people: belief and religion in early modern Ireland* (Manchester, 1997)

Gillespie and Neely R. Gillespie and W.G. Neely (eds), *The laity and the Church of Ireland, 1000–2000: all sorts and conditions* (Dublin, 2002)

HJ *Historical Journal*

HMC Historical Manuscripts Commission

IHS *Irish Historical Studies*

JEH *Journal of Ecclesiastical History*

JRSAI *Journal of the Royal Society of Antiquaries of Ireland*

NA National Archives, Dublin

NLI   National Library of Ireland

Phillips, *Church of Ireland*   W.A. Phillips (ed.), *History of the Church of Ireland from the earliest times to the present day* (3 vols, Oxford, 1933)

PRONI   Public Record Office of Northern Ireland, Belfast

RCBL   Representative Church Body Library, Dublin

Statutes at large   *The Statutes at large passed in paraliaments held in Ireland from 1310–1800* (21 vols, Dublin, 1786–1804)

TCD   Trinity College Dublin

Illustrations

appearing between p. 148 and 149

Contributors

Toby Barnard, fellow and tutor in history at Hertford College, Oxford since 1976, has published extensively on seventeenth- and eighteenth-century Ireland. His recent books include: *A new anatomy of Ireland: the Irish Protestants, 1649–1770* (2003); *The kingdom of Ireland, 1641–1760* (2004); *Irish Protestant ascents and descents* (2004) and *Making the grand figure: lives and possessions in Ireland, 1641–1770* (2004).

Richard Clarke has been bishop of Meath and Kildare since 1996. He published *Richard Whately: the unharmonious blacksmith* in 2002 and contributed to J. Guy and W.G. Neely (eds), *Contrasts and comparisons: studies in Irish and Welsh church history* (1999).

John Crawford is vicar of the St Patrick's cathedral group of parishes in Dublin and author of *St Catherine's parish, Dublin: portrait of a church of Ireland community* (1996) and *The Church of Ireland in Victorian Dublin* (2005).

Ciaran Diamond is a graduate of NUI, Maynooth, and is currently engaged on a Ph.D. at Trinity College, Dublin.

Adrian Empey is Principal of the Church of Ireland training college. He co-edited *A worthy foundation: the cathedral church of St Canice Kilkenny* (1985) and has published numerous articles on medieval Ireland.

Raymond Gillespie, associate professor of history at NUI, Maynooth, has published many books and articles on early-modern Ireland. The most recent include *Reading Ireland: print, reading and social change in early modern Ireland* and *Seventeenth-century Dubliners and their books*. He is joint editor of *The History of the Book in Ireland* (2006) and *The parish in medieval and early modern Ireland* (2006). With Canon Neely he edited *The laity and the Church of Ireland, 1000–2000*.

Marie-Louise Legg has published *Newspapers and nationalism, 1850–1892* (1999) and has edited *The Synge Letters* (1996); *The Census of Elphin, 1749* (2004) and *The diary of Nicholas Peacock* (2005). She is an honorary fellow of Birkbeck College, University of London.

Colm Lennon is associate professor of history at NUI, Maynooth. His publications include *Sixteenth-century Ireland: the incomplete conquest* (1994) and *The Lords of Dublin in the age of Reformation* (1989).

An Ulster man who has spent most of his working life as a schoolmaster-priest in England and Africa, **Alan Megahey** is now rural dean of Lovedon in the diocese of Lincoln. He has published on Zimbabwe, the history of education and Irish Protestantism, notably *The Irish Protestant churches in the twentieth century* (2000).

William Marshall was ordained and served a curacy in the Church of Ireland. He then worked in India as a member of the Dublin University Mission to Chota Nagpur. On his return to Ireland, he was a parish rector and afterwards vice-principal of the Church of Ireland Theological College.

Kenneth Milne published *The Irish charter schools* in 1996 and edited *Christ Church cathedral Dublin: a history* (2000). He is historiographer to the Church of Ireland.

The Revd **W.G. Neely** is rector of Keady, County Armagh, and a canon of St Patrick's Cathedral, Dublin. His publications include: *Kilkenny: an urban history, 1391–1843* (1989) and *Kilcooley: land and people in Tipperary* (1983, revised edition, 2005). He co-edited *The laity and the Church of Ireland, 1000–2000* (2003) with Raymond Gillespie.

Daithí Ó Corráin is a research fellow in the Centre for Contemporary Irish History at Trinity College, Dublin. His book *Rendering to God and Caesar: the Irish churches and the two states in Ireland, 1949–73* is to be published in 2006.

William Roulston is research officer of the Ulster Historical Foundation. He is author of *Researching Irish-Scots ancestors: the essential genealogical guide to early modern Ulster: 1600–1800* (2005) and co-edited, with Eileen Murphy, *Fermanagh: history and society* (2004).

Introduction

This volume is a companion to the earlier collection on the laity and the Church of Ireland.[1] Like the first, it blends several approaches. First, it seeks to portray the changing activities of the clergy over a millennium. As well as attempting clerical group portraits at particular moments – in the later middle ages, 1640, and in the eighteenth century – it includes studies of outstanding individuals. The latter encompass Tresham Dames Gregg, a turbulent priest in nineteenth-century Dublin, and his near-contemporary William Connor Magee, who rose to be archbishop of York. Other contributions address more specific issues. These include clerical responses to dramatic upheavals, such as the sixteenth-century reformation, the disestablishment of the Church of Ireland and the establishment of the republic of Ireland. These analyses are supplemented by looking at clerical involvement in education and scholarship and Irish Protestants' ministering outside Europe. Nearer home, the apparently mundane but vital and neglected subject of housing the Church of Ireland clergy is discussed.

Certain themes run through the essays. Clerics are seen as a group, in relation to the laity and to their counterparts in other confessions and countries. A persistent puzzle is how far the clergy were united by a sense of forming a coherent order, caste, estate or emerging profession. The commonalities of education, doctrine and vocation have to be set against the striking divergences in background (as between those born and trained in Ireland and Britain) and remuneration. Occasions for solidarity vanished during the long interval between 1713 when Convocation – the representative body of the Church of Ireland – no longer met alongside the Dublin parliament and the creation of the General Synod, together with subsidiary diocesan and provincial synods, after disestablishment. Many of the essays mention the recurrent difficulties of collecting tithes and other dues and the resulting antagonisms. Clerical claims to money could embitter relations both with those of other denominations and with their own congregations. Yet a modest competence was essential if the clergy were to discharge their scriptural and canonical obligations. Despite the frequent references to the financial embarrassments, the Church of Ireland lacks any systematic study of the economic problems of its incumbents comparable to Christopher Hill's classic.[2]

1 Gillespie and Neely.   2 C. Hill, *Economic problems of the Church from Whitgift to the Long Parliament* (Oxford, 1956); cf. S.G. Ellis, 'Economic problems of the church: why the reformation failed in Ireland', *JEH*, xli (1990), pp 239–65.

The nature of the evidence is such that complaints and struggles leave stronger traces than placid and amicable dealings. Several contributors reflect on the near impossibility of retrieving the routine pastoral and sacramental labours of clerics other than in the barest outline. Nevertheless, there are clear signs that, by the close of the seventeenth century, the Church was imposing higher standards and better discipline on its ministers and as an institution was stronger. These impressions await detailed proof. One matter central to the ability of the Church to act effectively was the training of its clergy. Also, by the early eighteenth century, the ministry of the Church of Ireland had become overwhelmingly the preserve of graduates – and indeed graduates of Dublin University. Yet, the nature of the theological and pastoral instruction that intending ordinands received in Trinity College has yet to be detailed.

If the matter of preparation remains mysterious in many of its aspects, the omission is linked to the continuing uncertainties about the backgrounds and circumstances of the clergy, other than the bishops of the seventeenth and eighteenth centuries.[3] A start is made with Dr Marie-Louise Legg's consideration of a manageable sample of incumbents from the dioceses of Ferns and Leighlin and Elphin during the eighteenth-century episcopate of the younger Edward Synge. Further investigations of this kind, utilizing the biographical material assembled, diocese by diocese, by J.B. Leslie early in the twentieth century, may in time result in a comprehensive prosopography of the personnel of the Church of Ireland.[4] Only then will it be possible to give definitive answers to such questions as the extent to which clerical dynasties were established, with sons, sons-in-law, nephews and grandsons following forbears into the sacred ministry. In addition, an exhaustive examination would help to establish whether the clergy were recruited primarily from the younger sons and cadets of landowners, from professional and mercantile families or even from the middling and humbler sections of Irish Protestant society. In addition the Church, as an emerging profession for graduates, could fruitfully be compared with with others like medicine, the law, public service (both civil and military).

Many contributors show the diverse backdrops to clerical lives: the confessional composition, size, emoluments and topography of ecclesiastical livings varied strikingly across the island. Obviously, ministering in a central Dublin parish differed from undertaking a cure in the strongly Presbyterian districts of Ulster or in the rural hinterlands of Connacht and Munster. Furthermore, periods of relative tranquillity alternated with times of turmoil, in which the clergy of the Church of Ireland might find themselves targets. Just how incumbents responded to the polit-

---

3 J. Falvey, 'The Church of Ireland episcopate in the eighteenth century', *Eighteenth-Century Ireland*, 8 (1993), p. 109; J. Falvey, 'The Church of Ireland episcopate in the eighteenth century', unpublished MA thesis, University College, Cork (1995); F.G. James, *Ireland in the empire, 1688–1773* (Cambridge, Mass. 1973), p. 131; P. McNally, ' "Irish and English interests": national conflict within the Church of Ireland episcopate in the reign of George I', *IHS*, xxix (1995), pp 295–314.   4 The unpublished material is in RCBL.

ical and physical challenges of growing Irish Catholic nationalism, the Union of 1801, the uprising of 1916, the War of Independence and subsequent civil war remain to be studied in detail.[5] In general, the earlier centuries, particularly of the reformation and the upheavals of the seventeenth century, have attracted more attention from historians than the equally stirring events of the nineteenth and twentieth centuries. There are signs that the neglect is gradually being repaired. The chapters here by Richard Clarke, John Crawford, Alan Megahey, Daithí Ó Corráin and William Marshall, together with their and others' publications, help greatly to open up the hitherto deserted wastes to expert historical mapping.[6] In common with all the contributions that follow, they offer models for subsequent enquirers.

The last is, indeed, a purpose of this collection: to stimulate fresh work. Developments in the Church of Ireland and how they are best narrated and analysed gain from being seen against parallel developments. Consequently, there is much to be learnt from comparing the experiences of the Church of Ireland clergy with their counterparts in the other Irish churches, and with their equivalents in Britain, continental Europe and beyond.[7] Approaches and interpretations appropriate to other places may not always fit the Irish situation. Even so, while the local and specific contexts of Irish endeavours need always to be remembered, insularity has to be avoided. Arguably the heyday of the Church of Ireland lay in the eighteenth century, when its legal privileges were matched by a more solid institutional structure. The same period in the annals of the Church of England has lately attracted searching attention.[8] There is much to be pondered in this work by histo-

---

5 For suggestions: P. Comerford, 'Church of Ireland clergy and the 1798 rising' in L. Swords (ed.), *Protestant, Catholic and dissenter: the clergy and 1798* (Dublin, 1997); D.W. Miller, 'Irish Christianity and revolution' in J. Smyth (ed.), *Revolution, counter-revolution and union: Ireland in the 1790s* (Cambridge, 2000), pp 195–210. More generally on Protestant apprehensions: J.S. Kelly, ' "We were all to have been massacred": Irish Protestants and the experience of rebellion', in T. Bartlett, D. Dickson, D. Keogh and K. Whelan (eds), *1798: a bicentenary perspective* (Dublin, 2003), pp 312–20. 6 R. Clarke, 'Imperfect with peace ... Lord Plunket and the disestablishment revision of the Irish prayer book' in J.R. Guy and W.G. Neely (eds), *Contrast and comparisons: studies in Irish and Welsh church history* (Keady and Welshpool, 1999), pp 115–34; John Crawford, *The Church of Ireland in Victorian Dublin* (Dublin, 2004); M. Maguire, 'The Church of Ireland and the problem of the Protestant working class in Dublin, 1870s–1930s' in *As by law established*, pp 195–203. 7 J. Bergin, 'Between estate and profession: the Catholic parish clergy of early modern western Europe' in M.L. Bush (ed.), *Social orders and social classes in Europe since 1500: studies in social stratification* (Harlow, 1992), pp 66–85; R. O'Day, *The English clergy: the emergence and consolidation of a profession, 1558–1642* (Leicester, 1979); A. Pettegree (ed.), *The reformation of the parishes: the ministry and the Reformation in town and country* (Manchester and New York, 1993); U. Pfister, 'Pastors and priests in early-modern Grisons: organized profession or side activity?' in *Central European History*, 33 (2000), pp 41–65; J.H. Pruett, *The parish clergy under the later Stuarts: the Leicestershire experience* (Urbana, 1978). 8 W.J. Gregory, *Restoration, reformation and reform, 1660–1828: archbishops of Canterbury and their diocese* (Oxford, 2000); V. Barrie-Curien, 'The Church of England in London in the eighteenth

rians of the Irish Protestant clergy.[9] The same is true of the many admirable enquiries into the theological and evangelical movements of the eighteenth- and nineteenth-century Church of England.[10] So far, Irish responses to changing fashions in theology, worship and churchmanship are only starting to be analysed.[11] The rare attempts to compare the Church of Ireland with the churches in England, Scotland and Wales bring numerous insights.[12]

If larger shifts in attitudes, whether theological or political, await fuller investigation, so too do some apparently humdrum ones. Exactly how clerical households were constituted and functioned, and how they were seen by parishioners and other locals are not always clear. Canon Empey and Professor Gillespie throw vivid light on the multifarious activities in which some clerics engaged. Dr Roulston brings to life the physical realities of the rectory and parsonage. Yet, as Dr Legg remarks, much of the weekly routine of the incumbent is hidden. If this applies most immediately to the performance of the required religious duties – catechizing, presiding over rites of passage, preaching, administering the sacrament and discharging (or not) other canonical tasks – the obscurity deepens around any bid to locate individual clergymen more firmly in the society and culture of their localities.[13] It is a matter of regret that it has not been possible to include any study of the wives and children of the clergy.[14] Illumination would undoubtedly be offered on that – and numerous matters – if the image of the Church of Ireland clergy in fiction was investigated. Here George Birmingham (Canon Hannay) is an obvious point of entry.

century' in P. Clark and R. Gillespie (eds), *Two Capitals: London and Dublin, 1500–1840*, Proceedings of the British Academy, 107 (2001), pp. 211–21; eadem, *Clergé et pastoral en Angleterre au XVIIe siècle: le diocèse de Londres* (Paris, 1992); eadem, 'The clergy in the diocese of London in the eighteenth century' in J. Walsh, C. Haydon and S. Taylor (eds), *The Church of England, c.1689–c.1833: from toleration to Tractarianism* (Cambridge, 1993), pp 86–109; eadem, 'Clerical recruitment and career patterns in the Church of England during the eighteenth century' in W.M. Jacob and N.Yates (eds), *Crown and mitre: religion and society in northern Europe since the Reformation* (Woodbridge, 1993), pp. 93–104.   9 Among more general studies: D.A. Spaeth, *The Church in an age of danger: parsons and parishioners, 1660–1740* (Cambridge, 2000); P.Virgin, *The Church in an age of negligence: ecclesiastical structure and problems of church reform, 1700–1840* (Cambridge, 1989).   10 P.B. Nockles, *The Oxford Movement in context: Anglicanism high churchmanship, 1760–1857* (Cambridge, 1997); B.W. Young, *Religion and enlightenment in eighteenth-century England: theological debate from Locke to Burke* (Oxford, 1998).   11 Joseph Liechty, 'Irish Evangelicalism, Trinity College Dublin, and the mission of the Church of Ireland at the end of the eighteenth century', unpublished PhD thesis, St Patrick's College, Maynooth (1987); Crawford, *The Church of Ireland in Victorian Dublin*.   12 P.H.M. Bell, *Disestablishment in Ireland and Wales* (London, 1969); S.J. Brown, *The national churches of England, Ireland and Scotland, 1801–46* (Oxford, 2001).   13 Starting points include: S. Durand, *Drumcliffe: the Church of Ireland parish in its North Sligo setting* (Manorhamilton, 2000); M. Moffitt, *The Church of Ireland community of Killala and Achonry, 1870–1940* (Dublin, 1999); K. Mulligan, 'A history of Churchill' in W. Laffan (ed.), *A year at Churchill* (Tralee, 2003), pp 11–19; L. Robinson, T. Robinson and N. Dorman, *Three homes* (London, 1938).   14 For one contribution: D.M. Hartford, *Among the gaiters* (Portlaw, Pitlochry and Madrid, 1970).

This volume, it is hoped, as well as describing and analysing the collective and individual endeavours of the clergy of the Church of Ireland for almost a millennium, should encourage others to fill the gaps and challenge and modify the interpretations. Fortunately, the toilers in the vineyard are doughty and determined. Moreover, they are helped by the relative abundance of documentation. Because numerous Church of Ireland dignitaries and incumbents resisted the imperialism that drew historical records into the Public Record Office, where they were destroyed in 1922, a pleasing amount survived. In recent years, a good deal has been deposited in RCBL and PRONI, where, thanks to expert cataloguing, they are generally accessible. In addition, as Richard Clarke and Daithí Ó Corráin demonstrate, important documents are to be found outside the obvious Irish repositories, such as Hawarden (the Gladstone papers) and Lambeth Palace Library. So, the pace of research and publishing, especially on the history of the Church of Ireland from the later eighteenth century can be expected to quicken.[15]

One particular contribution to recent scholarship deserves to be singled out: that of John Paterson, successively dean of Kildare and Christ Church, Dublin. He had hoped to contribute a chapter to this volume as he had to the earlier one.[16] In the event, he was able before he died only to prepare extensive notes on clerics – both outstanding and ordinary – from the mid-nineteenth century to recent times. These have proved invaluable to other contributors and some of his insights have been incorporated into their chapters. His publications attest to his wide-ranging interests and his understanding of many aspects of the Church of Ireland (present and past), which he served with distinction and devotion.[17] His support, ideas and companionship were much appreciated in the planning of this volume and its predecessor. He personified the same characteristics of the best of those described below. As a token of the contributors' great esteem a nd sense of loss, this collection is dedicated to John Paterson's memory.

---

15 The most recent and comprehensive survey is K. Milne (ed.), *A Church of Ireland bibliography*, Church of Ireland Historical Society (Dublin, 2005).   16 'Lay spirituality and worship, 1750–1950: a reading people' in Gillespie and Neely, pp 250–76.   17 They include: 'The Church of Ireland' in D.R. Holeton (ed.), *Our thanks and praise: the eucharist in Anglicanism today* (Dublin, 1995), pp 223–30; 'The Irish cathedrals: rural' in *Search*, 5 (1982), pp 12–14; *Kildare: the cathedral church of St Brigid* (Kildare, 1983); *Meath and Kildare: an historical guide* (Kingscourt, Co. Cavan, 1981); 'T.G.F. Paterson' in E.E. Evans (ed.), *Harvest home: the last sheaf* (Armagh, 1975), pp xvii–xx; (with R.B. McCarthy), *Saint Mark's, the history of a Dub lin parish* (Dublin, 1971).

Irish clergy in the high and late Middle Ages

Adrian Empey

> Also, the Churche of thys lande use not to lerne any other science, but he Lawe of Cannon, for covetyce of lucre traunsytory; all other science, whereof growe none such lucre, the parsons of the churche dothe despyce. They cawed more by the plough rustycall, then by lucre of the plough celestyall.[1]

In introducing our medieval clerical forbears, some preliminary observations are necessary. In modern parlance, particularly with the increasing emphasis on professional clerical training that occurred in the nineteenth century, we see clergy simply as professionals in much the same way as lawyers, doctors or teachers are categorized. Medieval clergy, especially parochial clergy, were not professionals in this sense. Their identity stemmed rather from membership of an estate of the realm, to which specific rights and duties were attached. The significance of this membership will become clear when we encounter clergy in the civil courts.

Moreover, membership was not defined as it is in popular understanding today by ordination, which was technically conferred only on the major orders of subdeacon, deacon, priest, and bishop. While the four minor orders – doorkeeper (*ostiarius*), lector, exorcist, and acolyte – were regarded as in some sense sacramental, they never the less conferred clerical status upon the office holder, and distinguished him by tonsure from lay society. Put simply, the distinction between the minor and major orders is the distinction between a 'clerk' and a 'Clerk in Holy Orders'. Unlike the major orders, there was no age limit on entry, and marriage was permitted for those in minor orders. The latter, entering at a very young age, may often have had an apprenticeship for major orders in mind, but there was no strict obligation to fulfil such a pious intention. It is impossible to estimate the numbers of Irish clergy who belonged to this minor clerical class, but the numbers of clerks who feature in the civil courts clearly suggest that they were quite numer-

---

1 Anonymous report, 1515, cited in Phillips, *Church of Ireland*, ii, pp 179–80; *State Papers, Henry VIII*, ii, p.16.

ous. As we shall see, they often appear as royal or local government clerks, while from the fourteenth century onwards the parish clerk is increasingly visible in parish records. Many clerks presumably 'melted away' in time into the general population. One way of shedding clerical status was for a clerk to marry twice – if, for example, his wife died – because serial marriage was technically regarded in canon law as bigamy.[2] It was for this reason that civil courts always enquired whether a clerk claiming benefit of clergy was *bigamus* or not.

The clerical proletariat was further augmented by an indefinite number of unbeneficed chaplains,[3] who became more numerous from the fourteenth century when parish churches were extended to accommodate chapels for both religious and secular guilds, and when the number of chantries increased exponentially.

What proportion of the population belonged to the clerical estate? Only the most approximate estimates can be proposed. By the end of the fifteenth century, there were about 2,500 parishes in Ireland, about twice as many as in Scotland. It has been suggested that in England the ratio of beneficed to unbeneficed clergy ranged between one to one or two to one.[4] Given the poverty of many Irish parishes, particularly in Gaelic areas, the ratio was perhaps less in Ireland: an estimate of 4000 secular priests may not be very wide of the actual mark. Most Irish monasteries and friaries were quite modest. Significant foundations like Holy Trinity, Dublin, later Christ Church Cathedral, seem only to have had eight canons in 1468, while St Thomas's, Dublin, mustered only twelve canons.[5] It is likely that monastic numbers were considerably higher in the thirteenth century. Stephen of Lexington, for example, reported a total of 110 religious at Mellifont in 1228, of whom sixty-eight had fled prior to his visitation, compared to eleven monks who were pensioned off at the dissolution.[6] If the number of regulars was about the same as beneficed seculars, and if we can suppose that there were at least as many clerks of every description as chaplains, we may hazard a guess of around 8,000 clergy by conservative estimate, and perhaps 12,000 by extending the ratio bands. Since we do not know what the population of Ireland was, one can only guess that a more precise measurement of 4 to 6 per cent of the population of Norwich being in major orders might be reasonably representative of the densities in Anglo-Norman towns in Ireland. One estimate of Scottish ratios of clergy to laity at the beginning of the sixteenth century is 1:32.[7]

---

2 Canon law distinguishes between serial marriage and polygamy. Strictly speaking, what civil law describes as bigamy is actually polygamy.   3 While the term chaplain usually signifies an unbeneficed priest, it can also mean a beneficed vicar in certain contexts.   4 Felicity Heal, *Reformation in Britain and Ireland* (paperback edn, Oxford, 2005), p. 65   5 H.F. Berry (ed.), *Register of the wills and inventories of the diocese of Dublin in the time of archbishops Tregury and Walton, 1457–1483* (Dublin, 1898), pp 172, 177–8. It would appear that all the canons were subject to the visitation enquiry, so these figures almost certainly represent the whole communities.   6 Barry W. O'Dwyer, *The conspiracy of Mellifont, 1216–1231*, Medieval Irish History Series, No. 2, (1970), p. 22; Newport B. White (ed.), *Extents of Irish monastic possessions, 1540–1541* (Dublin, 1943), p. 221.   7 Heal, *Reformation in Britain and Ireland*, p. 44.

   Before concluding this introduction, it is also important to remember that encounters between clergy and laity were by no means confined to the sacraments. Prelates were not only spiritual overseers: they were also feudal magnates exercising secular jurisdiction over their lay tenants. The archbishops of Dublin exercised extensive jurisdiction over large areas of the modern county of Dublin. Between 1257 and 1263, two juries claimed that the archbishop through his seneschal and bailiffs entertained in his court all secular pleas, except four pleas of the crown (rape, arson, treasure trove, and forestall), and that all royal writs within the archbishop's lordship were executed only by his bailiffs.[8] In short, except for the reserved pleas, the sheriff of the county and his deputies were excluded from the archbishop's extensive lordship. This means that a considerable proportion of the lay population of County Dublin had to pursue most civil pleas in the archbishop's seigniorial courts as distinct from his ecclesiastical courts. Similarly, the archbishop of Tuam at the assizes in Connacht in 1300 claimed to exercise within his lordship certain pleas of the crown, including the shedding of blood of Englishmen, *vetitum namium*, assise of bread and ale, measures and weights, hue and cry unjustly raised, among other pleas. He also laid claim to wreck of the sea, and to have power to distrain all his tenants to repair bridges and causeways in all his lands as he saw fit, to put his free tenants on oath, and to deliver to them articles to enquire of Irish felons. He further claimed to have gallows, trebuchet, pillory and tumbrel, and to have all pleas except homicide of an Englishman, arson, or rape.[9] Besides higher jurisdiction, bishops and abbots were lords of manors and towns, over which they exercised exactly the same manorial and municipal jurisdictions as lay lords. The bishop of Ossory, who had no claim to high jurisdiction in his demesne, was lord of eleven manors, comprising about 47,000 statute acres, including at least three towns, over which he exercised the normal seigniorial jurisdictions.[10] If we add the monastic lands of the diocese, including the abbatial town of Inistioge, the total area under ecclesiastical seigniorial jurisdiction amounted to some 70,000 statute acres.[11] Finally, we must not forget that the oversight of ecclesiastical courts impinged on the lives of the laity in matters such as marriage, wills, fornication and adultery. Here again the justiciary rolls reveal how effective such courts were in practice. In the assizes at Waterford in 1305, for example, it was revealed that Henry fitz John had tried to marry his cousin Olivia following the death of his wife, but because she was within the prohibited degrees he was forced to keep her 'as his concubine for many years in the parts of Connacht because the prelates of the

8 C. McNeill (ed.), *Cal. Archbishop Alen's register, c.1172–1534* (Dublin, 1950), pp 110–14.   9 *Cal. justic. rolls Ire., 1295–1303*, pp 316–17.   10 See Adrian Empey (ed.), *A worthy foundation: the cathedral church of St Canice Kilkenny* (Mountrath, 1985), p. 18. It is possible that he also had towns in the manors of Durrow, Tiscoffin, and Clonmore. See C.A. Empey, 'County Kilkenny in the Anglo–Norman period' in W. Nolan and K. Whelan (eds), *Kilkenny: history and society: interdisciplinary essays on the history of an Irish county* (Dublin, 1990), p. 80.   11 Empey, 'County Kilkenny in the Anglo–Norman period', p. 82.

bishopric of Waterford did not permit them to cohabit in that diocese'.[12] In this fourteenth-century version of 'to hell or to Connacht', it would seem they amounted to the same thing. In 1297 Nicholas Feysel complained at the assizes in Cork that the bishop had extorted two sums of money from him through the church court. It transpired that the bishop had laid a penance on him for committing fornication, but that Nicholas had made fine of forty shillings instead. Nicholas was much addicted to fornication, because the bishop charged and convicted him yet again of the same offence. Nicholas had to withdraw his claim, and face another sentence of excommunication until he paid the two penalties.[13]

I

To say that Irish clergy, particularly in the late Middle Ages, suffered from a poor image would be a considerable understatement. The judgments of contemporaries, long before the anonymous reporter in 1515, were anything but complimentary. In 1363, for example, the preface to a long list of Irish petitioners at the papal court in Avignon reads as follows:

> Whereas by reason of pestilence and wars in those parts, there is a great lack of clerks, and the value of benefices is small, the pope is prayed to expedite the petitions for the underwritten persons, inasmuch as this is the first roll he has received from them, and he must not be surprised that persons have no scholastic degrees, inasmuch as in all Ireland there is no university or place of study … he is therefore prayed to expedite the said petitions, especially as the petitioners are from the ends of the earth.[14]

Such low self-esteem on the part of some twenty petitioners is reinforced by the phrasing of some of the individual petitions. Odo Ohogan, diocese of Emly, sought a canonry in Killaloe in addition to the rectory of Tipperary, 'on account of the slender value of the benefices and the scarcity of fit persons, it is hardly possible to subsist on two benefices'.[15] His co-petitioner, Nicholas Venderal, a Cistercian monk of Chore (Chorus S. Benedicti, Midleton), already dispensed on account of illegitimacy, sought a further dispensation to be promoted to the dignity of abbot 'seeing that there is in Ireland a very great lack of fit persons for such dignities'.[16] All the petitioners had one thing in mind: personal advancement. 'They cawed more by the plough rustycall, then by lucre of the plough celestyall.' Indeed, or so it would seem.

Such dire reports on the state of Ireland in the fourteenth, fifteenth and early sixteenth centuries constituted a rich literature of lament, unrelieved by the slight-

12 *Cal. justic. rolls Ire., 1305–1307*, p. 112. 13 Ibid., *1295–1303*, pp 96–7. 14 *Cal. papal petitions, 1342–1419*, p. 467. 15 Ibid., *1342–1419*, p. 469. 16 Ibid., *1342–1419*, p. 469.

est hint of optimism: a combination of disaffected barons and wicked natives endeavoured ceaselessly to extinguish the loyal remnant of the Old English colony. What is unusual in the 1515 rendering of a well-worn theme is the suggestion that the Irish church, on account of its manifest failings, was 'muche cause of all the said mysse ordre of this lande'.[17] And yet the prophecies of doom never came even remotely close to fulfilment. One is reminded of the adage that while things may on occasion be desperate they are never hopeless in the affairs of our sister island, whereas in Ireland matters are always hopeless but never desperate. It is not till the publication of Richard Stanihurst's *Description of Ireland* in 1577 that we encounter a more upbeat assessment of the virtues of Old English Ireland.[18] The reason is not far to seek: political reports are, by their very nature, political. Stanihurst, on the other hand, was proud of his Old English heritage, and was not about to sell it short. As with affairs of state, so with affairs ecclesiastical: caution in the assessment of sources is simply not an option. It is essential, therefore, to assess the nature of the sources of clerical history before forming even the most general conclusions.

II

The fact that the overwhelming proportion of the records that shed light on the conduct of churchmen are judicial should put us on guard. If only the justiciary rolls remained, one could be forgiven for concluding that Irish clerics distinguished themselves more for theft and murder than any other endeavour. Granted that one would expect to find only clerical criminals represented in the assize rolls, occasionally the rolls permit fleeting glimpses of another, perhaps more typical, reality. In 1299, for example, Master Maurice de Bree, parson of the parish of Fennor, County Tipperary, impleaded John de Fresingfeld for impeding the collection of the fourth oblation, which Maurice insisted was his due.[19] John is described as a 'minister of the court', which may mean that he was formerly a justice itinerant, or held another position in the court at the time of the hearing.[20] While it is pos-

---

17 *State Papers, Henry VIII*, ii, p. 16.   18 See Liam Miller and Eileen Power, *Holinshed's Irish Chronicle* (Mountrath, 1979), especially chapter three; also Colm Lennon, *Richard Stanihurst: the Dubliner, 1547–1618* (Dublin, 1981), pp 70–87, 131–5.   19 *Cal. justic. rolls Ire.,1295–1303*, pp 219–20. We know that in England there were four annual oblations paid to the parish priest on some or all of the four festivals: Christmas, Easter, Whitsun, and the patronal festival. These consisted of levies of a ½d. or 1d. on all nondependent parishioners (see James Murray, 'The sources of clerical income in the Tudor diocese of Dublin, *c*.1530–1600' in *Archivium Hibernicum*, xlvi (1991–1992), pp 153–4). It is interesting to note that these customs also existed in the church *inter Anglicos* in Ireland, presumably at the three high festivals. It may be that the fourth oblation was mistaken as one of the traditional oblations.   20 We know that John was a justice itinerant at Cashel in 1305, and that he held other judicial offices around this time: keeper of the rolls and writs of the common bench (1296–7) and justice of the justiciar's bench (1302–3). See H.G. Richardson and G.O. Sayles (eds), *The administration of Ireland, 1172–1377* (Dublin, 1963), pp 144–5n., 166–7, 185.

sible that Maurice made the complaint because the articles of assize normally caused enquiry to be made about the conduct of the king's officers, it seems more likely that John was implicated because he was lord of the manor of Inchirourke and other tenements in the parish of Fennor.[21] As the most important parishioner – and probably patron of the parish – it seems that he took the side of the parochial community in this dispute.[22] Maurice's right to the three annual oblations, 'as other parsons in those parts have in their churches', was not in dispute. The problem arose with the fourth oblation, which had a very different origin. It eventually emerged that about twenty-four years earlier a former vicar of the parish, William OKewe, struck a certain skinner – earlier described as a *claviger*[23] – within the precincts of the church, drawing blood. The upshot of the whole affair was that the diocesan, the archbishop of Cashel, placed the church under interdict. In order for the vicar to be reconciled, the parishioners agreed to bear the charge themselves

> And because the parson was not rich and was much loved by his parish-
> ioners, he asked them to aid him to pay the procuration of the archbishop.
> They freely granted a certain courtesy (*curialitas*)[24] to be taken for seven
> years, as an oblation once a year … And he (John de Fresingfeld) says that
> the term is passed, and that he and the parishioners are unwilling to give
> that oblation further.[25]

The matter was finally resolved when the archbishop held an inquisition composed of laymen and clerks in the presence of Maurice and John, which upheld the case for the defendant. Having established that the fourth oblation was not paid prior to the reconciliation, the archbishop commanded that it should cease. Maurice was fined for making a false claim, but in the event the justice in assize decided to pardon him.

The least one can say about this case, which only incidentally sheds light on the internal politics of a rural parish, is that even rugged discipline on the part of the vicar was not sufficient to breach the bonds of affection that existed between parson and parishioners. Almost certainly, he came from the same social background as they did, with the result that few would have considered his behaviour unfitting to his office. Sensitive souls were probably rare enough in Fennor in 1299. There is every likelihood that such relationships were so common as to be normal, but since they are never the concern of the kind of judicial record on which we depend

---

21 E. Curtis (ed.), *Calendar of Ormond deeds, 1172–1350* (6 vols, Dublin, 1932–43), no. 481. John granted his manor of Inchirourke to Edmund Butler on 16 November 1313. See also nos 479, 481, 482, 484–5.   22 I have no evidence that the parish was impropriate to a monastic foundation, which leaves the possibility that the right of presentation belonged to the lords of Inchirourke. 23 Presumably the custodian of the church key. Normally this would have been the responsibility of the *ostiarius*, the lowest ranking cleric in minor orders.   24 I think this would be better translated as 'gratuity' (cf. *curialagium*=gratuity or gift).   25 *Cal. justic. rolls, 1295–1303*, p. 219.

almost entirely for our knowledge of the lower clergy, it never comes to the surface except by coincidence of a very random kind.

If the evidence of civil courts is problematic, exactly the same may be said about papal records. The petitioners had every reason to describe their situation in the most lurid colours, while delators inevitably cast their opponents in apocalyptical terms. In 1322, for example, the chapter of Armagh accused the archbishop, among other things, of acting while under pain of excommunication, imprisoning the prior of St Mary's, Louth, beating Alan, a priest, wounding Nicholas, a clerk, stealing and pawning sacred vessels. The complaint continues: 'he is charged with these and many other crimes, such as bloodshed, adultery, and incest'.[26] In the same year the dean and canons of Cloyne, imprisoned by the archbishop of Cashel, complained that he had conducted an extortionate visitation of Cloyne, 'taking not only procurations in kind, and many gifts … but also extorted besides £300'.[27] When the archdeacon of Cloyne protested, the archbishop imprisoned him, together with the precentor, treasurer, and chancellor, and seven named canons, placing the see under interdict. Various other allegations followed, and finally, for good measure, they added: 'He is said to be father of fourteen spurious daughters, to whom he has given dowers, and has married them to rich and noble men, thereby increasing his power, and oppressing the clergy and people of his province'.[28] In 1303, the dean of Annaghdown protested bitterly to Rome about various oppressive actions on the part of the archbishop of Tuam, adding for good measure that he kept about him 'slayers of clerks and other excommunicate persons, committing acts of simony, … and he has imprisoned and tortured a canon regular in priest's orders because he would not allow the archbishop's horse to enter the place where the sacrament of the eucharist and church ornaments were kept, forcing him to swear not to disclose it'.[29]

Examples of this kind could be multiplied almost indefinitely from papal sources, to say nothing of the endless petitions for dispensations by the sons of priests, nuns and monks. The total impression gained is one of an utterly corrupted clerical caste. While there can be no doubt that clerical concubinage was widespread, above all in Gaelic areas, we must be careful not to conclude *ipso facto* that the products of such illicit unions – or even those clergy who did not live in a celibate state – were unworthy in every respect. Moreover, we cannot take the petitioners at their word. In the complaints against the archbishops in 1322 some specific charges were made, no doubt appropriately overstated, but those relating to their moral character were vague in the extreme. Notoriety played an important role both in civil and ecclesiastical proceedings in the Middle Ages: for example, in the processes of the grand jury. One is reminded of the absurd charges made against the Templars, Boniface VIII, and, locally, Alice Kyteler. None of this amounts to credible evidence. This is not to say that the evidence of the papal reg-

---

26 *Cal. papal letters, 1305–1342*, p. 219.   27 Ibid., p. 228.   28 Ibid.   29 *Cal. papal letters, 1198–1304*, pp 610–11.

isters is valueless – often its intrinsic value lies in quite incidental details – but that in addition to discounting the notorious elements that were stock in trade, it is necessary to gauge what is frequently the concealed purpose of the petition. Is it, for instance, a collusive action?

Another puzzle deserves contemplation. What exactly did contemporaries expect of clergy, high or low? We know that one of the achievements of the Fourth Lateran Council in 1215 was a greater concentration on what was involved in the cure of souls. The exemplary episcopate of Robert Grosseteste, the elderly and scholarly bishop of Lincoln (1235–53), not only produced in 1239 his celebrated pastoral work, *Templum Domini*, as a primary statement of what a priest needed to know in order to discharge his care of souls, but also witnessed a famous clash with Pope Innocent IV over the attempted provision of the pope's nephew to a Lincoln canonry, in which Innocent was worsted.[30] The Council of Lambeth in 1281, where Archbishop Pecham produced an outline of Christian doctrine and morals in his *Ignorantia Sacerdotum*, is widely regarded as the high point of pastoral legislation in medieval England. The main purpose of this work was to prescribe a syllabus for preaching on the part of the parish priest. It was not until about 1320 that a much more elaborate explication of *Ignorantia Sacerdotum* appeared under the title *Oculus Sacerdotis*, commonly attributed to William of Pagula, a Berkshire parish priest. This classic manual set out at length how to examine penitents, to prescribe appropriate penance, modelled on the articles of faith, the ten commandments, and the seven deadly sins. It also explained how the priest should educate his parishioners in the essentials of dogma and morals – to wit the fourteen articles of the creed, the seven sacraments, the ten commandments, the seven deadly sins, and the seven works of mercy and the seven virtues.[31] While no examples of these manuals have survived in Ireland, we know that Archbishop Cromer of Armagh instructed all his clergy in 1526 to acquire *Ignorantia Sacerdotum*.[32] It is clear, therefore, that both expectations and duties of those who exercised the cure of souls were widely understood and articulated in the course of the thirteenth and fourteenth centuries. But for all that, and in spite of well-intentioned diocesan legislation, the reality as often as not belies the theory. Despite all the evils so frequently dwelt upon by petitioners in the papal court, the evidence of significant clerical crime in secular records, the widespread practice of concubinage, and the repeated collapse of conventual standards in Irish monasteries, there is little to suggest that laity were unduly disturbed or anti-clerical. How can one measure the distance between the rigorous ideal of *Templum Domini*, and the comment of a clerical annalist, noting the death in battle in 1444 of the martial bishop of Clonmacnoise, in which his son, archdeacon of the diocese, his two brothers, and the prior of Clontuskert also perished? We are talking theologically in terms of light years:

30 See Leonard E. Boyle, *Pastoral care, clerical education and canon law, 1200–1400* (London, 1981), pp 3–51.   31 Ibid., pp 81–108.   32 Henry A. Jefferies, *Priests and prelates of Armagh in the age of reformation, 1518–1558* (Dublin, 1997) p. 39.

God's blessing and the blessing of all saints and true Christians with that
bishop to his terrestrial (*recte*: celestial?) mansion ... for a common giver to
all the clergy of Ireland, and a special true friend to all the learned in the
Irish liberal sciences also was that eminent Lord Bishop.[33]

This is not the place to employ the sort of actuarial equations or their historical
equivalents to attempt to bridge this space. All we can do is to lay seriously to heart
the hazards of passing judgement on the lives and loves of clergy distanced from
us by the sixteenth-century reformations, the Enlightenment, and the religious
revivals of the eighteenth and nineteenth centuries. Unaware of the least irony, the
annalist reveals the depth of the psychological chasm separating the real and the
ideal even on the terms of the fourteenth century. If the religious *mentalité* of the
annalist was shared – as it almost certainly was – by the literate clerical readership
he was addressing, then how can we attempt to plumb the psychological abyss of
an uneducated laity where superstition, folk tradition and magic mingled unself-
consciously with elements of Christian belief? Is it the case that religious orthodoxy was at best the preserve of a small clerical élite in pre-reformations Europe?[34]
And where in this spectrum would we place the average medieval parish priest,
who probably had as much in common with the folk religion of his parishioners as
he had with the distantly-perceived outlines of official doctrine?

III

From a visual perspective, the most eye-catching reminder of our Christian heritage is the lost world of high and late medieval monasticism. Not only do these
ancient piles evoke dim nostalgic impulses inherited from our nineteenth-century
romantic heritage, but their rural seclusion stirs up images of a blessed tranquillity extinguished by Tudor rapacity and the ever-encroaching pressures of global-
ization.

It seems idyllic, but was it? It is impossible to read Benedict's great rule without
being astonished by its ambition. The rule endeavours to set down the fundamental principles for living in a community single-mindedly dedicated to the achievement of salvation summarised in seventy-three chapters. To get there, every norm
of human nature is inverted. As if the rules of obedience, silence, and humility are
not enough for a novice, chapter four details a further seventy-three 'instruments
of good works'. No compromises are made with the pecking order of the secular
world, even for monks in priest's orders. When and if a monk succeeds in mea-

33 See K.W. Nicholls, *Gaelic and Gaelicized Ireland in the Middle Ages* (2nd edn, Dublin, 2003),
p. 115.   34 For a discussion of the significance of medieval folk religion, see Raymond Gillespie,
Devoted people: belief and religion in early modern Ireland (Manchester and New York, 1997), pp
1–19.

suring up to these rigorous demands, he is reminded in the seventy-third and final chapter that he has only reached 'Go':

> Now, we have written this Rule that, observing it in monasteries, we may show that we have acquired at least some moral righteousness, or a beginning of the monastic life … Thou, therefore, who hastenest to the heavenly home, with the help of Christ fulfil this least rule written for a beginning; and then thou shalt with God's help attain at last to the greater heights of knowledge and virtue which we have mentioned above.

The history of this magnificent project is undoubtedly integral to the achievements of medieval culture and civilization. Without diminishing that enterprise, one must also acknowledge the reality that the movement not only failed repeatedly to exclude secular influences, but failed doubly in achieving that internal spiritual harmony that lay at the heart of the endeavour.

The great ceremony that signalled the completion of the first Cistercian monastery at Mellifont in 1157, attended by the archbishop of Armagh, seventeen bishops, and three kings, was clearly intended to excite expectations of a sweeping monastic reformation directed from Cîteaux. As nothing succeeds like success, no fewer than twenty-three daughter houses of Mellifont were founded in Ireland by the end of the century. Yet by 1202 reports were already reaching the abbot of Clairvaux that discipline was breaking down in a number of the affiliated houses. In 1216 Mellifont itself resisted a visitation sent from Clairvaux, and the abbot had to be deposed. The same visitors were greeted at Jerpoint with a riot organized by the abbot, assisted by four other Irish Cistercian abbots. In the course of the following years matters went from bad to worse: faced by a league of Irish monasteries, headed by Mellifont, in what came to be known as 'the Mellifont conspiracy', the general chapter decided in 1226 and 1227 to send high-ranking visitors to Ireland, with power to employ force by invoking armed assistance from the civil authority, to break up the entire Mellifont filiation, placing individual monasteries under the direct control of English or French houses. Things had reached such a pass that the abbot of Mellifont resigned for fear of his life at the hands of the brethren. When Stephen of Lexington visited the abbey in July 1228, he found that almost half of the monks had deserted, taking with them all the archives and sacred vessels. Eventually some of them were allowed to return, but others were exiled to English and French abbeys, banned for life from Mellifont. Worse was to greet Stephen when he attempted his visitation of Inishlounaght, County Tipperary, a daughter house. When a lay brother attempted entry, he was ambushed by the prior and an armed monastic community, stripped, beaten, and tortured. The prior was reported to have thrown off his cowl, with a scabbard around his neck, holding a sword and lance, promising to transfix with his lance any member of the community that yielded to the visitor. Stephen, on learning that the monks planned to murder him, wisely protected himself by travelling in the company of local magnates. At another daughter house, Maigue in County Limerick, a coup was engineered by a grandson of the king of Thomond, forcing out the abbot and all the English and foreign monks. Having fortified the monastery against the visitors, the coup was ended only by force and at the cost of some lives.[35]

While the ostensible reason for such extraordinary levels of indiscipline was attributed to ethnic tensions, the fact of the matter is that the rule was designed specifically to imbue the virtues of obedience, humility, and silence, to say nothing about the seventy-three 'instruments of good works'. Internal pecking orders abounded. In the case of Maigue, the inspiration for the coup was laid at the feet of one of the O'Brien dynasty: so much for the exclusion of secular concerns! The pattern was all too familiar. In 1307 the abbot of Mellifont complained the abbey had been seized into the king's hand because of

> The intolerable controversies and contentions now continually had between many monks, with very many hired men at arms, from the desire of obtaining the highest place, that each of them would be abbot by ousting his adversary, as well by conspiracies with other abbots, by those desirous of such honour, each one in turn with his accomplices. By which the abbey, which is of the advowson and patronage of the king, is almost destroyed; its land alienated to divers people; and its goods dissipated. And also it appears to the court that many abbots of other houses are by the Cistercian chapter overthrown on account of the maintaining of said ambitious persons.[36]

The same roll contains complaints that the abbot of Maigue continually alienated the tenements and goods of the abbey, and 'in hatred of the English tongue, to maintain that no monks of England may dwell there, as was accustomed'.[37] The repeated charges of property alienation by the monasteries clearly point to the subordination of the conventual interest to family interests: someone on the inside is fixing leases for family members on the outside.

Far from being safe refuges from a violent world, life in the cloister could be just as 'poor, nasty, brutish and short' as anywhere among the unredeemed. On 16 November 1306, for example, Brother Richard Sweetman, prior of St Peter's, Trim, was charged with the murder of Robert Mody, a fellow canon regular of St Augustine. The jurors upheld the charge, saying that on the festival of SS Peter and Paul (presumably the patronal festival of the priory), Richard and his brother William, 'complaining that they could not drink at their will', went out to the cloister armed with swords and other arms, verbally abused, attacked and killed Robert and one other canon.[38] Because of *lacunae* in the text, the sequence of events is not

---

35 For a full account of the Mellifont conspiracy see O'Dwyer, *The conspiracy of Mellifont, 1216–1231*; John Watt, *The church in medieval Ireland* (2nd edn, Dublin, 1998), pp 53–9.   36 *Cal. justic. rolls Ire., 1305–1307*, pp 350–1.   37 Ibid., *1305–1307*, p. 351.   38 Ibid., *1305–1307*, pp 508,

always apparent, but it seems clear that their victims stood in the way of their gaining access to the cellar, which they felt was their due at the patronal festival. While the testosterone factor doubtless played its part in violent situations, we should again note the family element and the ready access to an assortment of weaponry. It all seems a long way from St Benedict.

The state of conventual life reported by the jurors of the city of Waterford in 1537 left much to be desired:

> Item that in the same quarter of Tipperary howe James Butler abbot of Inislonaght & deane of Lysmore hath sundry tymes disobayed the kings writ & is a man of odyous lif, taking yerely and daily mennes wifs & burges daughters, & kepeth no devyne service but spendeth the goods of his churche in veluptuousytie & morgageth the lands of his churche & so the house is all decayed, & useth coygne & livery.[39]

The jurors of the town of Clonmel were no less uncomplimentary, reporting that

> The abbaye of Innyslawenaghte besides Clomell of great enormytie usethe no devyne service, but fewe masses by verbe; and the abbot of the same using his leman or harlot openly by daie and night to his pleasure, and every monke of his havyinge his harlot and household.[40]

The picture that emerges from these presentments is generally depressing. The once imposing Augustinian priory of Athassel, County Tipperary, founded by William de Burgh, was reported as having 'but few masses, with iiii chanons, and some of them using & having wifs and children'.[41] Even the archbishop of Cashel was reported as having 'riotously & with a company of malyfactors being in bote on the river of Waterford … spoyled & robbed a bote of Clomell charged with sylke & saffron & other merchaundise'.[42] The prior of the Kells, County Kilkenny, was likewise accused of supplementing his income by holding Waterford merchants to ransom, '& kepte them in irons longe tyme & after sent them to the cumssy … (and) there kepte to their sore ympoverishment'.[43]

The source of these manifest ills lies less within the cloister than without. It was no accident that the high-water mark of conventual life corresponded exactly to the period in the thirteenth century when monasteries were able to maintain a relative independence from the pressures of secular society due to a happy combina-

510–11.   **39** Presentment of the city of Waterford made before the king's commission in H.F. Hore and J. Graves (eds), *The social state of the southern and eastern counties of Ireland in the sixteenth century*, Annuary of the Royal Historical and Archaeological Association (1868–9), p. 202. **40** Ibid., p. 248   **41** Ibid., p. 248   **42** Ibid., p. 203   **43** Ibid., p. 204. The prior in question was Nicholas Tobin, whose powerful relatives owned Killahy Castle in Cumsey, County Tipperary, close to the Kilkenny border.

tion of effective episcopal, papal, royal and seigniorial oversight, as I have demonstrated elsewhere in my profile of the priory of Kells.[44] Even the most cursory familiarity with late medieval Irish sources will support the conclusion that most monasteries were in the firm control of local lords, to the extent that they are better understood as an extension of family interests. It is enough to note the names of abbots and priors at the time of dissolution. There can be little doubt that the increasing political chaos of Ireland from the mid-fourteenth century onwards contributed directly to the fate of monasticism. If it was difficult to maintain conventual standards in times of peace and stability, then it is unreasonable to expect such spiritual rigour in the Darwinian conditions of late medieval Ireland.

Conversely, where conditions were relatively stable as, for example, in the archdiocese of Dublin, the evidence points firmly in the opposite direction. When the priory of Holmpatrick, Skerries, was visited by the archbishop on 4 May 1468, the prior reported to the visitors that

> All the canons are obedient and subject to correction, and all the divine services are duly celebrated, according to the resources of the house; also the convent says that the prior has conducted and conducts himself with propriety in all matters, and governs the house well.[45]

While we do not have the actual articles of visitation, there is every reason to believe that they were both detailed and searching. Certainly the archbishop's Official was equipped with wide-ranging judicial powers, including the visitation of the clergy and laity of the diocese, with authority to enquire into their manners and life, to punish their crimes and reform their manners.[46] In the case of the visitation on the nunnery of St Mary of Grace Dieu on 6 May 1468, we are informed that the nuns were questioned one by one, no doubt to reduce the possibility of collusion:

> The prioress says that all the nuns are sufficiently subject to correction, and obedient, and the house is in a satisfactory state, and the divine offices are duly celebrated. Dame Alson Taylour (who appears to be either sub-prioress or else second in seniority) says that the prioress conducts herself with propriety in all things, and the house is in a satisfactory state. Dame Margaret Ward, Dame Katherine Haket, and Dame Anne Gelluys being questioned one by one as to the prioress and state of the house, make the same declaration as the said Dame Alson Taylour.[47]

---

44 C.A. Empey, 'The sacred and the secular: the Augustinian priory of Kells in Ossory 1193–1541' in *IHS*, xxiv (1984), pp 131–51, especially pp 145 ff.   45 See Berry (ed.), *Register of the wills and inventories of the diocese of Dublin*, p. 175.   46 See, for example, the powers conferred by the archbishop on his Official, John Warren, in 1482, in M.J. McEnery and Raymond Refaussé, *Christ Church deeds* (Dublin, 2001), no. 1034.   47 See Berry (ed.), *Register of the wills*

In like manner, the visitors were satisfied that St Thomas's, Dublin, was in good order. The canons regular there confirmed that 'the abbot is well conducted and is prudent both for the profit and hospitality of the house'.[48] We have therefore good reason to believe that where effective episcopal, political and social structures of governance were in place – as was clearly the case in the archdiocese – monastic communities maintained a very adequate standard of conventual life, probably right up to the dissolution. While the monasteries were not as frequently the subject of lay bequests in Dublin as the friaries or parish churches, they continued to be the object of fairly frequent benefaction in wills in the second half of the fifteenth century, which strongly suggests that they retained at least the respect of the laity.

We can gain an unusually detailed insight into the organization and daily operations of a community of Arroasian canons regular of St Augustine in the account roll of the priory of Holy Trinity (Christ Church), Dublin, between 1337 and 1346.[49] Theoretically, canons regular were not monks, but the constraints of living under a rule clearly hindered them from participating to any great extent in the governance both of the diocese and the royal administration in Dublin castle. The supply of such personnel therefore was drawn from the secular chapter of St Patrick's Cathedral. Thus we have in Holy Trinity a fascinating example of a religious community living cheek by jowl with the seats of royal and municipal government. It was, in fact, the only 'monastic' community within the city walls.

In spite of its monastic character, the members of the community were deeply immersed in the political, economic and social life of society at large. As proprietor of some 10,500 acres, chiefly in Grangegorman, Glasnevin, and Clonkeen (Kill o' the Grange), the prior was ranked among the most important lords of the county. These, along with their dependent lay tenants, were the responsibility of the seneschal, who was always a senior canon. The accounts reveal in minute detail how this considerable enterprise was efficiently managed. Holy Trinity was in addition the focal point of pilgrimage by virtue of its renowned collection of relics, including the staff of Jesus and a talkative crucifix.[50] It was naturally the focal point of much municipal piety, as can be clearly seen from the Book of Obits of the Confraternity of Holy Trinity which, as the editors aptly commented, 'reads like a roll-call of civic and gentry families who were prominent in the Dublin area'.[51]

But perhaps the most accurate measurement of how porous was the theoretical wall dividing sacred and secular is revealed by the priors' guest list. Those who were wined and dined by, or received 'gifts' from, the priors between 1337 and 1346 included senior royal officials such as Sir Thomas Wogan, escheator and justice

and inventories of the diocese of Dublin, pp 175–6. 48 Ibid., p. 178. 49 James Mills (ed.), *Account roll of the priory of the Holy Trinity, Dublin, 1337–1346*, with introduction by James Lydon and Alan J. Fletcher (Dublin, 1996). 50 Ibid., pp xv–xvii. For the talking crucifix, see also Gerald of Wales, *Topographia Hibernica*, Ch. 73. 51 See Raymond Refaussé and Colm Lennon (eds), *The registers of Christ Church Cathedral, Dublin* (Dublin, 1998), p. 21. For the obits see pp 40–86.

itinerant,[52] Walter of Islip,[53] Robert (Power), chancellor of the exchequer,[54] and Ellis of Ashbourne, justice itinerant (1337) and justice of the justiciar's bench (1329–31).[55] To add to the pageantry and sense of occasion, we hear the trumpeters of the justices being entertained in the refectory, while the justices themselves, one assumes, were dining with the prior.[56] We hear of the sheriff of Dublin, his brother and others including the sheriff's clerk being feasted in the prior's chamber on the feast of St Scholastica in 1337, and a gift from the prior to another sheriff, Michael Mongomery, in 1344.[57] Naturally, the comings and goings of the archbishop, [58] his officials[59], and an assortment of visiting monastic dignitaries are also registered in the accounts.[60] There are, unsurprisingly, references to the prior having his seneschal, kitchener, and cellarer dining with him, at which the management of the priory and its manors were probably discussed.[61] Some general sense of the activity of the prior can be gleaned for the accounts from Tuesday 20 to Sunday 25 January 1338:

> (Tuesday) In the sacristy[62], for the prior, the prior of Holmpatrick, John Passelawe, and others, at dinner, in wine 3*d*. Also in 2 pairs of gloves for gifts by command of the prior, 3*d*. (Wednesday) The feast of S. Agnes the Virgin. In wine bought for breakfast of the prior and Master Simon, chancellor of the archbishop, 3*d*. And the same day, in wine for the coming of John Welsshe (and) Walter Brayhenogh, proctors, to dinner there, 3*d*; in 2 cooked capons and roast meat, 8*d*. Same day at supper there, in ale, 2*d*.; roast meat, 2½*d*. (Thursday) In the prior's chamber for the coming of John de Grancet[63] and his chaplain to breakfast, in bread, 1*d*.; in wine, 3*d*.; a cooked capon, 3*d*. In ale at evening, 1*d*. (Friday) In wine bought for the prior's chamber, for the coming of Sir Thomas Wogan, escheator of Ireland, and Sir Elias de Asshebourne, justices itinerant, and other strangers, to dinner, 2*s*.(equivalent to four gallons of wine); in oysters, 4*d*.; 2 pounds of figs bought, 4*d*. Also at evening same day, in the prior's chamber, in ale, 1*d*. (Saturday) In oysters for the prior, seneschal, and cellarer, in

52 Lydon and Fletcher, *Account roll of the priory of Holy Trinity, Dublin*, p. 5.   53 Ibid., p. 42. Walter was treasurer of Ireland from 1314 to 1318, and again from 1322 to 1325. He had been a baron of the exchequer from 1309 to 1311, and escheator from 1309 to 1311.   54 Ibid., p. 18. Robert was chancellor from 1335 to 1340.   55 Ibid., p. 44.   56 Ibid., p 19.   57 Ibid., pp 7–8, 83. 58 See, for example, pp 74–6, 79, 86.   59 There are references to the archdeacon and his retinue, the chancellor, and the marshal of the archbishop, ibid., pp 3, 5, 116.   60 For example the prior of Holmpatrick, the prior of St Wolstan's, and the Dominican friars of Arklow. Ibid., pp 5, 10, 11.   61 See ibid., pp 6–7, when two such meetings occurred within three weeks.   62 Probably the sacristan's chamber.   63 John de Grancet was a wealthy citizen of Dublin, whose acts of piety are reflected in other Christ Church deeds (see Lydon and Fletcher, *Account roll of the priory of Holy Trinity, Dublin*, pp 148–51). I cannot, however, verify the claim in this notice that he had been a baron of the exchequer or justice of the king's bench, as no reference is made to him Richardson and Sayles, *The administration of Ireland, 1172–1377*.

the cellar, at dinner, 1*d*.; in wine, 3*d*. (Sunday) The feast of the Conversion of S. Paul. In salted eels bought for the prior, 8*d*.; in 2 plovers bought, 2*d*.[64]

All this suggests an easy familiarity with a broad spectrum of political, civic, and ecclesiastical business. As a significant spiritual lord, the priors were commonly summoned to parliament. In 1346 allowance was made to Brother John Dolfyn 'for expenses of the prior and his retinue to Kilkenny for the parliament, and for writs and arranging other necessary things, as appears in a schedule of particulars sewn to this roll, 22*s*. 8*d*.'[65] Certainly, to judge from his wardrobe as detailed in the Michaelmas account 1344, the prior and his retinue did not seek the anonymity of the crowd: included among the recently purchased items were a skin with fur for his mantle, a skin for his hood, two robes (one for Christmas and one for Easter), a skin for a surcoat, a pair of gloves, six coats, and two skins for his esquires. The order for his liturgical apparel included two amices, woollen cloth for making hoods and amices, a skin for the prior's great amice, and another one for the lesser, besides two rochets. To further enhance his image, the prior ordered a new table for his chamber, a dozen 'saucers' (*salsarii*)[66] of pewter, a dozen dishes, a dozen plates of pewter, and two platters.[67] Nor was the cuisine offered at his table in any way wanting. A random scan of the account roll will reveal wine and ale, oysters, figs, butter, cheese, fish, roast lamb, roast fowl, roast beef, pasties of baked fowl, mutton, hens, geese, capons, and chickens, all of them no doubt from the resources of the priory's manors.

It would be a mistake to conclude that such hospitality and concern for display are signs of spiritual decline. There is nothing to suggest that the liturgical *cursus* was other than it ought to have been. Rather the accounts suggest a well-organized institution of the kind that might be expected to support a well-organized conventual life. Canons regular were not Cistercians. There was, besides, the prestige of the priory to be considered in an aristocratic society where prestige was power, and power was influence. Just how that influence was mediated is revealed in a disarmingly frank manner by the seneschal in 1344, as he rendered account for 2*s*. 8*d*., 'in cloth bought and given to the purveyors of the chief justiciary of Ireland that they may be more favourable to us; to make hose of it for them'.[68] The accounts are replete with gifts showered upon officials of all kinds, which are almost certainly *douceurs* with past or future favours in mind. What looks to us like bribery, to con-

64 Lydon and Fletcher, *Account roll of the priory of Holy Trinity, Dublin*, pp 5–6. **65** Ibid., p. 111; cf. p.118. For details about this parliament see H.G. Richardson and G.O. Sayles, *The Irish parliament in the Middle Ages* (Philadelphia, 1964), p. 338. The prior was technically a tenant-in-chief of the king, as the lands of the priory were taken into his hand *sede vacante*. The prior seems normally to have been summoned to parliament. See H.G. Sayles and G.O. Richardson, *Parliaments and councils of medieval Ireland* (Dublin, 1947), pp xxvii–xxix. **66** Saucers contained salt or sauces in this period, and should not be confused with cups and saucers. **67** Lydon and Fletcher, *Account roll of the priory of Holy Trinity, Dublin*, pp 88–90. **68** Ibid., p. 92.

temporaries looked like wise and provident management. Nor should we overlook the less visible role that kinship almost certainly played in such a society. One wonders if Brother William de Assheburne was related to Sir Elias de Assheborn, the justice itinerant, who received a gift from the prior.[69] Certainly, no embarrassment is evident when the prior showed favours to his brother or to his kinsmen.[70] What the Christ Church account rolls reveal is a picture of experienced, competent, and worldly-wise priors, who were in no way disadvantaged by their celestial calling in dealing with the tough world of business and politics. Churchmen of this calibre had no need of twentieth-century insights into the theology of *aggiornamento*.

IV

In tracing the careers of parochial clergy, the key to advancement was beyond doubt patronage. Without an influential patron, it is unlikely that talent alone was sufficient for advancement. In the later Middle Ages having a degree in canon law was important in climbing the ecclesiastical ladder, but in order to obtain a university degree it was necessary in the first instance to have a benefice as a means of support.

All roads, then, led to the patron. As far as Anglo-Norman Ireland is concerned, the largest corporate patronage was held by the monasteries. When the Anglo-Norman lords established their lordships in the late twelfth century, they found no parochial system in existence, with the result that they were in a position to appropriate their tithes of their fiefs either to their own religious foundations, or to others of their choice. Occasionally they retained advowsons in lay patronage, but such parishes were the exception to the rule. The main exception to this pattern of ecclesiastical settlement were the tithes of the old termon lands, which generally the bishops succeeded in retaining for themselves along with their parochial patronage. Thus the number of parishes available to bishops for presentation was usually small, and more often than not confined to the cathedral prebends. In the case of the archdiocese of Armagh *inter Anglicos*, the archbishop had the right to collate two prebends and two rectories from a total of fifty-one parishes; eight benefices were held in lay patronage, while the rest, about 80 per cent, were monastic.[71]

All of this would appear to suggest that patronage was firmly in the hands of the clergy, but it was not that simple. The king, for example, would have had the direct control only over the advowsons of his demesne manors, assuming that he had not alienated them. However, his indirect control was far more extensive because bishops, and a significant number of important abbots and priors, held their lands in chief. This meant that when dioceses were *sede vacante*, the king was entitled to dispose of benefices and cathedral prebends that were vacant at the

---

69 Ibid., p. 111. For Brother William see p. 42, and *passim*.   70 Ibid., pp 14, 88–9. It is scarcely a coincidence that the seneschal was the prior's brother.   71 Jefferies, *Priests and prelates of Armagh*, pp 42–4.

time. The same rule applied in equal measure to the monasteries, though the effect was moderated by a more rapid system of election. It applied in equal measure to vacant advowsons escheated to the crown during the minority of a tenant-in-chief.

There is plenty of evidence to indicate that the crown exploited such windfalls to the full. Following the death of Maurice fitz Thomas in 1298, the lordship of Desmond was administered by the king until his son Maurice came of age in 1314. During the minority the king directed the bishop of Cloyne to admit his clerk, Henry of Thrapston, to the church of Moyale, which was vacant and in the gift of Maurice.[72] Thus the king was in a position to reward his clerk at Maurice's expense. This fortuitous appointment marked the beginning of the career of a distinguished royal servant. In 1300 Henry was reported to have served the king well as a chancery clerk. On 18 June 1301 he assumed the office of keeper of the rolls and writs of the common bench, which he occupied till 1307.[73] He held successively the office of keeper of the rolls and writs of the eyre (1310), keeper of the rolls and writs of the king's bench (1323), justice of the bench (1329), chancellor of the exchequer (appointed 15 October 1329, but possibly without effect), and baron of the exchequer (1328–30).[74]

It would be tedious to catalogue the careers of other successful royal servants. Such examples might include Geoffrey de Tourville, who seems to have begun his career as a clerk in the service of Archbishop Henry of London. He was a witness to the charter that created the offices of the dignitaries of St Patrick's Cathedral in 1213.[75] He was archdeacon of Dublin from 1227 to 1244, when he was elected bishop of Ossory, a position that he held till his death in 1250. He was successively chamberlain of the exchequer (1226–32), justice itinerant (1230), chancellor (1232–4), treasurer (1234–50), and deputy justiciar (1245).[76] A common link between many royal servants is their association with the chapter of St Patrick's, which supported the most important element in the royal administration in Dublin, in much the same way as the chapters of St Paul's and St Martin le Grand sustained the administration in London. In the course of the reign of Henry III we find among the canons no fewer than eight ministers or judges.[77] Robin Frame has noted that royal clerks rewarded by ecclesiastical preferment between 1318 and 1361 included five treasurers and eight barons or chancellors of the exchequer. These included prebends of St Patrick's, St Canice's, Cloyne, Lismore, and an archdeaconry in Meath.[78]

Such a system clearly fostered absenteeism and pluralism. No doubt some of the evils associated with absenteeism were mitigated by the appointment of conscientious vicars, but it was undoubtedly open to abuse. In 1306 the crown sued Richard de Feringes, the archbishop of Dublin, for removing Robert de Carleton,

---

72 *Cal. justic. rolls Ire., 1305–1307*, pp 305, 318, 390–1. 73 Richardson and Sayles, *The administration of Ireland, 1172–1377*, p. 185 and note 4. 74 Ibid., pp 108, 116, 157, 184, 189. 75 H.J. Lawlor, *The fasti of St Patrick's, Dublin* (Dundalk, 1930), pp 2–4. 76 Richardson and Sayles, *The administration of Ireland*, pp 78, 92, 98, 118, 132. 77 Ibid., pp 2–4. 78 Robin Frame, *English*

a royal clerk, from the parish of Tipperkevin. It was claimed that the king had appointed him to the parish while the see was vacant after the death of Archbishop John de Sanford (1294). Robert was duly inducted by the keeper of the spiritualities of the diocese, but since he neglected to be ordained within a year of receiving possession, Sanford's successor, William de Hothum, who died in 1298, deposed him, as was entitled to do in canon law. The real issue was whether, having dispossessed, the right of presentation should have reverted to the crown even though the see was no longer vacant. It seems that both Hothum and Feringes wanted to convert Tipperkevin into a prebend of St Patrick's, and that this royal appointment got in the way of their plan. While we do not know the outcome of the case, it is likely that the king won since we do not hear of a prebendary of Tipperkevin until 1344.[79]

Another route to clerical fame and fortune lay through episcopal favour. While lacking exact figures for each diocese, there can scarcely be any doubt that the archbishop of Dublin had by far the greatest number of parochial nominations with twenty-five of the twenty-seven canonries of St Patrick's at his disposal.[80] A casual glance through the roll of the clerks of Ireland in 1368 reveals the importance of episcopal patronage on the part of benefice-seekers at the papal court in Avignon. Of the fifteen Irish clergy seeking cures, seven petitioned for benefices in the gift of a bishop, while the remaining eight petitioned for prebends, which with few exceptions belonged to the bishop. In every instance, those in search of a prebend either possessed a degree in canon law, or claimed to be skilled in law, while none of the benefice-seekers had legal qualifications, one describing himself as 'a poor priest', and another as 'a poor clerk'.[81] It is therefore very clear that in order to secure a position in the cathedral chapter, it was almost essential to have a legal qualification of the kind that would attract the approval of a bishop in search of suitably qualified officials for diocesan administration.

Much could be said about papal provisions, the volume of which swelled enormously from the mid-fourteenth century, adding new levels of complexity to advancement in the church. That many petitions in the papal court were mischievous, not to say vexatious, is apparent from a strongly worded protest by Edward III in 1366, which claimed that such citations were 'moved by rancour rather than a desire to get their (the appellants') rights, so that it is easy for simple and suspected witnesses … to make false depositions in the absence of the parties.'[82] We may well suspect that the purpose of a petition was to frustrate an action in a lower court. Often dispensations were sought to legitimate situations *ex post facto*, presumably to fend off hostile bids. In the final analysis, however, when papal commendators were opposed by powerful local interests, as many found to their cost,

lordship in Ireland, 1318–1361 (Oxford, 1982), pp 99–100.   **79** See *Cal. justic. rolls Ire., 1303–1308*, pp 222, 262–3. For fuller details see Lawlor, *Fasti of St Patrick's, Dublin*, pp 171–2.   **80** Mary Ann Lyons, *Church and society in County Kildare, c.1470–1547* (Dublin, 2000), p. 64.   **81** *Cal. papal petitions, 1342–1419*, pp 467–9.   **82** *Cal. papal petitions, 1242–1419*, p. 534.

they were generally unsuccessful in making good their claims.[83] There were there-fore finite limits to the actual exercise of papal patronage: the volume of litigation was, perhaps more often than not, in inverse ratio to its effect. At the best, or so it would seem, a papal dispensation might be useful in pipping contenders to the post, all else being equal.

To whom could an aspiring cleric turn to secure a benefice, when these routes, for one reason or another, were not options? On the face of it, the monasteries were the major-power brokers since collectively they held more parishes than all others together. Unlike the bishop, abbots and priors had sufficient resources within their communities for supplying their administrative needs, as we have seen in the case of Holy Trinity, Dublin. In this sense, the parishes for which they had to find vic-ars were superfluous to their needs. Twelfth- and thirteenth-century bishops wel-comed the wholesale granting of rectorial tithes by pious laymen to monasteries precisely because it took clerical patronage out of lay control. In theory, monaster-ies could be presumed to appoint worthy vicars to discharge the cure of souls in dependent parishes. The reality could be very different. In the course of a metro-political visitation of the parish of Greenoge, County Meath, in 1355, it was reported that the abbot of St Thomas, Dublin, was cited for the poor state of the chancel, for which as rector he was directly responsible. But worse was to follow:

> Sir William Magenich, the chaplain of the parish, did not know how to read, sing, understand, or conduct his office in an appropriate manner (*con-grue*). He could not baptize or teach his parishioners. He was drunk every Sunday.[84] He was possessed of every vice. He celebrated a second marriage by pronouncing the collect 'propitiare' over Roger Froysell and Joan Marche ... He raged against his parishioners, threatening to beat many of them, and continually provoked them to anger ... He used the wax for his own use and sold the candles, giving bread that was blessed to numerous women. They said that the abbot of St Thomas, who is rector, appointed another chaplain of good reputation to serve there. He granted the custody of the church to Robert Beleyns, who barred the door (*firmavit*) on the instruction of the rector. Sir William thereupon caused a small boy to gain entrance through a window in the chancel, with the result that he occupied the church for three days against the command of the rector. He also put the pix with the Body of Christ in a place where rats and mice ate it ... [85]

How could a wealthy and powerful abbey so mismanage a dependent vicarage? While it may have been a case of simple bungling on the part of the monastery —

83 See, for example, the contested priorship of Kells priory in the fifteenth century, in Empey, 'The sacred and the secular: the Augustinian priory of Kells', pp 147–8.   84 The Latin is very corrupt here, but drunkenness is clearly the issue.   85 Brendan Smith (ed.), *The register of Milo Sweteman, archbishop of Armagh, 1361–1380* (Dublin, 1996), no. 158, p. 158.

monasteries were not uncommonly accused of being careless or incompetent in
their oversight of parishes[86] – two other possibilities present themselves. Greenoge
may have been so poor that no Anglo-Norman priest sought it: Magenich or
Maguiness is plainly an Irish name. Alternatively, the abbot may have yielded to
powerful lay interests. Just as the king, the bishops, and the monasteries exploited
the parochial church to reward their clerical officials or satisfy all kinds of lobby-
ists, so too local or regional lords sought to exploit the church for precisely the
same reasons. Monasteries did not exist in a political vacuum. We have already seen
how finely tuned Holy Trinity was to its political environment. Seeking favours
also involved granting them proportionately. We have also noted the tendency of
monasteries in the late Middle Ages to fall under the direct control of local lords
to the extent that the abbot or prior was as often as not a family member. In such
circumstances appointments to dependent parishes were as much part of the spoils
as were the possessions of the monastery. It is basically a question of political
physics. Powerful families were not interested in intruding their members into the
poorest parishes, but that does not mean that the needs of more humble clients
could be ignored. For proof of the pervasive influence of the earls of Kildare over
the monasteries and churches within their seigniorial sphere of influence, one can
do no better than to pursue the details in Mary Ann Lyons's excellent analyses of
the anatomy of power in their lordship in the latter half of the fifteenth, and first
half of the sixteenth, centuries.[87]

   The pervasive influence of lay interests was evident even before the structures
of episcopal, royal, and papal authority were eclipsed in the later fourteenth century. How the influence of a lay patron might be exercised is nicely illustrated in
the case of the parish of Maynooth, located at the centre of Geraldine power. In
1248 the archbishop of Dublin at the request of Maurice Fitz Gerald converted
the parish into a prebend of St Patrick's Cathedral. Maurice, however, was careful
to reserve the right of presentation, thereby giving him a platform from which he
could influence key appointments in church and state. Among the subsequent
prebendaries of Maynooth were John of Sandford, dean of St Patrick's (1275–84)
and archbishop of Dublin (1284–94). It should be noted that Sandford was also a
distinguished royal servant, serving as escheator of Ireland from 1271 to 1285, justice itinerant (1275), and keeper and deputy justiciar (1288–90). He was presented
by Maurice to Maynooth *c*.1281 while dean of the cathedral, and still occupied it
in 1290 when he was archbishop. One is left with the impression of a convenient
arrangement that suited all parties: Maurice, the king, the cathedral, and indeed de

---

86 The same visitation reported that the abbot failed to prevent animals from pasturing in the
churchyard of adjacent parish of Donaghmore, with the result that pigs continually 'violated' it
so that on one occasion they exhumed the body of a woman. Ibid., p. 157.   87 See Lyons, *Church
and society in County Kildare*, pp 79–96; idem, 'The foundation of the Geraldine college of the
Blessed Virgin Mary, Maynooth, 1518', in *Journal of the Kildare Archaeological Society*, xviii, pt 2
(1994–5), pp 134–50.

Sandford himself. Sandford was succeeded by Walter Wogan, who must have been a canon of St Patrick's, although he is not listed in Lawlor's *Fasti*.[88] Walter was later to be a justice of the king's bench and escheator, but does not seem on the basis of the extant records to have been involved in the royal administration in the 1290s. Walter's occupation of Maynooth was, however, destined to be short, for at some point before 1306 he was 'induced' to resign it by the patron, John fitz Thomas, in favour of his son, Thomas, and his tutor, Master Walter Walraund. Apart from providing his son with a significant rectorial income, it looks as if Thomas was a minor, which may account for the association with his tutor, who was certainly in clerical orders.[89] Assuming he was the same Thomas that succeeded his father as the second earl of Kildare in 1317, he must never have progressed beyond minor orders, if indeed he was ordained.[90]

The case of the disputed advowson of the parish of Kinneigh, diocese of Glendalough, in 1308 illustrates the extent to which proprietorial rights and bonds of kinship could become inextricably entangled in church matters. This bitter dispute had its origin in a royal intrusion during the minority of the wives of Nicholas le Norreys and Henry Baret, the patronesses of Kinneigh.[91] The royal appointment fell to Thomas de Yaneworth, who was duly inducted by the archdeacon of Glendalough. This was not at all to the liking of Nicholas and Henry, who intruded a rival candidate, Master Bartholomew de Eyteleye, presumably at the instigation of their wives, having obtained another judgement from John Cheure, the dean of Leighlin, whose subsequent reputation for dishonesty gives us good grounds for suspecting that bribery may have been involved.[92] Whereupon Bartholomew's brothers Richard and Thomas, together with the husbands of the patronesses and David le Poer, broke down the door of the church and threw out Thomas's belongings. Although Thomas appealed against the false judgement, he was not prepared to wait. Instead he sought redress from a powerful lord, Arnold le Poer,[93] promising him the fruits of the church in the autumn on condition that

88 *Cal. justic. rolls Ire., 1305–1307*, pp 252–3. See also Lawlor, *Fasti of St Patrick's, Dublin*, pp 127–8.   **89** In the papal taxation of 1302–06, the income of Maynooth was estimated to be £20 per annum, which certainly placed it among the wealthier parishes. *Cal. doc. Ire., 1302–1307*, no. 711, p. 237.   **90** There is, besides, no record of his being a prebendary of St Patrick's Cathedral.
91 The sisters clearly inherited the advowsons from their father, who was either a tenant-in-chef of the king, or else it was ward within a ward. In feudal law daughters inherited equal shares of their father's estate, when there was no male heir. I have not been able to identify their father, but would suggest that he may have been Waleran de Wellesley, lord of Kenegh, killed in 1303: see E. St J. Brooks, *Knights' fees in counties Wexford, Carlow and Kilkenny* (Dublin, 1950), p. 55. Brooks suggests the parish of Kicullen for the location of Kenegh, but I suspect he may be incorrect.   **92** In 1310 John was found guilty of forging a quitclaim in favour of his son Geoffrey, having broken into a chest containing the seal of the deceased bishop of Leighlin. For good measure, he also forged a letter under the same seal granting the archdeacon of Leighlin all the profits of visitation, half of the profits of the chapter, and all the profits arising from probate of wills. *Cal. justic. rolls Ire., 1308–1314*, pp 165–6.

he protected him against a renewed assault by Bartholomew, his kin, and the patronesses' kindred. Arnold wasted no time, and succeeded in ousting the Bartholomew's men from the church. Not to be outdone, Bartholomew's brother Richard offered another magnate, Thomas le Botiller,[94] the fruits of the church for a whole year if he managed to restore the church to Bartholomew, and hold it against all comers. Once again the tables were turned, Thomas le Botiller and the Eyteleye gang compelled Arnold's men to withdraw. To make his power more visible, Thomas le Botiller remained in force at the church for several days, having dispatched a force of kern to deprive Yaneworth of his tithes by confiscating sheaves of corn. When he finally departed, he left soldiers in charge of the church, who once again threw out Yaneworth's belongings.

While the episode has all the ingredients of a comic opera, the surprising thing is that no one was killed. It was no longer just a matter of settling rival claims to an advowson between rival claimants: the retinues of magnates, always prone to violence, were now involved, as was the prestige of the contending lords. On this occasion it so happened that there was a bloodless ending. Backed by Arnold, Yaneworth eventually succeeded in prosecuting his claim to Kinneigh, but not before the archbishop of Dublin and his vicar general, the dean of St Patrick's Cathedral, were drawn into the action.[95] The happy ending notwithstanding, we should note that two things about this case. First, it was only after a long process that the right of the crown against the precipitate actions of local lords in the form of the patronesses and their husbands was finally vindicated by means of an action moved by a more powerful lord, Arnold le Poer. In other words, the forms of canon law that emerged in the course of the church-state struggles of the twelfth century, designed to limit, if not eliminate, lay interference in ecclesiastical matters, should never be taken at their face value. In reality what we see both in Maynooth and Kinneigh is the extent to which the politics of church and society, whether at micro- or macro-levels, were inseparably fused. In the later Middle Ages, as the authority of the church's institutions diminished, the encroachment of secular interests, previously latent, emerges into the clear light of day. We may also note how easily a dispute involving minor lords quickly escalated into a wider

---

93 Arnold's power base was in Kilkenny and Waterford. He played an important role in the Bruce war in Ireland (see G.O. Sayles, *Documents on the affairs of Ireland before the king's council* (Dublin, 1979), nos 101–2, 104, 107). As seneschal of the liberty of Kilkenny in he played a major role in frustrating Bishop Ledrede's prosecution of Alice Kyteler (ibid., no 162). In 1327 he was involved in a baronial war with Maurice fitz Thomas of Desmond (see G.H. Orpen, *Ireland under the Normans* (4 vols, Oxford, 1920, reprinted 1968), iv, pp 221–6. It may be noted that the Butlers were allies of Maurice fitz Thomas in this war, so there may have been longstanding rivalries between them in the background of the Kinneigh affair.   94 Thomas le Botiller was presumably the brother of Edmund le Botiller, later earl of Carrick, and father of James, first earl of Ormond. Richard had sought him out at Tullow, one of the Butler's demesne manors.   95 *Cal. justic. rolls Ire., 1308–1314*, pp 14–16. The rectory of Kinneigh, or at least a third part of it, belonged to St Patrick's Cathedral (*Fiants Ire. Edw. VI*, no. 665)

dispute involving magnates. Even when a magnate had no direct interest in appointments, the dynamics of lordship were such that he could not be indifferent to the interests of his tenants or clients. The process of secularisation – or re-secularization – of the church in the fifteenth and sixteenth centuries is less a late medieval phenomenon than a natural development of the situation that had preceded it.

While we have good reason to suspect widespread lay involvement in ecclesiastical preferment at every level, it is less easy to identify the more indirect influence of kinship, particularly in Anglo-Norman areas where hereditary incumbencies were extremely rare.[96] But we would be rash to conclude that the interests of the kindred, in a society where kinship was the focus of loyalty and a system of mutual protection, were therefore absent. We have seen how it played a part in the alienation of monastic property, and how the problems at St Peter's, Trim, and at Kinneigh, involved members of the kindred who were not prepared to hold back when the going got rough. Occasionally we can catch glimpses of this unseen cloud of witnesses when, for example, in the assizes at Wexford in 1312 William fitz Adam Hay, a clerk, and William fitz Adam Hay Cam were charged with homicide and robbery. William the clerk was found guilty of aiding and abetting robberies, but not of homicide. He was therefore committed to the custody of the church. His kinsman, Adam fitz Adam Hay Cam, was found guilty on all charges, but was admitted to make fine of eight marks by the pledges of Richard fitz William Hay, John fitz Hamund Hay, and John fitz William Hay.[97] While we do not know what became of his clerical cousin, we can scarcely doubt that his kin were prepared to do no less for him. In such a society it is difficult to believe that kinship interests played a lesser role in the governance of the church than they did in the world of laymen. Like customary law, such things were so integral to social norms that they surface only as incidental records.

The routes to clerical preferment in Gaelic areas diverge markedly from the familiar structures of the Anglo-Norman church, partly because of the differing social structures, but more particularly because of the time-gap of almost a century that elapsed between the creation of the diocesan system in the twelfth century and the transfer of various lands and rights in canon law to the bishops.[98] The resulting compromises produced a system of ecclesiastical governance that enabled families to establish hereditary claims to certain parishes, chapter functions or erenachy, on the one hand, and families with an hereditary profession as churchmen, such as the Maguires already mentioned, on the other. Membership of a kin-group was therefore frequently the key to preferment, though it is important not to over-exaggerate the contrast with the Anglo-Norman church. In this regard Henry

96 See Katherine Simms, 'Frontiers in the Irish Church – regional and cultural' in T. Barry, R. Frame and K. Simms (eds), *Colony and frontier in medieval Ireland* (London, 1995), p. 180.   **97** *Cal. Justic. rolls Ire., 1308–1314*, pp 236–7.   **98** Simms, 'Frontiers in the Irish Church – regional and cultural', p. 184.

Jefferies has identified several Gaelic surnames that predominate among the clergy of the diocese of Armagh *inter Hibernicos* in the fifteenth and early sixteenth centuries. Of these, the O'Lougherans and the O'Connellans account for about a third of all the clergy in that part of the diocese.[99] This hereditary element was further reinforced by the widespread practice of concubinage. All these tendencies appear to have been compounded by the incapacity of bishops to enforce their authority when it was obstructed by powerful lords. While it is never easy to read the political realities underlying the formal processes of ecclesiastical courts, the numerous citations, excommunications and consequent absolutions of Richard O Raghallaigh (O'Reilly), bishop of Kilmore, by the archbishop of Armagh, between 1366 and 1368 indicate that without the support of powerful laymen the archbishop's efforts were continually frustrated by the bishop. On 12 June 1366 the archbishop summoned Richard to appear at his manor of Dromiskin for persisting in his obdurate rebellion in spite of the imposition of the sentence of excommunication.[1] While his fault is not specified, there is little doubt that it related to his adulterous and incestuous relationship with his cousin Edina O Raghallaigh, referred to in a letter dated 27 August 1366.[2] Two other members of the O Raghallaigh family surface in ensuing correspondence: Richard's brother Cathal, described as a *nobilis vir*, whose precise role is hard to determine,[3] and Philip O Raghallaigh, king of Brefni.[4] The bishop's relationship to the king is nowhere stated, but it would be surprising if there was none, since his brother was reckoned to be a *nobilis vir*. However, families ties, particularly in contested elections to the chieftainship, could equally involve family rivalries. Almost incredibly, in spite of his defiance of the archbishop, Richard appealed to him in September (1367?) to aid him against the oppression of the church in his diocese by Philip, thereby giving the archbishop the opportunity to lecture him on his canonical disobedience and moral notoriety over many years: it was not to be wondered that such evils had befallen the church in his diocese.[5] It was doubtless these circumstances that induced the bishop to submit yet again in January 1368, when the archbishop agreed to absolve him subject to penalties, and ordered the clergy to treat with Philip regarding the sequestration of the fruits of the bishopric.[6] A reasonable reading of the context would suggest that in order to bring the bishop to heel, the archbishop had allied himself with a rival faction of the O Raghallaigh clan, in this instance the king of Brefney, and that in such situations the authority of the church could only be sustained when allied to powerful regional lords.

---

99 Jefferies, *Priests and prelates of Armagh*, pp 73–5.   **1** Smith (ed.), *The register of Milo Sweteman*, no. 70. The dispute may be pursued in greater detail in nos 68–78, 99, 120–1.   **2** Ibid., no. 73. Edina McGau(?)ueran was daughter of his uncle and wife of McGuyer (no. 68). The charge of incest relates to sexual relations within the degrees prohibited in canon law.   **3** Ibid., nos 71, 120. **4** Ibid., nos 68 and 99.   **5** Ibid., no. 99.   **6** Ibid., no. 68.

V

In spite of their ubiquity, it is difficult to profile clergy among the ranks of the chaplains. For our immediate purposes, they may be defined as unbeneficed secular priests. They came in various forms: private chaplains, members of secular collegiate chapters, chantry chaplains, chaplains employed by religious and craft guilds, and parochial chaplains. In many respects, they were the workhorses of the late medieval church, existing for the most part on meagre fees. Literacy offered other opportunities such as teaching, though the evidence is hard to pinpoint, and, more certainly, in drafting wills and conveyances. There can be little doubt, however, that most of their income was derived from their priestly functions, particularly in satisfying an almost insatiable market for masses for the dead, which was such a marked feature of late-medieval lay piety.[7] This demand was common to all orders: only the wealthy could afford the services of a private chaplain, while ordinary parishioners had ready recourse to religious guilds to cater for their celestial welfare.

An example of how seriously the layman regarded his spiritual welfare is nicely illustrated by John of Grauntsete, a wealthy and influential citizen of Dublin, who breakfasted with the prior of Holy Trinity on 22 January 1338, accompanied by his private chaplain.[8] Only three years previously, the priory had entered into an agreement with John, a friend and benefactor for many years, whereby it undertook to provide two canon priests

> as long as the world shall last ... on every day to celebrate for ever divine offices ... for the welfare of the same John while he lives ... also for the souls of the said Alice (his deceased wife), their ancestors, heirs, benefactors, and all those for whom the same John and Alice are in any way bound, and of all the faithful departed.[9]

John was not a man to take chances. The agreement specified the wording of two collects to be said daily for him while he was alive, and two appropriately reworded collects to be said daily after his departure. Provision had to be made in the event that the two canons were prevented from carrying out their office through illness. Every missal from henceforth had to contain a rubric in the margin by the *secretum* of the mass: 'orate pro Johanne de Grauntsete et Alicia uxore ejus ac pro omnibus quibus tenentur'. Further provisions included a requirement that each year on All Saints Day and Quadragesima Sunday the agreement would be read in the presence of the entire community. Nor was this the limit of John's benefaction. In 1347 he was licensed by the prior to build a chapel in honour of the Holy Trinity in St Michan's churchyard, while in the following year he built the chapel

7 See Adrian Empey, 'The layperson in the parish: the medieval inheritance, 1169–1536' in Gillespie and Neely, especially pp 18–21.   8 See Mills (ed.), *Account roll of the priory of the Holy Trinity, Dublin, 1337–1346*, p. 5.   9 Ibid., pp 148–51.

del Marie du Grace on the bridge of Dublin.[10] In the final analysis, it was the widespread and compelling force of lay piety that sustained the existence of large numbers of chaplains, who were in almost every other respect superfluous to the essential operation of the ecclesiastical system.

Such agreements were common. Sometime around 1280, Lady Elinor Purcell granted 'for her charity and her soul' to the prior and canons of St Mary, Rathkeale, 'a tithe of all bread, ale, porks, wethers or sheep, the shoulder of each beef, and of all other victual expended in her court of Moycro (Croagh, County Limerick.)[11] In return the priory undertook to provide a chaplain in their church, who would intercede for her soul, and those of her parents, husband, and ancestors for ever. Similarly in 1235 Nicola de Tuyt entered into an agreement with the prior and brethren of the Hospital of St John of Newtown near Trim to maintain a priest at the presentation of Nicola or her successors to celebrate mass daily in perpetuity for her soul, her husband's, and for predecessors and successors. The chaplain so presented could be received as a brother, if he so wished.[12]

Most chantries lasted only for a fixed term, as designated by will, but where lady chapels existed in parochial churches – with or without guilds attached to them – it is likely that each would normally have been served by a chaplain. In 1471, for example, there were altars dedicated to St Mary, St Brigid, and St Thomas in the parish church of Clondalkin. Three years later we hear of three chaplains there, each presumably serving the side altars.[13] Only the most powerful lords had the capacity to fund perpetual chantries or secular colleges designed to do the same thing. A number of them are well known: for example, the colleges at Gowran, Youghal, Maynooth, and Ardee. In the case of Maynooth, the ninth earl of Kildare established rules for the governance of the college, with procedures for the appointment of a provost, vice-provost, five priests, two clerks, and three choristers to pray for his soul and those of his ancestors.[14] The most ambitious plan, however, was put forward in July 1305 by Richard de Burgo, earl of Ulster, who sought royal licence to create a college of twenty-four chaplains at his manors of Loughrea and Tipperbride 'to celebrate daily for ever for the souls of the said earl and his ancestors'.[15] When an inquest was held to determine whether such a licence would not be in the king's interest, the jurors replied that

> it would be much to the advantage of the king and country if such chantry
> should be established in one or other of these places, if for no other reason,
> for teaching of the boys of those parts where such learning is very scant.[16]

10 McEnery and Refaussé (eds), *Christ Church deeds*, no. 236; Mary Clark and Raymond Refaussé (eds), *Directory of historic guilds of Dublin* (Dublin, 1993), p. 32. 11 *Cal. justic. rolls Ire., 1305–1307*, p. 434. 12 See James Mills and M.J. McEnery (eds), *Calendar of the Gormanston register* (Dublin, 1916) pp 151–2. 13 Berry (ed.), *Register of the wills and inventories of the diocese of Dublin*, pp 98, 113. 14 For further information see Lyons, *Church and society in County Kildare*, pp 87–96. 15 *Cal. justic. rolls Ire., 1305–1307*, p. 141. 16 Ibid., *1305–1307*, p. 142.

That this proposal seems never to have been acted upon is not important from our perspective.[116] What is significant is the assumption on the part of the jurors that such an institution might be presumed to engage in teaching, as though it was their common experience. The proposition that chantries fulfilled a useful educational function is therefore not entirely fanciful. Fees earned by chaplains as tutors would not surface in legal or parochial records because that was not their purpose. Their educational role in society is consequently likely to be invisible in the extant records.

Since the parochial chaplain was neither rector nor vicar, he derived nothing from the normal sources of parish income such as tithes, glebeland, or the sort of customary dues we have encountered in the parish of Fennor. He may have received some share of the surplice fees for baptisms, burials, marriages, and the churching of women, although these dues would normally have been attached to the rectory or vicarage since they were rooted in parochial prerogative rights. He must consequently have depended on chantry fees and retaining fees from both religious and craft guilds. In St Werburgh's, Dublin, the chaplain of the St Mary Chapel was paid five shillings every quarter by the churchwardens.[18] It is clear from the medieval deeds of the same parish that there were normally two, and possibly more, chaplains in St Werburgh's in the fifteenth century.[19] Since they are not mentioned in the churchwardens' accounts, it is likely that they were maintained by private chantries or guilds. In 1482, for example, Sir Adam Gare, chaplain, conveyed a stone house with two cellars and a garden adjoining the city wall to Sir Thomas Laundy and Sir Elise Feld, also chaplains (probably representing the parish of St Werburgh) on condition that if the tenant should die without heirs they were to find a priest 'to sing at our Lady's altar for ever in the said church, for the souls of William Boxseworth, Margaret Bosseworth, and Dame Maude Plunket, and all their generation'.[20] The deed further provided that in the event of the deaths of William and Margaret, two other priests were to be appointed, one at the election of Dame Maude and the other at the election of the churchwardens of St Werburgh's. A broadly similar picture emerges from the deeds of the parish of St John, Dublin. In 1413 three chaplains are named in a lease, which corresponds to the terms of a will made by John Lytill in 1434, in which he bequeathed to Sir William fitz William, chaplain, his gown, bed, and personal deeds, and futher conveyed certain lands to be given in fee simple to him and to two other chaplains whom Sir William is to nominate. John made provision of a rent of forty shillings

17 While there is a reference to a house in Loughrea in need of repair in 1437, this seems to allude to the Carmelite friary rather than to a secular college. There seems to be a fundamental confusion in A. Gwynn and R.N. Hadcock (eds), *Medieval religious houses. Ireland* (London, 1970), p. 291.   18 Account of Patryke Daly Kendy and Richard Dowgyne, proketors of Seynt Warbrowe churche from 9 June 1510 to 4 August 1511, RCBL, MS 326.27.1.8, f. 1. Payments of five shillings are recorded for the 'mydsomer', 'Mygha'mas', 'Chrystmas', and 'Ester' quarters.   19 Henry F. Twiss, 'Some ancient deeds of the parish of St Werburgh, Dublin, 1243–1676' in *PRIA*, xxxv (1919), pp 282–315. See nos 81, 83, 85, 86, 90, 92.   20 Ibid., no. 36.

annually to provide a perpetual chantry of one priest in the chapel of St Mary in St John's church, where he desired to be buried.[21] What is clear from parochial deeds of this kind is the role that chaplains played – as did clerks – in such conveyances. Chaplains were commonly appointed executors of wills, and in the case of Sir William fitz William provision was made for payment to him of twenty shillings 'for his trouble as executor, and a like sum is left to James Yonge'.[22] In addition to being executors, both chaplains and parish clerks are commonly mentioned in wills as the recipients of bequests, which seems to point to close personal friendships formed in the intimate community of a small urban parish.[23] In 1439, for example, William fitz John Passavaunt, junior, included among his beneficiaries Geoffrey Calfe, chaplain. He also bequeathed his cup 'called piper' to John Clerke, chaplain, and another silver cup to his mother. Both John and his mother Johanna were designated executors of the will.[24]

VI

Although clerks were the lowest in the clerical estate, they were ubiquitous. Their usefulness in administration probably stemmed from the fact that with the possible exception of the parish clerk they were unencumbered by the ritual burdens imposed by ordination on the major orders. Thus we find them – as we have already seen – most prominently in the service of crown. But they were also essential to the functioning of local government, hence they are frequently mentioned in county administration and also in municipal government. Many of the more routine conveyances are attested by clerks in the service of mayor of Dublin, for example.[25]

The day-to-day involvement in the operations of local government presented clerks with many opportunities for corruption, with the result that their activities often came to the attention of the royal courts.[26] The assizes held before Thomas

---

21 John L. Robinson, 'On the ancient deeds of the parish of St John, Dublin, preserved in the library of Trinity College' in *PRIA*, xxxiii (1916–17), pp 175–244, nos 94 and 112. I cannot be certain that the naming of two, and sometimes three, chaplains in these parochial conveyances is indisputable evidence that they were attached to the parish. The repetition of many of the same names in other parochial deeds, however, inclines me to think they were parochial. 22 Ibid., no. 112. James Yonge is described as a clerk and public notary in another parish deed in 1411 (ibid., no. 86). 23 See, for example, *Calendar of Christ Church deeds*, nos 633 (1346) and 239 (1348). In both instances Sir Thomas Hamund, chaplain of St Werburgh's, received a bequest. 24 Ibid., no. 290. 25 Robinson, 'Ancient deeds of the parish of St John, Dublin', nos 2, 4, 5, 6, 7, 11, 12, 13, 15, 24, 26. 26 In these and the ensuing cases cited from the justiciary rolls, it is not always possible to be certain that the term 'clerk' always signified a clerk in minor, as opposed to major, orders, since the purpose of the court was simply to determine whether or not the person charged was justiciable in a royal court. That said, the court rolls are usually careful to signify the status of a cleric, for example to specify if he is a vicar, parson, chaplain, or canon regular.

fitz Maurice at Limerick and Ardfert in 1295 reveal just how endemic such corruption could be among the clerical ranks of the county administration. The list of the charges, largely upheld by the juries, is certainly a tribute to their inventiveness. Isaac Colom and Walter fitz Adam the clerk, were

> charged that when they ought to summon 12 (jurors) at Dublin or elsewhere, they caused to be summoned 40 or 60, and then took bribes from some that they might remain at home; and that when 12 rich men were chosen at Dublin or elsewhere, the said clerks, for bribes from the rich men, put in their place poor men who had not the means of going there, and so for default were fined. And when some by general inquisition were indicted, the said clerks for bribes showed the indictments to them, and withdrew those indicted from the indictments, and showed the names of the jurors to them (i.e. he disclosed the names of those who had indicted them), so that the jurors sustained great damage. And that Walter also made a false writ of replevin for John Goch *v.* Ric. le Chapillein, and they said that the writ was obtained in chancery ... [27]

Robert de Clahulle was charged among other things that when he was serjeant he extorted sheep from the people of his bailiwick in County Kerry, and marked them for sending to his house; that he attached people who were not indicted, pretending that they had been, 'who for fear made fine with him; and that he would not leave the houses of some until he had gifts ... of lambs, young pigs, wool.'[28] There was worse to come. Adam de Cantelup was charged with the murder of William fitz Adam fitz Yue on the bridge of Limerick. Acting as subsheriff of Kerry in lieu of his brother Richard, he stood charged of empanelling whom he wished and extorting bribes to release them from their duty. He took gifts from felons to let them evade capture. Like others, he summoned large numbers of jurors in order to exact bribes. He forged an inquisition in the name of a coroner to gain the acquittal of a felon charged with homicide. It was also alleged 'that when he hated any free tenant he would put him on some jury in the *iter* (eyre) of Limerick.'[29] While most of the convicted clerks were committed to prison and dismissed from the king's service, some were allowed to make fine, including the notorious Adam de Cantelup, perhaps unsurprisingly given his connection with the sheriff. Significantly the clan rallied to his aid: his pledges included seven Cantelups, and we can be fairly confident that others named had family connections.

For some reason or reasons not easy to discern, there is a much higher incidence of clerks appearing before the courts than of any other clerical category. Certainly criminous clergy of all kinds had their day in court. In 1300 three clerical conmen – 'false preachers' – were convicted by a jury for extorting money by means of false exommunications and 'feigned precepts'. The court was satisfied that they were

27 *Cal. justic. rolls Ire., 1295–1303*, p. 20.   28 Ibid., *1295–1303*, p. 21.   29 Ibid., *1295–1303*, p. 22.

clergy as they were committed to the custody of the archbishop of Cashel.[30] In 1311 two curious robberies occurred in the priory of Holy Trinity and the abbey of St Thomas. Philip le Clerk was charged and convicted of stealing the oblations of divers people for the aid of the Holy Land, breaking into the coffer of John of Exeter, and stealing a robe from the image of St Katherine. It appeared that this crime was aided and abetted by one of the canons, William de Clifford. Although they claimed clerical privilege, the court refused to hand them over to the archbishop's attorney on the ground that they were guilty of sacrilege. Brother Roger of Corbaly, a canon of St Thomas's, was more enterprising. He disposed of his habit, shaved his head, dressed in lay garments, broke into coffers, mutilated charters and muniments, and stole sixty pounds of silver.[31] Churches offered a natural attraction for robbers, not only because of alms collections and silver objects, but also because ordinary parish churches seem to have functioned commonly as deposit banks. In the same year as the Holy Trinity and St Thomas's break-ins, robbers broke into the parish church of St Michael, Athy, and helped themselves to the contents of nine chests belonging to named individuals, containing an extraordinary assortment of valuables.[32]

While instances of clerks robbing churches can be multiplied,[33] they were frequently charged with other crimes, including homicide. In July 1312 four separate charges were brought against clerks in the assizes in County Waterford, two involving homicide, a robbery in the cathedral, and the theft of animals.[34] But not all clerical crime was driven by violence or love of filthy lucre. While clerks were permitted to marry, they were no less tempted by the promptings of the flesh than other mortals. Thus in 1311 Adam, clerk of the bishop of Limerick, eloped with the wife of Nicholas Roth for six months, but made the mistake of robbing her of a linen apron, a gown and tunic, for which he had to face charges.[35] Less fortunate in the lottery of love was Stephen Oregan, a clerk from Youghal, who disregarded the explicit warnings of a cuckolded husband, and paid the price by being set upon and castrated, having been caught *in flagrante delicto*.[36] The demon drink was no less compelling when, for example, David Oketfagh, a clerk, was convicted with

---

30 Ibid., *1295–1303*, p. 334.   **31** Ibid., *1308–1314*, pp 211–12, 221–2.   **32** Ibid., pp 227–8. Items included forty ells of woollen web, half a bacon, two bushels of beans, items of clothing, as well as money and silver.   **33** In 1313 Matthew Bryan stole from a trunk in the church in Emly 'a great sum of money given to the land of Jerusalem' (*Cal. justic. rolls Ire., 1308–1314*, p. 274), while in the following year another clerk was convicted of robbing the priory of St John of Jerusalem without the Newgate, Dublin, and of killing a man there (Ibid., p. 315). In 1312 two clerks were charged with breaking into a chest before the altar of St John the Baptist in Holy Trinity, Waterford, and stealing a breviary and chalice (ibid., p. 250). In 1297 Walter fitz Nicholas the chaplain robbed seven chests in St Brigid's Cathedral, Kildare, to the value of 100 shillings. Not content, he went on to rob the Carmelite friary in the town (ibid., *1295–1303*, p. 189). This inventory is by no means exhaustive.   **34** Ibid., *1308–1314*, pp 249–51, 261.   **35** Ibid., *1308–1314*, p. 207.   **36** *Cal. justic. rolls Ire., 1305–1307*, pp 376–7. Stephen brought the action against the husband, claiming damages – perhaps understandably – of £1000. He was awarded £20.

other malefactors of robbing two boats on the Shannon of twenty-seven gallons of beer and forty gallons of wine.[37]

In seeking to determine what lay behind this catalogue of crime, the judicial records provide no clues. Two possibilities come to mind. First, we have already noted how closely both secular and regular clergy were bound up with the lay society in which they subsisted, not least by ties of kinship. Clerks occupied a particularly ambiguous position, since the great majority were in what we would now term secular employment, which exposed them to precisely the same pressures and temptations as laymen. The fact that they were normally married with families to feed meant that in reality they had rather more in common with the laity than with the clerarchy. Second, they had none of the support systems that parochial or regular clergy normally enjoyed, not even the sacramental opportunities that were available to unbeneficed chaplains. Most of them therefore existed on casual fees for services rendered, rather than on a salary. They may well have been drawn to crime by desperation. The evidence of the courts generally confirms the impression of poverty. In 1311, for example, Richard and John Cogeho were convicted of trading in stolen property; their forfeited property was valued at only 15*s*. 6*d*. and 2*s*. respectively. They had no free land.[38]

We gain a different, if somewhat distant, impression of the parish clerk from parochial records and wills. Given the paucity of extant parochial sources for the medieval period, it is difficult to trace the evolution and development of this clerical office.[39] The remoter origins of the order need not detain us. In the diocese of Reims in 878, rural deans were required to enquire 'whether the presbyter has a clerk, who can keep school, or read the epistle, or is able to sing as far as may seem needful to him?' Gregory IX put universal shape on the office in lieu of regional practice in his Decretals in 1230, requiring every priest who had the charge of a parish to have a clerk, who would sing with him, read the epistle and lesson, be able to keep school and admonish the parishioners to send their children to church to learn the faith.[40] Robert Grosseteste, bishop of Lincoln (1235–53), laid down that every parish of sufficient means should have a deacon or subdeacon, but in the rest 'a fitting and honest clerk to serve the priest in comely habit'.[41] That singing and reading were the normal expectations of clerks in Ireland is clearly suggested by a case in the assizes at Drogheda in 1311, when a clerk was convicted of stealing a horse from the abbot of Knock. Although no ordinary or his representative appeared in the court to claim him, the court was satisfied that he was indeed what he claimed to be 'because it was found that Gilbert reads and sings'.[42] Apart from assisting the curate in the administration of the sacraments and in the liturgy,

---

37 *Cal. justic. rolls, 1308–1314*, pp 205–6.   38 Ibid., *1308–1314*, p. 188.   39 For a brief, if not entirely satisfactory, summary description of the parish clerk, see N.J.G. Pounds, *A history of the English parish* (Cambridge, 2000), pp 187–90.   40 Cuthbert Atchley, *The parish clerk, and his right to read the liturgical epistle* (London, New York and Bombay, 1903), p. 12.   41 P.H. Ditchfield, *The parish clerk* (London, 1907), p. 17.   42 *Cal. justic. rolls Ire., 1308–1314*, p. 208.

parish clerks normally exercised the office of holy-water bearer (*aquae baiulus*). To
judge from the will of Robert North, a parishioner of St Werburgh's, Dublin, the
parish clerk was a well-established parochial officer by the mid-fourteenth century, if not earlier, and it is from about this time too that he features more regularly
in parish deeds.[43] In some respects the notarial involvement of chaplains and clerks
is impossible to distinguish. In 1405, for instance, James Yonge, clerk and notary
public, certified a statement by John Lytill about the circumstances of his arrest for
refusing to sign and seal certain documents.[44] Six years later another member of
the Yonge family, John, also a clerk and notary public, certified another deed in
relation to the same John Lytill.[45] It would appear from such collections of parish
deeds that certain families had a strong clerical tradition. Besides the Yonges, a
deed in 1467 mentions both William Bron (Brown), chaplain, and Thomas Bron,
clerk, playing a leading role in a conveyance.[46] Since the surviving parochial material is legal in nature, it contains no clues as to the clerk's liturgical involvement.
However, Richard Walsh, canon of Holy Trinity, recalled in his will in 1504 that
'when clerk of St Werburgh's, he went with the curate, Sir Henry Mulghan, to
administer the last sacraments to Richard Wydon'.[47] Richard's career as a canon of
Holy Trinity is in itself an interesting comment on the choices that faced clerks:
whether to proceed to major orders, or to marry and remain in minor orders.
There is plenty of evidence, not least the parochial deeds already discussed, that
many clerks had wives and children. The impression conveyed in parochial sources
is that the clerk was an important and respected parish officer in the later Middle
Ages. Both literacy and his visible role in the sacramental life of the community
marked him out from the ordinary mass of the laity. It may be that an effective
clerk was able to earn a good living by using his clerical skills in notarial and teaching activities. Certainly the last will and testament of Nicholas Suttowne in 1478
strongly suggests a person of comfortable means:

> (He) leaves his body to St Warburge's Church to be buried, and a crucifix;
> the house where he lives, the new rent on the key, and a third part of his
> goods to his wife for jointure; he leaves legacies to the monastery of the

---

43 His will, dated 1346, includes a number of bequests, including one to Sir Thomas, his parish
chaplain, and one to John, the parish clerk, 'for the building of Holy Trinity and St Patrick's
churches, and proving his will, and to Master Adam, the clerk.' (McEnery and Refaussé (eds),
Christ Church deeds, no. 633). A deed from the parish of St John, Dublin, dated 1364, mentions
two clerks by name, and two chaplains (Robinson, 'On the ancient deeds of the parish of St John,
Dublin', no. 50, p.189). One cannot be certain that the clerks are parochial. In general, where conveyances involve chaplains and clerks, the probability is that they are of parochial rather than
municipal provenance. City officials are notably absent from the lists of witnesses in such deeds.
The frequency of references both to chaplains and clerks increases considerably in the fifteenth-
century deeds of St Werburgh's, St John's, and the parishes of St Catherine and St James.   44
See Robinson, 'On the ancient deeds of the parish of St John, Dublin', no. 68, p. 192. Cf. p. 194.
45 Ibid., no. 85, p. 194.   46 Ibid., no. 127, p. 200.   47 *Christ Church deeds*, no. 380.

monks of the B.V.M, the four orders of friars, his five boys, the prison at the castle and the lepers, for victuals, the poor of St John without the Walls, Dublin, Anne White, Walter Holme, John Waltir, the poor of Rechell Street, Simon Walshe, clerk, a priest to celebrate for him for three years the trental of St Gregory, his father for his blessing, Justice Dowedall for restitution, Philip Bermynham to look after his wife, children and rents; to Walter Ryan, James Clerke, and to Adam Gary: should his heirs die without issue he bequeaths one half of his lands in England and Ireland to St Warburge's Church for the support of a priest to pray for the souls of himself, his wife, etc., and the other half to the abbot and monks of St Mary near Dublin; he leaves 6*s*. 8*d*. to his rector for forgotten tithes, and constitutes John Suttown, his son, and Anne Cusack, his wife, executors, Walter Champflour, abbot of St Mary's, to be supervisor and tutor over his children.[48]

If Nicholas was wealthy in virtue of inherited wealth, why would he have sought to be a parish clerk? One wonders if a clerk through involvement in conveyancing may not have been able to speculate successfully in property? Whatever the source of his wealth, he seems to he very far removed by his circumstances from the kind of clerks presented in the assizes.

VII

The dismal condition of the Irish Church in the late Middle Ages was acknowledged even by contemporaries, and not only in the oft-cited anonymous report in 1515. A half-hearted attempt was made by Henry VII in 1496 to implement a comprehensive reform programme in the Irish Church, in response to which Pope Alexander VI appointed a number of English bishops – Canterbury, Durham, London, and Bath and Wells – to oversee the process.[49] There can be little doubt that endemic warfare, power struggles within as well as between the great lordships, the feebleness of royal government, the ineffectiveness of both papal and episcopal oversight, ethnic strife, poverty and widespread dilapidation, contributed to a context in which lay and ecclesiastical interests competed – too often one and the same – for supremacy. To this heady cocktail, one must acknowledge the widespread practice of concubinage.

The only ray of light in this picture of unrelieved gloom, revealed by recent scholarship, is the remarkable renaissance of the late medieval friars – Franciscan, Dominican, and Augustinian – whose preaching made a profound impact on the laity. Between 1426 and 1539, the Irish Observant Franciscans established no less than forty-eight friaries, mostly in Connacht and Ulster.[50] The evidence of the

48 *Christ Church deeds*, no. 327.   49 See Lyons, *Church and society in County Kildare*, p. 55.   50 Colman N. Ó Clábaigh, 'Preaching in late medieval Ireland: the Franciscan contribution' in Alan

majority of late medieval wills, in the form of bequests to 'the four orders of friars' provides incontrovertible evidence of the universal esteem in which they were held by the laity. Later, the bitter comments of Protestant reformers about their influence may be taken as a tribute by an adversary.

But whence came their popularity? The mendicant orders drew their sustenance directly from lay giving – not from inherited wealth. One has only to review the evidence of the dissolution to see how modest was their realisable wealth, in marked contrast to that of the monasteries.[51] Indeed, it was precisely the lack of dependence on fixed forms of wealth that made them so difficult to suppress. Thus the mendicants did not create a new lay piety: that pre-existing piety was what produced the necessary support for these new foundations in the first instance. Besides, recent scholarship has also correctly stressed the important role played by late-medieval lay patrons in the endowment of parish churches in the dioceses of Armagh *inter Anglicos*, and Kildare.[52] Jefferies concluded from his survey of the parishes of Louth that the lack of serious complaints made against the parish clergy in the Armagh registers may be seen as evidence that they 'served their parishioners to at least a minimum standard acceptable to the church authorities, and more importantly, to their congregations'.[53] He emphasised the fact that church courts and visitations were regular and effective, to the extent that parishioners could, and sometimes did, sue the clergy when they were amiss.[54] Besides, lay piety found its expression in other ways, especially in membership of religious confraternities and in the evidence afforded by wills. My own research into the Irish laity in this period, particularly in the context of late-medieval parochial development, has led me to very similar conclusions.[55] Mary Ann Lyons has also rightly stressed the active piety and involvement of lay patrons in Kildare in the late-fifteenth and early-sixteenth centuries, not only by the earls of Kildare but also by other leading county families.[56]

The truth of the matter is that Irish society in late medieval Ireland was enormously complex, given the proliferation of internal frontiers, and the cultural complexities of lordships and dioceses that straddled ethnic boundaries. That this variety confounded outsiders should not be a source of wonderment. Since the internal politics of Ireland were necessarily confusing, why should conditions in the church be any the less confusing? In this context we must learn to live with the

J. Fletcher and Raymond Gillespie (eds), *Irish preaching, 700–1700* (Dublin, 2001), p. 82. **51** For example, the Franciscan friary, Dublin, was extended at 55s. in 1540 (*Extents Ir. mon. possessions*, p.78); the Austin friary, Dublin, at £7 3s. 2d. (ibid., p. 79); the Carmelite House, Dublin, at 53s. 8d. (ibid., p. 121); the Dominican House, Athy, 32s. (ibid., p. 173); the Carmelite House, Kildare, at 8s. 1d. (ibid., p. 168). **52** See Lyons, *Church and society in County Kildare*, pp 79–108; also Jefferies, *Priests and prelates of Armagh*, pp 2–56; idem, 'The role of the laity in the parishes of Armagh *inter Anglicos*, 1518–1553' in *Archivium Hibernicum*, lii (1998), pp 73–84. **53** Jefferies, *Priests and prelates of Armagh*, p. 55. **54** Jefferies, 'The role of the laity in the parishes of Armagh', pp 76–81. **55** Empey, 'The layperson in the parish: the medieval inheritance, 1169–1536', pp 7–48. **56** Lyons, *Church and society in County Kildare*, pp 79–108.

apparent contradiction that the acknowledged evils of the Irish Church were directly attributable, on the one hand, to the crude exploitation by the laity who sought to gain control of the church as an extension of their seigneurial interests, while at the same time they could be generous patrons where they perceived their celestial interests to be at risk.

Such anomalies are not made easier to comprehend by the nature of the sources themselves. We have already acknowledged the problems raised both by the evidence of the assizes and the nature of the papal registers. Such material is not calculated to throw light on the quality of clergy who never get entangled in legal processes, with the result that we are left with a very negative profile of late-medieval clergy. These ambiguities are perfectly illustrated by the case of the chaplain from hell, William Magenich, which we have already discussed. The archiepiscopal visitation could be regarded as evidence of low standards in high places. That, indeed, was the purpose of the articles of visitation. What the articles do not ask for is evidence of good behaviour and faithful pastoring. A closer reading of the evidence reveals that only two of the eighteen charges made in the course of examining nine parishes relate to clergy: one to the misdeeds of William, and the other to Roger Ballivus, vicar of Dompmore, who allowed animals to pasture in the cemetery. In three of the nine parishes, the jurors reported 'nothing but good' (*nichil nisi bonum*). Significantly, while charges of fornication and adultery are frequently cited in relation to parishioners, none of the nine or more clergy are so charged, although there is an implication that William's relations with 'many women' were at least ambiguous.[57]

A more nuanced estimate of the Irish clergy in the later medieval period would suggest that just as there were islands of relatively good governance in the land – or more exactly lands – of peace, so too there were areas of relatively good governance in the church, and that there was a strong correlation between the two. Where political and ecclesiastical conditions allowed church courts – so essential to clerical discipline – to function, there we can expect to find at least adequate clerical and conventual standards being observed. Indeed, the extant deeds of some of the Dublin parishes we have considered, including the medieval churchwardens' accounts of St Werburgh's, suggest a high level of parochial performance, not in any way inferior to other parts of Latin Europe. While standards might be expected to be adequate in Dublin, the evidence of John Kempe's will in 1471 suggests that even in the comparatively remote rural parish of Hollywood in the diocese of Glendalough, perilously close to the Irish of the Dublin Mountains, the parish church of St Canice had a vicar, two chaplains, a clerk and a fraternity:

> I bequeath my soul to Almighty God, the Blessed Virgin Mary and all the
> saints, and my body to be buried in the church of St Canice of Hollywood
> … Item I leave to the Fraternity of Hollywood 2 acres of rye. Item, I leave

57 Smith (ed.), *The register of Milo Sweteman*, no. 158.

to the vicar of the same, a like field of rye, with one hog. Item, I leave to the chaplain of the parish 12*d*. Item, to the chaplain of souls 12*d*. Item, to the chaplain of Grallagh 12*d*. Item, I leave to the chapel of Grallagh half an acre of rye. Item, I leave to the church of Westpalstown the like … Item, I leave to the four orders of friars of Drogheda 16*d*. Item, I leave to the clerk of Hollywood one measure of rye … Item, I leave to Friar Bull of Drogheda one hog. Item, I leave for my soul six priests with two clerks without (choir) boys, and 5 pounds of wax (*sic*). Item, for a burial place 12*d*.[58]

To judge from the livestock and crops mentioned, it looks as if John was a tenant of the manor of Hollywood. It is also apparent from his legacies that he enjoyed a good relationship with the parochial clergy. While we may wonder about the level of the vicar of Hollywood's education and accomplishment, it is quite apparent from the terms of the will that John was content with whatever ministry he had to offer. Much the same impression is conveyed by considerable numbers of wills in this period.

For all its manifest problems, the Irish church showed significant signs of life at those points where the church's institutions were closest to a far-from-indifferent laity, particularly at the level of its parochial structures and its mendicant friaries. Furthermore, much of what was good about the church is concealed behind a screen of documentary sources that fail to do it full justice. One could stand the traditional view of the late-medieval Irish church on its head by concluding that what is remarkable about important aspects of the church is not that it was so bad, but rather that it was so good in such hostile and unpromising circumstances. What is to be wondered is that it was not very much worse.

VIII

In a book dedicated to the clergy of the Church of Ireland, it is reasonable to ask what relationship has the Church of Ireland to the pre-reformations church? We understand by the term 'reformations' that radical reform and spiritual renewal were the common experience of western Christian Europeans in the course of the sixteenth century, with a lot of outworking in the succeeding century. When the dust, conflict and confusion of this enormous spiritual upheaval finally settled, western Christians found themselves in opposing religious camps, and sought to draw hard theological boundaries around their respective encampments. This was not the way it was meant to be: each reforming party thought in terms of a reforming process that would encompass the whole western church. The idea of permanent division in the church took some time to establish itself, even if the realities

58 Berry, *Register of the wills and inventories of the diocese of Dublin*, pp 14–15.

later appeared to point in that direction for a considerable time. But such a broad statement as this is fraught with historical difficulties, because it presupposes – albeit in a limited way – that a determined pattern or outcome existed in a time of confusion It is only with hindsight we presume to see a pattern taking shape that was somehow invisible to contemporaries. It is fair to say that no professional historian would sleep easily on such a view. History has no inevitabilities. All historical events are contingent: their eventual outworking has at least as much to do with the variable possibilities that existed at the time of their occurrence, as they have with what actually happened, assuming that in itself is determinable. One of the debates that arose when the theological boundary-drawing process got under way in the controversies of the early seventeenth century concerned the relationship of the post-reformations Irish churches with the medieval past. At issue was the desire to demonstrate which side in the religious conflict was the rightful claimant to the faith of St Patrick. As is always the case is such debates, the real issue concerned the present, the past being conceived purely in terms of an idealised present. The time is surely past for anyone in the twenty-first century to revisit a debate that was not only rhetorical, but anachronistic. In terms of theological genealogy, all one can say is that the churches of the sixteenth century have their common roots in the theological traditions of the western church. How one measures that relationship is a theological, not an historical, issue.

The most obvious historical continuity from the perspective of the Church of Ireland has to do with the structures that the church has inherited from the Middle Ages. As a consequence of the Tudor reformation, the Church of Ireland inherited the diocesan and parochial system, which was substantially the creation of the twelfth-century reform movement with its thirteenth-century outworkings. Even the lay forms of organisation, such as the vestry and the election of churchwardens, are part of that heritage. However, it is equally important to recognise some disjunctions too. Unlike England, where much of the fabric of the medieval parochial church is remarkably well preserved, the wars and the general political dislocation of the sixteenth and seventeenth centuries produced the devastation and desertion of the fifteenth-century network of parish churches that are still such a marked feature of our rural landscape. There is, therefore, a hiatus, more profound in its implications than the dissolution of Irish monasteries, separating the great late-medieval parochial development from the slow restructuring of the Church of Ireland in what Alan Ford has termed 'the second Reformation'. The tragic destruction of that heritage is, in many respects, emblematic of the separate post-reformations' histories of the Catholic and Protestant communities that share, however indirectly, in that common heritage.

2

The ministry of the Church of Ireland, 1536–1636

Colm Lennon and Ciaran Diamond

When, in 1536, the Irish parliament legislated for a church of Ireland to replace that of Rome as the established ecclesiastical authority within the state, the existing parishes and clerical personnel came under new management. Until 1547, however, the Catholic orthodoxy of King Henry VIII, now supreme head of the church, determined that no theological or doctrinal changes be disseminated under the auspices of the early Reformation, and the Protestant regime of his son, Edward VI's reign (1547–53) proved to be too short-lived for widespread parochial reform to be undertaken. After a brief reversion to Roman Catholicism in Queen Mary's reign during which the traditional liturgy and priesthood were consolidated, the Church of Ireland was re-established by statute as the state church under Queen Elizabeth I in 1560, and Protestantism was affirmed as the religion of that church. Thereafter the onus of evangelization in the parishes would fall on the ministers of the Church of Ireland, with consequent demands placed upon their ability to preach the word of God and teach the reformed doctrines.[1]

In this essay the nature and quality of the first three generations of Reformation clergy in Ireland will be assessed. The ministry of the first and second generations, that is, from 1536 to approximately 1600, was characterised largely by continuity from the pre-Reformation era, and the implications of this continuum bear scrutiny in the light of the slow progress of the reform before the seventeenth century. Presaged by certain trends in the later Elizabethan era, profound change began to set in among the clergy of the Church of Ireland in the early decades of that century, as reflected particularly in the pattern of appointments to cathedral benefices,

---

1 For information on the statutory and institutional arrangements relating to the early Reformation in Ireland, see B. Bradshaw, 'The Edwardian Reformation in Ireland, 1547–53' in *Archivium Hibernicum*, xxxiv (1976), pp 83–99; B. Bradshaw, 'The opposition to the ecclesiastical legislation in the Irish Reformation parliament' in *IHS*, xvi (1968–9), pp 285–303; H.A. Jefferies, 'The early Tudor Reformation in the Irish Pale' in *JEH*, lii (2001), pp 34–62; H.A. Jefferies, 'The Irish parliament of 1560: the Anglican reforms authorised' in *IHS*, xxvi (1988), pp 128–41; J. Murray, 'Ecclesiastical justice and the enforcement of the Reformation: the case of Archbishop Browne and the clergy of Dublin' in *As by law established*, pp 33–51.

whose incumbents were in many cases responsible for the cure of souls in parishes throughout Ireland. To gain an overall perspective on the transformation of the Anglican ministry in post-Reformation Ireland, it is worthwhile to examine the background of the new appointees as well as the pattern of patronage to benefices down to the 1630s, as a supply of suitably-qualified graduate clergy began slowly to become available. The question of the extent to which impropriation of parishes stunted the development of a stable ministry was a perennial one for the Church of Ireland during the early modern period.

II

The Protestant Reformation was not the original cause of raised expectations of clerical standards in Ireland and elsewhere, though it and the other confessions did shape significantly the resulting programme of training and accomplishment after the great religious scission. In calling for improvements in the *mores* of the ministry throughout Christendom, the Christian humanists, led by Erasmus, had been to the fore in the movement for priestly excellence since the early sixteenth century. His mouthpiece, the goddess, Folly, castigated the parochial as well as the regular clergy: 'These fine fellows insist they have properly performed their duty if they reel off perfunctorily their feeble prayers, which I'd be greatly surprised if any god could hear or understand'.[2] Erasmus's friend, John Colet, dean of St Paul's in London, had rallied his clergy in 1512 by endorsing St Bernard's exclamation: 'The dignity of priests … is greater than either the king's or the emperor's: it is equal with the dignity of angels'.[3] In Ireland, Archbishop George Cromer of Armagh instructed all his clergy to acquire a copy of the work entitled *Ignorantia Sacerdotum* in 1526.[4] Widely used in England in the later middle ages, the book was a schematic guide for priests in carrying out one of their principal obligations, the religious instruction of the laity.[5] Cromer's requirement of individual ownership of the catechism on the part of his priests indicated that it was available for purchase in the northern Pale, though, as non-graduates predominantly, the clergy may not have been regular book-buyers. That cultural shifts associated with the northern Renaissance were beginning to affect the eastern region of Ireland is evident from the circulation of print and its associated educational applications, and the parochial clergy were looked to to be mediators of the new learning through instruction and sermons, even if they themselves had not studied theology at an advanced academic level.[6]

2 A.H.T. Levi (ed.), *Collected works of Erasmus*, xxvii (Toronto, 1986), p. 140.   3 Cited in F. Heal, *Reformation in Britain and Ireland* (Oxford, 2003), p. 43.   4 H.A. Jefferies, *Priests and prelates of Armagh in the age of reformations, 1518–1558* (Dublin, 1997), p. 52.   5 See E. Duffy, *The stripping of the altars: traditional religion in England* (London, 1992), pp 53–4.   6 For evidence of the influence of Christian humanism on Ireland, see B. Bradshaw, *The Irish constitutional revolution of the sixteenth century* (Cambridge, 1979), pp 48, 54–5.

A prescription for linkage between the ministers of the newly-established Church of Ireland and pedagogic and cultural reform was decreed in an act for the English order, habit and language of 1537. In keeping with the general aim of promoting English speaking and customs throughout the island, the bishops were bound to extract an oath from newly-ordained clergy that they themselves would use English and endeavour to 'move, educate and teach' all others within their cures to do the same. Furthermore, the ordinaries were to require all newly-appointed benefice-holders to swear that they would learn and instruct in the English tongue and use it in the bidding prayers in the liturgical service and for preaching (if they could preach). The final requirement of newly-installed benefice-holders in the act was that they should establish schools within their parishes for education in and through English. These measures were passed within the framework of King Henry VIII's new status as 'supreme head and governor' of church as well as state, as he aspired to advance Ireland to 'an honest Christian civility and obedience'[7]. And, at least in the archdiocese of Armagh *inter Anglicos* down to the later 1540s, inquisitions were regularly held to identify priests who had failed to maintain schools, several being fined for offences against the act of 1537.[8]

Of coeval significance with the effects, short-term or long-term, of the drive to foster educational reform under clerical sponsorship are the implications of the act for the English order, habit and language for the ministry of the Church of Ireland itself. Explicitly affirming the co-extensiveness of political, social and religious reform under Henry VIII's sovereignty in church and state, the statute laid down the parameters of the anglicization of Ireland, a core policy of the Tudor and early Stuart rulers. From the beginning, the Reformation was associated with the propagation of English social and cultural forms, and it was expected that the priests who served the parishes would not just be English-speaking but also active agents for the anglicizing of their communities. In circumstances in which a very large cohort of the clergy who were absorbed within the Church of Ireland in 1536 were monoglot Irish-speakers, the gulf between aspiration and reality in terms of acculturation in Englishness through clerical mediation was ominously wide *ab initio*. Nor did the gulf grow any narrower as the century wore on. After several decades during which the balance between English- and Irish-speaking ministers did not change significantly, and when eventually Anglican religious leaders began to take seriously the question of systematic reform of the ministry, the archetypical model for the creation of a satisfactory priesthood was the act for English order of 1537. According to the ecclesiastical commission charged with reform in 1594, failure to enforce this act was the cause of 'great frowardness, perverseness and dangerous diversity among our people in Ireland, and especially in the clergy'.[9] Thenceforth, the association of the good pastor with Englishness was to be more than an aspira-

---

7 *Statutes at large*, i, 119–27; Tony Crowley (ed.), *The politics of language in Ireland, 1366–1922* (London, 2000), pp 21–3. 8 Jefferies, *Priests and prelates of Armagh*, pp 144–5. 9 Ford, *Reformation*, pp 33–4.

tion and become instead the *sine qua non* of effective evangelization within the parishes.

Thus the politico-cultural aims of the state government were intertwined with the ecclesiastical authorities' drive to reconstruct the ministry of the Church of Ireland after 1600, especially in respect of the transmission of the Word of God in the English vernacular. The linguistic issue in Ireland was in fact a complication of the process of creating a reformed priesthood within Anglicanism, which emphasised very heavily the communicative skills of the individual pastor. Generally throughout the zone of Reformation Protestantism there was envisioned a qualitative difference between the role of the pre-Reformation Catholic priest and that of the reformed minister.[10] Whereas the former may well have been an upright moral exemplar for his flock, his personal characteristics were irrelevant to his mediating of the Eucharist and the other sacraments to them. In the view of the reformers, the principal functions of the minister were pastoral. He was expected to preach the Word effectively and instruct his parishioners in the precepts of religion. While late medieval clergyman may have performed these tasks conscientiously, a premium was to be placed by Protestant reformers on professional and academic training for those who ministered in the parishes. The ideal minister then was a university graduate, a clear and cogent orator in the pulpit, a reverent liturgist, a good teacher and a paternal parochial figure of unspotted life, suitable to inspire the members of his congregation within and outside the church.[11]

The challenge of creating such paragons was faced in the later Tudor realms of Ireland and England, though from significantly different starting-points. Leaving aside the question of English-speaking, and despite systemic difficulties in promoting the priesthood as an attractive career, the latter country at least had an educational infrastructure incorporating institutions for the nurturing of suitable new ordinands. Moreover, for the most part, the engagement of the lay patrons of benefices throughout much of England with educational and religious reform led eventually to the routine presentment of well-trained graduates to benefices. Thus, although the number of well-paid posts for ministers was proportionately small after 1558, the conditions existed in England by the early seventeenth-century for the accelerating of the ecclesiastical prospects of high quality incumbents.[12] Ireland, by contrast, suffered from an educational deficit at all levels, but particularly at the highest until the foundation of Trinity College in 1592. Also, the breakdown of relations between the state authorities and the lay elites throughout the island in the late sixteenth century worked to the detriment of Anglican reform of the system of patronage of clergy. Ultimately this was to lead to the haemorrhaging of resources and talented youngsters to the reviving Roman Catholic priest-

10 Heal, *Reformation in Britain and Ireland*, p. 5.   11 R. O'Day, 'The reformation of the ministry' in R. O'Day and F. Heal (eds), *Continuity and change: personnel and administration of the Church in England, 1500–1642* (Leicester, 1976), pp 55–6.   12 See R. O'Day, *The English clergy: the emergence and consolidation of a profession, 1558–1642* (Leicester, 1979), especially chapter 10.

hood. Thus, even allowing for the notoriously chronic poverty of Irish benefices, the agencies and will for the production of new recruits to the Church of Ireland ministry were lacking in Ireland throughout most of the period under review.[13]

The parochial clergy that the Church of Ireland involuntarily took over in the sixteenth century were extremely mixed in terms of backgrounds and outlook. They ranged from the priests of mainly English descent 'inter Anglicos' to the hereditary erenaghs of the church among the Gaelic. As in the case of a modern corporate take-over, in which the new management aspires to forge a fresh image for its personnel, even at the expense of shedding large numbers of the existing work-force, the Anglican authorities wished ultimately to create a new parish ministry, but they were compelled to carry on with the inherited incumbents. Mechanisms for depriving contumacious or pluralist clergy came into existence under the court of faculties,[14] but the problem down to the 1590s and beyond was that there were no suitable replacements for displaced priests. Thus, it was upon the shoulders of the pre- and early Reformation clergy, themselves unreformed, that the burden of ministering within a Protestant church fell for the decades after 1560.

Perhaps underrated in terms of their contribution to the Church of Ireland,[15] the bulk of the so-called 'native' ministry or indigenous clergy did succeed, in spite of varying levels of discomfiture felt with Anglicanism, in delivering a continuous pastoral and sacramental service to their parishioners, though in a traditional mode. Availing of the spirit of the dispensatory clause ordained in the act of uniformity of 1560, many used Latin as the language of the service, and not just in Irish-speaking districts, and thus cloaked any innovativeness in religious observance in a reassuring medium.[16] In Gaelic and marcher districts, Irish-speaking congregations were communicated with, if not preached to, in their vernacular.[17] For members of the uxorious hereditary clergy of the pre-Reformation Gaelic church, adherence to the Church of Ireland offered legitimacy for wives and children,[18] though there is little enough evidence of the issue of clerical marriage bulking large in this transitional phase.[19] Even in thoroughly anglicized inner Pale centres in

13 See Ford, *Reformation*, pp 63–72; A. Clarke, 'Varieties of uniformity: the first century of the Church of Ireland' in W.J. Sheils and D. Wood (eds), *The churches, Ireland and the Irish*, Studies in Church History, xxv (Oxford, 1989), pp 105–19.   14 Ford, *Reformation*, pp 34–5.   15 This is allowed by A. Ford, 'The Protestant Reformation in Ireland' in C. Brady and R. Gillespie (eds), *Natives and newcomers: essays on the making of Irish colonial society, 1534–1641* (Dublin, 1986), p. 54.   16 Jefferies, 'Anglican reforms authorised', pp 133–4: J. Murray, 'The Tudor diocese of Dublin: episcopal government, ecclesiastical politics and the enforcement of the Reformation, *c.* 1534–1590', unpublished PhD thesis, Trinity College, Dublin (1997), p. 220.   17 Even in parts of Meath in 1576, the clergy were largely Irish-speaking reading ministers, according to Sir Henry Sidney's report of Bishop Hugh Brady's visitation of his diocese: E.P. Shirley (ed.), *Original letters and papers in illustration of the history of the Church of Ireland during the reigns of Edward VI, Mary and Elizabeth* (London, 1851), pp 14–19.   18 Katharine Simms, 'Frontiers in the Irish church – regional and cultural' in T. B. Barry, Robin Frame and Katharine Simms (eds), *Colony and frontier in medieval Ireland: essays presented to J.L. Lydon* (London, 1995), p. 199.   19 Jefferies,

Dublin and east Meath, conformity to Protestantism on the part of many parish clergy was seen as only skin-deep.[20]

Although the advancement of the Reformation in the parishes could not reasonably have been expected of an untrained ministry, the attitude towards its members on the part of Protestants from England who came to Ireland was extremely harsh. Indeed, it is largely upon the views of these unsympathetic observers, moved in some cases by ethnic prejudice as well as religious zeal, that the negative verdict on the post-1560 generation of the clergyman of the Church of Ireland has been based. At best, the residual clergy, comprising for the most part those were ordained before 1558, were regarded as 'so void of knowledge of God and his will, that they know not his commandments' by Dean Robert Weston of St Patrick's Cathedral, Dublin,[21] as 'ignorant papists', by Archbishop Adam Loftus,[22] or as 'old bottles [who] cannot away with this new wine' by Bishop Brady.[23] Many curates were believed by Andrew Trollope to 'carry around a Latin version of the Book of Common Prayer but read little or nothing of it or can well read it, but they tell the people a tale of Our Lady or St Patrick'.[24] In almost half of the parishes of Meath, one of the wealthier Irish dioceses, Sir Henry Sidney reported to Queen Elizabeth I that the incumbents were 'Irish rogues, having very little Latin, less learning and civility' who lived on 'the gain of masses, dirges, shrivings and such like trumpery, godly abolished by your majesty'.[25] At worst, the 'native' clergy were described by their English critics as 'Irish rogues and Romish runagate priests', fitter to keep hogs than serve in the church'.[26]

Reference to the 'Romish' nature of the priests focuses attention on the alternative clerical system that was slowly coming into being by the late years of the sixteenth century. Many of the conformist clergy who had been absorbed into the Church of Ireland eventually became domiciled in the Roman Catholic ministry once the Tridentine revival of the priesthood began in earnest.[27] Agents of the Counter-Reformation had been just as critical of the standard of the early Elizabethan ministry in Ireland,[28] and signs of reform of education and priestly standards were manifest with the return of the first seminarian graduates from the continent in the 1590s. Thus, pressure came on many of the remaining Catholically-inclined incumbents in the parishes to forsake their benefices 'to become massing priests because they are so well entreated and so much made of amongst the people'.[29] Uncommitted to the Reformation, these ministers followed

Priests and prelates of Armagh, p. 166; Murray, 'The Tudor diocese of Dublin', pp 176, 207–9. **20** James Murray, 'The diocese of Dublin in the sixteenth century' in James Kelly and Dáire Keogh (eds), *History of the Catholic diocese of Dublin* (Dublin, 2000), pp 107–11. **21** M.V. Ronan, *The Reformation in Ireland under Elizabeth, 1558–1580* (London, 1930), p. 261. **22** Ibid., p. 360 **23** Shirley (ed.), *Original letters*, p. 162. **24** Heal, *Reformation in Britain and Ireland*, p. 435. **25** Shirley (ed.), *Original letters*, p. 16. **26** Heal, *Reformation in Britain and Ireland*, p. 435; Ford, *Reformation*, p. 32. **27** The process is described in Ford, *Reformation*, pp 36–40. **28** See, for example, Ronan, *Reformation in Ireland under Elizabeth*, p. 362. **29** Ford, *Reformation*, p. 39.

the tendency of their recusant congregations to identify fully with their Roman Catholic fellows among the lay leaders and seminary-trained clergy.

By the 1590s there was emerging among the Protestant leaders in Ireland a vigorous movement for the creation of a new ministry in the Church of Ireland. Prompted in part by the chronic manpower crisis caused by the dying off or defection of the old-style ministers, this campaign was of a piece with the Anglican resurgence adumbrated by the foundation of Trinity College in 1592. Making use of the mechanisms of the court of faculties and the court of high commission, the agents of Archbishop Loftus initiated a visitational process in many dioceses to deprive contumacious clergy and replace them by newcomers, if necessary from England.[30] Already such a programme was beginning to bear fruit in the shape of the appointments of English graduate clergy to the chapter of St Patrick's Cathedral, Dublin, under Loftus's patronage.[31] Less successful was the attempt to recruit Irish-speaking clergymen to be trained in the English universities for the ministry in the Gaelic western dioceses. While some graduates of Gaelic background were produced by the turn of the century, the level of their commitment to the state church was questionable.[32] Overall, the standard of native ordinands remained low in the period before Trinity College began to produce its first graduates. Normally recourse was had to the appointment of lectors or reading ministers, instead of preaching ministers.[33] Exacting criteria for candidates for the priesthood simply could not be applied, given the shortage of potential recruits, a situation compounded by the fact that ministers in Ireland were not required to wait for a year between ordination as deacon and priest.[34] It was thus to England that the Protestant leaders in Ireland turned in the early seventeenth century for the nucleus of a new ministry for the Anglican church.

The early years of the seventeenth century witnessed the extension of English power over the entire island of Ireland and the prospect of a reformed ministry being instituted throughout the parochial system of the established church. The intentions of the new Stuart administration for the ministry of the Church of Ireland are evident in instructions of 1604 to the Irish Council for the 'reformation of the clergy and establishing of a learning ministries in Ireland'. These memorials called for non-preaching clergymen to be deprived of their *commendams* and the appointment of preachers in their place. The memorials also gave directions for the provision of a sufficient income for 'learned ministers'. Their income was set at a minimum of £100 or 100 marks a year.[35] However, these intentions were hindered by two related problems: the lack of preaching ministers and the lack of livings capable of supporting such ministers.[36]

---

30 Ibid., pp 33–5.   31 Murray, 'The Tudor diocese of Dublin', p. 301; Ford, *Reformation*, p. 33.
32 Ford, *Reformation*, pp 41–6.   33 See O'Day, 'Reformation of the ministry', pp 59–61.   34 Alan Ford, 'The Church of Ireland 1558–1634: a puritan church?' in *As by law established*, pp 52–68.   35 *CSP, Ireland, 1603–6*, pp 241–2.   36 Ford, *Reformation*, p. 64.

The extent of these problems and the attempts to solve them are revealed in a series of royal visitations and inquiries between 1615 and 1634. The 1615 visitation covered the ecclesiastical provinces of Dublin, Cashel and Tuam and found that in the 24 dioceses within this area there were only 161 preachers and 364 reading ministers. In 1622 a commission was established to enquire into the state of Ireland and this included a thorough examination of the church. This examination covered all four ecclesiastical provinces, which comprised 2,492 parishes throughout the realm. The Commissioners calculated that 380 preachers served these parishes. Although Alan Ford has identified problems with these figures, he estimates that between 1615 and 1622 the number of preachers increased by about 52 per cent.[37] A further regal visitation was held in 1634, and by then preaching ministers outnumbered reading ministers by about 20 per cent.[38] It is evident from these visitations that in the first three decades of the seventeenth century the number and quality of the Church of Ireland ministry were increasing.

During this period the character of the clergy underwent significant changes. This is apparent in a profile of a specific segment of the clergy: the members of the cathedral chapters. Although the chapters of the thirty-two Irish cathedrals contained high-status and well-paid clergymen, such as the deans of Christ Church and St Patrick's cathedrals in Dublin, most cathedral clergymen were primarily parochial clergymen. Between 1600 and 1634, 556 clergymen were appointed to livings in the Irish cathedral system.[39] Almost forty-five per cent of these clergy-

---

37 Ibid., pp 66–7. 38 Ibid., p. 67. 39 The figures are based on a database of the cathedral chapters. The sources used to compile the database include: clerical succession lists, dioceses of Ardagh; Elphin; Kildare; Kilfenora, Clonfert and Kilmacduagh; Killala and Achonry; Killaloe; Kilmore; Leighlin; Limerick; Meath; Tuam, RCBL, MS 61/2/1; 5; 7; 8; 9; 10; 11; 12, 1–2; 13; 14, 1–2; 15; *Alumni Dublinenses*; P.J. Anderson (ed.), *Officers and graduates of University and King's College, Aberdeen, 1495–1860* (Aberdeen, 1893); W.M. Brady, *Clerical and parochial records of Cork, Cloyne and Ross* (3 vols, Dublin, 1863–4); *A catalogue of the graduates in the faculties of arts, divinity and law graduates of the University of Edinburgh since its foundation* (Edinburgh, 1858); J. Foster, *Alumni Oxonienses, 1500–1714* (4 vols, Oxford, 1891); J.B. Leslie, *Ardfert and Aghadoe clergy and parishes* (Dublin, 1940); J.B. Leslie, *Armagh clergy and parishes* (Dundalk, 1911); J.B. Leslie, *Clergy of Connor from patrician times to the present day* (Belfast, 1993); J.B. Leslie, *Clogher clergy and parishes* (Enniskillen, 1929); J.B. Leslie, *Derry clergy and parishes* (Enniskillen, 1937); J.B. Leslie, *Ferns clergy and parishes* (Dublin, 1936); J.B. Leslie, *Ossory clergy and parishes* (Enniskillen, 1933); J.B. Leslie, *Raphoe clergy and parishes* (Enniskillen, 1940); J.B. Leslie, *Supplement to 'Armagh clergy and parishes'* (Dundalk, 1948); J.B. Leslie and H.B. Swanzy, *Biographical succession lists of the clergy of the diocese of Down* (Enniskillen, 1936); J.B. Leslie and R.H. Wallace, *Clergy succession list of the diocese of Dublin and Glendalough* (Dublin, 2002); *Munimenta alme Universitatis Glasguiensis: records of the university of Glasgow from its foundation till 1727* (Glasgow, 1854); W.H. Rennison, *Succession list of bishops, cathedral and parochial clergy of the dioceses of Waterford and Lismore* ([Waterford], 1920); St J.D. Seymour, *Succession of parochial clergy of the united diocese of Cashel and Emly* (Dublin, 1908); H.B. Swanzy, *Succession list of the diocese of Dromore* (Belfast, 1933); J. Venn and J.A. Venn, *Alumni Cantabrigenses*, part 1 (4 vols, Cambridge, 1922–7); C.A. Webster, *The diocese of Ross: its bishops, clergy and parishes* (Cork, 1936).

men never attained the rank of a dignitary.[40] Most prebendaries in the Irish cathedral system did not reside at their cathedral but instead lived on the benefice that provided their income. It was also common for treasurers, chancellors and archdeacons to reside on the principal rectory that formed the corps of their living. There was therefore a close connection between the members of the cathedral system and the parishes. Moreover, most Irish cathedrals had the functions of parochial churches, particularly those located in rural areas: at Kilmore and Ardagh, for example, the dean exercised the role of the parish incumbent. Therefore, it is suggested that the 556 clergymen can be seen as a representative sample for the Church of Ireland ministry in the early seventeenth century.

The development of a coterie of English graduate clergy in St Patrick's cathedral, Dublin, in the 1590s has already been identified in the first part of this chapter. The emergence of a university-trained clergy, primarily from England, is the principal development within the Church of Ireland clergy in the early Stuart period. Table One gives a percentage breakdown of the geographical origins of the 556 cathedral clergymen appointed between 1600 and 1634.[41] Although it is highly probable that most of the clergymen in the unknown category came from England or Ireland, the patronyms suggest that the proportion of those from England far outweighs those from Ireland. Therefore, the percentages according to clergymen from England are probably under-represented. Nevertheless, the most interesting development revealed by the table is the decrease in the number of clergymen originating in Ireland. The vast majority of the clergymen who came from Ireland possessed patronyms that suggest a Gaelic Irish origin and were appointed to livings along the western seaboard. Above all the statistics demonstrate the gradual abandonment by the Gaelic Irish of service to the Church of Ireland and their replacement by clergymen from England.[42]

Table 1
Geographical origins of clergy (percentages)

Country of origin	*1600–9*	*1610–19*	*1620–34*	*1600–34*
Ireland	28	19	15	19
England	19	16	19	17
Scotland	4	4	8	6
Wales	2	1	0.5	1
Unknown	47	60	57.5	57

40 The ranks of dean, archdeacon, precentor, chancellor or treasurer.   41 The figures in Table 1 are the minimum ones. The information in the clergy succession lists has been cross-referenced with other sources and where there is doubt, the information is classified as unknown, even if the succession lists have indicated otherwise.   42 Ford, *Reformation*, pp 106–27.

With regard to the educational attainment of the clergy, at least 60 per cent of the study group attended university and 90 per cent of those were graduates. Table Two gives a breakdown of the universities attended by the study group. Of particular significance is the proportion of clergymen who attended the indigenous university, Trinity College, Dublin, and the increase is the proportion of graduates from there who received their first ecclesiastical appointment between the first and second decades of the seventeenth century. This was a period when the number of clergy was expanding rapidly and within the cathedral chapters the number of appointments doubled.[43] It was during this period that Trinity College, Dublin, began to fulfil its role as a national seminary for the Church of Ireland. The figures also demonstrate that of the two English universities, Cambridge was the principal contributor of graduate clergymen to the Church of Ireland even though it was the smaller of the two. The puritan ethos, which characterised this university, was also evident in Trinity College, Dublin, and the proportion of clergymen educated in such an environment is significant. As a consequence the ministry of the Church of Ireland in the early seventeenth century adopted a distinctive identity that was strongly Calvinist in outlook.

Table 2

Universities attended by clergy (percentages)

University	1600–34	1600–9	1611–19	1620–34
Cambridge	15	19	14	14
Oxford	11	12	11	11
Trinity College Dublin	20	11	20	24
Scottish	5	4	3	8
Known to have attended university	9	7	9	10
Not known to have attended university	40	47	43	33

As the educational standards of the ministry improved, the clergy began to form themselves into a profession. The emergence of a distinctive vocational and social group among the clergy set them apart from the rest of society through common training, regulations and style of life.[44] This development was recognised by contemporaries: in 1615 Lord Deputy Chichester wrote that he had always cherished the profession of the Ministers of the Gospel.[45] This process was also encouraged through diocesan visitations. In 1623 and 1629 visitation articles for the province of Armagh included a query as to whether minister was a 'common resorter to taverns or alehouses giving himself to drinking, ryoting and playing at cards, dyce, or

---

43 112 cathedral clergymen were appointed between 1600 and 1609 compared with 216 between 1610 and 1619. 228 were appointed between 1620 and 1634.   44 O'Day, *The English clergy*, pp 1–2.   45 *CSP, Ireland, 1615–25*, p. 23.

other unlawful game, or is he a striker, dueller, dancer or hunter'.[46] In effect this
visitation article sought to separate the clergy from the laity. These principles were
eventually codified in the 1634 Canons of the Church of Ireland. Article 42 directed the clergy not to go to or stay in taverns or alehouses. Furthermore, the dignity
of their calling required them to avoid 'base or servile labour' or idleness. Instead
ministers were ordered to devote their time to hearing or reading Holy Scriptures
or occupying themselves with academic exercises. Above all, the separation of the
clergy from the lay people was most evident in the style of dress. The style of
clothing was to give the appearance of decency, gravity and order. The article suggests that clergymen wear 'scholarlike' apparel and even directed them not to wear
'any light coloured stockings'.[47]

The 1634 canons also point to the emergence of another important development: the evolution of clergymen as local administrators for the state. Article 46
required a registry of births, weddings and burials performed in each parish
church to be kept and presented to the bishop annually.[48] Increasingly the parish
was seen as a convenient unit by the authorities to which to delegate regulatory
tasks such as the supervision of poor relief and the maintenance of roads.[49]
Consequently, in addition to their religious duties, the clergy were expected to
oversee functions of a civil nature such as the collection of cesses and the provision
of local education and welfare services.[50] Thus the ministry of the Church of
Ireland was not only identified with the English administration because of their
religious outlook, but also because they performed administrative functions for the
state authorities.

As a consequence of the ethnic and educational background of the new ministers and the changing role assigned to the clergyman by both church and state, the
relationship between the ministry and the local community altered. Until the end
of the sixteenth century the parochial clergy were usually from the local community. Their successors were somewhat different: most clergymen came from outside the locality and expounded a new doctrine.[51] Furthermore, in Gaelic Irish
areas the new clergy were by and large unable to communicate with their parishioners and the new clergy's unwillingness to learn the native tongue undermined
any attempts to perform their pastoral functions.[52] These developments increasingly alienated the local community and in some places led to outright hostility. In
1607 the bishop of Cork, Cloyne and Ross, William Lyons, wrote to Lord Deputy
Chichester on the state of the church in his diocese and observed 'an English min-

46 Visitation articles, 1623 and 1629, article 3 (consulted on Early English books online:
http//eebo.chadwyck.com).   47 *Constitutions and canons ecclesiastical* (Dublin, 1634), article 42.
48 Ibid., article 46.   49 T.C. Barnard, 'Parishes, pews and parsons: lay people and the Church
of Ireland, 1647–1780' in Gillespie and Neely, p. 73; R. Gillespie (ed.), *The vestry records of the
parish of St John the Evangelist, Dublin, 1595–1658* (Dublin, 2002), p. 9.   50 G.V. Jourdan, 'The
rise of the puritan and planter classes, 1613–1625' in Phillips, *Church of Ireland*, p. 562.   51
Clarke, 'Varieties of uniformity', p. 118.   52 Ford, *Reformation*, p. 148.

ister must be beholden to the Irishry, his neighbour love him not, especially his profession and doctrine'.[53]

Further hostility arose over the issue of tithes, as some laymen resented the exactions demanded by clergymen who did not minister to them.[54] Tithes were a particularly contentious matter in Ulster where the authorities introduced a new system of tithes and dues based on the English system in the early seventeenth century. The local populace saw these fees as innovatory and this led to resentment and alienation from the clergy.[55] In 1614 there were reports of an Irish minister, a convert to Protestantism, who was murdered by some of his neighbours. While some attributed the murder to sectarianism, there were others who believed that he was killed because 'he was severe in demanding his tithes'.[56] The following year a minister was murdered with forty-four wounds because of a tithe dispute in Ulster.[57] There were also tensions over church fees for christenings, marriages and funerals. These tensions are apparent in a petition of 1628 on behalf of the subjects of Ireland, which gives details of attempts by the clergy to exact their fees from husbandmen and their use of administrative structures to compel the husbandmen to pay.[58]

The changing nature of the relationship between the local community and the newcomer clergymen was also evident in the laity's partial control of parochial patronage. The period from 1539 to 1604 witnessed a significant increase in the number of church livings controlled by laymen.[59] According to the report of the 1622 Commissioners, roughly half of the 2,492 parishes of Ireland were impropriate.[60] However, this underestimated the scale of the problem: Alan Ford has identified regional variations ranging from 50 per cent of parishes impropriated in the province of Cashel to 80 per cent in the province of Tuam, and a national rate of 60 per cent.[61] The self-interest of impropriators resulted in the diversion of ecclesiastical income away from the employment of active reforming graduate clergymen to other purposes. In many parishes minimal payments were made to uneducated curates to serve the cure and in other parishes impropriators refused to pay for any curate. As confessional identity solidified in the early Stuart period, Old English gentry and merchants, who had acquired the rights to church incomes in the Tudor period, diverted these resources towards the employment of Roman Catholic clergymen.[62]

In 1604 Sir John Davies observed that patrons of ecclesiastical livings took the greater part of the income and that priests and Jesuits were among those who were

53 *CSP, Ireland, 1606–8*, p. 180.   54 O'Day, *The English clergy*, p. 191.   55 Ford, *Reformation*, p. 149; G.J. Hand and V. Treadwell (eds), 'His Majesty's directions for ordering and settling the courts within the kingdom of Ireland, 1622', *Analecta Hibernica*, xxvi (1970), pp 211–12.   56 *CSP, Ireland, 1611–14*, p. 538.   57 *CSP, Ireland, 1615–25*, p. 23.   58 *CSP, Ireland, 1625–32*, pp 337–8.   59 S.G. Ellis, 'Economic problems of the church: why the reformation failed in Ireland', *JEH*, xl (1990), p. 255.   60 BL, Add. MS 4756, f. 19.   61 Ford, *Reformation*, p. 68.   62 Ibid., pp 36–40. Ellis, 'Economic problems of the church', pp 255–7; C. Lennon, 'The Counter-reformation in Ireland, 1542–1641' in Brady and Gillespie (eds), *Natives and newcomers*, p. 84.

getting the most benefit of clerical benefices.[63] In 1612 the Commission to examine the abuses in Ireland observed that religion was being undermined by impropriations because church livings were not able to maintain ministers and preachers, and church buildings remained in disrepair.[64] Subsequently, there were calls for impropriators to be compelled to use their income for the employment of competent clergymen and these included Sir Thomas Ryves's polemic *The poore vicars plea for tithes*.[65] Ryves maintained that every minister of the church should receive a sufficient allowance from the tithes of his own parish for which they performed preaching and other divine services. When these payments were paid to somebody else, Ryves suggested that then both the minister and the laymen were being defrauded because the minister could not perform his function.[66] In 1624 the dean of Limerick, George Andrews, preached against 'devourers of church livings' and encouraged his audience to augment the church with their wealth.[67] However, progress was not made until the lord deputyship of Thomas Wentworth, when, in 1635, an act of parliament provided for the restitution of impropriations to the ministry.[68] It also envisaged greater episcopal and administrative scrutiny of appointments to those livings.[69] And by 1636 Lord Deputy Wentworth was able to report to the king that significant improvements had been achieved with regard to impropriations.[70] By that stage, however, lay patronage of ecclesiastical livings and their hostility to the newcomer clergy had hindered the acceptance and development of the Reformation in Ireland.

The clergy also shared responsibility for hindering the Reformation in Ireland by alienating the church's landed inheritance. In 1613 Sir John Davies contended that clergymen were robbers of the church and as a result there was often very little left for their successors.[71] During the latter half of the sixteenth century clergymen, whose commitment to the Reformation could best be described as ambiguous, granted long ambivalent leases at low rents for high entry fines to their friends and families. As a consequence, the generation of clergymen appointed in the early Stuart period found their livings impoverished. Although the authorities attempted to limit the length of ecclesiastical leases to twenty-one years through proclamations, acts of state and statutory provisions, almost all the clergy found it necessary to hold livings in *commendam* so as to obtain a sufficient income.[72] In 1606 William Lyons, bishop of Cork, Cloyne and Ross, observed that the preachers he had brought over from England required five or six livings each so as to have an adequate income.[73] The authorities recognized that by trying to solve the problem

---

63 *CSP, Ireland,1603–6*, p. 143.   64 *CSP, Ireland,1611–14*, p. 446.   65 *CSP, Ireland,1615–25*, pp 276, 416; T. Ryves, *The poor vicars plea for tithes* (London, 1640).   66 Ryves, *The poor vicars plea*, pp 144–51.   67 G. Andrews, *A quaternion of sermons* (Dublin, 1625), pp 102–4.   68 Ford, *Reformation*, p. 68.   69 10 and 11 Car I, c. ii, *Statutes at large*, pp 136–40.   70 C. McNeill (ed.), *Tanner letters* (Dublin, 1943), p. 9.   71 HMC, *Report on the manuscripts of the late Reginald Rawdon Hastings esq.*, iv (London, 1947), p. 12.   72 TCD, MS. 1188; *CSP, Ireland,1608–10*, p. 238; 10 and 11 Car I, c. iii, *Statutes at large*, pp 142–4.   73 *CSP, Ireland, 1608–10*, pp 179–80.

of low income, another problem – pluralism – arose. As a result, the authorities in 1623 cautioned that pluralities should be used sparingly and that when parishes were united, the parish churches should only be a distance of four miles from one another.[74] During the reign of James I, letters patent often contained *commendam* clauses citing the smallness of the income of the living as a reason for the granting of multiple livings. Some of the grants also indicated that parishes were united on account of their closeness to one another: in 1611, John Bradish was appointed to the vicarages of Modeligo and Kilmolash in the diocese of Lismore on account of the smallness of their incomes and their mutual proximity.[75] However, this did not preclude clergymen from receiving livings elsewhere: Bradish would later be appointed to livings in the diocese of Cork, which he held alongside his livings in the diocese of Lismore.[76]

Bradish was subsequently condemned to death by the assizes at Tallow in 1621 for murdering a fellow clergyman, a vicar whose surname was Ledisham.[77] Because of the demand for clergymen in the early seventeenth century, rigorous standards were often not applied when ministers were being selected. As a result, Ireland developed a reputation as a receptacle of 'English runagates'.[78] In 1629, Sir John Bingley observed that the Protestant clergy in Ireland were a 'set of very profane and drunken fellows who neglect their services'.[79] Similarly, the Scottish traveller, William Lithgow, observed in the early 1630s that the Church of Ireland had admitted clergymen who were unsuitable to be pastors, although he did note that the church possessed many sound and religious preachers who lived exemplary lives.[80] These views reflected the higher expectations that society had for the clergy. In 1624, the dean of Limerick, George Andrews, called on ministers to reform themselves so that they might shine as lights in the midst of 'a crooked generation'. In a subsequent sermon, preached before the lord deputy and state officials, he called on the laity to encourage good preachers and pastors.[81] Indeed Andrews would have been encouraged by the compliments on the quality of preaching in Ireland, and particularly in Dublin, made by various commentators, including Barnaby Rich, Stephen Jerome and William Brereton, in the early seventeenth century.[82]

In the century that followed the creation of the statutory Church of Ireland, three generations of clergymen attempted to grapple with the implications of the Reformation. Before the seventeenth century, there was little in the way of reform.

74 *CSP, Ireland,1615–25*, p. 417.   **75** *Cal. pat. rolls, Jas I*, p. 193.   **76** Brady, *Clerical records*, i, p. 133.   **77** Rennison, *Dioceses of Waterford and Lismore*, p. 70, note.   **78** Ford, *Reformation*, p. 75.   **79** *CSP, Ireland,1625–32*, p. 442.   **80** G. Phelps (ed.), *The rare adventures and painful peregrinations of William Lithgow* (London, 1974), pp 254–5.   **81** Andrews, *Quaternion*, pp 8, 103.   **82** W. Brereton, *Travels in Holland, the United Provinces, England, Scotland and Ireland*, ed. E. Hawkins, Chetham Society (London, 1844), pp 143–4; *Calendar, Carew MSS, 1601–3*, p. 432; S. Jerome, *Ireland's jubilee, or joyes to paean* (Dublin, 1624); B. Rich, *A new description of Ireland* (London, 1610), p. 55.

Consequently, the first two generations were able to maintain a traditional outlook and retain the allegiance of the local community. After 1600, the Church of Ireland developed a more distinctive protestant outlook. As a result, the traditional clergy began to be replaced by a ministry characterized by its university education and Englishness or (in some cases) Scottishness. The reformation of the ministry resulted in a graduate clergy who were largely English in origin and who became alienated from the indigenous community. Their enthusiasm for the process of Anglicizing Irish society hampered their pastoral role. Instead both Gaelic Irish and Old English élites sought and received spiritual comfort and guidance through the missionary activities of the Counter-Reformation seminary priests. In contrast, the ministry of the Church of Ireland was reluctant to pursue missionary activity and instead confined itself to ministering to the settler communities. Ultimately these developments led to the emergence of a church that was above all characterized by its exclusivity.

3

The Church of Ireland clergy, *c.*1640: representation and reality

Raymond Gillespie

Attempts to define and anatomise social groups in early modern Ireland have become much more difficult in recent years. Well-worn categories such as 'Old English', 'native Irish' and 'New English' have been shown to be much more contingent and complex than was previously thought. Many of those who seemed to belong to coherent ethnic groups have, on closer inspection, turned out to behave not as the sociologically minded expect. Individuals of one ethnic grouping can be discovered adhering to the confessional position or political views of another. One possibility for resolving this dilemma is to utilise the idea of social orders employed by others in contemporary Europe to understand Irish society. Adopting this sort of approach highlights the significance of one of those orders: the clerical estate of the established church.

The Church of Ireland clergy are easy to identify in the social landscape of seventeenth-century Ireland. The most obvious characteristic was their ordination which separated this group from those around them. Ordination conveyed a set of rights distinguishing the clergy from those not in holy orders. The clergy had the right to meet in their own assembly, Convocation, at the same time as parliament, to regulate their own affairs and to tax themselves. Conveniently for historians they feature in records parallel to those of the civil administration. The documentation associated with episcopal visitations, for instance, makes it possible to observe the Irish clergy as a body in a way that records of, for example, the peerage as a social order do not. In addition clergy as individuals had recourse to the civil administration and hence they appear in, for instance, the depositions taken after the rising of 1641 which allows a reconstruction of some aspects of their lives.

I

At one level the social meaning of ordination gave coherence to the clergy of the Church of Ireland in the early seventeenth century.[1] A century earlier the profes-

---

1 This essay does not consider the theological significance of orders but the analysis in P.F. Brad-

sional clergy were part of an international organisation, a corporation of clerks, with a supreme magistracy in Rome. As such, clergy were very much part of the public world and advancement in the Irish church, as elsewhere, was obtained by a knowledge of and training in canon law. Canon law was central, at least in the Pale area of Ireland, to thinking about the early stages of Catholic reform under Queen Mary in the 1550s and in reducing those parts where the church seemed aberrant in form to the European norm.[2] As part of the reform process the emphasis on canon law disappeared to be replaced by a concern about theology, driven by a view of the church not as an organisation with delegated divine power but dependent directly on the actions of God. Theological education, therefore, became far more important than it had been before. Increasingly in the early seventeenth century that meant for those who served in Irish parishes a theological education in England or, in a few cases, Scotland, since Trinity College, Dublin had only been recently established. By the 1630s preaching ministers, who were usually university graduates, outstripped the number of reading ministers who had predominated in 1615.[3] That clerical estate may have been given even greater coherence by another development. The reform process in England had reduced a complex system of major and minor orders into two: those of priest and deacon. Thus clerical distinctions, and educational achievements, became less pronounced by the 1640s than they had been before and the broad outline of a new reformed clerical group can begin to be discerned.

During most of the early seventeenth century the Irish clergy had a number of opportunities to shape the image of this clerical group. Clergy of varying backgrounds met on a number of occasions. At episcopal visitations those clergy from a diocese who appeared in response to an episcopal summons would have had an opportunity to compare experiences and establish common interests. A common sense of endeavour might be promoted by the bishop's sermon on the occasion. Almost none of those have survived. One which has, that of Henry Leslie, bishop of Down, in 1636, is probably untypical since it was devoted to an attack on the Presbyterian dissenting clergy in his diocese, a problem that was not widespread outside Ulster.[4] Again the assize was a secular gathering but one that clergy and bishops might attend. As well as meeting each other, one of their number would reflect on an issue of the day in the assize sermon.[5] Whether or not there were opportunities for clergy to meet between these annual visitations or assizes is not clear.

On a smaller scale those in cathedral chapters had an opportunity to encounter each other although how frequently chapters met outside Dublin is not recorded.

shaw, *The Anglican ordinal: its history and development from the Reformation to the present day* (London, 1971) also applies to Ireland where the same ordinal was in use.   2 James Murray, 'The Tudor diocese of Dublin: episcopal government, ecclesiastical politics and the enforcement of the reformation, 1534–1590', unpublished PhD thesis, TCD (1997), pp 72–89, 162–7.   3 Ford, *Reformation*, p. 67.   4 Henry Leslie, *A treatise on the authority of the church* (Dublin, 1637). A second edition appeared in 1639.   5 For example see Thomas McCrie (ed.), *The life of Mr Robert Blair* (Edinburgh, 1848), pp 77–9.

Clearly in larger cities, such as Dublin or Cork, parish clergy were well known to each other. In Dublin, for instance, the clergy of the city regularly borrowed books from the library of James Ussher, bishop of Meath and later archbishop of Armagh, and probably encountered one another in the process.[6] In the rural world, isolation was much more of a problem. The life of Robert Blair, who held the living of Bangor in County Down during the 1620s and 1630s, described how clergy of one diocese debated current issues such as the relationship of nonconformity to the established church through letters, but whether such contacts were a common practice or confined to east Ulster is not known.[7] Blair also described how some of the more godly clergy would travel to listen to each other preach and hence form friendships. Again, clergy might travel to preach in each other's parish churches and thereby provide variety for listeners. During the religious revival in east Ulster in the 1630s, the godly clergy of that area shared one another's pulpits and clearly knew each other well.[8]

Against this image of the Church of Ireland clergy as a coherent body must be set the very real divisions within the clerical estate. The primary function of the clergy was to provide pastoral care for the inhabitants of the 2,492 parishes which contemporaries reckoned made up Ireland. However not all ecclesiastical livings were equal. At its simplest the ecclesiastical hierarchy created divisions between the bishops, their senior clergy (such as cathedral deans and members of cathedral chapters), the parish clergy and those, such as curates, with no benefices at all. Not all curates were poor but in comparison to incumbents they were worse off. In 1641 Robert Dunster, the curate in Hackettstown in County Carlow, had losses in the rising of £113 10s., of which £40 was his stipend. His rector, John Watson, listed his losses as being £1,769, including his living worth £90 per annum.[9] However, even among the parish clergy where status might declare them equal, the income of their parishes proved they were not. For historical reasons across Ireland parishes varied a great deal in size and hence in income. In the core of the Pale, in regions such as the diocese of Meath, there were many small parishes and for these to produce a sufficient income to maintain one family it was necessary for clergy to hold two or more parishes. In some cases these were so far apart as to create problems in fulfilling pastoral duties.[10] Such problems were common. One clergyman in the early 1640s had property in Clare but his four livings, together worth a modest £130, were scattered over Limerick and Cork.[11] Thus the solution to the problem of providing sufficient maintenance for clergy created another, that of pluralism.

The problem of clerical income was compounded by the difficulty of impropriations. A large number of parishes outside Ulster were in lay hands and the

6 Elizabethanne Boran, 'The libraries of Luke Challoner and James Ussher, 1595–1608' in Helga Robinson-Hammerstein (ed.), *European universities in the age of Reformation and Counter Reformation* (Dublin, 1998), pp 109–15.   7 McCrie (ed.), *Life of Mr Robert Blair*, p. 82.   8 Ibid.   9 TCD, MS 812, ff 11, 41.   10 BL, Add. MS 4756, f. 20v; Ford, *Reformation*, pp 71–2.   11 TCD, MS 829, f. 221.

income of the incumbent in the hands of the impropriator. As the commissioners surveying the state of Ireland in 1622 explained

> And concerning the maintenance of the ministry we find it in most places to be small, in so much that parsons and vicars presentative are enforced for want of means to supply several cures whereby they are all the worse served and the stipendiaries and curates in churches appropriate as they are appointed at the pleasure of the owner of such appropriations so from them they receive slender allowance, some allowing but 40*s* a year, some less and none in any proportion fit for any service.[12]

The problem was most acute in Connacht where, according to the visitation of 1634 some 92 per cent of livings in the archdiocese of Tuam were impropriate as opposed to 70 per cent in the ecclesiastical province of Dublin.[13] According to Thomas Ryves in his tract on tithes in Ireland of 1620, most of these Connacht livings were worth under £2 and many not worth above 15*s*.[14] There were exceptions for the well connected. Thomas Johnson, vicar of Turlough in County Mayo, deposed in 1641 that his living was worth £30 a year and Gerald Byrne reckoned his living worth £70 a year. In County Galway some of the more attractive livings were said to be worth £100 a year but these seem to have been among the richest.[15] While some attempt was made by Lord Deputy Wentworth and Bishop Bramhall of Derry to recover impropriations in the 1630s, it made little impact in the areas worst effected, being confined mostly to Ulster and Munster. Furthermore those who held impropriations often wanted those clergy dependent on them to fill the livings, thus restricting opportunities. In County Down settler landlords such as Sir Hugh Montgomery and Sir James Hamilton brought clergy with them from Scotland to fill livings.[16] Such clergy lived under the protection of their patrons. At Carrickfergus an English puritan, Mr Hubart, lived 'under the protection of the old Lord Chichester' and at Bangor James Hamilton supported the Presbyterian Robert Blair. Such patrons could have an important effect on the style of parish ministry, encouraging some practices, such as the subjects of sermons, and discouraging others.[17] One godly minister in the midlands, Richard Olmstead, was urged to put his sermons into print by his patrons, Sir Charles Coote and Adam Loftus, since they approved of them and wanted them to be more widely available.[18]

Pastoral care in a parochial setting was not the only option open to ordained clergy. At least some of the larger Protestant households maintained chaplains. At Lisburn the chaplain to the Conway household, Philip Tandy, was also its librarian.[19]

---

12 BL, Add. MS 4756, f. 19.   13 Ford, *Reformation*, pp 88–9.   14 Thomas Ryves, *The poor vicar's plea* (London, 1620), p. 124.   15 TCD, MS 831, ff 150v, 166; TCD, MS 830, ff 130, 134. 16 George Hill (ed.), *The Montgomery manuscripts* (Belfast, 1869), p. 61; T.K. Lowry (ed.), *The Hamilton manuscripts* (Belfast, 1867), pp 33–4.   17 McCrie (ed.), *Life of Mr Robert Blair*, pp 58, 60–1.   18 Richard Olmstead, *A treatise of the union between Christ and the church* (Dublin, 1627), sig. A3; Richard Olmstead, *Sion's tears leading to glory* (Dublin, 1630), sig. A6.   19 *Cal. SP, Ire-*

More usually chaplains, in addition to saying morning and evening prayers, acted as tutors to the children of the household. The godly Steven Jerome, who was chaplain to the earl of Cork as well as holding a number of livings, described the regime in the household in the 1630s, 'no day being permitted wherein besides domestic prayer with the family and in private in your chambers, the scriptures with the best sermons and theological tractates were not read to you or by you'.[20] The result was a generation of Boyle children who were, by any standards, exceptionally pious and inclined towards the godly end of the spectrum of Protestant belief. Some relationships did not run as smoothly. In 1632 the Calvinist Lord Mountnorris asked William Laud, archbishop of Canterbury, to recommend a 'sober man and a good scholar' as a chaplain. The appointee, James Croxton, soon proved out of step with Mountnorris's theological views and was dismissed in 1634.[21]

The opportunities for clergy in education were not limited to that of tutor in a great household. Sixteenth-century legislation had created a network of parish and grammar schools in Ireland and that had been supplemented in the early seventeenth century by the creation of Royal Schools as part of the plantation schemes in Ulster and in Wicklow. Here the income of a clerical schoolmaster could vary a great deal according to how the land with which the school was endowed was managed. In the 1640s Raphoe Diocesan School was estimated to provide an income of £40 per annum while the Clogher Diocesan School was worth £240 a year. Armagh brought an annual income of £80 when the lands were leased in 1635. It was possible for clergy to do well in this world. Ann Bullingbrooke, the widow of the master at the Dungannon Royal school, listed losses of £400 in 1641, which was about average for an Ulster deponent.[22] Outside the planted areas the position was less clear. Many parishes seem to have had schools, although these were often run by the incumbent or the curate of another parish as a way of supplementing their incomes. In 1641 Robert Sheppley of Birr listed his income from the school at £50 a year which he held with two livings worth £100 per annum, while the curate of Kilberry in Meath drew £30 a year from the school in Trim to supplement the £14 provided by his curacy.[23] Again at Lisburn the master of the school in the 1630s, Thomas Halsam, also seems to have undertaken some pastoral and preaching duties to judge from the entries in his notebook although whether or not he was paid for these is not clear.[24]

The divisions within the clergy were not simply those of status or finance. There were real problems of different theological and ideological stances within the Irish

land, 1633–47, pp 118–19, 129.   **20** S[teven] J[erome], *The soul's centinell ringing an alarm against impiety and impenitence* (Dublin, 1631), dedication.   **21** Patrick Little, 'Providence and posterity: a letter from Lord Mountnorris to his daughter, 1642' in *IHS*, xxxii (2000–1), p. 560.   **22** Raymond Gillespie, 'Church, state and education in early modern Ireland' in M.R. O'Connell (ed.), *O'Connell: education, church and state* (Dublin, 1992), pp 47–8.   **23** TCD, MS 814, f. 83; MS 816 f. 180. For other clergy schoolmasters who held schools with their livings, but without separate valuations see TCD, MS 834, f. 83, MS 831, f. 166; MS 813, f. 232.   **24** PRONI, Mic 1/5.

clerical body. The early seventeenth-century Church of Ireland was inclined to the godly end of the spectrum and as a result emphasised the commonalities of Protestants of different traditions in opposition to Catholicism. As Henry Leslie, bishop of Down, said in a sermon at Drogheda in 1622 'contention extinguishes the very life of religion which is brotherly love and therefore they who make so much ado about ceremonies had need to take heed that in the meantime they lose not that which is most precious ... let us labour to reconcile ourselves and at length to embrace unity'.[25] In this world it was easy to accommodate those Scots clergy of a Presbyterian disposition, even radicals such as Robert Blair at Bangor in County Down, within the Church of Ireland. The Presbyterian Robert Blair on being appointed to the vicarage of Bangor in 1623 wished to make his position clear to the bishop of Down, Henry Echlin. He informed the bishop that he was 'opposite to episcopacy and their liturgy'. Echlin declared that he would 'impose no conditions upon you' save that he was required by law to ordain Blair. To this Blair objected, but Echlin found what seems to have been a common solution by asking 'will you not receive ordination from Mr Cunningham and the adjacent [presbyterian inclined] brethren and let me come in amongst them in no other relation than a presbyter?' To this Blair could not object.[26] The bishop was within his rights in acting in this way. The 1615 Articles of the Church of Ireland did not require subscription to the Articles on either ordination or admission to a living. Moreover in the Irish Articles, article 36 from the English Thirty-Nine Articles, which dealt with consecration of bishops, was silently dropped again leaving room for a broadly based consensus. However, the 1665 Act of Uniformity required episcopal ordination and assent to the Book of Common Prayer and the Thirty-Nine Articles.

The differences that this attempt at comprehension introduced within the Irish clerical body were all too visible by the 1630s. In Ulster those of a Presbyterian background who had been inducted into Church of Ireland livings ran foul of the reforming moves spearheaded by Bishop Bramhall of Derry and were forced out of their livings. In other parts of the country there were similar tensions between those who were loyal to the established church and those who were increasingly worried that it was temporising with Catholicism. Such tensions came to a head in Dublin in the early 1640s where a group of godly clergy including Faithful Teate and Steven Jerome had been preaching violently anti-Catholic sermons in city. In late 1642 following a sermon preached by Jerome in Christ Church cathedral, in which he claimed the Irish rising was a punishment for Charles I's marriage to a Catholic daughter of Jezebel, the authorities took action. Teate left Dublin, Jerome was imprisoned and the chancellor of Christ Church, John Harding, who had arranged the sermon, was unfrocked. Harding became a Baptist minister and his son a Presbyterian. Teate's son became an Independent minister in Dublin.[27] In

25 Henry Leslie, *A treatise tending to unity* (Dublin, 1622). p.50.   26 McCrie (ed.), *Life of Mr Robert Blair*, pp 59–60.   27 Raymond Gillespie, 'The crisis of reform. 1625–60' in Kenneth Milne (ed.), *Christ Church Cathedral, Dublin: a history* (Dublin, 2000), pp 204–5.

such ways did the tensions within the early seventeenth-century ministry become clear and provide the framework for the emergence of indigenous Irish dissent which was fuelled by the Cromwellian administration of the 1650s.

II

If, when observed from within, the Church of Ireland clergy was both a reasonably coherent body and a deeply splintered one, when viewed from without they seemed rather different. The Irish clergy did not lack detractors. One of James I's chaplains preaching before the king at the beginning of the seventeenth century declared of the Irish church that 'divers hold reverend places in that church that are unworthy of the meanest rooms, blind guides, that were never acquainted with the things of God; others like Isachar, a strong ass couching down between two burdens, finding rest good and the land pleasant'.[28] Commissioners in 1613 agreed, claiming that there was a 'small number, less sufficiency and little residence of ministers'.[29] In the early 1640s there was no shortage of those to impugn the actions of the Church of Ireland clergy believing that they were happy to blow with any wind of change and convert to Catholicism, if necessary. One clergyman, Daniel Harcourt, claimed in 1643 that he was forced to take up his pen to defend the Irish clergy 'in regard some clamatious tongues have charged the Irish English clergy to adhere to the Romish faction and fictions, which they had done they had saved their lives and estates'.[30] Despite Harcourt's protestations there was evidence to suggest that some did exactly that. In the depositions taken after the insurrection there are examples of such conversions. In Limerick it was claimed that the vicar of Kilmallock, the chancellor of Emly (who seems to have been of native Irish stock from his name) as well as a number of other clergy converted. In Leix it was said that the daughter of Bishop Pilsworth of Kildare had converted and in Monaghan the curate of Clones 'revolted from the faith and went to mass'.[31] How much of this was simply propaganda prompted by the insurrectionists is not clear, but it does seem that some clergy were only loosely affiliated to the institutional Church of Ireland.

There was no shortage of high profile examples to demonstrate the apparent truth of such generalisations about clerical laxity. John Atherton, later bishop of Waterford and Lismore, already had a murky past before he came to Ireland in the late 1630s and that would emerge in his trial in 1640 when a litany of sexual crimes from looking at 'lewd pictures' through incest and adultery to buggery was recited. There were also dark hints that others in the church might be similarly inclined.[32] Again Steven Jerome, the godly chaplain to the earl of Cork, had a

28 J. Hopkins, *A sermon preached before the king's majesty* (London, 1604), sig. C5v.   29 *Cal. pat. rolls Ire., Jas I*, p. 399.   30 Daniel Harcourt, *The clergies lamentation* (London, 1643), p. 15.   31 TCD, MS 829, ff 209, 221, 273; MS 814, f. 56; MS 835, ff 30, 62.   32 Aidan Clarke, 'A woeful

murky past in England having been forced to leave his parish there because of an alleged rape on a woman.[33]

Even if one were not prepared to believe such salacious stories there were those who saw trouble for the clergy just around the corner. Thomas Ryves in an analysis of the workings of the inadequate finances of the Irish church in the early 1620s saw all manner of problems in store. Inadequate finance would result in an unlearned ministry and hence 'the decay of all religion' or worse 'if there be no maintenance there will be no ministry'.[34] Even if the ministry did survive this trial it would be inadequate for its task. The commissioners enquiring into the state of Ireland in 1622 had set out what they expected of the parish clergy. Ministers were to preach, administer the sacraments and in addition it was ordered that 'more care be taken in every parish that those that do come to church may be instructed in the principles of true religion by their ministers who both by example and doctrine may become better guides to your people there in many places of the kingdom, where we heard too much offence given by the careless performance of their duties'. Moreover clergy were 'to keep hospitality, a thing much tending to the advancement of religion especially in this kingdom' and the poor were to be relieved in the absence of a poor law. Buildings were to be maintained and the clergy were to be learned despite the fact that 'in Connaught and in other places they are as ignorant as poor'.[35] Clergy were also expected to maintain the lifestyle of gentry. Thomas Ryves, for instance, described the problems of the minister who had 'to live in the fashion of a minister ... to maintain his wife and children when he is alive, to provide for them after his death, to pay servants' wages and over and above all this to keep hospitality'.[36]

Such views were based on unrealistic expectations. A more realistic view of what parish clergy were at least expected to do was set out in the questions posed to churchwardens by the bishops on visitation using the canons of 1634 as a guide.[37] Here bishops were concerned that their clergy be resident, that they keep the church property in good repair, that they read the services according to the Book of Common Prayer and that they catechize. They were equally concerned that they preach regularly and that the sermons would be appropriate 'to the behoof of their hearers' and that the teaching be good, with no popish doctrine. At least some clergy agreed with this. William Ince, preaching in 1640, urged his peers to make their sermons clear so that they could be understood, and that they 'would

---

sinner: John Atherton' in Vincent Carey and Ute Lötz-Heumann (eds), *Taking sides?: colonial and confesional mentalités in early modern Ireland* (Dublin, 2003), pp 138–49.   **33** Steve Hindle, 'The shaming of Margaret Knowlsey: gossip, gender and the experience of authority in early modern England' in *Continuity and Change*, ix (1994), pp 394–411.   **34** Ryves, *The poor vicar's plea*, pp 145, 146.   **35** BL, Add. MS 4756, ff 19v, 21, 22v, 64v.   **36** Ryves, *The poor vicar's plea*, p. 121.   **37** *Articles to be enquired of by the churchwardens and questmen of every parish in the lord primate's visitation metropolitical* (Dublin, 1640); *Articles to be enquired of by the churchwardens ... in the ordinary visitation of the Right Reverend ... George ... lord bishop of Cloyne* (Dublin, 1639).

both please and instruct' and asked his hearers to 'excuse the homeliness of a fable and let the goodness of the moral win your pardon of the tale itself'.[38]

Some were more cynical about their role as preachers. Richard Olmstead in the 1630s muttered darkly about people who desired novelty rather than edification from sermons and 'go from sermon to sermon to know something to be able to discourse and find table talk'.[39] Perhaps more serious in the eyes of the bishops was the requirement that the sick be visited, the dead buried, marriages solemnised appropriately and that holy communion be administered three times a year as required by canon law. Earlier visitation articles expanded on this by restricting the administration of communion to those not 'openly known to be in debate and out of charity with their neighbours or defamed with any notorious crime and not reformed', but in the more Arminian world of the late 1630s that had been abandoned.[40] It was these issues rather than preaching that were liable to provoke complaints from the laity.[41] Above all, clergy were to adopt an appropriate lifestyle. They were not to be involved in 'bare or servile labour', they were to dress 'gravely and decently' and not resort to taverns, play cards or dice or become usurers. However in many cases clerical finances did not permit the rigid adherence to these injunctions and many were indeed farmers and lent money at interest as a way of managing their clerical incomes as the next section of this essay will suggest. Practical needs made the realities of Irish clerical life rather different from the ideal prescribed by the church.

III

The evidence therefore suggests that there were different perceptions of the Irish clergy about 1640. While the clergy's view of themselves, insofar as it can be ascertained, was a fairly positive one, those outside the clerical body had a rather less favourable assessment of their abilities and motivations. It is difficult to make any real judgments about which of these perspectives is correct, or in what balance to mix them in any synthesis. One clergyman, Revd Devereux Spratt, in Kerry seems to have had a positive experience. Graduating from Oxford in 1635, he went to Castleisland in County Kerry where his grandfather was the incumbent. He served briefly as tutor to Sir Edward Denny's sons in Tralee and 'after by persuasion of friends I entered into the function of the ministry'. Whether he had already been ordained in England or was ordained in Kerry is not clear, but if the latter it does suggest rather limited preparation for life in the Irish church. For Spratt, preaching lay at the core of his ministry and 'this way of preaching I followed, and continued a few years in that town [Tralee] joining myself to the people of God;

38 William Ince, *Lot's little one* (Dublin, 1640), pp 58, 155–7.   39 Olmstead, *Sion's tears*, pp 102, 105–6.   40 *Articles given in charge to be inquired upon and presented to the churchwardens* (Dublin, 1623).   41 Gillespie, *Devoted people*, pp 26–7.

setting apart many days of humiliation to meet the Lord in the way of his judgements'. His ministry was interrupted only by the rising of 1641 by which stage he had become chancellor of Ardfert and held two other parishes also.[42] Even the godly might be pluralists.

A contrast is offered by Robert Blair. A convinced Presbyterian, Blair fled Scotland after the introduction of the Articles of Perth in 1619 and in 1623 was inducted as vicar of Bangor by Viscount Clandeboy, who held the patronage of the living. From his account of his ministry he preached frequently, up to four times a week, dealing not with scriptural texts but with 'fundamentals' such as heaven and hell. He visited his parishioners and instructed them and administered the sacraments. He also acted as the spiritual leader of the community, leading prayers when the harvest was threatened and establishing local discipline. In all this he acted in the same way as Spratt seems to have done in his parish. Blair was different in one respect in that he was one of the initiators of an evangelical revival which originated in south Antrim in the late 1620s and spread throughout east Ulster. In this sense he betrays a sense of mission not evident in Spratt's writings.[43]

Revealing as the autobiographies of Spratt and Blair are of the actions and attitudes of some parish clergy they are far from typical. The writings of both men belong to a particular genre. They are spiritual autobiographies, intended to chronicle the relationship of the writer with God and record the blessings they received as a way of confirming their membership of the elect. As such they were characteristic of the 'hotter sort' or godly clergy. Such men were in short supply in early seventeenth-century Ireland. More typical, perhaps, was the parish clergyman who was preoccupied with the daily round of collecting tithes, maintaining church property and carrying out his pastoral functions to Protestant communities of varying sizes across the island. In addition such clergymen had to make a living for themselves and their families and as such they became part of the secular world of commerce and agriculture. It is difficult to reconstruct this world because most clergy regarded their lives as ordinary and therefore not worth recording. However, in one body of material, the depositions taken on oath after the insurrection of late 1641, a number of clergy told stories about their experiences and listed the losses that they had sustained, hence providing a way into the material world in which they moved.[44] Over 180 clergy can be identified by themselves as such in their depositions although others may have made statements but did not describe themselves as clergy. More detailed analysis at local level may bring these to light.

Within this body of evidence there was clearly a wide range of experiences and responses. For some on the godly wing of the church, the rising conformed to a theologically conditioned world in which Catholics were to be identified with the

42 St John D. Seymour (ed.), *Adventures and experiences of a seventeenth-century clergyman* (Dublin, 1909), pp 15–16.   43 McCrie (ed.), *Life of Mr Robert Blair*, pp 59–102.   44 For this body of evidence see Aidan Clarke, 'The 1641 depositions' in Peter Fox (ed.), *Treasures of the library, Trinity College Dublin* (Dublin, 1986), pp 111–22.

Antichrist and a rising was inevitable. In this scenario, the Church of Ireland clergy were depicted as martyrs. Daniel Harcourt's 1643 pamphlet was written to defend exactly this view. Harcourt chronicled in some detail the murders of ministers and their hardships in the early 1640s claiming that 'this martyrology is part of that ministry', since through their sufferings the clergy 'have sealed their zeal for the Gospel by the effusion of their bloods, confusion of estates, taking a miserable exile with John to Patmos where I hope God will reveal himself to them in their straightness to their comfort and His glory'.[45] Those who reflected on the events through which they lived saw clear patterns. Roger Puttock, the minister at Navan, County Meath, who claimed to have lost livings worth over £200 a year, lands he held on lease and personal goods worth £1,250, saw the hardships of Protestants as a punishment from God for 'doting before on Rome and her idolatries, now her cruelties cause a great loathing of her and her doctrine. Before we were wedded to the world, now weaned from it'.[46] Among the depositions, that made by Robert Maxwell, archdeacon of Down and later bishop of Kilmore, represents well this mentality. It would achieve some notoriety by being included, in an edited form, in Sir John Temple's anti-Catholic history of the rising, published in 1646.[47] Maxwell's long and rambling deposition, a good deal of which is misremembered and in some places invented, contained evidence of the 'barbarous' cruelty of the Irish and claimed the murder of 154,000 Protestants in the early stages of the rising. Equally it was replete with stories of providential wonders such as the appearance of ghosts walking on the river after the drowning of Protestants at Portadown and strange lights being seen in the sky on the night that his brother was murdered.[48] All this provided concrete evidence of God's providence at work in protecting a chosen people: the Irish Protestant settlers. Equally it provided evidence that the Irish Catholic cause could not prevail against the elect. Above all, it was deeply anti-Catholic and anti-native Irish.

Similar sentiments can be detected in other clerical depositions. One minister in Wexford clearly believed that he had been singled out for special treatment since 'because he was a Protestant minister he was put in prison in a most dark and loathsome dungeon', the smell of which, he claimed, poisoned him.[49] In this case the circumstances are complicated by the fact that he seems to have been native Irish in origin (on the basis of his name) and that background may have increased animosities. A curate in Cavan believed that he was 'by them [the rebels] hated not only as a minister ... [but] because he was an Englishman'.[50] In Ballyboughal in County Dublin, the minister might have had good reason to hold similar views when one man set mastiff dogs on him and he escaped only by fleeing into the church.[51] Yet

45 Harcourt, *The clergies lamentation*, p. 15.   46 TCD, MS 816, f. 132; *Good and true news from Ireland being a copy of a letter sent by Mr Roger Puttock ... to a brother of his* (London, 1642), sigs a2–a2v.   47 John Temple, *The history of the ... rebellion in Ireland* (7th edn, Cork, 1766), pp 189–95. 48 TCD, MS 809, f. 9.   49 TCD, MS 818, f. 31.   50 TCD, MS 833, f. 275.   51 TCD, MS 810, f. 168.

again John Goldsmith, parson of Burrishoole in County Mayo, claimed that he was 'much maligned' and hated because he continued to exercise his ministry after the outbreak of the rebellion notwithstanding the good relations he had with his Irish neighbours up to that point.[52] However such sentiments were not common. Looking for special marks of providence, as Maxwell did, was potentially a dangerous occupation since it led into the realm of metaphysical speculation in which journey all manner of difficulties might be encountered. In March 1642 Faithful Teate, the godly Church of Ireland minister from Ballyhaise in County Cavan, told a story about the apparently miraculous survival of his baby son while the family fled from Cavan.[53] The story was told without comment, although a later pamphlet imposed an interpretative frame inserting the providential explanation before the story that 'to some of his servants the Lord hath extended marvellous great providence and mercy'.[54] The story of the strange survival of Faithful Teate's son did not disappear. It reappeared in a section of Isaac Ambrose's *The three great ordinances of Jesus Christ* (published in London in 1662) but in this case an interpretative frame was provided by Ambrose through placing the story in a section entitled 'Ministrations of and communion with angels'. According to Ambrose, the story came from Faithful Teate himself.[55] This is a much more personal story that was the result of Faithful Teate's longer term reflections during the 1640s and 1650s on the strange survival of his son and an attempt to find a language and context within which to explain that very individual experience. It introduced an angel to explain the workings of God's providence in a way that might have been otherwise inexplicable. This was, however, a dangerous strategy since angels were regarded by many as popish and Teate's speculations were seen by some as confessionally disloyal and dangerous.[56]

The violent views of Maxwell and others do not represent the entire picture. There is evidence in the depositions of a rather more nuanced view of relations between the Church of Ireland clergy and the Catholic inhabitants of Ireland. In Tyrone an Irish woman out of 'a common act of goodwill' travelled six miles to warn a minister's wife about the rising and to suggest he leave the area 'lest he might be killed'.[57] This strain of thought is most clearly spelt out in the deposition made by George Creighton, the minister of Lurgan in County Cavan, in 1643.[58] Creighton described his experiences from the evening of 23 October 1641 when a group of armed men arrived at his house demanding admission. Creighton feared an assault but instead the insurgents had come to reassure him that he would not be harmed, since he was Scottish rather than English, and to confiscate his

---

52 TCD, MS 831, f. 148, partly printed in Mary Hickson (ed.), *Ireland in the seventeenth century* (2 vols, London, 1884), i, p. 384–5. 53 TCD, MS 832, f. 79v. 54 G.S., *A brief declaration of the barbarous and inhumane dealings of the northern Irish rebels* (London, 1641), p. 9. 55 Isaac Ambrose, *The three great ordinances of Jesus Christ* (London, 1662), pp 233–5. 56 For a fuller analysis of this case see Raymond Gillespie, 'Imagining angels in early modern Ireland' in Peter Marshall and Alex Walsham (eds), *Angels in the early modern world* (Cambridge, 2006). 57 TCD, MS 839, f. 1. 58 Printed in J.T. Gilbert (ed.), *A contemporary history of affairs in Ireland* (3 vols, Dublin, 1871), i, pp 525–46.

arms. He used this privileged status to invite nine neighbouring English families to take up residence with him for protection and later offering food and shelter to those fleeing to Dublin. In late 1641 and early 1642 he estimated that he helped 4,500 people. As he explained it, he 'saw that this was the will of God' and his presence on the road and his supply of provisions were providential. Creighton's relationship with the insurgents was complex. At one level he knew many of the insurgents well, and indeed had a long-running property dispute with one of them, the earl of Fingal. Creighton traded on his good relations and the fact that he was a 'kind neighbour' to the local O'Reilly family to stave off pressures from others, such as Fingal, to have him evicted or murdered. He cultivated more friendships among the O'Reillys and even claimed some kinship with them through the earl of Argyll. All this gave Creighton a certain status in the locality even though it was an area under the control of the insurgents and one in which Catholicism was the dominant religious affiliation. How typical the case of Creighton was is uncertain for want of detailed depositions by other clergy. The evidence of his experience at least suggests some attempt to create accommodations within pre-existing theological divisions, although from the evidence of his deposition there was no doubt in Creighton's providential mind that in the longer term God was indeed working out the destruction of the Irish and that the Protestants were God's chosen people.

Such complex 'self-fashioning' through the telling of stories was rare among those clergy who made depositions in the early 1640s. Most were content to relate what material possessions they had lost at the hands of those involved in the war and to name those that they thought were responsible for plundering them. In most cases they recognised those who robbed or threatened them as being from the local community although in other cases the culprits came from further away and were strangers. The making of this sort of deposition was not a random affair. By the time depositions were taken some clergy were dead while others had fled the country and hence could not depose. As a consequence there is a geographical imbalance in the clergy's depositions available as evidence. Less than 10 per cent of the surviving clerical depositions come from Ulster, although it had a greater share than this of the Church of Ireland clergy to judge from the 1634 visitation. By contrast 20 per cent of the clerical depositions came from an arc from Waterford through Kilkenny to Tipperary and Limerick, an area in which the Church of Ireland was relatively weak according to the visitations. The same pattern appeared in Counties Meath, Westmeath, Louth and Kildare which were centres of recusancy but had a large number of depositions made by Church of Ireland clergy. This, in part, may reflect the pattern of violence in the early months of the rising. In areas such as Ulster the dislocation and sectarianism was such that relatively few clergy stayed in their parishes to make depositions while in other areas, such as Tipperary, clergy were not intimidated to leave. The result is a rather skewed form of the geography of ministry when dealing with the evidence of the depositions alone.

Recording losses implies that one had possessions to lose and hence the poorest clergy who owned little escaped the net of the commissioners taking the depositions. Nor were there depositions from the very wealthy. Few bishops, or their agents, recorded their losses. What the depositions capture, therefore, is the material world of the middling ranks of the parish clergy. However the estimates of losses in these documents are fraught with dangers. They are neither statistically representative of the clergy as a whole nor is it possible to be sure that the lists of losses capture all the possessions of an individual. Yet, enough survives to indicate that even within this restricted world there was a considerable spread of mammon. At the top of the economic pyramid were people such as Michael Smith, archdeacon of Clonfert, who claimed losses of over £10,000 as a result of the 1641 rising.[59] At the base of the pyramid was the curate, dependent on a rector or impropriator for his income. The unfortunate John Potter, curate of Affane in County Waterford, listed his losses in 1641 as his curacy worth £3 10s., household stuff worth £1 10s., a cow worth 4s., and £1 worth of hay. Between the extremes of curate and archdeacon there was a wide spread of wealth, most clergy noting their total losses at well below £1,000, depending on the wealth of the parish and the acumen of the minister in managing his assets.

Clerical wealth of this sort came from a range of sources. Most obviously a living provided financial support through the income from tithes and other dues and possibly glebe land attached to a church which could be farmed to produce cash. Richard Runcorn in Westmeath, for instance, had eighty acres of glebe attached to his living, all of which he claimed was under wheat and worth £130 whereas the living itself brought in £80 a year.[60] What clergy reckoned their livings to be worth and what they actually received are two different things. Arrears of tithes were clearly a problem. Essex Digby, the incumbent of Geashill parish in County Offaly, claimed in 1641 that his two livings were worth £300 a year but that arrears of tithes from 1638 to 1640 (admittedly bad years) were £150; Randal Adams of Westmeath declared his arrears of tithes to be £100 for a living worth £200 a year.[61]

Collection of tithes was made more difficult by the complex law relating to them and customary arrangements varied from region to region in Ireland. Some attempt had been made to bring order to this maze of rights and duties in the parliament of 1613–15, but this had failed and by the 1630s only Ulster had a coherent scheme for tithe collection, despite the demands from the commissioners investigating the state of Ireland in 1622 for such reform.[62] Moreover, tithes were not always easy to collect, especially in areas dominated by dissenters or Catholics. Bishop Bramhall of Derry, for instance, noted in 1634 that in parts of Down the clergy 'never use tithing for fear of scandal'.[63] Again the 1622 commissioners com-

---

59 TCD, MS 830, f. 143.   60 TCD, MS 817, f. 77.   61 TCD, MS 814, f. 75; MS 817, ff 4v-5.
62 G.J. Hand and V.W. Treadwell (eds), 'His Majesty's directions for ordering and settling the courts within his kingdom of Ireland, 1622' in *Analecta Hibernica*, 26 (1970), pp 211–12.   63 *Cal. SP, Ireland, 1633–47*, p. 88.

plained that in Ulster tithes were difficult to collect because people frequently moved about, thereby evading the legal process for collecting arrears to apprehend them and it suggested reform in the law of tithes.[64] For such reasons some land-lords abandoned tithes and maintained the clergy directly. Sir Hugh Montgomery in County Down 'considered that the contentions (which too frequently happen) concerning tithes, might breed dislike and aversion between people and the minister; therefore he gave unto the incumbents salaries, with glebes and prequisites or book money (as they are commonly called) for marriages, christenings, burials and Easter offerings, the clerk and the sexton also had their share of dues' and an adjoining landlord, Sir James Hamilton, maintained his clergy 'liberally'.[65] While this made for ease of collection of dues, it also had the effect of increasing landlord control over appointments to parishes. For those clergy who had to collect their own tithes, one possibility was to employ a tithe proctor from within the local community. In Cavan, Faithful Teate used Hugh Brady of Cullentroe as a tithe proctor by which means Brady was 'raised by him [Teate] from poverty to a rich estate and succour'.[66] A second possibility was to farm the tithes as John Sterne did with the tithes of one of his parishes and Henry Bolton with the tithes of another midland parish.[67] It may also be what the dean of Clonfert, Samuel Pullein, referred to when he spoke of arrears of rent of the vicarage of Knockgraffon in his deposition in 1642.[68] How widely this technique was used can only be guessed in the absence of systematic evidence.

Tithes as a form of income had both advantages and disadvantages. In towns they were difficult to assess and special arrangements had to be made for the maintenance of the ministry in Dublin. In the countryside, they tended to be collected after harvest so that a large proportion of the parish incumbent's income appeared over a short period of time and hence he had large cash balances on hand. However, in the depositions that related to events in the immediate post-harvest period in the autumn of 1641 few listed large sums of cash among their losses. Clergy clearly found ways of investing their cash to provide a stream of income. Here a number of strategies were possible. Perhaps the simplest investment solution was to engage in money lending, although this was disapproved of by the ecclesiastical authorities. Most clergy listed among their losses debts that were not recoverable as a result of the rising. In many cases the amounts were small and must be regarded as normal transactional debts in an economy that was short on specie. In some cases, however, the proportion of debts to other possessions was very high. One third of the losses of the vicar of Mainham, in Kildare, Richard Jordan was in debts; in Roscommon, Philip Taylor, the incumbent of Kilbride, listed debts worth £1,460 among total losses of £1,852.[69] Again in Armagh the widow of the vicar of Loughgall listed debts of £1,208 out of total losses of £2,349. Such debts were clearly built up over

64 BL., Add. MS 4756, f. 22.   65 Hill, *Montgomery manuscripts*, p. 55; Lowry, *Hamilton manuscripts*, p. 34.   66 TCD, MS 832, f. 79.   67 TCD, MS 814, ff 75v, 76v.   68 TCD, MS 821, f. 30. For another example of this see TCD, MS 816, f. 124.   69 TCD, MS 813, f. 232; MS 830, f. 8.

time since the living was said to be worth only £248 a year.[70] In the larger cities lending money was clearly an important outlet for accumulated clerical wealth. In Limerick, for instance, one incumbent of a living worth £70 a year had total losses of £291, of which £208 was in debts; and a number of Cork clergy had losses that were largely debts.[71] Debts on this scale can only be seen as the result of systematic money-lending which generated interest. Such activity was certainly an attractive, if frowned upon, activity for clergy who had large cash balances on hand in an economic system which had few institutional ways of moving surpluses from those wanting to borrow to those needing to do so. There are no details in the depositions on interest rates or other conditions of lending but given that prevailing interest rates were very high the potential profit was considerable, albeit risky.[72]

The second method of investing income was to purchase property. Almost all the clerical depositions itemise agricultural activity carried out by the incumbents of livings. This takes the form of lists of losses of livestock or corn, sometimes still in the ground. This may be the result of incumbents farming the glebe land attached to the living. Not all adopted this solution to managing their land. In some cases glebe land was set on lease. One incumbent leased his 846 acres of glebe at 2s. 6d. an acre.[73] However by the 1640s clergy also began to purchase or lease farms for their own use, thus benefiting from the volatile land market in Ireland. At the upper end of the economic spectrum this could represent considerable amounts of property. Henry Dodwell of Sligo had land worth £333 in Sligo and £596 in Roscommon.[74] Ambrose Aungier, chancellor of St Patrick's in Dublin, held land in Callan in County Kilkenny on which he had erected a number of buildings and John Harding, his counterpart at Christ Church Cathedral in Dublin, had lands on lease in County Armagh.[75] The dean of Clonfert also had land in Ulster.[76] More typical was John Watson of Hackettstown in County Carlow who had acquired 534 acres in Carlow with a mill. The land was stocked with forty-one milch cows, a bull and forty-eight young cattle as well as a number of sheep and horses. He also claimed to have lost £40 worth of corn and hay.[77] Some of the more affluent clergy had what can only be described as considerable ranching operations. Michael Smith, archdeacon of Clonfert, listed among his 1641 losses 1,060 wethers, 1,000 ewes, 140 cows and a bull. There was no corn listed, suggesting that he did not develop an arable aspect to his farming operations. It may be that this livestock was pastured elsewhere and simply fattened for market rather than as part of a long-term farming operation.[78]

Some deponents went as far as to calculate the profit which they made from the land that they leased from others. Roger Gwinne in Kilkenny calculated that he

70 TCD, MS 836, f. 50.   **71** TCD, MS 829, f. 132; MS 824, f. 249.   **72** Michael MacCarthy-Morrogh, 'Credit and remittance: monetary problems in early seventeenth-century Munster' in *Irish Economic and Social History*, xiv (1987), pp 5–19.   **73** TCD, MS 814, f. 75v.   **74** TCD, MS 831, f. 58.   **75** TCD, MS 809, ff 291, 305.   **76** TCD, MS 821, f. 30.   **77** TCD, MS 812, f. 41. **78** TCD, MS 830, f. 143.

made £20 profit on land that he leased for £100 and £5 profit on a £25 lease. Given that his living was worth £50 a year this represented a substantial contribution to his income.[79] Roger Puttock of Navan likewise listed over £100 profit on the land he leased, his living being valued at £200 a year.[80] In Cork another incumbent noted that a farm he leased was worth £30 above the landlord's rent, or about two-thirds the value of his income from the parish.[81] In Monaghan, one incumbent made almost as much from the land he rented from the earl of Essex in Farney as he did from his living although the incumbent of Lissard in County Longford realised only £25 profit a year on his land when his livings were worth £99.[82] Such endeavours clearly added substantially to the income of at least some of the parish clergy willing to speculate in the land market. For such men farming was as important as prayer for survival.

If something of clerical income can be constructed from the depositions, so too can something of clerical expenditures. Clergy spent their income in a wide range of ways. In some cases these purchases were related to their calling. A case in point is books. Clergy were professionally involved with books. At the simplest they would be expected to own a Bible and Book of Common Prayer but in practice many owned more than this. Since they were meant to have a least a modicum of learning many clergy bought books as a way of keeping in touch with new theological ideas, promoting spiritual growth or even practical manuals of agriculture or medicine. Unfortunately we know little about exactly what they bought since no list exists of an early seventeenth-century parish minister's library.[83] However, the lists of losses by clergy usually contain a total estimate of the value of their books. Of those who reported losses of books in their depositions roughly half were clergy, suggesting their practical engagement with print. Using the valuations provided by the clergy for their book losses it seems that their books accounted for between 3 and 16 per cent of their total losses, with most being above 5 per cent which is substantially more than the losses of books noted by gentry.[84]

Less obviously related to the clerical estate was the expenditure on what might be described as improvements to their property. Many clergy claimed losses as a result of improvements carried out on their property that they could no longer benefit from after the rising. Philip Chappel, vicar of Whitchurch in Waterford, claimed that he had improved his land by erecting buildings worth £13 from which he thought he would get an additional 30s above the head rent if he leased it.[85] Others also itemised expenditure on improvements in their depositions: £2 10s. by John Crawford the incumbent of Dunshaughlin on his land, £5 by William Sarsfield in Cork and £40 by Andrew Hayes in Tipperary.[86] Yet others detailed build-

---

79 TCD, MS 814, f. 121.   80 TCD, MS 816, f. 132.   81 TCD, MS 823, f. 28.   82 TCD, MS 834, f. 88v; MS 817, f. 199.   83 A list survives of the books of Bishop Jones of Meath in the 1660s in RCBL, MS 25, ff 98v.–101.   84 Raymond Gillespie, *Reading Ireland: print, reading and social change in early modern Ireland* (Manchester, 2005), pp 69–70.   85 TCD, MS 820, f. 156.   86 TCD, MS 816, f. 100; TCD, MS 825, ff 43, 77; MS 821, f. 33.

ings or houses that they had constructed on leased land, which was to improve its value. The rector of the parish of Kilbarry in County Leitrim claimed to have built fourteen houses on his land worth £826, while Essex Digby at Geashill itemised ditching, fencing and enclosing as well as building stone houses as among his improvements.[87] Improvements to property were not simply to do with money. Improvements in agricultural practice introduced by clergy are also noticeable. In the parish of Clane in County Kildare the incumbent, Edward Pearse, was careful to note that the cows among his losses were of 'English breed' rather than the inferior Irish cattle. Other clergy did likewise.[88] Some were interested in agricultural innovation. One incumbent in Tipperary listed 'garden fruits' among his losses, suggesting he was experimenting with new crops or possibly fruit trees.[89]

Improvements to property were usually closely linked to the acquisition of high status goods. Most clerical depositions listed pewter or brass among the losses but a number specifically mention the loss of plate or gold rings.[90] William Meales, the dean of Clonmacnoise, itemised 'gold rings, a jewel and some coin' as well as a clock and a watch among his losses and William Lightbourne in County Kildare listed 'a very good library of choice books, gold, silver, plate, jewels, rings, damask, diaper, holland, [and] linen' among his losses.[91] Also in Kildare, Christopher Goldbourne included a pair of virginals in his list of losses.[92] Ownership of luxuries, such as plate, and unusual goods, undoubtedly gave clerical buyers a certain amount of pleasure but their motives were more complex. Buying such materials from England and continental Europe, perhaps through Dublin, provided the clergy with a link to a wider world of manners and civility advanced by Protestantism. Such goods acted as symbols of their status but also provided them with tangible ways of expressing their links with England or Scotland. Such goods were symbols of how the clergy were changing the face of Ireland with modern and English fashions in landscape improvement as well as the world of fashionable and modern possessions. As a result of their religious profession, clergy desired to improve the world both materially and morally. Moreover, many had the financial resources, from tithes and the profits of land, to achieve their objectives. They used the money from tithes and from their lands to invest in the symbols of status and civility. The spread of Protestantism and the realisation of cultural and material change went hand in hand.

IV

The idea of the clergy of the established church as a culturally determined order rather than a socio-economic grouping holds a good deal of promise for dissection of the clerical body at various points in its life cycle. Over time the shape of the

---

87 TCD, MS 831, f. 5; MS 814, f. 75.   88 TCD, MS 813, ff 273, 382; MS 824, f. 238.   89 TCD. MS 821, f. 28.   90 TCD, MS 814, f. 48; MS 821, f. 18; MS 834, f. 10; MS 836, f. 50; MS 829, f. 221; MS 816, f. 177.   91 TCD, MS 816, f. 87; MS 813, f. 225.   92 TCD, MS 813, f. 273v.

Irish clerical body would change from the image set out here. In the later seventeenth and early eighteenth centuries the emergence of Trinity College, Dublin as the main training ground for Irish clergy would give a coherence to that body that had not existed before and set it on the track towards becoming a profession. In the years before 1640, however, the Irish clergy might well be characterised, as one of their number described them, as 'weavers and tapsters and other mechanic clergy'.[93] The clerical estate in the early seventeenth century may have been defined by the rite of ordination but it contained within it an enormously wide social range of rich and poor, pious and profane people. Like most others when the opportunity arose they succumbed to the potential of profit, through land speculation and money lending, in a way that those wanting a more godly reformation might disapprove of. Yet those who disapproved did little to solve the practical problems of survival that these clergy grappled with on a daily basis. What was expected of these men was considerable but the resources provided for them to realise those expectations were slight. It is, perhaps, astonishing that they achieved as much as they did.

93 Ince, *Lot's little one*, p. 164.

4

'Almoners of Providence': the clergy, 1647 to c.1780

T.C. Barnard

In 1647, Protestant episcopacy was abolished in Ireland, the Book of Common Prayer proscribed and a Directory of Worship substituted.[1] These measures copied what had occurred already in England as the Westminster parliament tightened its grip; it also showed how far ecclesiastical policy in Ireland was determined in England. By 1646, the English parliament, having defeated Charles I, was confident enough to direct its attention onto Ireland. There, since 1641, a large part of population had thrown off effective English authority and instead submitted to a Catholic government based in Kilkenny. On behalf of Charles I, a lord lieutenant, Ormond, had preserved a precarious hold over Dublin and its environs. Elsewhere, in Ulster, beleaguered Protestants had put themselves under the protection of Scots, themselves in rebellion against the king. In Munster, some Protestant settlers looked to the Westminster parliament as more likely than Charles I to save them from the insurgent Catholics. In this confused situation, the clergy of the Church of Ireland faced pressing difficulties. From the start of the trouble, they, together with their families and property, had been particular targets of aggression from Catholic neighbours. Leaders, notably Henry Jones, dean of Kilmore, and then, successively, bishop of Clogher and Meath, organized an astute campaign to advertise and maybe magnify clerical sufferings. However, the propaganda published on their behalf in London did not immediately ease their plight. Numerous clergy were obliged to abandon their parishes, heading either for the comparative safety of Dublin or for the uncertainties of exile in Britain. The wills of several, written during the 1640s and 1650s at locations scattered across England, hint at the varied responses to the tribulations.[2] Often, it was not only their personal prop-

---

1 St J.D. Seymour, *The Puritans in Ireland, 1647–1661* (Oxford, 1921, reprinted 1969), pp 1–19.
2 Will of Theophilus Buckworth, proved 21 May 1653, PRO, PROB 11/225, 36; will of B. Culme, 20 May 1645, proved 1 Feb. 1657[8], ibid., PROB 11/272, 17; will of John Richardson, 9 Aug. 1654, TCD, MS 2156; will of George Synge, 9 Aug. 1652, PRO, PROB 11/240, 274; will of Henry Tilson, ibid., PROB 11/244, 84.

erty but also the church buildings in which they had officiated that were taken over by the Catholics of the neighbourhood.

Victory over Charles I, completed only in 1648 and culminating in his execution early in the following year, allowed the English parliament to mount a campaign of reconquest in Ireland. This was achieved by 1652. Ireland was brought back to English and Protestant control. So far as the adherents of the established church were concerned, one disaster – Catholic dominance – was replaced by a second: the imposition of a religious settlement which allowed a degree of pluralism among Protestant sects but did not tolerate the practice of Protestantism as it had been established by law before 1647. Some ministers from the pre-war Church of Ireland adjusted to the situation and accepted postings and salaries from the new revolutionary regime. Others continued clandestinely to observe the now forbidden liturgy, but under fear of denunciation and punishment.[3] A third option was for the clergy to remain in exile. Those who followed the last course included former leaders, such as John Bramhall, the bishop of Derry, who passed much of the 1650s in continental Europe close to the king (Charles II) and his court. In 1660, it seemed that the sufferings of the steadfast were ended. Charles II was restored, and with him the episcopal churches of England and Ireland. Bramhall was advanced to the archbishopric of Armagh. The process of restoration was statutorily concluded with the passage in 1665 of the Act of Uniformity.[4]

Notwithstanding the apparent return to the pre-war days, the intervening decades of the 1640s and 1650s had left indelible marks. The clergy, having suffered humiliations, losses and uprooting were frequently embittered: either against the Catholics whom they regarded as the authors of their woes or against the Protestant sectaries who had taken advantage of the confusion, or indeed against both. Presbyterians and Catholics were sometimes accused of having formed an unholy alliance to topple monarchy and Protestant episcopacy. Clerical victims were consoled by reinstatement in their old positions and in some cases, such as Michael Boyle, Jeremy Taylor, Griffith Williams and Thomas Otway, by elevation to bishoprics and other dignities in Ireland.[5] In the main, they adopted an uncompromising attitude towards their opponents, and were fierce in enforcing legal requirements of religious conformity.

Nevertheless, the clergy, having endured the privations of the war and its aftermath, drew divergent lessons from it.[6] In particular, they were warned of the con-

---

3 *A declaration of the Protestant clergie of the city of Dublin, shewing the reasons why they cannot consent to the taking away of the Book of Common Prayer, and comply with the Directory* (Dublin, 1647); R. Gillespie, 'The crisis of reform, 1625–60' in K. Milne (ed.), *Christ Church Cathedral, Dublin: a history* (Dublin, 2000), pp 207–10; *Lord Inchiquins Queries to the Protestant clergy of the province of Munster with theyr answer to the said queeres* (The Hague, 1649). 4 *A declaration of the Lords Spiritual and Temporal, and the Commons in this present Parliament of Ireland assembled, concerning ecclesiastical government and the Book of Common-Prayer* (Dublin, 1661); *Statutes*, iii, pp 139–49. 5 J.I. McGuire, 'Policy and patronage: the appointment of bishops, 1660–61' in *As by law established*, pp 112–19. 6 R. Armstrong, 'Protestant churchmen and the Confederate

sequences of Protestant disunity and of the fragility of the Protestant interest in an Ireland where most inhabitants remained Catholic. The importance of union among the fractured Protestant churches and of a more dynamic response to the business of evangelizing were urged. Some who had compromised by accepting government stipends during the 1650s now compromised again by conforming to the re-established Church of Ireland. Notable in this regard were two, Edward Worth and Henry Jones. Worth was consecrated bishop of Killaloe; Jones resumed his place as bishop of Clogher and in 1661 was translated to Meath. In general, men of their kidney tended to be more lenient towards their separated brethren in the hope of enticing them back into the legal fold. So, from the 1660s, the ministry of the Church had to accommodate divergent attitudes and approaches. The divergences persisted throughout the next century.

A second legacy all too apparent from 1660 was that the Church of Ireland faced different challenges from those of the early seventeenth century. Its main competitor was still Catholicism. Its resurgence during the 1640s under the aegis of the Confederation of Kilkenny, with a resident hierarchy, regular and secular priests officiating, and church property repossessed, warned of how rapidly the latent strength of Catholicism could be mobilized. The Catholic church, despite ferocious penalties directed against its personnel in the 1650s, was suspected still to have the potential to take over Ireland. The suspicions seemed to be proved in succeeding decades, as official policy to Catholicism altered from persecution to connivance and indulgence, and culminated in its open profession during James II's reign. A high point was marked by the king's presence at mass in the Dublin cathedral of Christ Church in 1689.[7] Yet, for all these alarming advances in the visibility and strength of the Catholic clergy, they failed to secure two victories that they craved: to oust the Protestants from their privileges as the state church and from legal possession of the property of the established church. Despite the disappointments for Catholics, enough happened between 1685 and 1691 to demoralize the clergy of the Church of Ireland and to make them fear that it was only a matter of time before the last two Catholic objectives were achieved.

The Catholic *revanche* between 1685 and 1691 was briefer and less terrifying than the earlier ascendancy of the 1640s. Even so, the fear that the resurgent Catholics might attack the personnel and property of the Church of Ireland with the same ferocity as in and after 1641 led to schemes to publicize the sufferings. The bishop of Meath, Anthony Dopping, assumed a function similar to that of Henry Jones in collecting accounts of depredations on clergy and churches.[8] The two troubled periods, especially when considered together, chastened thoughtful Protestants and cast sombre shadows throughout the eighteenth century. Among

wars' in C. Brady and J. Ohlmeyer (eds), *British interventions in early modern Ireland* (Cambridge, 2004), pp 230–51. 7 K. Milne, 'Restoration and reorganization, 1660–1830' in Milne (ed.), *Christ Church Cathedral Dublin*, pp 270–3. 8 T.C. Barnard, 'Ireland, 1685–1691', in a volume edited by T. Harris and S. Taylor (forthcoming).

both clergy and laity, responses to the chilling experiences varied from the wish to disable Catholic rivals so completely that the priesthood would wither and die, thus denying Catholicism in Ireland its essential nutriments, to a concern that the Protestants put their own house in order the better then to address the intractable problem of the Catholic majority. The contradictory attitudes all had their impact on policy after 1692. Laws were passed that were intended to take an axe to the roots of official Catholicism. Further statutes improved the Church of Ireland, institutionally and financially. Other initiatives suggested that at least a section of the clergy wished to tackle endemic problems among its own adherents and among the larger population. Some clergy continued to explore means through which the debilitating competition between themselves and dissenting pastors might be turned into fruitful cooperation against Catholicism. A few ministers of the established church interested themselves in moderating the apparently negative approach to Catholicism, even proposing devices through which it could be given legal toleration.

Catholicism remained the inescapable presence, which throughout the seventeenth and eighteenth centuries the clergy had to acknowledge. Hopes that it would be weakened by military defeats and the sustained legal attacks of the 1650s and early eighteenth century proved illusory. Indeed, official enquiries, notably in the 1730s and 1760s, suggested the reverse: Catholicism exhibited the same alarming vitality that had enabled it to take over in the 1640s and after 1685. Moreover, although the laws decreed otherwise, Catholic priests outnumbered the clergy of the established church, and presided over a system of schools, religious houses and unobtrusive chapels. In 1731, Bishop Robert Howard of Elphin echoed the gloom of his mentor, Archbishop King of Dublin, when he predicted that 'popery is the gulf that may swallow us at last'.[9]

To this hazard was added a new one after 1660: that of Protestant dissent. Before 1641, owing to the dense settlement of eastern Ulster by Scots, their distinctive Presbyterianism had also been imported. Awkward compromises contained the potential problem of separatism, but even before the war the strains were threatening to crack apart the Protestant community. The effect of the war, bringing to Ulster a Scottish army of covenanters, and the subsequent waves of Scottish immigration into the region planted Presbyterianism more securely, so that by 1659 there were five presbyteries in Ireland. Determined bishops of the established church, such as Jeremy Taylor, consecrated bishop of Down and Connor in 1661, wielded the legal weapons in the hope of eradicating Presbyterianism. They failed. Instead, with renewed immigration of Scots, Presbyterianism continued its growth. With alternative structures and sustained by intimacy with Scotland and

9 Bp R. Howard to H. Howard, 3 June 1731, 23 Dec. 1731, 27 Jan. 1731[2], 16 March 1731[2], 22 April 1732, NLI, PC 227; cf. Abp W. King to Lord Carteret, 22 June 1727; same to Abp W. Wake, 22 June 1727, TCD, MS 750/8, 213, 214.

its own tight discipline, Presbyterianism constituted the principal worry for many clergy of the established Church throughout Ulster.[10]

The threat was both ideological and practical. Presbyterians denied the scriptural bases on which the government and ceremonies of the Church of Ireland were founded. They also resisted the efforts of the ministers to extract monies for religious services, such as marriage and burial, over which the Church of Ireland claimed a monopoly, and for their own and their buildings' upkeep in the form of tithes, ministers' money and parish cesses. Clergy of the established church who provoked or resisted the nonconformists could find themselves engaged in unedifying and continuous battles.

The Presbyterians were the largest and most coherent denomination to emerge from the confusion of the mid-seventeenth century, but not the only one. English Presbyterians, Religious Independents, Baptists and Quakers all survived from the 1650s. But none had the geographical concentration enjoyed by the Presbyterians in the north nor indeed the tight discipline and sustaining links with a parent church outside Ireland. Even so, the other sects irritated the clergy of the Church of Ireland, especially those bent on turning the nominal monopoly over religious services into a reality. Dublin and the larger towns were the districts where Protestant separatists caused the most unease. In the countryside, Quakers were irksome because of their habit of refusing to pay tithes to support ordained ministers. By the early eighteenth century, the disappearance of virtually all the substantial landed patrons of Protestant dissent turned it into less of an irritant. However, the arrival of Methodism in Ireland in the 1740s confronted incumbents with a fresh challenge that showed signs of eroding support among humbler members of the conformist congregations. Church of Ireland clergy varied in their responses to these threats. Often, in their different localities, they faced very different challenges. Also, their perceptions of the threat varied. Accordingly, if some seized the cudgels offered them by the law and belaboured rivals, others contented themselves with servicing those who remained faithful, and tried to ignore the rest.

II

The alarms of the mid-seventeenth century and of the 1680s reminded that the Protestants in Ireland were a vulnerable minority and, moreover, one which, because of the crises, was deeply fragmented. Perceptive clerics, as well as counselling that the breaches be repaired as swiftly as possible, schemed to improve the

---

10 E. Furgol, 'The military and ministers as agents of Presbyterian imperialism in England and Ireland, 1640–1648' in J. Dwyer, R.A. Mason and A. Murdoch (eds), *New perspectives on the politics and culture of early modern Scotland* (Edinburgh, 1982), pp 95–115; R. Gillespie, 'The Presbyterian revolution in Ulster, 1660–1690' in W.J. Sheils and D. Wood (eds), *The churches, Ireland and the Irish*, Studies in Church History, xxv (Oxford, 1989), pp 159–70.

organization and personnel of the Church of Ireland. To this end, they worked through parliament. In the 1660s, bishops had been more concerned to block suggestions that might lessen the privileges of their church than to modernize it. In the 1690s, although the bishops in Ireland again faced the prospect of being forced to tolerate Protestant dissenters – along the lines of the recent measure in England – they stopped the bill. Instead, they pushed others designed to fortify the Church. The resulting statutes would make parishes more manageable by dividing the large and uniting the small and sparsely populated, would require clergy to reside and make it easier for them to do so with better arrangements for building houses and providing glebes. In some places, notably Dublin and Cork, help was given to build churches where they were wanting.

At the same time, zealous bishops sought to correct abuses that threatened to bring their church into discredit. Negligent and scandalous dignitaries were disciplined or removed. Particular attention was directed on a trio in eastern Ulster who blemished the reputation of the established Church: a worry given the strength of Scottish Presbyterianism in the region. Thomas Hacket, the long-absent bishop of Down and Connor (he preferred to live by the River Thames in Hammersmith), was removed. Protracted proceedings eased out the archdeacon of Down, the Revd Lemuel Matthews.[11] Most sensational of all were the allegations levelled against the dean of Connor, Thomas Ward. Between 1678 and 1693 he had become a serial adulterer. In pursuit of his prey he had frequented a fiddler's house in Carrickfergus and numerous taverns. He, too, was prised out.[12] These embarrassing incidents did not entirely end the problem of clerical misdemeanours. At Lismore, the dean, William Jephson, angered his superiors with his absences and neglects, but was protected by highly placed friends among the laity.[13] Inevitably, scandals still occurred in the eighteenth century, but, in general, the more rigorous supervision introduced by the bishops of the 1690s, such as King, Foy and Palliser, continued and made a Matthews or Ward a rarity among the beneficed clergy.

More intractable was the issue that had long been identified as a, if not *the*, prime obstacle to an effective ministry: its maintenance. In Ireland, even more than in England, the notional value of livings bore little resemblance to the revenue that could be collected. Some of the difficulty arose from the extent of lay impropriation, which meant that the lay owner of a living was entitled to some or all the tithes. The parlous situation in the dioceses of Ferns and Leighlin, itemized by Bishop Edward Synge in 1736, is analyzed below by Marie-Louise Legg.[14] Elsewhere, two-

---

11 Proceedings against Revd Lemuel Matthews, RCBL, MS 531; *To the Honourable the Commons of England in Parliament assembled, The humble petition of Lemuel Matthews* [Dublin, ?1702]. 12 'An abstract of the pleadings and process in a cause instituted ... against Thomas Ward', RCBL, MS 566; J.B. Leslie, *Clergy of Connor from Patrician times to the present day* (Belfast, 1993), p. 643.   13 T.C. Barnard, *A new anatomy of Ireland: the Irish Protestants, 1649–1770* (New Haven and London, 2003), pp 89, 92, 93.   14 See below, chapter 6; E. Synge, *Two affidavits in relation to the demands of Tythe-Agistment in the diocese of Leighlin* (Dublin, 1736), pp 17–18.

thirds of the tithes in the see of Clonfert were said to be in the hands of Lord Clanricarde in 1682. So many livings in Killaloe were impropriate to Lord Thomond
that 'he is a manner the bishop of the diocese'.[15] In the westerly bishopric of
Ardagh, Lord Westmeath had a comparable strangle-hold.[16] In addition to the clerical poverty that then resulted, in the case of Clanricarde (and numerous others) the
impropriator was a Catholic.[17] Lay-people in receipt of the rectorial and vicarial
tithes paid an allowance to the unfortunate who performed divine service in the
parish. Lay-people were not the sole offenders: non-resident and negligent clergy
sometimes collected the emoluments as rector and vicar and then allowed a pittance
to a curate. Further financial troubles arose from fluctuating agricultural conditions.
During the harsh 1740s, the yield of the tithes in the north Cork parish of Kil-
shannig fell from £300 to barely £100. However, when in the last quarter of the
century agricultural prices improved in south Munster, some clergy benefited.[18]
Parishioners of a different persuasion understandably resented and might resist
paying to maintain a minister whose services they did not attend, especially when
they were also charged to support their own priest or pastor.

As well as principled objections to the levy, there were others that made nominal supporters of the Church of Ireland reluctant to contribute. Tithes bore dis-
proportionately on modest and poor producers, and, in times of dearth, might
make the difference between subsistence and indigence, especially for those in the
countryside. Further squabbles erupted over which products were liable. Trivial as
it might seem, in the diocese of Derry in 1683, the recalcitrant were threatened
with prosecution in the bishop's court for refusing to pay the tithe on rabbits.[19]
Such demands should not be minimized as grievances that estranged the laity from
the clergy of the established Church. Regional and altering patterns of agriculture
and rural industry meant that there were determined attempts to ensure that potatoes, flax and cattle were subject to assessment. Again, the campaigns by individual bishops and clergy to enforce their interpretations of the law of tithes caused
anger and violence.[20] Edward Ledwich, drawing on his experience as incumbent of
Aghaboe in the diocese of Ossory during the 1770s, contended that he received no
more than half his entitlement. Furthermore, the notional rates on different commodities were seldom paid in full. Yields were further depressed by the dishonesty
of tithe-proctors, who contracted to collect on behalf of the incumbent and then
pay him a fixed sum, and the unceasing chicanery of 'welders'.[21] Problems of this
kind were widespread and meant that the notional valuation of a living was often

15 PRONI, DIO 4/4/4.   16 E. Reader to Bp W. Smythe, 13 Oct. 1693, NLI, PC 436.   17 Bp
E. Wolley to Bp A. Dopping, 24 Oct. 1682, Armagh Public Library, Dopping MSS, 1/33.   18
D. Dickson, *Old world colony: Cork and south Munster, 1630–1830* (Cork, 2005), pp 219, 284,
287–8.   19 PRONI, DIO 4/5/3, no.5.   20 T.C. Barnard, 'Parishes, pews and parsons: lay people and the Church of Ireland, 1647–1780' in Gillespie and Neely, pp 70–103; P. Delany, *An essay
towards evidencing the divine original of tythes* (London, 1748).   21 E. Ledwich, *A statistical
account of the parish of Aghaboe in the Queen's County, Ireland* (Dublin, 1796), pp 53–4.

optimistic. Bishop Berkeley thought that one living within his diocese of Cloyne was worth £80 p.a.; the new incumbent valued it at only £60.[22]

Reasonably enough, by the eighteenth century, bishops saw that the existing haphazard approach to tithes was ineffectual and divisive. Accordingly, they organized a measure which would end the confusion by enacting a new law. This attempt – in 1735 – revealed with embarrassing clarity the selfishness of landed proprietors sitting in parliament.[23] For all their professed devotion to the Church of Ireland and their willingness to protect it legislatively against its rivals, they were not prepared to tax themselves and their neighbours more heavily on behalf of the clergy of the established church. The bishops, chastened by the public rebuff over tithes, consoled themselves with modest devices to better their conditions. However, the essential financial problem remained, so that it continued to cause dissension between incumbents and parishioners and to lead to more comprehensive assaults on the failings of the clergy of the established church. Once more clerics reacted variously: some aggressively, so provoking more attacks – both literary and physical – on the establishment; others moderated their ambitions and demands in order to avoid dangerous confrontations.[24] The battle worsened an endemic anticlericalism. In 1736, one clergyman predicted, 'an evil spirit threatens the present constitution of the church next session with something not pleasing'.[25] When, in 1739, subscriptions were solicited among country gentlemen for a new edition of Sir James Ware's works, the subscribers, on discovering the book was about bishops, 'called for their money again'.[26] By 1741, a cleric, endeavouring to secure the tithe on flax, contended that the defaulters 'appear to be in an advanced flight towards rebellion'.[27]

III

In putting their house in better order, the clergy of the Church of Ireland had most success in the areas where they enjoyed greatest control over their own destinies.

22 Bp G. Berkeley to Lord Perceval, 17 Nov. 1742, BL, Add. MX 47013B, f. 92; Revd R. Brereton to same, ibid., f. 97; A.A. Luce and T.E. Jessop (eds.), *The works of George Berkeley, bishop of Cloyne* (9 vols, London, 1948–57), viii, p. 266.   23 Paper on tithe agistment, 1737, BL, Add. MS 21,132, ff. 49–53; 'Short hints on the tithe bill', ibid., ff. 66–7; M. Bric, 'The tithe system in eighteenth-century Ireland', *PRIA*, lxxxvi, C (1986), pp 271–7; *Prescription Sacred: Or, reasons for opposing the new demand of herbage in Ireland* (n.p., 1736); *Some reasons against the bill for settling the tyth of hemp, flax, &c. by a Modus* (Dublin, 1734).   24 Bp R. Howard to H. Howard, 22 May 1736, NLI, PC 227; M. Bric, 'Priests, parsons and politics: the Rightboy protest in County Cork, 1785–1788' in C.H.F. Philpin (ed.), *Nationalism and popular protest in Ireland* (Cambridge, 1987), pp 163–90; Dickson, *Old world colony*, pp 448–52; A.P.W. Malcomson, *Archbishop Charles Agar: churchmanship and politics in Ireland, 1760–1810* (Dublin, 2002), pp 190–1.   25 Revd J. Smythe to W. Smythe, 14 Dec. 1736, NLI, PC 449.   26 J. Blaymires to W. Harris, 30 Jan. 1738[9], Physico-Historical Society papers, Armagh Public Library.   27 Revd R. Lestrange to W. Smythe, 24 Aug. 1741, 23 Sep. 1741, NLI, PC 449.

The complement of clergy grew. By the mid-eighteenth century, the total was estimated variously between 800 and 1,200. The higher figure may have represented those in orders, but not necessarily beneficed. By 1817, the number of incumbents was said to be about 1,200.[28] It has been calculated that there was a ratio of one Church of Ireland minister for every 312 members of the church. At the same time, there was thought to be one useable church building to roughly the same number of Church of Ireland worshippers.[29] Overwhelmingly, the church was manned by university graduates. Notwithstanding repeated laments that the bench of bishops groaned under the weight of prelates imported from England, the bulk of the diocesan clergy had been born and educated in Ireland, usually at Trinity College, Dublin.[30] The larger Protestant population made it easier to recruit ordinands from within Ireland. By the early nineteenth century, the process had culminated in a situation in which 64 per cent of the clergy in the diocese of Cork are known to have been born in either the city or county of Cork. In this diocese, and those of Cloyne and Ross, less than 4 per cent were English by birth.[31]

A denser network of schools across Ireland and the expanded size and vitality of Dublin University meant that higher standards could be demanded of those intending to enter the ministry. It still depended on bishops to decide just what requirements they should impose before they ordained candidates and licensed incumbents.[32] Even in the eighteenth century, they veered between laxity and severity. In 1781, one cleric revealed that he had just been ordained deacon by the bishop of Raphoe. Arriving with a testimonial and certificate of his bachelor's degree from Oxford university, the bishop had had no option.[33] A meeting of the archbishops and bishops in 1791 apparently regulated more strictly the training of would-be clergy at Trinity. The step suggested that most Church of Ireland clerics were now instructed in the college. Those preparing for the diaconate had to study Grotius, Archbishop Secker's lectures, Jortin's *Discourses concerning the truth of the Christian religion*, and Gilbert Burnet on the Thirty-Nine Articles. They would also be examined on their knowledge of the Old and New Testaments, with special attention to their chronology and geography. In addition, each candidate would be asked to write in Latin on a sacred subject and be quizzed about their

---

28 Barnard, *New anatomy*, pp 81–2, 361; R. Barton, *Lectures in natural philosophy* (Dublin, 1751), p. xi; J.C. Erck, *The Irish Ecclesiastical Register* (Dublin, 1817), pp 32, 60, 98, 114. 29 S.J. Connolly, *Religion, law and power: the making of Protestant Ireland, 1660–1760* (Oxford, 1992), pp 179–80. 30 Barnard, *New anatomy*, pp 81–101; J. Falvey, 'The Church of Ireland episcopate in the eighteenth century', *Eighteenth-Century Ireland*, 8 (1993), p. 109; J. Falvey, 'The Church of Ireland episcopate in the eighteenth century', unpublished MA thesis, University College, Cork (1995); F.G. James, *Ireland in the empire, 1688–1773* (Cambridge, Mass., 1973), p. 131; P. McNally, ' "Irish and English interests": national conflict within the Church of Ireland episcopate in the reign of George I', *IHS*, xxix (1995), pp 295–314. 31 I. d'Alton, *Protestant society and politics in Cork, 1812–1844* (Cork, 1980), pp 61–2. 32 S. Burdy, *The life of Philip Skelton*, ed. N. Moore (Oxford, 1914), pp 38–41; R. Howard to W. Howard, [between 1727 and 1728], NLI, PC 227. 33 A.T. Hamilton to earl of Abercorn, 5 Oct. 1781, PRONI, D 623/A/44/137.

knowledge of the Greek New Testament. Various commentaries on the Bible were recommended. Intending priests were to read Samuel Clarke on natural and revealed religion, Hamilton on the attributes of the supreme being, and Wheatley on the Book of Common Prayer. Inevitably, the candidates varied in the assiduity with which they pursued the set curriculum; similarly, bishops differed in the rigour with which they tested the hopefuls.[34]

Instruction was improved, at least notionally, after 1718 thanks to a special lecturership in divinity endowed by Archbishop William King.[35] Trinity College had been founded as a Protestant seminary. During the second half of the seventeenth century, its popularity as a finishing school for the sons of prospering Protestants grew, but it did not lose its clerical purpose. It has been calculated that during the first half of the eighteenth the college was producing annually between eight and eighteen graduates who might then be ordained. Indeed, the supply exceeded the vacancies, so helping to explain the log-jam which obliged aspirants to queue for benefices. The frustrated languished long in curacies, or made shift as tutors and schoolmasters, while constantly alert to chances of preferment.[36] Sons tended to follow fathers into the Church. About a fifth of those who matriculated as members of the college between 1685 and 1750 had a clergyman as father.

Such was the growth of the Protestant population in Ireland that there was no shortage of recruits to the sacred ministry. At first sight this happy situation appears at variance with the monotonous complaints about the long and costly preparation and the protracted spells spent by many of the well-qualified in meagrely paid curacies, to be followed by repeated struggles to secure an equitable tithe. One aggrieved cleric reckoned that it had cost £91 to keep him at school for seven years and £280 for another seven years at Trinity College. When other disbursements were included the total neared £400. As an investment it was ill-rewarded by long service as a curate, paid anything from £20 to £50 p.a.[37] The grievance persisted throughout the century. In 1787, 'the curates of Ireland' related how in the countryside they were obliged to keep a horse and servant. They were disabled by their indigence from the duties of hospitality and charity. Often they had no house of their own and had to pay a yearly £15 or £30 for lodgings. More rhetorically, they contrasted their own plight with that of the 'fat rector lolling in his easy coach, wallowing in the filthy puddles of pride and luxury, perhaps never seeing his church or parishioners or caring about them'.[38] Although there was some sympathy for the curate's lot, superiors sometimes contended that

34 A. Erck, notebook, RCBL, MS 103, pp 365–6.   35 D. Hannigan, 'The University of Dublin, 1685 1750: a study of matriculation records', unpublished MA thesis, St Patrick's College, Maynooth (1995), pp 23–5; R.B. McDowell and D.A. Webb, *Trinity College Dublin, 1592–1952: an academic history*, 2nd edn (Dublin, 2004), pp 41, 161–2. Cf. d'Alton, *Protestant society and politics in Cork*, p. 62.   36 Hannigan, 'The University of Dublin, 1685–1750', pp 77–8.   37 Philocurus to ?Bp T. Rundle, *c.*1735, PRONI, D 668/E/38; 6 Geo I, c. xiii (*Statutes at large*, pp 542–3).   38 'Curates of Ireland' to ?Bolton, 30 Feb. 1787, NLI, MS 15,811.

the poor underlings were authors of their own woes. With unrealistic expectations, the obscure and poorly connected insisted on being ordained. They then burdened themselves with wives and children.[39]

Financial incentives alone hardly explain why the hopeful continued to train for holy orders. The absence of enough alternative careers which united status and respectability may help account for the continuing flow of ordinands. Some allowance also must be made for the contemporary feeling that the church, if it was akin to the professions of the law and medicine in demanding arduous and expensive preparation, differed in being viewed – at least by some – as a vocation. Repugnance was expressed towards those without any such sense of a higher call who nevertheless sought ordination. Occasionally, bishops scrupled to ordain particular applicants. Nathaniel Foy, bishop of Waterford and Lismore, wished for more searching examination of qualifications after thirteen had been ordained by a fellow bishop. He regretted that acceptance for the ministry was still governed 'by relations, recommendations and other respects'.[40] Bishops in neighbouring sees quarrelled when one ordained a candidate rejected by the other. However, the concern led to closer scrutiny of would-be deacons.[41] Archbishop King, for example, refused to lay hands on the son of Judge Hely, despite his being recommended by Lord Drogheda. In the event, another bishop, prevailed upon by Lords Conway and Hillsborough, obliged.[42] There could also be problems when hopefuls were recommended by English and Welsh bishops for Irish preferments.[43]

The ministry of the Church of Ireland reproduced and, in some respects, intensified the economic stratifications in Irish Protestant society. Solidarity in labouring in the same vineyard was vitiated by the unequal rewards and indeed by the differences between pleasant and insalubrious areas within the plantation. Against these divisions must be set some forces making for greater clerical cohesion. A common purpose in striving to spread a particular version of evangelical truth and common enemies to that endeavour ought to have united all. Then, too, most clerics shared the experiences of being educated in Ireland and of reading the troubled history of the Protestants there. They studied and then preached from standard translations of and commentaries on the Bible. But, cutting across and sometimes destroying any sense of a unified caste were assorted economic and cultural circumstances. One bishop thought the clerical estate 'so varied and diffused a body of men' that it lacked unity.[44]

---

39 T.C. Barnard, 'Improving clergymen, 1660–1760', in *As by law established*, p. 140; Barnard, *New anatomy*, pp 82–3.   40 Bp N. Foy to?, PRONI, DIO 4/15/2/3, p. 2.   41 Bp R. Tenison to Bp W. Smythe, 17 July 1696, NLI, PC 436; Barnard, 'Improving clergymen', pp 140–1.   42 Abp W. King to W. Flower, 11 April 1727, TCD, MS 750/8/187–8; Bp H. Downes to Bp T. Vesey, NLI, de Vesci MSS; unknown to unknown, O'Hara MSS, 24 Dec. 1747, NLI, MS 20,385.   43 Certificate to Bp W. Lloyd for H. Williams, 1 April 1693; Bp W. Lloyd to Bp W. Smythe, 10 April 1693; H. Williams to same, 26 June 1693, NLI, PC 436.   44 Bp R. Howard to H. Howard, 22 May 1736, NLI, PC 227.

By the latter part of the seventeenth century, most intending clergymen were prepared at Trinity College in Dublin. Despite its dominance, its impact varied according to the time when the tuition took place. The college enjoyed a renaissance in the two decades after Charles II's restoration, the effects of which are apparent in a generation of Irish-educated bishops – Anthony Dopping, Nathaniel Foy, Samuel Foley, William Palliser, William King and John Stearne – who took a lead in the statutory and voluntary initiatives of the 1690s. Frequently they had been trained by rigorous tutors imported from England: Richard Lingard, Henry Dodwell, Robert Huntington and Narcissus Marsh.[45] Even within this cohort of graduates there were striking differences in churchmanship: for example, between Palliser, archbishop of Cashel and a promoter of the high church ideals in Queen Anne's time, and King, successively bishop of Derry and archbishop of Dublin. Furthermore, the ethos of the college could alter dramatically, almost from decade to decade. The kind of ecclesiastical and secular politics professed by George Berkeley, a fellow from 1707 to 1724, and Patrick Delany, reputedly the most popular tutor in the 1710s and 1720s and also a Tory, was replaced by ideas more in tune with 'the revolution principles' for which the university and its fellows were applauded.[46] By 1744, the institution was in such good order and odour that it was suggested that a wayward but well-connected youth take rooms in the college, 'not to do his duty [i.e. read for a degree], but to have gentlemen of good character to converse with him'.[47]

A serious gap in our knowledge of the formation of the clergy is the practical preparation given in the routine requirement to write and deliver sermons. A good delivery clearly mattered if the divine message was to be communicated effectively in buildings with erratic acoustics. In these unheated and often leaky spaces, it was hard to keep the attention of auditors. Model sermons could be bought from booksellers for use by those uncertain of their own powers of composition. Experienced clergymen built up a stock of addresses, suited to specific festivals and texts. Occasionally they stipulated that they be burnt after they had died, presumably to prevent illicit recycling. Just as fashions in theology altered, so too did the recommended styles of sermons. In the 1680s, Edward Wetenhall, the bishop of Cork, reflected on the matter. He endorsed the injunction from Corinthians, 'In the church, I had rather speak five words with my understanding, that is being understood, that I might reach others, than ten thousand words in an unknown tongue.'

45 T.C. Barnard, 'Provost Huntington's injunctions to the schoolmasters', *Hermathena*, cxix (1975), pp 71–3; T.C. Barnard, 'Reforming Irish manners: the religious societies in Dublin during the 1690s' in Barnard, *Irish Protestant ascents and descents*, pp 143–78; 'The life and travels of the Right Revd and learned Dr Robert Huntington', *Gentleman's Magazine* (1825), pp 11–15, 115–19.   46 *Letters written by his excellency Hugh Boulter, D.D., Lord Primate of all Ireland* (2 vols, Dublin, 1770), i, pp 47–8, 51–2, 54–5. Insights into Delany's outlook come from his *Revelation examined with candour*, 2nd edn. (2 vols, London, 1733); *Eighteen discourses and dissertations upon various very important and interesting subjects* (London, 1766).   47 K. Conolly to J. Bonnell, 7 July 1744, NLI, PC 434.

He then added his wish to respect 'the capacity of the most, and that I am sure is of the unlearned'. He applauded a cohort of 'profoundly learned divines and excellent preachers' in the preceding generation. They included three – Ussher, Bramhall and Taylor – who had been bishops in Ireland. Wetenhall further approved of some trained in the English universities – often clandestinely – during the 1650s. Yet, he decried the emergence in recent times of florid preachers who 'cannot descend to speak plain and easy truths and practicals'. Sermons now veered from the 'flaunting and romantick' to 'the spruce and curious'. Wetenhall intended to caution his colleagues and brethren, but it is likely that many of his reflections were occasioned by developments in England rather than in Ireland.[48]

More than half a century later, Delany, high in regard as a preacher in early Hanoverian Dublin, reflected on the same matter. His model was a mentor at Trinity College, Peter Browne, who moved from the provostship to be bishop of Cork in 1710. Delany contrasted the manner and content of Browne's discourses with what had come into vogue subsequently. Delany contended that recent trends in preaching alienated auditors and so weakened the church. In particular, he regretted that, under the influence of mathematical reasoning, a 'cold, dry, didactic way' had spread into preaching. It was all very well to collate texts methodically, so clearing difficulties and proving points, but it introduced a chilliness that repelled church-goers.[49] Delany by his example might seek to reverse the decline, but, since he had few equals in eloquence and his ministry was confined chiefly to Dublin, Downpatrick, Bath and other English pulpits, his impact was limited. Delany urged his fellow clerics to perform social and civil duties being simultaneously 'almoners of providence', relieving 'every social distress', and, at least ideally, 'the greatest benefactors to mankind'.[50] Despite his exhortations, congregations continued to be treated to the inaudible, incoherent, unorthodox or nothing at all, as well as to the impassioned and inspirational. The shortcomings allowed renovative movements, such as evangelicalism and Methodism, to take hold, and to achieve what the luke-warm mumblers of the established church could not: that sinners be washed clean in 'the laver of regeneration'.[51]

Delany had been a powerful presence at Dublin University, and had his clerical successors. In 1758, four of the seven senior fellows of the college were in holy orders. The clerics tended to a suavity that enabled them to pass muster in the polite society of the city.[52] The tradition of Delany was continued by John Lawson, by the 1750s a senior fellow of the college. He lectured and wrote on oratory and geometry.[53] He combined mastery of these subjects with fame as a preacher.

---

48 E. Wetenhall, *Six sermons preached in Ireland, in difficult times* (London, 1695), sig. [A3v–A4v]. 49 Delany, *Eighteen discourses and dissertations*, pp xii–xiv; [P. Delany], *The present state of learning, religion and infidelity in Great-Britain* (London, 1732), pp 6–8, 11–15, 27–33. 50 Delany, *Eighteen discourses and dissertations*, p. 236. 51 Delany, *Divine original of tythes*, p. 33; P. Delany, *Sixteen discourses upon doctrines and duties, more peculiarly Christian* (London, 1754), pp 327–8. 52 Barnard, *New anatomy*, p. 108; McDowell and Webb, *Trinity College Dublin*, p. 44. 53 John

The latter reputation contradicted Delany's insistence on a strong delivery. Lawson compensated for the weakness of his voice 'by the energy and pathos of his delivery'.[54] In demand in Dublin parishes, Oxford and London, as well as in the college chapel, he stressed charity and upheld the existing social and political orders. He reminded members of the House of Commons that the state had the right and a duty 'to entrust those only who profess the national religion with places of great authority and influence'. He also argued that those who, under cover of liberty of conscience, 'advance tenets impious and shocking, contrary to the general belief and reason of mankind' must be restrained. Similarly, Catholics with awkward political loyalties should be punished, not as heretics, but as bad subjects. Lawson was prepared to concede that early English rulers had been at fault in ruling by force and not by law – 'a method of proceeding equally cruel and unpolitic'. This mismanagement had been corrected belatedly. Like others of the cloth he detected the spread of civility into Ireland, with 'peace, plenty and humanity'. But he still cautioned against Protestants dropping their guard. The objections against Catholicism as both political and theological system remained. Lawson insisted that 'every true Protestant...must alike fear and oppose a superstition which esteems impious and idolatrous, destructive of reason and liberty, and highly displeasing to God'. Such unyielding sentiments might be timely in a Dublin church in 1746 when the outcome of the Young Pretender's descent on Scotland was uncertain. However, it was thought appropriate to print Lawson's sermon in 1776. The balance that Lawson recommended – between winning Catholics 'to the truth by humane methods, by kindness and instruction', and maintaining vigilance – was approved by most Church of Ireland congregations.[55]

On hearing or reading Lawson's sermon to parliament, sceptics might wonder how much kindness and instruction were directed towards Catholics by the Church of Ireland clergy. Periodic endeavours to equip intending clergy to preach in the Irish language invariably excited controversy and were virtually abandoned for a couple of generations after 1715.[56] Furthermore, whatever moderation might be shown towards docile Catholics by products of late seventeenth- and early eighteenth-century Trinity, such as the elder and younger Edward Synges, gave way to an obdurate attitude during the turbulence of the 1780s and 1790s.[57]

Lawson, *Lectures concerning oratory* (Dublin, 1758); idem, *Appendix de Linearum geometricum proprietatibus generalibus tractatus* ([?Dublin], undated); W.B. Stanford, *The classical tradition in Ireland* (Dublin, 1976), pp 52–4.   54 [John Lawson], *Occasional sermons upon the following subjects*, 2nd edn (London, 1776), p. v.   55 [Lawson], *Occasional sermons*, pp 269, 271; John Lawson, *A sermon preached in St Andrew's, Dublin, before the Honourable House of Commons; on Tuesday, the 23d of October, 1753* (Dublin, 1753).   56 T.C. Barnard, 'Protestants and the Irish language, c.1675–1725', *JEH*, 44 (1993), pp 243–72, reprinted in Barnard, *Irish Protestant ascents and descents*, pp 179–207.   57 The fullest treatment is Joseph Liechty, 'Irish Evangelicalism, Trinity College Dublin, and the mission of the Church of Ireland at the end of the eighteenth century', unpublished PhD thesis, St Patrick's College, Maynooth (1987). See, too: S. Small, *Political*

In addition to the Irish Protestant seminary of Trinity College, a second institution – Convocation – brought together numerous clergy. As in England, so in
Ireland, Convocation met at the same time as parliament. In Dublin, this happened
in 1661–1665 and again between 1704 and 1713.[58] The meetings undoubtedly
encouraged questions of shared interest to be aired. Many – particularly the economic problems of the Church – were ones that affected the whole clerical body.
Others reflected sectional and partisan concerns, and weakened any community of
purpose. Moreover, the structure of Convocation, divided between an upper house
of bishops and a lower of elected representatives of the subaltern clergy, helped to
expose disagreements. Some arose from the different preoccupations and perspectives of the bishops, especially when they were lately imported from England.
Also, the bishops were prone to quarrel among themselves. Similar – and worse –
contentions disturbed the lower house, numbering 150, especially during the sessions in Queen Anne's reign.[59]

Numerous issues came into play: rivalries between those of English and Irish
background, differences of outlook based on age, education, theological orienta-
tion, personality, affinity and even the geography of Ireland. A perennial argument
was over whether to regard Catholics or Protestant dissenters as the greater danger to the Church of Ireland. Evaluations of the threats could be coloured by the
location in which an individual ministered: throughout Ulster, Presbyterians
seemed the more formidable; elsewhere, the Catholics worried the Church of Ireland clergy. Convocation offered a vehicle through which the lower clergy might
recover some of the emoluments and prestige lost to the laity. However, its
provocative resolutions alarmed ministers and bishops who realised the importance
of cooperation with powerful Protestant laymen. The intemperance and indiscre-
tion of ardent clergymen, both inside and outside Convocation between 1704 and
1713, copying inflammatory tactics from their counterparts in England and allying
with the currently ascendant Tory interest, not only separated them from more
cautious colleagues but tarnished the reputation of the whole order.[60]

In 1714, with the accession of George I, the political climate changed abruptly,
and strident Tories, whether in state or church, lost favour. Nervous church leaders, headed by Archbishop King, feared that the Whigs, now ensconced in power,
would exact revenge on the entire Church. The archbishop denounced the preachers who tactlessly inveighed against King George as bent on overturning the established Church.[61] The prediction was unduly pessimistic. Nevertheless, King and

thought in Ireland, 1776–1798: republicanism, patriotism and radicalism (Oxford, 2002), pp 156, 160,
163.   58 Some records of 1661 Convocation in TCD, MS 1038; Bodleian, Carte MS 64, f. 287.
59 Abp W. King to Abp W. Wake, 12 Sept. 1713, Christ Church, Oxford, Wake MSS, 12/385.
60 D.W. Hayton, 'The High Church party in the Irish Convocation, 1703–1713' in H.J. Real and
H. Stöver-Leidig (eds), Reading Swift: Papers from the third Münster symposium on Jonathan Swift
(Munich, 1998), pp 117–40; D.W. Hayton, 'High churchmen in the Irish Convocation' in Hayton, Ruling Ireland, 1685–1742: politics, politicians and parties (Woodbridge, 2004), pp 131–58.
61 Abp W. King to Bp W. Lloyd, 20 Nov. 1714; same to Bp St G. Ashe, 26 Feb. 1714[15], same

his like were correct to the extent that the legal monopoly of the Church of Ireland was eroded, first by an act allowing a degree of toleration to the worship of Protestant dissenters in 1719 and then (in 1737) one acknowledging the legality of marriages solemnized by dissenting ministers.

IV

The absence of Convocation after 1713 reduced clerical cohesiveness and combativeness. Thereafter there were few formal occasions on which numerous clergy met. The bishop's visitation required incumbents in each diocese to assemble annually. The gathering was an occasion for admonition, exhortation and refreshment. It may have accentuated the gulf between the bishop, eager to impress with his learning and hospitality, and the underlings, strangers to such indulgences.[62] Nor did it encourage coordination across separate dioceses. Less formal groupings based on neighbourhood and friendship are glimpsed occasionally – for example, through clerical wills. In 1752, the Revd Thomas Brereton of Downpatrick, in addition to bequests to kindred, remembered three colleagues in the district. The Revd Humphrey Adams would receive ten guineas and Brereton's best short academic gown, tippet and two hats; the Revd Ralph Cumine was to have the long gown, linen bands, tippet and Brereton's 'new big coat'.[63]

After 1714, there were few public signs of clerical coordination, other than the bishops in the Lords moving as a phalanx behind a specific scheme. There, the spiritual peers supplied invaluable ballast for the administration. Nevertheless, divergences persisted. Some were rooted in the experiences and controversies of Queen Anne's time. Tory bishops toned down their strident opinions. In time, the survivors from Anne's reign – Smythe of Limerick, Vesey of Ossory, Browne of Cork and Milles of Waterford – although blessed with longevity went to their celestial rewards. Henceforward, disagreements on the episcopal bench owed more to the differing perspectives of those of Irish and English upbringing than to political affiliations. It was parliament that saw the campaigns to improve the material lot of the established Church: campaigns which usually united the bishops but pitted them against an inveterately anti-clerical laity.[64]

Political parsons did not vanish after 1714. The acutely polarized politics of Tories and Whigs gave way to more subtle variations of emphasis and tactic. Issues

to Bp C. Crow, 17 May 1715, TCD, MS 2536, 117, 196, 283.   **62** For the sociability on these occasions: T. Barnard, *Making the grand figure: lives and possessions in Ireland, 1641–1770* (New Haven and London, 2004), p. 350.   **63** Will of Revd T. Brereton, 8 June 1752, PRONI, D 671/D8/5/5. For Adams and Cumin, see J.B. Leslie and H. Swanzy, *Biographical succession lists of the clergy of diocese of Down* (Enniskillen, 1936), pp 73, 134, 141, 161, 162; E. Parkinson, *The city of Downe* (Belfast and London, 1928), pp 65, 66.   **64** For activity in the House of Lords, see Falvey, 'The Church of Ireland episcopate'; F.G. James, *Lords of the ascendancy: the Irish House*

capable of exciting strong and opposed views survived: how far, if at all, legal penalties against Catholics and Protestant nonconformists should be relaxed; how much latitude should be allowed to idiosyncratic and unorthodox opinions; how far English influence over the doctrines, practices and personnel of the Irish church should extend. Other than in the Upper House or through pamphlets and sermons, there were no obvious outlets for the clergy to pursue political programmes. Nor, until the 1780s, did the issues in debate have the same urgency as the earlier controversies. Then, the linked worries over tithes and threats to what was coming to be conceived of as 'the Protestant Ascendancy' goaded the clergy into action.

The parish clergy did not abstain from politics. In the main, they appeared in different arenas and used altered methods from those of their predecessors before 1714. In the absence of Convocation and with the dangers of Tory opinions being pilloried as Jacobitism, clergymen were generally discreet. Two main developments can be discerned. Clerical controversialists from the earlier era tempered their tone. Also, activists diverted their energies into struggles that seemed local, even parochial, but which often possessed national ramifications.

Three examples suggest how committed Tories accommodated themselves to the Hanoverian world. Archbishop King, although vituperative about clerical Tories, happily helped a Dublin incumbent, John Francis of St Mary's, the non-resident dean of Leighlin and 'a stiff Tory'. Even Francis's fondness for claret was not seen as a bar. Rather he was recommended after thirteen years' service, with a wife and seven children to support, for being 'popular in his parish and in good graces with them, especially for the fair sex for his preaching'. He was said not to obtrude his politics in his sermons. King alleged that he did not want to see Francis being forced to beg in his old age.[65]

Toby Caulfield and William Perceval also acclimatized themselves to the changed atmosphere of George I's reign. Both also personify the importance of kinship and connections in rising within the Church. Caulfield was the grandson of a peer, Lord Charlemont. As a younger son of a younger son, he had to fashion a career for himself. He followed the familiar *cursus honorem*: schooling at Kilkenny College; then Trinity College Dublin, from which he graduated BA in 1694. Two years later he was beneficed in the remote diocese of Killala.[66] This he saw as the prelude to better livings.[67] Possible routes for escape from the west included a chaplaincy to a regiment, on a naval vessel, or to the lord lieutenant.[68] On visits to Dublin, he mingled with potentially helpful patrons.[69]

of Lords and its members, 1600–1800 (Dublin, 1995), pp 131–49; A.P.W. Malcomson, *Archbishop Charles Agar: churchmanship and politics in Ireland, 1760–1810* (Dublin, 2002).   **65** Abp W. King to Duke of Bolton, 8 March 1717[18], TCD, MS 2535/103; Bp J. Evans to Abp W. Wake, 14 March 1717[18], Christ Church, Oxford, Wake MS 12/245; Hayton, 'The High Church party in the Irish Convocation', p. 129.   **66** Cotton, *Fasti*, iv, pp 87, 111; J.B. Leslie, *Raphoe clergy and parishes* (Enniskillen, 1940), p. 34.   **67** T. Caulfield to K. O'Hara, 20 Aug. 1696, NLI, MS 20,388.   **68** T. Caulfield to K. O'Hara, 31 July 1697, NLI, MS 20,388.   **69** T. Caulfield to K.

Partly from shared convictions and partly from opportunism, Caulfield attached himself to the circle around the second duke of Ormonde.[70] With the duke appointed lord lieutenant in 1703, this seemed a shrewd move, and soon resulted in his appointment as a domestic chaplain, often the prelude to ascent within the ecclesiastical hierarchy.[71] A chief merit of Ormonde, in the eyes of Caulfield and those of many contemporaries, was his sympathy for Irish Protestant interests. Caulfield was dismayed that partisanship divided the members of parliament. 'The country and court parties' were a regrettable phenomenon, and would soon mutate into the denominations of Whig and Tory. At this juncture, Caulfield's inclination, like many among the clergy, was towards the court, so long as it was embodied in Ormonde and the Tories, whom Ormonde led.[72] Meanwhile, Caulfield was achieving greater prominence within the church, signalled with his selection to be a proctor in Convocation for the diocese. His opinion of the current acrimony in church and state was summed up when he wrote jestingly, 'you know I am not over precise or singular and therefore comply with the fashion of the age, for I love conformity, uniformity and any formity but occasional conformity'.[73] Caulfield's dislike of occasional conformity – the practice whereby Protestant dissenters escaped the penalties of the 1704 Test Act – was of a piece with his Tory attitudes: earlier, he had spotted and decried Presbyterian political influence during the 1703 election.[74]

Views that had recommended Caulfield in Queen Anne's reign could blight in that of her successor. Caulfield adapted and received modest preferments – a prebend of Raphoe in 1716, vicar-general of Killala in 1724 and, the following year, archdeacon of Killala.[75] In many respects, Caulfield's career typified what awaited those able to buy the academic grounding to prepare for ordination. Kinship and connections stopped him from mouldering in total obscurity. In County Sligo, he took his share of the local duties, including secular ones, that fell to the small élite of prosperous Protestants. As early as 1703, he hired a curate.[76] In turn, he established a tradition of clerical service, with his son taking holy orders and continuing in the vicinity.[77]

Complementary to Caulfield's career is that of another ardent Tory. William Perceval returned to Ireland in the entourage of an English lord lieutenant, Rochester. Perceval, like Caulfield, announced his adherence to the 'court party' in Dublin.[78] Perceval belonged to an extensive kindred, divided between England and Ireland. He had formed useful contacts while a tutor at Oxford: the university pre-

O'Hara, 28 Nov. 1699, 27 Feb. 1702[3], NLI, MS 20,388.   70 T. Caulfield to K. O'Hara, 9 Oct. 1699, 18 and 28 Nov. 1699, 16 July 1702, NLI, MS 20,388.   71 T. Caulfield to K. O'Hara, 26 Sep. 1703, NLI, MS 20,388.   72 T. Caulfield to K. O'Hara, 19 Oct. 1703, 2 Nov. 1703, NLI, MS 20,388.   73 T. Caulfield to K. O'Hara, 5 May 1713, NLI, MS 20,388.   74 T. Caulfield to K. O'Hara, 9 Oct. 1703, NLI, MS 20,388.   75 Cotton, *Fasti*, iii, p. 372; iv, pp 87, 111.   76 T. Caulfield to K. O'Hara, 9 Dec. 1703, NLI, MS 20,388.   77 Indenture (draft) of C. O'Hara and Revd Adam Caulfield, June 1751, NLI, MS 20,388; Cotton, *Fasti*, iv, p. 111.   78 W. Perceval to A. Charlett, 13 Dec. 1701, Bodleian, Ballard MS 36, f. 21.

ferred by Irish Protestant grandees for their sons. Perceval endeavoured to keep in good repair his links with the influential in England. He hoped that more Oxford graduates would be sent to reinforce the Irish church. His remark that 'such are much wanted here and wished for by us who know the difference between an Oxford and an Irish education', and his contempt for 'Irish breeding and understanding' hardly endeared him to Irish-born colleagues.[79] Perceval himself, after his spell at Oxford, was in danger of forgetting that he was a second son of the Percevals of Templehouse in County Sligo.[80]

Back in Ireland, Perceval ingratiated himself with the powerful. William Palliser, the archbishop of Cashel, made him archdeacon of Cashel.[81] Next, Robert Rochfort, former Speaker of the Irish House of Commons, took him up. Rochfort built a church on his estate in County Westmeath. Perceval, who had prompted the action, preached at the consecration of the building. The quick publication of the sermon suggested that it was designed as propaganda for the interlocking High Church and Tory causes. The tract was fierce in its insistence that tithes, too frequently applied to secular purposes, should be devoted to proper ones.[82] In Convocation, Perceval had already propelled himself into the leadership of the Tory churchmen. He aimed for the chairmanship of the lower house in any future session.[83] In the event, it was decided – in Ireland as in England – not to summon Convocation after 1714, for fear of further contentions. Perceval, realising that the new government reviled opinions such as his own, avoided Dublin and lived quietly on his cure in the midlands.[84] Yet, he still followed public affairs avidly. Moreover, the introduction of a regular stage coach from Kinnegad greatly eased his trips to the capital.[85] In 1719, during an alert over a possible Stuart invasion, he feared that his correspondence might be intercepted and opened.[86]

Perceval moderated his views enough to reassure patrons in Ireland. He declared unequivocally, 'I am a zealous advocate of the established Church ... but I am no Pretender's man'.[87] Midlands obscurity was soon exchanged for the Dublin parish of St John's and a prebendal stall in Christ Church cathedral: dignities valued at

---

79 W. Perceval to A. Charlett, 10 May 1707, 5 Aug. 1710, Bodleian, Ballard MS 36, ff. 39, 60; S.J. Connolly, 'Reformers and highflyers: the post-revolution church' in *As by law established*, pp 157–8; Hayton, 'The High Church party in the Irish Convocation, 1703–1713', pp 117–40, especially 135–6, 139.   80 J. Anderson, *A genealogical history of the house of Yvery* (2 vols, London, 1742), ii, p. 325.   81 Abp W. Palliser to W. Perceval, 8 Feb. 1700[1], 22 Aug. 1702, PRONI, D 906/58, 62.   82 W. Perceval to A. Charlett, 7 Nov. 1701, 20 Dec. 1712, Bodleian, Ballard MS 36, ff. 16, 78; W. Percival, *A sermon preach'd at the consecration of Christ-Church, in the County of West-Meath ... Sunday 18 Jan. 1712/13* (London, 1713).   83 W. Perceval to Bp T. Vesey, 13 Sep. 1715, NLI, de Vesci MSS, J/3A.   84 W. Perceval to Bp T. Vesey, 8 Jan. 1714[15], NLI, de Vesci MSS, J/3A; same to A. Charlett, 18 April 1717, Bodleian, Ballard MS 36, ff. 102v–3.   85 W. Perceval to Bp T. Vesey, 8 Jan. 1714[15], NLI, de Vesci MSS, J/3A; same to K. O'Hara, 21 Nov. 1717, 27 and 28 Nov. 1718, NLI, MS 20,385.   86 W. Perceval to A. Charlett, 20 Nov. 1718, 29 April 1719, Bodleian, Ballard MS 36, ff. 107v, 108.   87 Lord Perceval to W. Perceval, 3 March 1721[2]; W. Perceval to Lord Perceval, 14 April 1722, BL, Add. MS 47,029, ff. 109, 114v.

£250 p.a.[88] Back in the capital, he threw himself eagerly into the varied activities of a large parish. Some, such as educational charities, stemmed naturally from the concerns of the clergy. Others, notably participation in the Dublin Society, suggested wide-ranging cultural interests that were a legacy of his Oxford days. Membership of the Society strengthened and extended his network of helpful and congenial connections. In 1732, Perceval entertained an English visitor with accounts of the chief collections in Dublin. Perceval was adjudged a fine gentleman, 'as lively and good company as ever I met with'.[89] Perceval composed verses on his Christ Church colleague, Henry Aldrich, probably a formative influence in his zest for collecting and architecture, and on the book-lined study of John Stearne, when dean of St Patrick's.[90] Perceval reminds of the clergy's contribution to the cultural life of Protestant Ireland. That contribution, it can be argued, is disproportionate to the numbers of the clergy.

Perceval also shows how an apparently unrepentant Tory could be rehabilitated and flourish in the Church of the 1720s and 1730s: his transition resembled similar ones made by Tory laymen. Yet, Perceval did not repudiate old acquaintances and kept his ties with grander kinsfolk and acquaintances in good repair. He visited George Mathew, a recent convert from Catholicism, and admired Mathew's new and magnificent house at Thomastown. He kept up with his former Oxford pupil, William Flower, the future Lord Castle Durrow, another notable builder. He was prepared to trade on his friendships in England with Bishop Atterbury of Rochester (another Christ Church connection) and Bishop Smalridge of Bristol.[91] Atterbury, subsequently implicated in a Jacobite Plot, would be obliged to flee abroad. Perceval further proclaimed a continuing respect for Henry Dodwell, a powerful influence in Trinity while a fellow between 1662 and 1666 and then in Oxford, but subsequently shunned by many for his refusal to take the oaths of allegiance to William and Mary. Perceval maintained a correspondence with Dodwell long after the latter had fallen from grace.[92] He also acknowledged friendship with the popular Tory don, Patrick Delany.[93]

V

The political activism of clergymen during Queen Anne's reign did not cease. Of necessity, it found new occasions and means of expression. Erstwhile Tories either

88 W. Perceval to Lord Perceval, 31 Oct. 1721, BL, Add. MS 47,029, ff.78–78v.   89 J. Loveday to T. Hearne, 9 July 1732, Bodleian, MS Rawlinson Lett. 15, f. 129; J. Loveday, *Diary of a tour in 1732 through parts of England, Wales, Ireland and Scotland*, Roxburghe Club (Edinburgh, 1890), p. 49.   90 W. Perceval, *Elegia in obitum reverendi Henrici Alderich* (n.p, [1760]), in Bodleian, Ballard MS 50, f. 68; Foxon, P 175, reprinted in W. Scott (ed.), *The Works of Jonathan Swift* (Edinburgh, 1814), i, pp 272–4.   91 W. Perceval to K. O'Hara, 25 May 1718, NLI, MS 20,385.   92 W. Perceval to H. Dodwell, 2 Sep. 1704, 26 Feb. 1704[5], Bodleian, St Edmund Hall MS 9, pp 95–110, 137–47; J. Loveday to T. Hearne, 9 July 1732, Bodleian, MS Rawlinson Lett. 15, f. 129.   93 W. Perceval to K. O'Hara, 25 May 1718, 29 June 1718, NLI, MS 20,385.

lay low or adjusted. Whigs had less reason for reticence. Indeed, their stance between 1688 and 1691 and again from 1710 to 1714 was vindicated. Reasonably they expected rewards. A few were advanced to the bishops' bench; more were invited to preach on the red-letter days dedicated to the new regime. Defence of 'revolution principles' and the Hanoverian succession rolled readily from their tongues. Yet, all expectations were not satisfied. Disappointments were easily blamed on the influx of Britons into the highest reaches of the Church of Ireland. These complaints overlooked the extent to which even the middling ranks – the cathedral deaneries – and the connected establishment of Trinity College were occupied by clerics of Irish breeding and formation.[94] Frustrations generated a patriotism that ranged from invective against mistaken British politicians and policies to constructive schemes to improve Ireland.[95] The satires and antics of Jonathan Swift represented one extreme; the involvement of the Revd Samuel Madden in the nascent Dublin Society and of Archbishop Boulter and Bishop Maule in the Incorporated Society, the other pole.[96]

How the clergy contributed still to public life and political argument can be suggested by a few examples. Clerical involvement was as likely to arise from anxieties shared with other owners of property and lay beneficiaries of confessional privileges as from their specific calling. As recipients of the legal privileges of the Church of Ireland ascendancy, incumbents were willing and fluent apologists for the system. In County Cork, the Revd Rowland Davies accumulated a variety of duties: successively dean of Ross (1679 to 1710) and of Cork (1710 to 1722), vicar-general of the latter diocese, and also registrar of the vice-admiralty court of Munster. As registrar, he is to be found presiding over enquiries at Skibbereen into shipwrecks and what had become of the cargoes. Davies amassed land. Alarmed by James II, he joined others of substance in England: a precaution that enabled him to make useful contacts, publicize the sufferings of the Irish Protestants (and his own family) and lobby in England for the relief of Ireland (and himself).[97]

---

94 Barnard, *New anatomy*, pp 98–9; McNally, '"Irish and English interests"', pp 295–314.   95 On the mutations, see Hayton, *Ruling Ireland*; E. Magennis, *The Irish political system, 1740–1765* (Dublin, 2000); P. McNally, *Parties, patriots and undertakers: parliamentary politics in early Hanoverian Ireland* (Dublin, 1997), pp 174–95.   96 For the varied responses: Barnard, 'Improving clergymen'; Barnard, *Making the grand figure*, pp 22–4, 172–4; M. Dunlevy, 'Samuel Madden and the scheme for the encouragement of useful manufactures' in A. Bernelle (ed.), *Decantations: a tribute to Maurice Craig* (Dublin, 1992), pp 21–8; D.W. Hayton, 'Did Protestantism fail in eighteenth-century Ireland? Charity schools and the enterprise of religious and social reformation, c.1690–1730' in *As by law established*, pp 166–86; J.S. Kelly, 'Jonathan Swift and the Irish economy in the 1720s', *Eighteenth-Century Ireland*, vi (1991), pp 7–36; P.H. Kelly, 'The politics of political economy in mid-eighteenth-century Ireland' in S.J. Connolly (ed.), *Political ideas in eighteenth-century Ireland* (Dublin, 2000), pp 105–29; S. Madden, *Reflections and resolutions proper for the gentlemen of Ireland* (Dublin, 1738); Kenneth Milne, *The Irish charter schools 1730–1830* (Dublin, 1997), pp 11–52; F. Mulligan, *The founders of the Royal Dublin Society* (Dublin, 2005), pp 13–17.   97 R. Caulfield (ed.), *Journal of the Very Revd Rowland Davies, LL.D., ... March*

Refugees, such as Davies, aspersed those who had remained with their flocks during the crisis as covert if not overt Jacobites. The supposedly guilty included Davies's own diocesan, Edward Wetenhall. Davies and his companions projected themselves as untainted by any collaboration with James II and so fit to head the post-war church.

Davies, on poor terms with successive bishops of Cork, in common with other deans of similar background, enjoyed considerable authority within his locality. Not only had he seen the Catholic threat in the 1680s, but he warned loudly of continuing dangers. He was quick to publish his prophetic and cautionary sermons; quick, too, in insisting that the Protestants' legal ascendancy from which he profited handsomely be maintained. Dean Davies was followed into the Church and succeeded in some of his livings by a son, Boyle Davies. The younger Davies was as voluble as his father in airing his anti-Catholicism and political preferences. Fervour for particular candidates during the municipal battles in the city of Cork earned him the sobriquet of 'Dr Zealwag'.[98] Cupidity brought the accusation that Davies, like his father before him, 'won't say Amen for brass or copper, nor bury the dead unless thou art paid'.[99]

The same themes of political engagement, local power and nepotism recur in the biography of another well-connected cleric in County Cork, St John Browne. A younger brother of Jemmet Browne, bishop of Cork from 1745 to 1772, St John Browne came of a family prominent in the city of Cork and was educated nearby at Midleton College. He then proceeded to Dublin University. Browne soon allied with a local landowner and MP, Thomas Adderley, and revelled in politics.[1] In 1744, Browne bestirred himself during a parliamentary by-election. A decade later, he piled timber, in the shape of a pamphlet of his own, on the fire that flared up in the borough of Bandon. A contemporary denounced Browne as the 'archsycophant' to Primate Stone.[2] In doing so, the opponent suggested links, both concrete and ideological, between the local and the national. Incumbents other than Browne exerted themselves on behalf of specific candidates in parliamentary and municipal elections. The activists included Dean Charles Massy in Limerick, Dean Arthur St George and Dean William Handcock in Athlone. How far their interventions were motivated by principle and how far by family feeling and local feud-

8, 1688–9, to September 29, 1690, Camden society (London, 1857).   **98** Alexander the Coppersmith [W. Boles], *Milk for babes, meat for strong men*, p. 24; Barnard, *New anatomy*, pp 89–93; H.E. Jones, 'The descendants of the Very Revd Rowland Davies, LL.D., dean of Cork', *The Irish Genealogist*, 3 (1956–67), pp 424–38; *A letter from Obadiah Shepherd to Alexander, the Copper-Smith* [Cork, *c*.1731], pp 16–17.   **99** Alexander the Coppersmith, *Milk for babes, meat for strong men*, p. 26.   **1** St J. Browne to S. Bagshawe, 30 June 1758, John Rylands Library, Manchester, B 2/3/562; Brady, *Clerical records of Cork, Cloyne and Ross*, i, pp 125, 142, 158; ii, pp 436–9.   **2** St J. Browne to E. Southwell, 8 June 1744, NA, M 3036; H.G., *A just and true answer to a scandalous pamphlet call'd a genuine letter from a freeman to George Faulkner* (Dublin, 1755), annotated copy in RIA, Haliday pamphlets, 255/15; G.H., *A genuine letter from a freeman of Bandon to George Faulkner* (Dublin, 1755).

ing is often hard to decide. It was supposed that the clergy of the established church inclined towards the administration of which they were at once props and stooges. Accordingly, the alignment of Browne with Archbishop Stone, a leading defender of an insensitive British administration in Dublin, was thought natural by some 'patriotic' contemporaries. But, in the mid eighteenth-century skirmishing between placemen and patriots, the clergy of the established Church were no more likely than their predecessors in Queen Anne's reign all to chant an identical political creed.

Larger questions about the direction and nature of policies for Ireland were hard to detach from calculations about local and family matters. A rampant dynasticism apparently governed the recorded behaviour of the Davies, Browne and Perceval families. Browne naturally enough wished to provide for children and consolidate the standing of the family. He could afford to enter one son at Westminster school; for another, the Latin school in Bandon sufficed, at least as a beginning.[3] Church livings featured in the planning. Two of St John Browne's sons were ordained: one rose to be chancellor of Ross, a dignity once occupied by his parent; a second also held livings that his father had enjoyed, before migrating to the diocese of Canterbury. Meanwhile, Bishop Browne saw to it that two of his sons were beneficed in his diocese. The elder of Bishop Browne's sons, the Revd Edward Browne, in turn fathered three sons who entered the Church of Ireland.[4]

The Revd William Perceval exhibited the same proclivities. Of his three sons, schooled at Mullingar, two followed him into the Church of Ireland.[5] The third became a lawyer.[6] One of the offspring, the Revd Kane Perceval endured drudgery as a curate of St Michan's in Dublin.[7] To escape this lowly station, the curate solicited the backing of his grander relations in England. He also had access to the most important politician of the day, Henry Boyle, Speaker of the House of Commons.[8] In 1747, the archbishop of Dublin presented Kane Perceval to the prebend of Powerscourt in County Wicklow, worth £100 annually. Four years later the archbishop made him vicar of Castleknock, a benefice valued at £250 p.a. Concurrent with the quest for professional advancement had been the pursuit of personal satisfaction. The latter was achieved by Kane Perceval's marriage in 1751 to an heiress of Huguenot ancestry, reputedly with a fortune of £1,800 and the prospect of more. In addition to her money, she was adjudged a prudent and well-

3 St J. Browne to S. Bagshawe, 21 Nov. 1758, 26 Oct. 1759, 5 Feb. 1760, John Rylands Library, Manchester, B 2/3/563, 565, 566.   4 Brady, *Clerical records of Cork, Cloyne and Ross*, i, p. 142; ii, pp 428–9, 445.   5 W. Perceval to K. O'Hara, 23 May 1717, 12 Sep. 1717, 21 Nov. 1717, NLI, MS 20,385.   6 W. Perceval to Col. Foley, 4 Feb. 1732[3], PRONI, D 906/78.   7 K. Perceval to Lord Perceval, 5 Oct. 1742, BL, Add. MS 47,008B, f. 15v; J.B. Leslie and W.J.R. Wallace, *Clergy of Dublin and Glendalough* (Belfast, 2001), p. 966.   8 K. Perceval to Lord Perceval, 16 Feb. 1741[2], 6 July 1742, 7 Aug. 1742, 12 Oct. 1742, 14 June 1743, 5 June 1746, 17 March 1746[7], BL, Add. MS 47,008B, ff. 7, 11, 13, 17, 25, 32, 35; R. Purcell to Lord Perceval, ibid., Add. MS 47,002A, f. 145; Powerscourt vestry book, 1660–1760, RCBL, P. 109.1.1.

behaved young lady.[9] Kane Perceval's younger brother, the Revd Charles Perceval, sought backing from his Perceval relations, recently elevated to the earldom of Egmont.[10] He gained preferment in the north of County Cork, the Egmont area of influence. There, in 1747, Charles Perceval received the living of Mitchelstown and was collated to Castlelyons and Clondulane in 1751. The first station was reckoned to be worth £120 or £130 yearly.[11] He, too, improved his circumstances by a shrewd marriage to a Miss Squire, 'the only daughter of a frugal clergyman, well beneficed, and brings him every shilling of 5000'.[12]

VI

Examples of the unedifying hunt for preferment and to provide for sons remind of characteristics to be found in both the Church and other secure and prestigious occupations throughout the eighteenth century. In part, but only in part, the need for would-be clergymen to prostrate themselves before supposed superiors reflected the amount of lay patronage in the Church of Ireland. It mirrored the situation in the Church of England following the sixteenth-century reformation. Together with the impropriation of tithes to lay-people, it created an often unwelcome and even demeaning subservience of the clerical estate to lay patrons. Clerical reformers schemed to recover some of what had been lost. Concerted attempts to do so were resisted fiercely – and successfully. It was left to individual clerics to try to turn the system to their advantage. Patrons of livings in Ireland were liable to be besieged by aspirants. Toby Caulfield and the Percevals have already shown how this was done. Hopefuls sought a word in the right quarter – either at Dublin Castle or in the passage-ways of St James's Palace in London.

The crown retained the rights of presentation to many dignities, but not all. Bishops were important in this respect; so, too, were some lay peers. A family well placed in both regards was the Veseys. The venality of John Vesey, archbishop of Tuam, had become a byword by the 1690s. A son, Thomas Vesey, advanced first to a baronetcy and then to a bishopric, burnished the tradition. In 1725, Sir John Staples, himself the third baronet, thanked his cousin, Bishop Vesey, for the favour of a living, the rectory of Knocktopher in the diocese of Ossory, 'which has [made] me easy in my fortune, and has been the cause of my being happily married and I hope settled in this country for life'. It looked as if Vesey was running a benefit society for other baronets.[13] Staples' promotion contrasted with the plight of a

---

9 K. Perceval to Lord Perceval, 7 April 1747, 25 July 1751, 31 Dec. 1751, BL, Add. MS 47,008B, ff. 39, 53, 54; W. Perceval to same, 24 Aug. 1751, ibid., f. 135; Cotton, *Fasti*, ii, pp 154, 157, 178. 10 W. Cooley to Lord Egmont, 2 Sep. 1748, BL, Add. MS 47,006, f. 53.   11 K. Perceval to Lord Perceval, 16 June 1747, BL, Add. MS 47,008B, f. 40; W. Cooley to same, 26 June 1747, ibid., Add. MS 47,005B, f. 118; Brady, *Clerical records of Cork, Cloyne and Ross*, ii, p. 270.   12 W. Cooley to Lord Perceval, 15 June 1744, BL, Add. MS 47,004B, f. 77.   13 Sir J. Staples to Bp T. Vesey, 22 Jan. 1724[5], NLI, de Vesci MSS, J/23; J.B. Leslie, *Ossory clergy and parishes*

curate in the same diocese, on whose behalf the doubling of his stipend from £15 to £30 was sought. Another curate, Thomas Hodson, was commended for behaving 'with great diligence and fidelity, and a general approbation, under the discouragement of a small income and a numerous family'.[14] However, Hodson never merited the same treatment as Staples.

Lay control of ecclesiastical patronage is shown, too, in an account (compiled in 1755) of what was enjoyed by another family of grandees, the Boyles, earls of Cork and Burlington. The Boyles, by now permanently absent from Ireland and their lands passing to the dukes of Devonshire, notionally still controlled seven advowsons in south Munster. In value, the livings stretched from Mothill, at an estimated £300, to a pair worth only £40 each. It was thought that the Boyles had formerly presented to three other livings, including Carrick, reckoned to yield £400 yearly. However, the rights had been assumed by the Butlers, dukes of Ormonde. At Mogeely, because the bishops of Cloyne had named the last three incumbents, the Boyles' claims had been extinguished. A third incumbency was also in danger of being lost to the bishop. One beneficiary of the Boyles' patronage was Isaac Gervais. His links with the family extended over sixty years and had been tightened when he accompanied the young Lord Burlington on an extended European tour between 1714 and 1716.[15] For this service, Gervais claimed that he had been promised an annuity of £200 for life. Observers felt that his demands were exorbitant, but characteristic of 'an Irishman and a churchman'. Gervais held two of the Boyles' livings worth in all £240 and the deanery of Tuam, 'by the interest of the family'. In addition, a son, Henry Gervais, enjoyed another of the livings, said to yield an annual £150.[16]

Dean Gervais was dissatisfied and railed against what he regarded as the shabby treatment by his patrons and against the favour shown to interlopers from England. He complained exaggeratedly that with the appointment of each new viceroy, 'near 100 chaplains will be recommended, every one by his friend'. Others concurred. The bold, on news of a vacancy – 'a carcase after which the spiritual crows have long gaped' – might speed from Dublin to London to seek the living directly from the lord lieutenant. The viceroy appointed in 1755, Lord Hartington (soon to be duke of Devonshire) had just inherited the Boyles' Irish properties. Accordingly, Gervais argued that as 'an ancient retainer of the family', it would be humiliating if he did not receive a mark of favour.[17] The family felt a sufficient obligation

(Enniskillen, 1933), pp 162, 314.   **14** W. Andrews to Bp T. Vesey, 18 Jan. 1728[9], 25 July 1729, NLI, de Vesci MSS, J/24; W. W[orth?] to Jane Bonnell, 1 July 1725, NLI, PC 435; Leslie, *Ossory clergy and parishes*, p. 286.   **15** I. Gervais to Sir R. Wilmot, 29 Dec. 1753, Chatsworth, Devonshire letters, 387.0; *Alumni Dublinenses*, p. 322; J. Ingamells, *A dictionary of British and Irish travellers in Italy, 1701–1800* (New Haven and London, 1997), p. 160.   **16** 'List of advowsons in the gift of the family'; A.T. Abdy to Lady Cork and Burlington, 17 Aug. 1755, Chatsworth, Devonshire letters, 367.7A; Luce and Jessop (eds), *The works of George Berkeley*, viii, pp 267, 277, 310–11; W.H. Rennison, *Succession list of the bishops, cathedral and parochial clergy of the dioceses of Waterford and Lismore* (Waterford, [1920]), pp 68, 78, 126, 157, 162, 181, 206, 210.   **17** I. Gervais to Lord Hartington, 5 Sep. 1755, Chatsworth, Devonshire letters, 387.1.

to entertain him at Burlington House in London.[18] In addition (and in common with others of the cloth well-entrenched in a locality), Gervais had adroitly exploited the chances to improve his fortune, through leases and bargains, at the expense of his nominal but absent overlord. Again, it is the place of the clergyman in the local economy and society and his ability to turn it to advantage that come across in Gervais's story, not misfortune. Even so, Gervais repined. Maybe the charms of Lismore palled and the memories of the Veneto faded, but his presence in the pulpit, as of others who had travelled far, while not conforming to canonical requirements, was an unexpected boon for his congregation.

The important, self-important, cantankerous and combative vie for attention. The meek and mild, who, to the best of their abilities, fulfilled their duties, are silent. The diversity of Church of Ireland clerics, in condition and contribution, is captured by an English clergyman, the Revd John Burrows, who visited Ireland in 1773. Burrows' clerical cameos include a bishop, curates and several ministers. The visitor shared his passage on the yacht from Holyhead to Dublin with the bishop of Waterford, Richard Chenevix. Burrows commented, 'I never saw a more tottering, infirm, decrepit old man.' The prelate, a bishop for more than thirty years, was railed at by two peeresses for taking the berths on the vessel that they wanted.[19] In Ulster, Burrows met the first chaplain of the lord lieutenant, destined for a bishopric. He commented on this clergyman, George Lewis Jones, ''tis a settled behaviour, a formed manner, a sort of suppressed dignity, which, tho one ought not to condemn, does not give pleasure'. In addition, the observer recorded that the wife of the bishop-to-be, 'on the credit of a round apple face, which she had in her youth, and on having been a winter in Paris, she will be but an uncomfortable bishop's wife and will be very fantastically dressed'.[20] Jones was successively bishop of Kilmore and Kildare. Burrows, descending through the clerical hierarchy, characterized the archdeacon of Clogher, John Maxwell as an ecclesiastical Sir Walter Elliot (as caught by Jane Austen), 'well descended and well allied, and well preferred himself'. The archdeacon was said to be 'a very handsome old man, far gone in the descents, alliances and preferments of other people, particularly in the families of the first settlers and planters of Ireland'. He had fathered another cleric, dismissed as 'an idle, talking' man 'about town'.[21] Burrows was disappointed not to meet Edward Bayley, archdeacon of Dublin and dean of Ardfert (1766 to 1785), accounted the most eloquent preacher of the day.[22] Instead he had to content himself with less impressive clerics: Roper, 'a country clergyman made out of an officer', and adjudged 'illiterate'; and Dr Welch, a curate, ridiculed as 'a wretched instance of the married clergy'. Welch supplemented his stipend by serving as tutor to Lord Blayney's heir. The dependence was advertised embarrassingly

18 I. Gervais to Sir A. Abdy, 6 Sept. 1755, Chatsworth, Devonshire letters, 387.2.   19 J. Burrows, Journal, NLI, MS 23,561, pp 26–7.   20 Ibid., p. 95.   21 Ibid., p. 85.   22 Leslie and Wallace, *Clergy of Dublin and Glendalough*, pp 382–3.

by Welch continuing to eat at the Blayneys' table, where the curate cut a figure 'so woebegone, and so humble'.

Burrows' impressions led him to generalize about the condition and position of the clergy of the established Church of Ireland. In particular, he believed that, because they enjoyed larger incomes than their English counterparts, they were accorded greater outward respect. At the same time, they exerted little spiritual influence and were already unpopular among the Protestant laity for their greed over tithes.[23] Burrows elaborated on the financial situation. Livings were worth between £400 and £1200, with the average annual value close to the lower figure. He contended that the incumbents, with these generous emoluments, preferred to pass their days in more amusing places than their rural parishes. Bishops, possessing even greater means, were turning into objects of envy, if not hatred, among the gentry. Hitherto lay people had rented much episcopal property on easy terms – 'bishops' leases' – but recent increases in the value of land had encouraged bishops to cash in by trying to raise their own rents. In consequence, the anti-clericalism that had flared up from time to time – in the House of Commons and elsewhere – was again directed onto the bishops.[24] Lady Echlin, commenting in 1760, tended to confirm Burrows' strictures. Bishops failed to follow the scriptural models of Titus and Timothy. Lady Echlin contended that 'a bishop must be vigilant, not given to wine, not greedy of filthy lucre, not covetous, for the love of money is the root of all evil'. But she concluded that the bishops of her own day 'seem to maintain a quite different opinion of this dangerous sweet root, tempting and pleasant to taste like the fatal apple'.[25]

Reformers continued to fret about clerical shortcomings. Worry over the unabashed worldliness of some combined with the attacks (both ideological and physical) throughout the 1780s and 1790s, the elaboration of the idea of Protestant ascendancy, the Union of 1800 and Catholic relief, to urge improvements. In 1810, Thomas O'Beirne of Meath warned that 'everything must depend on the character of the minister. He, whose conversation is the small talk of the drawing room; the gossiping of mornings of idleness, and evenings of trifling amusement; whose reading, if he claims any, is confined to productions for the stage or toilet, or to gleanings from the periodical works that compose the libraries of those who shrink from the dullness and fatigue of serious application and study; he who affects praise for being so much a gentleman in society, as cautiously to keep out of sight the clergyman and the minister of the gospel; he whose weekly occupation is confined to his farm and his stock, or whose talk on all occasions is of horses and dogs, and the sports of the field, in which he excels…would only raise a smile of disdainful pity, or a frown of disgust'.[26]

23 Ibid., pp 43–4.   24 Ibid., pp 103–4.   25 Lady Echlin to C. Tickell, 14 Feb. 1760, Tickell Mss, no. 83, private collection, Devon.   26 T.L. O'Beirne, *Charge delivered to the clergy of the diocese of Meath* (Dublin, 1810), pp 12–13.

If the testimony a Catholic commentator of the 1840s is to be believed then a new seriousness had entered into the Church of Ireland ministry. It was said that, 'the old cursing, swearing, foxhunting, drinking, gambling, whoring, pheasant-shooting parsons have disappeared...the gentlemen are at length beginning to be as it were full of feeling and compassion for their wandering brethren, and the most strenuous efforts are being made by them to decoy our poor people from the religion of their fathers'.[27] Throughout the eighteenth and into the nineteenth century, there were enough of the profane and negligent to lend veracity to the stereotype. The worldly, plunging into secular affairs, overshadow the diligent delving laboriously in their obscure vineyards.

This account, unfairly but perhaps inevitably, has concentrated on the former to the detriment of the latter. Yet, some of the evidence reviewed above indicates bouts of reform, notably during the 1670s and 1690s, which raised clerical standards in at least some dioceses. There was a natural tendency for the strenuous reformers of the early nineteenth century, to overlook or minimize the steady improvements throughout the eighteenth century. Those changes, frequently modest and sometimes hard to perceive, when aggregated meant that many of the clergy were better equipped for their tasks, thanks to education, housing and emoluments.

27 O'Sullivan, 'Praxis Parochi', pp 390–2, Kerry Diocesan Archives, Killarney, quoted in N. Yates, *The religious condition of Ireland, 1770–1850* (Oxford, 2006).

5

Accommodating clergymen: Church of Ireland ministers and their houses in the north of Ireland, *c.* 1600–1870

William Roulston

The homes of Church of Ireland ministers do not, on the whole, excite much attention now. It was not always so. At one time proper accommodation for Anglican clergy was considered a matter of national importance, resulting in acts of parliament and government grants. This chapter looks at the houses of Church of Ireland clergymen in the north of Ireland from Plantation to Disestablishment, focussing in particular on the period between 1690 and 1810. It is broken into two main sections. The first considers the attempts by the government and the Church of Ireland to provide proper housing for Anglican clergymen during this period and assesses whether the different initiatives devised and implemented were successful. Drawing on a range of sources, the rest of this chapter examines the houses themselves in terms of design, construction, contents and surroundings.

I

The Reformation, which had its formal beginnings in Ireland in the 1530s, made little impact on the northern province of Ulster until the early seventeenth century. The final eclipse of Gaelic power in the north of Ireland in 1603, followed by official and unofficial plantation schemes resulting in the influx of thousands of settlers from England and Scotland, made possible the extension of Protestantism to the region. Having consolidated its position as an institution, the Church then sought to introduce a Protestant pastorate at parochial level. To achieve this it needed to recruit ministers and secure for them a sufficient income. The leading ecclesiastic in Ulster in the first decade of the seventeenth century, George Montgomery, appointed bishop of Derry, Raphoe and Clogher in 1605, submitted a series of proposals to James I in 1608–9, including the recommendation that each parish be endowed with convenient glebe lands derived from non-church lands confiscated by the crown.[1]

The king responded positively and under the terms of the scheme for the official plantation in Ulster an order was included that for every 1,000 'plantation' acres in a parish, one townland of glebe should be allocated to the church. How this worked in practice can be illustrated by taking the parish of Donagheady in County Tyrone. Here a 2,000 acre estate was granted to the first earl of Abercorn and a 1,000 acre estate to his brother, Sir Claud Hamilton of Shawfield. Thus three townlands of glebe were assigned to the Church of Ireland in this parish.[2] It is important to emphasise that these allocations of glebe applied only to those counties directly affected by the 'official plantation scheme', that is, Armagh, Cavan, Donegal, Fermanagh, Londonderry and Tyrone. In counties Antrim, Down and Monaghan the provision of glebes was much poorer; in some parishes there was none at all.[3] At this stage there was no real attempt to encourage clergy to build on their glebes.

The first opportunity to assess clergy accommodation in the north of Ireland in the seventeenth century comes with the 1622 visitation, frequently referred to as the 'Royal Visitation'.[4] This visitation reveals that relatively few houses had been built by the clergy on their glebes. In areas where glebe-lands were remote from the church, clergymen who wished to reside in their parishes were forced to build houses elsewhere. In Langfield parish, County Tyrone, the glebe was said to be in 'a wild place and remote and very unfit for the incumbent to dwell in'. In Conwal parish, County Donegal, the rector had built a house on lands owned by the bishop of Raphoe near the site of the parish church, the glebe-lands being 'far distant from same'. Similarly in the nearby parish of Clondahorky the incumbent had 'built a good house near the … church upon a quarter of land he hath in lease from the bishop', the glebe-lands being remote from the church. The dean of Raphoe, Archibald Adair, had also built a house on land leased from the bishop.

Those clergy who had chosen to live in the parish to which they had been appointed, but who had not started to build, had to find alternative accommodation. In the parish of Clogher, County Tyrone, for example, the dean lived in a friend's house. In very few instances the local landowner was involved in providing accommodation for a minister. In Drumglass parish, County Tyrone, Sir Arthur Chichester, by 1622 the lord treasurer, had allocated a site for the parsonage and provided the necessary building materials. This coincided with his sponsorship of a new church in the town he was developing at Dungannon. The only indication of an attempt to build an early seventeenth-century parsonage on the

1 H.A. Jefferies, 'George Montgomery, first Protestant bishop of Derry, Raphoe and Clogher (1605–10)' in H.A. Jefferies and C. Devlin (eds), *History of the diocese of Derry from earliest times* (Dublin, 2000), p. 155.   2 W.J. Roulston, 'The Ulster plantation in the manor of Dunnalong, 1610–70' in C. Dillon and H.A. Jefferies (eds), *Tyrone: history and society* (Dublin, 2000), p. 284. 3 E.D. Atkinson, *Dromore: an Ulster diocese* (Dundalk, 1925), p. 131.   4 'Royal Visitation', 1622, PRONI, DIO/4/23/1/1.

site of a pre-Reformation predecessor is in the parish of Tamlaghtard where adjacent to the ruins of an 'old vicarage house' a new timber house had been built. The possible reuse of a medieval parsonage is suggested by the phrase 'in repairing' to describe the minister's house in Creggan parish, County Armagh.

The first moves to require clergy to build on their glebes came in 1626 when each incumbent granted 120 acres of glebe-land within two miles of the parish church covenanted for himself and his heirs and successors 'to build a sufficient mansion of stone, thirty feet in length, twenty in height and eighteen in breadth, English standard measure, within the walls'.[5] Lack of relevant documentation means that it is impossible to assess the impact of this rule. Nonetheless, the move indicates a growing realisation on the part of the authorities that clerical residence was crucial to the furtherance of Protestantism in Ireland. This view is illustrated in a letter of August 1635 from John Bramhall, bishop of Derry, to Viscount Chichester. Referring to a parish in Inishowen, County Donegal, the bishop wrote that 'doubtless the residence of a minister would be a great inducement to invite planters thither'.[6]

It may be presumed that nearly all the houses of the clergy in Ulster were destroyed in the 1641 rebellion. During the Restoration period there was very little attempt to encourage clergy to build on their glebes, though occasionally concerns were voiced about the problem of clerical residence. A visitation of Derry diocese from 1670 concluded that the reason that so many rectors were not resident in their parishes was due to 'there not being houses fit to be hired, fit to reside in' or houses belonging to the parish.[7]

From the end of the seventeenth century there were more concerted efforts to improve accommodation for the clergy. The coincided with, and was part of, a wider movement to reform the Church of Ireland.[8] The bishop of Meath, Anthony Dopping, included lack of clerical residence as one of the four reasons he put forward for the failure of the Church of Ireland to make a real impact in the island.[9] In the united diocese of Down and Connor it was said in 1693 that the lack of resident clergy led to the neglect of 'divine service, hospitality and relief of the poor'.[10] The attitude of some senior clergy in the diocese did not help matters. For example, in 1697 Archdeacon Leslie rather bizarrely concluded that his curate in Kilclief, County Down, was able to serve the parish better by not living in it.[11] In some cases the parishioners themselves were prepared to assist with building a home for their minister so as to encourage him to live amongst them. Edward Goldsmith, minister in Magheragall, County Antrim, claimed in 1694

5 J. Morrin, *Calendar of the patent and close rolls of chancery*, iii (Dublin, 1863), pp 176–7.   6 T.W. Moody and J.G. Simms (eds), *The bishopric of Derry and the Irish Society of London, 1602–1705*, i (Dublin, 1968), p. 202.   7 Notes from a 1670 visitation of Derry diocese, PRONI, T/1075/8, p. 24.   8 J.C. Beckett, 'The government and the Church of Ireland under William III and Anne' in *IHS*, ii (1941), pp 280–302.   9 J. Brady, 'Remedies proposed for the Church of Ireland (1697)' in *Archivium Hibernicum*, xxii (1959), pp 163–73.   10 Visitation of Down and Connor, 1693, PRONI, DIO/4/5/3, no. 23.   11 Revd Henry Leslie to Bp William King, 18 October 1697, TCD, MS 1995–2008/544.

that the parishioners there had 'taken such a liking' to him that they promised to help him build a residence.[12]

In the diocese of Derry Bishop William King worked, with reasonable success, at improving the number of resident clergy. He was clearly of the opinion that the Church needed its ministers living in their parishes, writing in 1693 that the 'pluralists of this diocese are not better men than the unalists [those who held only one living]'.[13] One of the reasons for King's determination on this issue was his preoccupation with challenging the spread of Presbyterianism in his diocese. In 1700 King wrote to Dean Bolton complaining of the fact that between Inishowen and the parish of Donaghmore there were no resident rectors and the growth of dissent could be directly attributed to this.[14] At the same time, King was aware of the difficulties of living in a remote part of the north of Ireland with few amenities. In 1693 the London-born rector of Clondevaddog parish in County Donegal, Robert Lloyd, wrote to King to tell him that he was trying to settle in 'this remote northern rough country'.[15]

In the early 1690s King and a number of other bishops had prepared a bill to provide all benefices with sufficient glebe-land and a glebe-house.[16] In the event, nothing came of this. The efforts of King and others eventually bore fruit when in 1698 the Irish parliament, recognising that the homes of the clergy were destroyed in frequent wars and acknowledging that residence was difficult unless there was some inducement to build, passed an act that allowed an incumbent to recoup two-thirds of his outlay on building a glebe-house when he left the parish.[17] This was the first of a series of acts passed first of all in the Irish legislature and after 1800 in the London parliament designed to encourage and facilitate the construction of glebe-houses.

In visitations, bishops encouraged their clergy to take advantage of this act.[18] One who rushed to build was the Revd Nathaniel Cooper, rector of Inver, County Donegal, who was able to provide a certificate to his bishop in 1702 which declared that he

> did make, build & erect a dwelling house, outhouses & other necessary improvements on the glebe belonging to the said church of Enver [sic], which said dwelling house, outhouses and other improvements are fit and convenient for the residence of his successors …[19]

---

12 Register of the archbishops of Armagh, 1690–1719, PRONI, DIO/4/2/15.   13 Visitation of Derry diocese, 1693, PRONI, DIO/3/26.   14 Revd John Bolton to Bp William King, 8 March 1699[1700], TCD, MS 1489/1/157.   15 Revd Robert Lloyd to Bp William King, 15 May 1693, TCD MS 1995–2008/277.   16 J.C. Beckett, 'William King's administration of the diocese of Derry, 1691–1703' *IHS*, iv, no. 14 (1944), p. 168.   17 10 William III, c. 6.   18 'Directions for an ordinary visitation of Armagh', 25 July 1702, PRONI, DIO/4/29/2/ 1/2, no. 8.   19 Certificate presented by Rev Nathaniel Cooper, 1702, in box of miscellaneous papers, PRONI, D/668/D.

The amount expended by Cooper was £90. However, in 1729 it was found that the house had been 'ill built and is now in a ruinous condition'.[20]

Whatever the hopes of the reformers, the 1698 act did not result in a large-scale campaign of glebe-house building, leaving many vexed and frustrated at the spurning of this initiative. In 1720 Bishop Nicolson of Derry complained to Archbishop Wake:

> The truth is, the clergy of this kingdome have so universally neglected their old palaces and glebe-houses that canonical residence is one of the greatest rarities (or miracles) in the land. We have a wholesome law for the reimbursement of two parts in three of any summ of money expended in the repair of such houses, and yet, in spight of all this encouragement an Irish bishop (rector or vicar) chooses to live in a cabine on a lay-farm sooner than upon any inheritance of his church.[21]

In 1725 a further act was passed which increased the proportion of the outlay that could be recovered by successive clergymen to three-quarters.[22] Two years later a third act concerning clerical residence was passed.[23] Difficulties in enforcing the earlier acts, particularly in cases of insolvency, necessitated another act in 1735.[24] Acts of this type were unknown in England. When forwarding the 1735 bill to London, Archbishop Boulter of Armagh acknowledged that it was 'wholly different from any law in England' and hoped that 'it may not be thrown out by the gentlemen of the law on your side, by reason of their not knowing the necessity and use of it here'; he followed this up by a lengthy defence of the clauses in the act.[25]

The concerns expressed about the effectiveness of these acts are borne out by the surviving visitations from 1733 for a number of northern dioceses – Clogher, Derry, Dromore, Kilmore and Raphoe – which reveal that many of the problems of the early seventeenth century persisted.[26] Non-residence was still a problem in many parishes. For example, the dean of Raphoe lived in Londonderry, ten miles away from his parish. Arthur Workman, curate of Seapatrick, County Down, lived with his sister at Waringstown in the neighbouring parish of Donaghcloney. If clergy were resident they often did not live in a house on the glebe. In the parish of Clonleigh, County Donegal, the rector lived in a rented house in the town of Lifford. At the same time, the situation in most of the north of Ireland was better than in many southern dioceses. In Elphin diocese, for example, there was only one parsonage in 1720 and that was the dean's residence.[27]

20 Visitation of Raphoe diocese [1729], RCBL, GS/2/7/3/34.   21 Bp William Nicolson to Abp William Wake, 3 May 1720 Christ Church, Oxford, Wake MS 13/172 (copy in PRONI, MIC/240/1, xli, pp 332–3).   22 12 Geo. I, c. 10.   23 1 Geo. II, c. 15.   24 9 Geo. II, c. 13.   25 *Letters written by His Excellency Hugh Boulter D.D.* (2 vols, Dublin, 1770), i, pp 114–6.   26 Visitations of Derry, Dromore and Raphoe, 1733, RCBL, GS/2/7/3/34; visitations of Clogher and Kilmore, 1733, PRONI, DIO/4/24/2/1.   27 Bp Henry Downes to Abp William Wake, 13 September 1720, Christ Church, Oxford, Wake MS 13/198.

Clerical residences continued to be provided through the beneficence of local landowners or parish patrons. The 1733 visitation of Kilmore diocese found that in Belturbet, in Annagh parish, County Cavan, the patron of the parish, Dr Maxwell had recently bought 20 acres in the town with a house on them which he granted to the incumbent and his successors as a parsonage. The house had lately been put into repair and alterations made to it. In Belfast Lord Donegall built 'an excellent house' for the vicar adjoining the churchyard.[28]

While the number of glebe-houses built in this period was not as large as had been hoped, the efforts of those who had chosen to build should not be ignored. The spirit of improvement displayed by a number of clergymen is captured well in the following letter of 1728 from Vere Essex Lonergan, rector of Saintfield for the past twenty-one years, to Michael Ward of Castleward:

> When I came here ... [t]here was a despicable hole of a parsonage house, upon a glebe of twelve acres without improvement or inclosure. I thank God I have now ... the best parsonage-house and office-houses, gardens and inclosures about my glebe, and the cheapest to my successors of any in the diocess.[29]

Commentators saw a clear connection between the extension of Protestantism into a locality and the advance of accepted norms of order and decency associated with civilised society. The *Dublin News-Letter* of October 1737 carried the following notice about Creggan parish, County Armagh: 'The Country ... is now growing every Day more and more into a peaceful and Protestant settlement, in which ... the decent repair of the Parish Church, and a good Parsonage House lately erected ... have not a little contributed'.[30] Others chose to emphasise the negative aspects of absentee ministers. For Nicholas Archdall, the non-residence of the rector meant that the parish was left to an 'ignorant, drunken curate ... an example of the most stupid ignorance and abandoned morals'.[31] There is no doubt that Archdall was generalising unfairly about Church of Ireland curates, many of whom laboured hard in difficult circumstances. But by heightening concerns about the evils of non-residence agitators hoped to convince the ecclesiastical authorities of the necessity of forcing ministers to live in their parishes.

Acts of parliament were not the only means by which the civil and ecclesiastical authorities sought to encourage glebe-house building. After 1711 the Board of

---

28 Revd Daniel Beaufort's journal of a tour around Ireland, 1787–8, TCD, MS 1019, p. 54.   29 Revd Vere Essex Lonergan to Michael Ward, 17 June 1728, PRONI, D/2092/1/3, p. 117.   30 *Dublin News-Letter*, 25–28 October 1737, quoted in E. McParland, *Public architecture in Ireland, 1680–1760* (New Haven and London, 2001), p. 19.   31 N. Archdall, *An alarum to the people of Great Britain and Ireland in answer to a late proposal for uniting these kingdoms, shewing the fatal consequences of such an union, to the constitution, laws, trade and manufactures of both kingdoms; how destructive to the Protestant religion established in Ireland, and how little beneficial to England* (Dublin, 1751), p. 15.

First Fruits provided direct financial assistance towards improving the infrastructure of the Church of Ireland. Initially this was confined to granting money towards the purchase of glebes and the building of glebe-houses, and only later was money spent on churches. The first grant of money for a glebe-house came in 1726 and between that date and 1764 sixty-four grants were made, eighteen of which related to the province of Ulster. The standard grant in this period was £100.[32] In the north of Ireland early grants were made for the following glebe houses: Armoy (1729), Killowen (1729), Errigal Truagh (1731), Magheradrool (1733) and Donaghadee (1734). The actual fund available to the Board was fairly small to begin with. In 1724 Henry Maule complained that, as the fund was only £400 it would not 'in 400 years answer the want of clergy in respect to glebes, without which the necessary residence of the clergy can never be practicable'.[33]

Later augmentations substantially increased the fund. In the 1777–8 session, the Irish parliament voted to provide the sum of £6,000 to the Board of First Fruits. This was the first annual grant to the Board and it continued until the abolition of the Irish parliament in 1800; from 1785 to 1800 the grant was a steady £5,000 per annum.[34] This sizeable increase in the funds available to the Board allowed it to grant £100 to 116 glebe-houses in Ireland, £11,600 in all, between 1791 and 1803. This compares with £500 granted to eighty-eight churches in the same period – a total of £44,000. Following the Act of Union the Board received an annual grant from the UK parliament, initially the same as that issued by the Irish parliament. Its fund was increased by a further £46,863 as a result of compensation paid by the government to the Church for the loss of ecclesiastical boroughs.

It is important to emphasise that for a minister to receive a grant from the Board of First Fruits, he must have already built the glebe-house and expended at least the equivalent of two years' of his own income on it. In the early nineteenth century a number of schemes were devised to make it easier for a minister to receive money for building a glebe-house. Lord Redesdale, the lord chancellor of Ireland between 1802 and 1806, promoted a initiative that would enable the commissioners of the first fruits to advance money for building glebe-houses which would be repaid in instalments without interest.[35] In this way Redesdale reckoned that 360 glebe-houses could be built in Ireland as a whole in the following twenty years. The agitation by Redesdale and others resulted in the passing of not one but two bills designed to facilitate glebe-house construction. One of the most important aspects of these legislative changes was that the Board of First Fruits was enabled to issue loans to aid building work, not simply make grants once the work had been completed.

The Board was, however, rather slow to adopt this facility, and instead more or less continued with its practice of making grants: by 1808 only eight glebe-house

32 Papers relating to the Board of First Fruits, PRONI, DIO/4/11/2/27.   33 Revd Henry Maule to Abp William Wake, 22 December 1724, Christ Church, Oxford, Wake MS 14/231.   34 Akenson, *The Church of Ireland*, p. 115.   35 Lord Redesdale to Spencer Perceval, 17 May 1803, PRONI, T/3030/7/5.

loans had been issued. A further act of 1808 consolidated the Board's funds into a single account. It was now allowed to lend or grant money for churches and glebe-houses at its own discretion. This was accompanied soon afterwards by a substantial increase in the annual grant made by the UK parliament.

With greater opportunities and encouragements to build arguments for non-residence gradually weakened. Clerics who did not want to reside in their parishes were forced to come up with more ingenious excuses. On being appointed to Tullycorbett parish in County Monaghan in 1801, Howard St George asked to be excused from residing there as he already had three houses and the responsibility of maintaining a fourth would be too much for him.[36] In some circumstances ill-health and infirmity were accepted as valid reasons for non-residence. For the aged and infirm Dr Smyth, rector of Enniskillen, residence at his house in Santry near Dublin was preferred to his northern glebe-house, which was 'so damp and so much injured by the snow' that he could not possibly live there.[37] Even the conscientious Philip Skelton was forced in his declining years in the 1780s to live in Dublin rather than his County Tyrone parish.[38]

The continued incidence of pluralism was an obvious impediment to clerical residence. When Francis Houston was appointed to the parishes of Killowen in County Londonderry and Dunsfort in County Down in the mid-1750s he was faced with the option of where to live. Attempts to procure suitable accommodation in the parish of Dunsfort were not successful. Writing to the bishop of Down and Connor in 1757, Houston outlined his options as being a house in Downpatrick five miles from Dunsfort or a house in Killough three miles away. The latter was rejected on the grounds that it was 'one of the coldest and most exposed places in the country'.[39] Instead Houston chose to settle in Killowen 'where it is almost impossible [that] I should be happy or easy'.[40]

Neglect of building when the opportunities afforded it was regarded as a serious matter. The Revd George Bracegirdle, rector of Donagheady in County Tyrone (1753–68), eschewed living in his parish for the greater comforts and conveniences of the nearby town of Strabane. When he died his family were left in serious financial difficulties as a result of unpaid dues from the parishioners. Representations to the patron of the parish, the earl of Abercorn, to intervene on the family's behalf were met with a chilly response. In reviewing the situation Abercorn had been 'forced to reflect how happy it would have been for Mr Bracegirdle's family if they could have prevailed upon him to have built upon his glebe'.[41]

Criticisms of clerical non-residence were also being voiced by ordinary parishioners. In 1785 or thereabouts, the Church of Ireland inhabitants of the parish of

36 Letters and copies of letters to the bishop of Clogher from various (often unnamed) correspondents, many undated, PRONI, D/1208/3. 37 Ibid. 38 S.J. Connolly, *Religion, law and power: the making of Protestant Ireland* (Oxford, 1992), pp 184–5. 39 Revd Francis Houston to Bp Arthur Smyth, 10–20 November 1757, PRONI, D/668/E/38. 40 Ibid. 41 Earl of Abercorn to Revd William Barker, 15 May 1768, PRONI, D/623/A/19/31.

William Roulston

Jonesborough, County Armagh, complained to the archbishop of Armagh that they were being neglected by their non-resident rector.[42] Unless he was obliged to live in the parish the parishioners warned that they would be

> under the necessity (however disagreeable to them and contrary to their religious opinions) to apply to some clergyman of another persuasion, who they have no doubt will cheerfully pay them every proper attention, and not allow their sick to die without proper advice and comfort, or the dead to be interred without the attendance of a clergyman.

Little would appear to have been done about this, however, until the appointment of the Revd Archibald Kidd in the early nineteenth century. When Kidd arrived in Jonesborough he 'found extreme difficulty and inconvenience in obtaining a lodging therein'.[43] An obvious obstacle was that there was no glebe in Jonesborough, a parish that had only been created in 1760. Through a grant from the Board of First Fruits a small glebe of six acres was bought and in 1815 Kidd successfully petitioned the archbishop of Armagh to be allowed to build a glebe-house.

The Ecclesiastical Inquiry of the 1830s provides an opportunity to examine at parochial level the provision of glebe-houses across Ireland.[44] The following table focuses in particular on the eight northern dioceses of Ireland and plots the decade of construction of the glebe-houses then in existence in these dioceses.

Table 1

Glebe-houses in the northern dioceses of Ireland in 1836

Period	Armagh	Clogher	Connor	Derry	Down	Dromore	Kilmore	Raphoe	Total
Pre-1741	4	0	0	5	1	0	3	1	14
1741–50	0	1	0	0	1	0	0	0	2
1751–60	1	0	0	2	0	1	0	0	4
1761–70	2	2	0	1	0	0	0	1	6
1771–80	10	9	1	6	2	0	1	4	33
1781–90	13	2	0	4	2	3	1	3	28
1791–1800	8	2	1	6	1	1	0	2	21
1801–10	6	0	3	2	0	4	2	1	18
1811–20	17	6	10	4	16	4	15	9	81
1821–30	8	12	10	5	2	5	6	6	54
1831+	1	1	0	4	0	0	2	0	8
Not known	2	1	2	3	1	2	0	0	11
None	17	9	23	14	10	4	9	6	92

42 Petition of Protestant inhabitants of Jonesborough, n.d. [*c.*1785], PRONI, DIO/4/32/J/1/4/1.   43 Memorial of Revd Archibald Kidd to Abp William Stuart of Armagh, 25 March 1815, PRONI, DIO/4/32/J/1/5/1.   44 *Third report of His Majesty's commissioners on ecclesiastical revenue and patronage in Ireland* (hereafter *Ecclesiastical Inquiry (Ireland)*), H.C. 1836, xxv.

Some caution should be exercised when analysing at this table. Dates of construction have been taken at face value; no doubt many are inaccurate. About half a dozen were built 'upwards of 100 years ago' (or words to that effect) and these have been placed in the pre-1741 category. In some cases the postulated date of construction seems almost fanciful. The glebe-house in Killashandra, for example, was believed to have been built 200 years earlier. It may have been a building of some antiquity, but it is unlikely to have been that old.

One important point to note is that nearly one in four benefices was still without a glebe-house. This proportion varied from diocese to diocese. In Connor it was nearly half, while in Dromore less than a sixth of the benefices were without a glebe-house. In benefices lacking a glebe-house alternative accommodation was often available. Some rectors were accommodated in lodgings. Others constructed some form of habitation that met their needs, but which could never be considered a glebe-house. In Errigal parish, County Londonderry, the glebe-house had been condemned as unfit for habitation and 'an old office has been converted into a temporary residence by the present incumbent at his own expense'.

It must be acknowledged that the building works recorded in the inquiry cannot be assumed to represent the first time that a benefice was provided with a glebe-house. Clearly many of the glebe-houses recorded in the inquiry were replacements for earlier habitations. Despite these limitations the table nonetheless provides us with an idea of periods of considerable activity with regard to the provision of glebe-houses. The first was the period 1771–90; sixty-one glebe-houses constructed in this period were still in use in 1836. Again we ought to note the variation between dioceses: twenty-three of these glebe-houses were in the diocese of Armagh, while only one was in Connor diocese. There followed something of a falling off in glebe-house construction. In the first decade of the nineteenth century only eighteen glebe-houses were built, but this was to rise dramatically to eighty-one between 1811 and 1820. Half the glebe-houses in Kilmore diocese were built in this decade, and nearly two-thirds of those in Down. Further research is needed at local level fully to understand these variations over time and space.

By 1830 the great age of glebe-house building was over. Thereafter glebe-houses were built sporadically and rarely on the same scale as their predecessors. During the Disestablishment debate in the late 1860s, the possession of glebe-houses proved a contentious issue. The Church of Ireland argued that these houses should automatically remain the property of the church, pointing out that much of the money that had been spent on building had come from the private funds of ministers.[45] Gladstone's bill, however, gave the Church no more than the first option of purchasing the glebe-houses back from the government at the rate of twelve times the annual value of the building. This was opposed by the House of Lords, but the only concession to the Church on this matter was the reduction in the purchase rate from twelve years to ten.[46] In the end almost all the glebe-houses in the

45 Akenson, *The Church of Ireland*, pp 253–6.   46 Ibid., pp 256, 267.

possession of the Church prior to 1870 were repurchased, in many cases with the financial support of the local parish.[47]

II

The above consideration of the schemes designed to promote glebe-house building provides a framework within which the houses of the clergy can be further examined. Many of the parsonages built in the period covered by this essay have already been noticed by architectural historians, though these have tended to be the more distinguished homes still in existence even if no longer in the possession of the Church.[48] Lesser dwellings and demolished rectories are usually ignored and there is as yet no single volume dealing exclusively with the homes of the Irish clergy. Maurice Craig has written of clerical residences: 'the characteristic glebe-house is a two storey, three-bay house with a basement, a hipped roof and either two stacks or a single stack, well set about with trees and with a yard at the back ... for the most part they are very simple, very appropriate, and very well built'.[49] Detailed investigation will probably bear out Craig's generalisation, particularly when applied to parsonages built in the late-eighteenth and early-nineteenth centuries, but his observation should not be allowed to mask the fact that there was considerable variation in the scale and quality of the houses when viewing the period as a whole.

It is also important to distinguish between those houses built specifically as clergy houses and those which were occupied by ministers in other capacities. Few clerics lived in the sumptuous surroundings enjoyed by Samuel Madden, rector of Drummully in County Fermanagh. In his home was a 'beautiful gallery for music' and a hall and parlour 'almost covered with fine pieces of painting, several of which are originals, done by the names that have been most famous over Europe'. In the words of a contemporary cleric, the Revd William Henry, his house was 'finished with a classical taste and elegance'.[50] Madden, however, was a rather untypical clergyman, even in an age when aristocrats filled pulpits. In addition to being rector of Drummully he was the owner of a large estate in the parish, Manor Waterhouse, which he had inherited from his father John. As has already been noted, there were other Church of Ireland ministers during this period who were landowners in the parish they served and who resided on these temporal concerns. Clergy were also known to rent gentry houses as temporary accommodation. For example, the Revd Patrick Delany, dean of Down, lived for a time at Mount Panther, an Annesley house near Dundrum, County Down.[51]

47 Ibid., p. 315.   **48** See the works of C.E.B. Brett, *Buildings of County Antrim* (Belfast, 1996), *Buildings of County Armagh* (Belfast, 1999), *Buildings of North County Down* (Belfast, 2002); the numerous publications of the Ulster Architectural Heritage Society; and A.J. Rowan, *The buildings of Ireland: north-west Ulster* (London, 1979).   **49** M. Craig, *Classic Irish houses of the middle size* (London, 1976), pp 38–9.   **50** Description of County Fermanagh by Revd William Henry, *c.*1739, PRONI, T/2521/3/1, p. 46.   **51** A. Day (ed.), *Letters from Georgian Ireland: the corre-*

Of the early clergy houses we know nothing save what brief written descriptions have survived. Nonetheless it is possible to detect a certain consciousness on the part of some of the new clergymen, particular those of English origin, to introduce house designs from their homeland. In Tullycorbett parish, County Monaghan, the minister had built by 1622 a 'reasonable English house'.[52] At the same time in Cappagh parish, County Tyrone, the incumbent, Gervase Walker, who it seems was born in Nottinghamshire, had built a 'mansion house of timber after the English fashion'.[53] Walker also held the neighbouring parish of Badoney, and while he made no attempt to build a house, he 'bound his tenant to build one house after the English manner, which is in building'. Elsewhere there are references to obligations on the part of tenants of glebe-lands to build in an English style.

Of houses built during the Restoration period there is even less information. One that stood out was the house built by Edward Walkington, rector of the parishes of Arboe and Artrea in Armagh diocese, prior to his promotion to bishop of Down and Connor in 1695. It was destroyed in the events of 1689–91 and all that remained in 1703, when Thomas Ashe visited it, were the cellar walls. He described the house as having had 'many pretty and convenient apartments in it' and had been told that 'it was the prettiest box of a house, thereabouts, nothing like it'. The outbuildings had included a stable for sixteen to eighteen horses with good racks and mangers.[54]

Hazlett House at Liffock near Coleraine in County Londonderry has traditionally been regarded as a clergy house built in the early 1690s as part of Bishop King's attempt to encourage clerical residence in his diocese. Dendrochronology has confirmed the date of the house, though documentary evidence has not been forthcoming to show that it was built for a cleric. The house itself is a single storey thatched cottage – now owned by the National Trust – and might very possibly have been the residence of Archdeacon Golden when visited by the Delanys in 1758. Mrs Delany described his house as 'the cabin a lowly one, but elegantly neat'.[55] The word cabin should not be regarded as a derogatory term for a house. In reference to the house of Edward Bayley, treasurer of Down, known as Belville in 1744, Mrs Delany wrote: 'They live in what is called in this country "a cabin" – that is a house of one floor and thatched; it is situated very near the sea, with a pretty neat court before it; the outside promises very little, but the inside is quite elegant, as much as I saw of it, which was the hall, a large parlour, drawing room and a bed-chamber.'[56] In 1733 the glebe-house in Termonamongan parish, County Tyrone, was described as 'a thatched cabin'.[57] The rector at this time was

spondence of Mary Delany, 1731–68 (Belfast, 1991), p. 210.   **52** PRONI, DIO/4/23/1/1.   **53** Ibid.   **54** Thomas Ashe, 'View of the archbishopric of Armagh', 1703, PRONI, T/848/1.   **55** Day, *Letters from Georgian Ireland*, p. 153.   **56** Ibid. See also N. Roche, 'A contemptible habitation: some contemporary views of cabins from the sixteenth to the nineteenth centuries' in T. Reeves-Smyth and R. Oram (eds), *Avenues to the past: essays presented to Sir Charles Brett on his 75th year* (Belfast, 2003), pp 235–52.   **57** RCBL, GS/2/7/3/34.

William Hamilton who had a small landed interest in the parish where he lived: there was little incentive, therefore, for him to build anything grander.

Single storey houses seem to have been commonplace for clergy residences for much of the eighteenth century. In 1753 the newly appointed rector of Donagheady parish, County Tyrone, the Revd George Bracegirdle, described the glebe-house as having a

> parlour twenty feet square out of which two tolerable rooms with beds; in one of them a chimney and closet; a large kitchen open to the roof, two other little rooms where the servants lay – these all on a floor – your Lordship knows in this country they have not the art of building a staircase. I must not forget a very good cellar and also six magnificent sash windows in front.[58]

His overall impression of the house was that it was convenient for a single man only and not for a minister with a family. His predecessor in the parish, Archdeacon Andrew Hamilton, had in fact built the house with sufficiently thick walls to allow for the addition of a second storey, but had never got around to doing this. Simpler still was the dwelling of the curate in Kildrumsherdan parish, County Cavan, which was described in the 1733 visitation as a 'farm house' with walls of lime and stone and a thatched roof standing on one of the glebes.[59] In having his own house at all this curate was in a better position than many of his station. The Revd Philip Skelton lived a rather nomadic life as a curate in the diocese of Clogher, lodging initially in the grandeur of Manor Waterhouse (the aforementioned home of his rector, the Revd Samuel Madden), to be followed by a rudimentary farmhouse in Pettigo; later he lodged with a doctor in Enniskillen and a shopkeeper in Fintona.[60] Few were as fortunate as the curate in Cappagh parish, County Tyrone, for whom the rector, Dr Gibson had built 'a neat thatched cabin with offices, fields and enclosures'.[61]

Lacking sufficient resources to build a new dwelling from scratch several ministers contented themselves with making additions to existing buildings.[62] This, however, did not always make for good houses. In 1742 the glebe-house in Seagoe parish, County Armagh, was noted as being 'part ... built with stone and lime, part with brick, and part with clay and straw wrought into a kind of mortar called mudd ... Some part of the said house is covered with shingles, but the greatest part is thatched with straw.'[63] As might be expected, this curious amalgamation of building materials and modes of construction varied considerably in condition: 'that part which is built with stone and brick is in good repair; the other part is mostly in a ruinous way, both timber and walls being almost rotten and decayed'.

58 Revd George Bracegirdle to earl of Abercorn, 29 December 1753, PRONI, D/623/A/30/206. 59 PRONI, DIO/4/24/2/1.   60 T.C. Barnard, *A new anatomy of Ireland: the Irish Protestants, 1649–1770* (New Haven and London, 2003), p. 87.   61 TCD, MS 1019, p. 5.   62 RCBL, GS/2/7/3/34; TCD, MS 1019, p. 37.   63 A. Dawson, 'A terrier of the parish of Seagoe, diocese of Dromore, 1742: a fragment' in *Ulster Journal of Archaeology*, iii (1897), p. 225.

Despite the undoubted simplicity of many of the glebe-houses, more formal architecture was beginning to make an appearance from the early eighteenth century. Probably the finest clergy residence from the first half of the eighteenth century is Oakfield near Raphoe, County Donegal. Built as the deanery in 1739 it has been described by Alistair Rowan as 'jewel of its district, perfectly preserved and perfectly unexpected for its date'.[64] He uses the design of this house as an example of the provincial time-lag between parts of rural Ireland and the mainstream of architectural developments. The house is a square, two-storey block with symmetrical facades of five bays on the east, south and west and a yard to the north. The hipped roof is wide-eaved and features three dormer windows over the centre bays on the east and west fronts. The main door features a Tuscan aedicule. The entrance front has been compared to Inigo Jones' design for Lord Maltravers' house at Lothbury in London.[65] However, this dates from 1638, fully one hundred years earlier than Oakfield.

Other important glebe-houses from the early to mid eighteenth century include the deanery at Clogher, County Tyrone, of about 1750 with its central Venetian window and, in the same county, the rectory at Drumquin featuring a central pedimented porch of two storeys.[66] According to a date-stone the latter was built in 1762 by the Revd Arthur Benson who is believed to have rebuilt the parish church during his incumbency. The church, however, with only faint hints at Classicism, is a much more modest structure than the glebe-house.[67] This phenomenon of glebe-house outshining church in terms of scale and quality may be observed in many other parishes in the north of Ireland.[68]

By building in the appropriate style clergy were demonstrating their awareness of current architectural trends and their willingness to put these into practice on their glebes. As the house of the clergy improved in quality and increased in scale so they featured in the travelogues and descriptive histories of the period. In 1739 one observer of architecture and society, the Revd William Henry, described the rectory at Donaghmore, County Donegal, as 'one of the finest glebe-houses in the Kingdom'.[69] A few years later Walter Harris commented that the cruciform church in Killyleagh, County Down, and the good parsonage near it 'look well together'.[70] In architectural terms many of the finer glebe-houses were on a par with the homes of the gentry. The desire of some ministers to be accommodated on this scale is hardly surprising given that many clergy were from the landowning families or had aspirations to enter landed society.[71] Furthermore, it was considered

64 Rowan, *North-west Ulster*, p. 43.   65 Ibid., p. 471.   66 Ibid., pp 42, 254.   67 The church is now in ruins.   68 For the simplicity of many churches in the north of Ireland in the early eighteenth century see W.J. Roulston, 'The provision, building and architecture of Anglican churches in the north of Ireland, 1600–1740', unpublished PhD thesis, Queen's University, Belfast, 2 vols (2003), i, chapters 6–8.   69 Revd William Henry, 'Hints towards a natural and topographical history of the counties of Sligo, Donegal, Fermanagh and Lough Erne', c.1739, NA, M 2533.   70 W. Harris, *Antient and present state of the county of Down* (Dublin, 1744), p. 76.   71 T.C.

important that ministers set a good example to their parishioners in the way they lived. They were, after all, viewed as 'agents through whom politeness and civility were to be disseminated across the Irish hinterlands'.[72]

The sums of money expended on new glebe houses varied considerably, reflecting to some extent at least the resources available to individual ministers. In Kilmore parish, County Armagh, the rector had built by 1622 a new parsonage with a stable and barn as well as planting an orchard at a total cost of £200, a not inconsiderable sum for the time. One hundred years later glebe-houses were being built for significantly less than this. In Ballinderry parish, County Londonderry the Revd John Forbes (*c.*1693–1725) built a house costing £90, while in Culdaff parish, County Donegal, the 'stone & lime & thatched' parsonage was valued at £75 in 1733.[73] In Ballymore parish, County Armagh, on the other hand, the Revd William Godley (1733–40) was able to present a certificate for building work to the value of £1,000. The aforementioned deanery at Raphoe cost £1,680. This was bettered by John Hall, rector of Ardstraw in County Tyrone who by 1719 had built a 'good convenient parsonage house, garden, office houses and other convenient improvements' at a cost of £1,700.[74] When the bishop of Derry called on Dr Hall in the autumn of 1721 he referred to his house as a 'palace'.[75]

Hall's building activities in the Ardstraw did not stop with his parsonage. He solicited and secured the financial support of Trinity College, Dublin – the patron of the parish – as well as 'several persons of quality and others' towards the construction of a new church; between them they had given £189 18s. 6d. by 1723.[76] Hall's own cash contribution to the new church is not known (it is unlikely to have matched the money he spent on the parsonage), but the monument erected to his memory after his death in 1735 proclaimed that 'the church was rebuilt under his care, and he contributed largely to it'.[77] While Hall's generosity to the parish of Ardstraw is undoubted, it must be borne in mind that he was a man of some means. In addition to holding Ardstraw he was the rector of a parish in Raphoe diocese and had been a vice-provost of Trinity College, Dublin. In addition, through marriage he had acquired a considerable fortune.[78] Hall was, therefore, in a much better position to contribute lavishly to the rebuilding of a parish church and the construction of a new rectory than many of his contemporaries who laboured in much less favourable circumstances. Hall's example should alert us to the fact that frequently those who built the more impressive houses were able to do so because of additional sources of revenue. The bishops may have sought to

Barnard, 'Improving clergymen, 1660–1760' in *As by law established*, p. 146.   72 T.C. Barnard, *Making the grand figure: lives and possessions in Ireland, 1641–1770* (New Haven and London, 2004), p. 109.   73 Commonplace book of the archbishop of Armagh, 1768, PRONI, DIO/4/29/7/2/1; RCBL, GS/2/7/3/34.   74 RCBL, GS/2/7/3/34.   75 Bp William Nicolson's diaries, PRONI, MIC/69/5, xxxvi, p. 69.   76 RCBL, GS/2/7/3/34.   77 A tablet in the church is inscribed, 'Rebuilt by Dr John Hall 1724'. J.B. Leslie, *Derry clergy and parishes* (Enniskillen, 1937), p. 95.   78 Ibid., p. 95.

impress on their ministers that building was a duty, but whether the clerics responded was in many instances based on a series of external factors beyond the bishops'
control.

Attitudes to what was appropriate for a glebe-house were subject to change during the course of the period under review. In Monaghan parish in the mid-1830s
it was 'reported that there is a house upon the glebe; but that owing to its being
thatched and otherwise not built according to law, it cannot be deemed a glebe-
house'.[79] This rejection of the habitation on Monaghan as a true glebe-house on
account of its roof covering is curious given that glebe-houses elsewhere are known
to have been thatched at this time. The glebe-house in Drung, County Cavan,
reckoned to have been about 100 years old according to the Ecclesiastical Inquiry,
was described in the contemporaneous Ordnance Survey memoir of the parish as
having been thatched.[80] Elsewhere thatch continued to be used as a roof covering
for glebe-houses into the nineteenth century.[81]

The design of most glebe-houses in this period was not the work of a professionally trained architect. As with other dwellings, as well as most churches, the
appearance of the building was due to the imagination of the interested amateur.
Many of the clergy were keenly interested in architecture – one of the earliest
architectural treatises published in Ireland was the work of an Anglican minister –
and Toby Barnard has commented that the bishops and wealthier clergy 'exerted
a disproportionate influence over the reception of Classical architecture into Ireland in the later seventeenth and early eighteenth centuries'.[82] Nonetheless it is
important to acknowledge that men operating under the title of architect were
increasingly employed to work on projects relating to glebe-houses. In 1737, for
example, Bishop Francis Hutchinson accepted the estimate of William Needham,
whom he described as an 'eminent architect' for repairs to the parsonage of
Rasharkin, County Antrim.[83]

Thomas Cooley, the most distinguished architect working in the diocese of
Armagh in the later eighteenth century, prepared a ground plan for a typical glebe-
house, but there is no evidence that he designed any surviving parsonage.[84] In
Derry diocese, Michael Shanahan, architect to the earl bishop, designed a number
of glebe-houses.[85] Lissan glebe-house was built to designs by the distinguished
John Nash. John Bowden who designed many churches in Ireland in the early
nineteenth century was the architect of Jonesborough rectory, built c.1815. William
Farrell may have been the architect of the rectories at Maghera, Raymunterdoney

79 *Ecclesiastical Inquiry (Ireland)*, p. 143.　80 A. Day and P. McWilliams (eds), *Ordnance Survey
memoirs of Ireland, vol. 40, Counties of South Ulster, 1834–8* (Belfast, 1998), p. 20.　81 PRONI,
D/1208/3.　82 Barnard, 'Improving clergymen', p. 146.　83 Bp Francis Hutchinson's notebook,
c.1729–c.1739, Diocesan Offices of Connor and Down and Dromore, Belfast (recently transferred
to PRONI, D10/1/22).　84 Brett, *Buildings of County Armagh*, p. 120.　85 P.J. Rankin, *Irish
building ventures of the earl bishop of Derry* (Belfast, 1972), p. 44; *Belfast Newsletter*, 29 January
1773, 21–25 April 1775.

and Erganagh in Cappagh parish.[86] Farrell was one of the most active architects in the north-west in the first half of the nineteenth century, being employed to design a range of public buildings as well as work for the landed gentry. He was probably the same as the 'Mr Farrell' who in 1815 was requested to repair the roof of the glebe-house at Chanterhill near Enniskillen which had been damaged in a storm.[87] Significantly, the same letter refers to his work for Lord Ely, a patron for whom William Farrell is known to have worked.

The names of the builders of the earliest glebe-houses have not found their way into the documentary record and we can only guess at their identities by surmising that some of the men responsible for building churches and houses for laypersons were involved in the construction of glebe-houses. From the middle of the eighteenth century contracts for building glebe-houses began to be advertised in newspapers. As an example, the following notice appeared in the *Londonderry Journal* on 22 January 1773:

> Notice is hereby given to all persons who may choose to contract for the building of three new glebe houses which are this year to be erected upon the glebes to the parishes of Magilligan, Balteagh and Bovevagh all in the neighbourhood of Newtown Lemavady in the County of Londonderry that they may send their proposals for the same to the Revd Mr Bristow in Coleraine expressing the price for which they will build stone walls with lime and sand by the statute perch of 20 feet long and 18 inches thick and 1 foot high they finding all materials: [1] for brick walls of nine inches thick, twenty-one feet long and one foot high; [2] for reveail'd door and windows and thorough arches each; [3] for chimney funnels each; [4] for wall plaistering and ceiling per yard all stuff found; [5] for door cases from 4 to 6 and half inches square and about 6 feet 6 inches by 3 feet 3 inches in clear.

The choice of site was governed by a number of factors. When searching for a suitable location for his deanery, Dean Delany considered one site because it had a source of fresh water.[88] Proximity to water was, however, to the detriment to the glebe-house in Donegal town. In the 1830s it was found to be 'small and inconvenient and ill-finished, and being situate at the foot of a hill, with the walls against the banks, the under apartments are constantly flooded for one half of the year which renders them quite damp and useless'.[89]

The building process has left little record. What has survived indicates that it did not always run smoothly. About 1780 Frederick Augustus Hervey, bishop of Derry and earl of Bristol, wrote to Archdeacon John Monck in a tone of exasperation:

---

86 Rowan, *North-west Ulster*, pp 411, 430, 476.   87 PRONI, D/1208/3.   88 Day, *Letters from Georgian Ireland*, p. 209.   89 *Ecclesiastical Inquiry (Ireland)*, p. 431.

You are the veriest archpriest that ever I knew, and unless you were possessed of the powers of Pope Benedict the 14th I do not conceive how you can convert the stones with which the masons build your house into bread for the builders; for money they can get none out of you. You lay no more golden eggs, and we have nothing for it, but to kill the goose and open her belly. In short, dear Goose, if we don't gut you we will certain skin you, though I believe you are as hard as flint …

In case Monck should have been left puzzled as to what the bishop was getting at, Hervey continued: 'In plain English, if you don't pay your masons and carpenters, I will pay them for you'.[90]

Joseph Ferguson, curate in Ballymoyer parish, County Armagh, was rather dismissive of the quality of those who were responsible for parsonages when wrote in 1816:

The glebe-house was erected, like most other buildings of the same description, in a manner reflecting little credit either on the skill of the architect, or the attention of the superintendent. These houses are generally built by contractors, who contrive to make them appear fair to the eye, but care not if they should tumble to the ground after they have received the money.[91]

Ferguson's comment was clearly coloured by his own experience of a glebe-house. The poor condition of other parsonages had more to do with neglect than with poor construction. In 1787 Beaufort found the glebe-house in Maghera, County Londonderry, 'so antique as to all built with and floored with oak and has had three or four different additions and yet is very ruinous and bad, Lord Strangford having neglected the house, destroyed the glebe and cut down the trees'.[92] Neglect was not the only reason for the dilapidated condition in which some glebe-houses ended up. In Magheracloone parish, County Monaghan, misuse rather than disuse was to blame. Here the glebe-house had fallen into disrepair by the end of the eighteenth century: 'the walls are separate from each other and the roof separate from the walls – only the remains of one solitary floor entirely rotten'. Upon investigation it was found that

it was not merely the hand of time that was so expeditious in forming the ruin as the miserable conduct of a degraded clergyman, a Mr King, who used in Mr Cummin's time to keep a private still in the house and malt on

90 Bp Frederick Hervey to Revd John Stanley Monck, n.d. [*c*.1780], PRONI, T/1638/35/2. 91 W. Shaw Mason, *A statistical account or parochial survey* (3 vols, 1814–19), ii, p. 84. 92 TCD, MS 1019, p. 37.

the floors and in the course of this nefarious business as the boards decayed from wet, he tore them up and burned them and even carried away a choice loft over the stable for the same purpose.[93]

The contents of the homes of ministers allow for a glimpse into the material culture of the clergy and here also we can draw comparisons with the landed elites, though again generalisations need to be guarded against. The items found in many glebe-houses in this period matched those met with in the homes of the gentry, and were way beyond the means of the great majority of parishioners. When the contents of the house belonging to the late rector of Coleraine were being auctioned off in 1739 the items put up for sale included gilt leather chairs and mahogany tables.[94] The possessions of other eighteenth-century clergymen also speak of comfort and elegance and indicate well furnished houses.[95] The contents of the home of the Revd George Cope of Drumcree, County Armagh, included walnut framed chairs, a mahogany dining table, carpets and silk curtains.[96] In Dunboe, County Londonderry, Archdeacon Golden's possessions included 'some very fine pieces of China'.[97] These were used for drinking tea, itself a luxury beyond the reach of most. In his will of 1752 the Revd Thomas Brereton of Downpatrick was able to differentiate between his best and second best tea kettle and chest bequeathed to his sisters, Mrs Beateman and Mrs Ervin. The latter was also left his 'Escriptore' [escritoire] and silver table spoons.[98] The possession of silverware was a further indication of gentility.

The studious built up their own personal libraries, some of which were of considerable extent. By the time of his death in 1781 James Hamilton, rector of Donagheady, had acquired over 2,000 volumes, 700 of which were in French, 200 in Greek and Latin and the rest in English.[99] In 1834 Dr Ussher, rector of Tullyaughnish, was reckoned to have had the best library in County Donegal.[1] Curiosities were also collected and put on display. In the glebe-house of Aghadowey parish, County Londonderry, there was once 'over the mantelpiece of the drawingroom ... a beautiful piece of sculpture, representing Socrates discovering his pupil Alcibiades in the haunts of dissipation, which been brought from Italy by the Earl of Bristol'.[2] Card playing seems to have been a popular pastime among certain

---

93 PRONI, D/1208/3. Another letter in the same collection, this time written by a John Wright and dated 30 August 180(4?), noted that the glebe-house had become 'irretrievably ruinous', adding that it had been constructed of 'bad materials upon an improper foundation'.   94 *Belfast Newsletter*, 11 May 1739.   95 'A valuation of the goods of the Revd Mr Robt Letherburrow, late of Drumcree, taken & made 4 May 1737', PRONI, T/808/15298.   96 Ibid., 20 June 1758. For other examples from the pages of the *Belfast Newsletter* see the editions of 7–10 May 1776, 30 September–4 October 1785, 9–12 October 1787 and 27–30 July 1790.   97 Day, *Letters from Georgian Ireland*, p. 153.   98 Will of Revd Thomas Brereton, 8 June 1752, PRONI, D/671/D8/5/5.   99 Revd Thomas Burgoyne to earl of Abercorn, 18 September 1781, PRONI, D/623/A/44/132.   1 A. Day and P. McWilliams (eds), *Ordnance Survey memoirs of Ireland, vol. 38, Parishes of County Donegal I, 1833–5* (Belfast, 1997), p. 89.   2 Leslie, *Derry clergy and parishes*, p. 89. In 1884 it

members of the clergy; Beaufort noted four card tables at Dr Gayer's house when he stayed there in 1787.[3] Concerns about adequately protecting their homes and possessions led some ministers to take out insurance policies. In the late eighteenth century Dunboe glebe house was insured with the Hibernian Insurance Company for £600 – it had cost £837 to build – £400 of which was for the house and £200 for the contents.[4]

The domestic life of an eighteenth-century Irish parson has often been viewed as one comfort and indolence. The somewhat dissipated lifestyle of the Revd John Nixon, as revealed in a diary of 1769–70, is well known, but should not be assumed as typical of an eighteenth-century parson.[5] Certainly those who could afford to do so, such as the Delanys at Mount Panther, enjoyed entertaining on the grand scale.[6] Here they had salmon, lobster, trout and crabs delivered to their door every day, while at nearby Dundrum French white wine, vinegar, Hungary water and capers could be had.[7] The importance attached to cooking and having the proper means to do so can be seen in the inventory of goods possessed by the Revd Robert Letherburrow of Drumcree. The contents of Letherburrow's kitchen included numerous pots, copper saucepan, frying pan, dripping pan, crocks, spits, pestle and mortar, brass grater and even a rolling pin, amongst a multiplicity of utensils.[8]

This account of glebe-houses in the north of Ireland cannot be allowed to pass without some mention of the ancillary buildings and gardens that stood alongside or surrounded these dwellings. As with other habitations, the setting of the house was considered important. Criticisms were levelled at those who had done little to improve the environs of the glebe-house.[9] Many clergymen took a keen interest in gardening and planting. In another example of the transplantation of English norms to early seventeenth-century Ulster, the rectors of Kilmore and Loughgall in County Armagh both laid out orchards.

By the first half of the eighteenth century the craze for planting and improving glebe-land was in full swing. Charles Este, rector of Derrynoose (1726–30), County Armagh, 'planted a great number of forest trees in a regular manner on the glebe of Madden, laying out and draining the ground'.[10] William Smith, rector of Loughgilly (1704–14), in the same county, in addition to laying out gardens and an orchard, 'enclosed and quicked the whole glebe of about 60 Irish acres and divided it into parks'.[11] Dr Gibson, rector of Cappagh, County Tyrone, took care to ensure that the gardens and orchards which surround his house were 'well sheltered with walls, hedges and trees'.[12] In Seagoe parish in 1742 there was a 'kitchen

was bought by Archbishop William Alexander and brought by him to the palace at Armagh. 3 TCD, MS 1019, p. 56. 4 Certificate of insurance for Dunboe glebe-house, n.d., in box of unsorted materials, PRONI, D/668/C. 5 M. Hill, 'Protestantism in County Fermanagh, c.1750–1912' in E.M. Murphy and W.J. Roulston (eds), *Fermanagh: history and society* (Dublin, 2004), p. 392. 6 Day, *Letters from Georgian Ireland*, p. 222. 7 Ibid., p. 210. 8 PRONI, T/808/15298. 9 TCD, MS 1019, p. 86. 10 PRONI, DIO/4/29/7/2/1, f. 38. 11 Ibid., f. 76. 12 TCD, MS 1019, p. 3.

garden containing about two English acres of ground, well inclosed and planted'.[13] Such gardens had an important use, supplying the table of the minister and his household with fresh fruit and vegetables. The Delany's garden supplied them with gooseberries, currants and potatoes.[14]

Laying out a garden was not without its problems. The Revd William Wolsley, appointed to Tullycorbett parish in 1784, wrote to his bishop in 1798 that he had improved the glebe-house and planted a large number of trees around it so that it was 'one of the most comfortable residences in the diocese'.[15] He added that before he arrived in the parish there was no garden so he had enclosed an English acre with a brick and stone wall. Unfortunately, the brick makers had 'imprudently' allowed the fire to go out before all the bricks had been properly burnt, with the result that he had to rebuild the wall at a cost to himself of £200, money that should have gone to his large family: he had thirteen children.

The ancillary buildings associated with a glebe-house reflecting the fact that most parsonages were the foci of working farms. In 1721 a terrier of the parish of Comber, County Down, recorded that, in addition to the glebe-house, there was a barn, stable, cow house and brew house, 'all in sufficient repair'.[16] At Seagoe there was a cowhouse of brick and lime; three stables and a barn, the walls whereof are of mud, all thatched'.[17] In addition, the former glebe-house was now being used as an out-house. In a few instances coach-houses were constructed.[18] While some attempt may have been made to separate farm buildings from the dwelling, this was not always practicable. When visiting the rectory in Cappagh parish, Beaufort noted that the entrance to the house was 'in the yard of offices'.[19]

Those who could afford it constructed ornamental buildings in their gardens. In Ardstraw parish Dr Leland built a 'pretty summer house'; in the 1830s it was believed that this was a converted O'Neill castle from the late medieval period.[20] A unique edifice in the environs of a clergyman's dwelling, so far as is known, was the work of William Green, rector of Killesher, who went so far as to construct a 'handsome chapple of ease, sclated & well fixed which he designs for his burial place & family'.[21]

Since 1870 a great many rectories have been sold, with the result that relatively few of the houses of the clergy constructed in this period are still in the possession of the church. The sheer scale of these houses means that many are impracticable for the domestic needs of a twenty-first-century clergyman and his family. A number

13 Dawson, 'Terrier of the parish of Seagoe', p. 225.　14 Day, *Letters from Georgian Ireland*, p. 210.　15 PRONI, D/1208/3.　16 Comber vestry minute book, PRONI, MIC/583/36.　17 Dawson, 'Terrier of the parish of Seagoe', p. 225　18 P. O Mordha, 'Some priests and parsons of the Clones area, 1620–1840' in *Clogher Record*, ix (1977), p. 239.　19 TCD, MS 1019, p. 3.　20 A. Day and P. McWilliams, *Ordnance Survey memoirs of Ireland vol. 5. Parishes of County Tyrone I, 1821, 1823, 1831–6* (Belfast, 1990), p. 9.　21 J. or T. Dolan, History of Fermanagh, 1718–9, NLI, MS 2085, p. 125.

of glebe-houses have found new uses as guest-houses or similar forms of accommodation. The list of losses among glebe-houses is long and depressing. It includes Kilskeery glebe house, built in 1775, and now demolished. Others are in imminent danger of collapse. Termon House, near Carrickmore, County Tyrone, built 1815 by the Revd C. C. Beresford for £3,293, has been unoccupied for some years now. With the guttering clogged by vegetation, damp is becoming a major problem and one that will probably be the ruination of the house before long. The former glebe-house in Donaghmore parish, County Down, featured in a recent Ulster Architectural Heritage Society publication of historic buildings at risk of destruction.[22] Badly conceived alterations have disfigured a number of houses. Of the inappropriate changes made to Lissan rectory, the architectural historian, Alistair Rowan has lamented: 'A sad instance of misapplied zeal and the consequences of inadequate state protection of Irish monuments'.[23] It is to be hoped that a proper understanding and appreciation of these buildings and the part they played in Irish society may result in greater protection of these edifices. Even by restricting itself to one part of Ireland, this study has only scratched the surface of what may be uncovered about the homes of the Anglican clergy. It is to be hoped that there will be those who prepared to take this study further.

22 [H. Hossack, W. J. Roulston et al.], *Buildings at risk*, vol. 4 (Belfast, 1997), p. 62.   23 Rowan, *North-west Ulster*, p. 363.

6

The parish clergy of the Church of Ireland in the eighteenth century

Marie-Louise Legg

We know little about the daily life of the men who were the backbone of the Church of Ireland in the eighteenth-century. The problem has been, at bottom, the lack of archival sources. If the clergy wrote books, few – other than printed sermons – have survived; little of their correspondence has been preserved and only a few of their published sermons remain.[1] Visitation papers exist only sporadically, and eighteenth-century Ireland does not seem to have its own Parson Woodforde, with his diary of hospitality and neighbourliness. Nor does it have its equivalent of Francis Kilvert of Clyro, whose introspective diary of suppressed passions and natural observation illuminates his world in rural Wales in the mid-nineteenth-century.[2]

The problems faced by clergymen appear to have been monumental. They were poor, even if on paper they might seem quite well off. They often had no suitable place to live. Their parishioners were frequently dispersed over wide areas and in unions of many parishes: a situation particularly acute in the countryside, where Protestants were few. We know almost nothing about their pastoral ministry. The identification of suitable candidates to serve the church, given their lack of income and the daunting size of their task, depended not necessarily on their suitability for office, but more on locality and the bishop's knowledge of particular candidates as relations, at university, or in other dioceses. After reviewing the problems faced by ministers in the first half of the eighteenth-century, I want to examine what we do know about the process of choice and presentation in two dioceses where Edward Synge was bishop for twenty-nine years, from 1733 to 1762.

1 An exception is the sermons of Revd Joseph Story, an Englishman who became bishop of Killaloe and later Kilmore. J.B. Leslie, *Ferns clergy and parishes: being an account of the clergy of the Church of Ireland in the diocese of Ferns, from the earliest period, with historical notices of the several parishes, churches, etc.* (Dublin, 1936). 2 R.L. Winstanley (ed.), *The diary of James Woodforde* (5 vols, Oxford, 1924–31); Francis Kilvert, *Kilvert's diary*, ed. W. Plomer (3 vols, London, 1938–40).

One way of overcoming the gaps in the archives is by looking at the careers of those who entered the church. The background of the young men who became clerics was fairly predictable. Of the seventy-four students of Trinity College, Dublin who entered the church between 1733, when Edward Synge became bishop of Ferns and Leighlin, and 1762, when he died as bishop of Elphin, eighteen were described as sons of gentlemen, twenty-two as sons of the clergy, five as sons of professional men, four as sons of farmers and three as the sons of merchants. One was the son of a barrister. For twelve the parental occupation is not known.[3] In gentry families it seems to have been mainly younger sons who took orders.[4] Some sons would have inherited personal wealth or married into wealthy families. Muschamp Vesey was the youngest son of John Vesey, archbishop of Tuam, Edward Synge's predecessor. Through family connections (he was a relation by marriage of the Colcloughs) he became rector and vicar of Abbeyleix, Queen's County, the seat of his brother, Sir Thomas, bishop of Ossory from 1714 to 1730.[5] Many clergymen were the sons of clergymen and, like the children of doctors who know the demands of their parent's profession, they understood the life they faced on ordination. On the other hand, one Ferns clergyman was a son of a Dublin butcher and one a son of a shoemaker.[6]

By the second quarter of the century they were probably born and educated in Ireland and went to Trinity College, having been taught by a local master or family tutor. As Toby Barnard has shown, education to become a clergyman was expensive.[7] Having taken a BA, an aspiring clergyman had to wait for three to four years before ordination.[8] He could not be ordained before the age of 24.[9] Some held that priests should first be deacons, but this was not always the case. Deacons could minister to a parish in all rites except that of communion. Under the Act of Uniformity, if he remained as a deacon he faced a future as a curate.[10] But before ordination a certificate of learning and good behaviour was required.[11] Concerned about the good reputation of his clergy, Archbishop Marsh always enquired into candidates' learning and morals.[12] In 1694, much to his embarrassment, Jonathan

3 *Alumni Dublinenses.*   4 Of a sample of 30 families in *Burke's landed gentry of Ireland* (London, 1958), there were 54 children who became clergymen in the eighteenth-century. Of these 38 (70.37 per cent) were younger sons.   5 Muschamp Vesey was related to Caesar Colclough through his wife Henrietta, daughter of Agmondisham Vesey. Henry Echlin, rector of Clonegal, was a son of Sir Henry Echlin and married Jane Moore, granddaughter of the earl of Drogheda. Colclough family tree, www.fortunecity/colclough; Leslie, *Ferns clergy*, p. 196.   6 Thomas Barton, prebendary of Aghold, was the son of Thomas, 'lanius' (butcher). James Tasker, rector of Ardcolm was a son of James, 'calcearius' (shoemaker). Both were born and educated in Dublin. *Alumni Dublinenses*, pp 47, 800.   7 T.C. Barnard, *A new anatomy of Ireland: the Irish Protestants, 1649–1770* (London, 2003), p. 82.   8 Averaged over the 60 clergy who served in the diocese of Ferns and that of Elphin between 1733 and 1762, the mean stay was 6 years.   9 Bishops had to be at least 30 years old, but deacons could be 23. [John Johnson], *The clergy-man's vade mecum* (London, 1709), pp 42–4.   10 Louis Landa, *Swift and the Church of Ireland* (Oxford, 1954), p. 8.   11 Ibid., p. 6.   12 In 1690 Marsh wrote cryptically after the consecration of

Swift was asked by Marsh for a personal reference from Sir William Temple before he could be ordained, first as a deacon and then a priest, by the bishop of Kildare in Christ Church Cathedral, Dublin.[13] To guide the new incumbent, many handbooks were written to aid him in his career, dealing with some of the duties and the difficulties that he might face.[14] John Johnson's manual dealt not only with the hierarchy, doctrine and worship of the church, but also considered clerical 'privileges and hardships'. The clergy were not bound to serve on juries and their goods were free of toll at fairs and markets.[15] As well as the duty to read the Book of Common Prayer, to administer the sacrament and to preach, they had to read certain acts of parliament and proclamations to the congregation. They were counselled to reside in one parish if they ministered to more than one, and were given help on how to extract their tithes. One piece of advice throws light on the behaviour of some congregations: there was guidance on dealing with 'striking, brawling and disturbances during divine service'.[16] Post-reformation patrons of Church of Ireland parishes seem not to have met together to consider possible candidates for the clergy, as did the puritan clergy and patrons in early seventeenth-century England. Ireland, with its relative shortage of Protestant graduates, had to rely on other methods. Patrons appointed relatives, friends, and friends of friends. They appointed local men and the children of local men and other clergy. Favouring one's relations was one means of ensuring that the incumbent was known to the patron and, it was hoped, reliable. The circle of friends extended to university contemporaries.

Lay impropriators often had the advowson of local parishes. We know a lot about the politics of the hierarchy of the Church of Ireland. What we do not know is the confessional affiliation of many of those laymen who possessed advowsons. Nor do we know when the advowsons were donative – needing no approval from the bishop – or presentative, where the candidate was examined by the bishop or his archdeacon.

Having been collated to a parish, a candidate had to pay a sum calculated on the value of their new living to the clerk and registrar of faculties in Dublin. Henry Duncan paid £20 to hold the rectory of Mayacon, diocese of Ferns. He already held the rectories of Baltinglass and Ballynule, diocese of Leighlin. Bartholomew Vigors paid £24 to be dean of Leighlin Cathedral together with the rectory of

William Fitzgerald as bishop of Clonfert, 'in which consecration I had no hand ... nor may I ever be concerned in bringing unworthy men into the Church'. Raymond Gillespie (ed.), *Scholar bishop: the recollections and diary of Narcissus Marsh, 1638–1696* (Cork, 2003), p. 37.   **13** Joseph McMinn, *Jonathan's travels: Swift and Ireland* (Belfast, 1994), p. 23.   **14** As well as John Johnson's guide, [M.R.], *The parson's vade mecum* (London, 1693); Sir Simon Degge, *The parson's counsellor, with the law of tithes or tithing* (London, 1676); George Meriton, *The parson's monitor* (London, 1681); Walter Morgan, *The parson's jewel, or Morgan's qualify'd incumbent* (London, 1705); William Watson, *The clergy-man's law: or the compleat incumbent* (3rd edn, London, 1725).   **15** *The clergy-man's vade mecum*, pp 134–5.   **16** Watson, *The clergy-man's law*, p. 180.

Shankill. These sums took a large bite out of their prospective income.[17] A new minister's induction was usually performed by neighbouring clergy in a ceremony which gave him possession of his church. Even if the church was, as so often in Ireland, in ruins it was enough to lay the new incumbent's hand on the church wall.[18] The incoming minister now faced the realities of survival in the parish. Clerical income was dependent on rents and tithes, on unions of parishes, on family money, and (rarely) on marrying a rich wife.[19] The parish clergy in towns fared rather better, as those in even small towns could diversify into schoolmastering and tutoring.

'Where a Religion is established ... and without Religion no Society can subsist... society is under a moral obligation of supporting the Ministers...', wrote a layman in 1767,[20] but parish clergymen in eighteenth-century Ireland frequently faced financial difficulties. An observer remarked in 1749 that the 'bulk of the clergy' lived on £300 a year or less. Even then, only one in a hundred enjoyed this level of income and £200 a year was considered 'handsome'.[21] Bishop Edward Synge said that one of his clergymen had an income of £100 a year, despite serving three parishes.[22] Curates were in worse circumstances. Though considered to be gentlemen 'born of gentlemen', they might be rewarded with £30 a year, forced to board in 'a farmer's house' and unable to marry.[23] It was noticed that 'great livings are given to a few men who have powerful friends and independent fortunes'.[24] Certainly clergy with rich patrons ready to take them into their households found themselves in good case. One example was the Revd Daniel Letablère. Letablère was a Huguenot whose father had served at the battle of the Boyne. On graduating from Trinity College Dublin in 1748, he was taken up by the Kildares and presented by them to the livings of Rathangan and Larabryan. He later became a prebendary of Yagoe and of Maynooth in St Patrick's cathedral, Dublin, and ended his life as dean of Tuam. When the Kildares came to Dublin in the summer, Letablère was in their train.[25] Good connections with Dublin Castle and with the hierarchy of the Church of Ireland were inestimably valuable. The golden road to success for a young clergyman was to begin his career as chaplain to the lord lieutenant or to an archbishop.[26]

---

17 Registry of the faculties granted since 19 July 1745, Marsh's Library, MS Z.3.5.34/197. 18 [Johnson], *The clergy-man's vade mecum*, p. 78. 19 Henry Echlin, son of judge Sir Henry Echlin, became rector of Clonegal and married a grand-daughter of the earl of Drogheda. Leslie, *Ferns clergy*, p 136. 20 *The rights of the clergy of Ireland candidly considered by a friend to the constitution* (Dublin, 1767), p. 5. 21 *A letter from a layman to the clergy of Ireland* (Dublin, 1749). 22 Edward Synge, *Two affidavits in relation to the demands of tythe-agistment in the dioces of Leighlin; with an introduction* (Dublin, 1736), pp 16, 17. 23 *A letter from a layman* (Dublin, 1749), p. 10. 24 Ibid., p. 7. 25 M-L. Legg (ed.), *The Synge letters: Bishop Edward Synge to his daughter Alicia Roscommon to Dublin, 1746–52* (Dublin, 1996), pp 13, 117–18n. 26 F.G. James, 'The Church of Ireland in the early 18th century', *Historical Magazine of the Protestant Episcopal Church*, xlviii (1979), p. 437.

The income of the clergy was received through glebe harvests, rents and tithes. The product of tithes in kind he would sell on the open market. The first two might be sure, though only in years of good harvest, but tithes were uncertain. Comparing the lot of the parish clergy in England with those of Ireland, Swift described the comfort of the English clergy, with rich farmers paying their easily collected rent and tithes. The English clergyman lived in a house and with a barn in good repair, and no entertainment was expected from him 'beyond a pot of ale and a piece of cheese'. His congregations were full on Sundays of 'plain cleanly people', who spoke his own language.[27] In Ireland the toll on clergy incomes taken by impropriators was significant. Because of his interest in tithe agistment, Edward Synge, when bishop of Ferns, took some trouble to find out about the income of the clergy in three of the four ecclesiastical provinces. Like his father before him, he found that hundreds of their houses, churches and glebes had been destroyed in the wars.[28] Further, a 'change of culture and subtractions of Tythe and Agistment' had reduced the value of livings. He gave one example of a living reduced from £350 to £100 a year. Some of his clergy in the former diocese of Leighlin received only the small tithes and in others the impropriator allowed them only 40s. a year.[29] One example were the rectorial tithes of the parish of Aghourd, but they were impropriate to the Colclough family, who provided just £32 a year for a curate out of £300 a year. The church there had been in ruins 'from time immemorial'.[30]

Throughout the century and beyond, there were protests against these low levels of income, and ideas were put forward for their reform and augmentation. One clergyman suggested a sliding scale over and above the tithe should be added. The Revd Arthur Forde of Lurgan petitioned the lord chief baron in 1750, saying that the average Easter offering was 4d., and suggesting that traders, retailers and hucksters of the parish should pay a shilling more at Easter in lieu of their personal tithes. Shopkeepers should be asked for 2s. 6d. a year and those with gardens one penny.[31]

The quality of life of the Irish clergyman depended also on the size and, importantly, the location of his flock. Connolly has calculated that in 1728, when 600 incumbents and 200 curates ministered to a Church of Ireland population of 'at most' 250,000 people, the established church had a ratio of one clergyman to every 312 church members, and he judged this ratio to be 'perfectly respectable'.[32] This would have been true if the Church of Ireland population had been evenly distributed around those churches that were in good repair with resident ministers. But their distribution was by no means even across Ireland. Both geography and history had scattered Protestant worshippers and their churches unevenly.

27 Dean J. Swift's observations on the bill for the clergy's residing in their livings, NLI, MS 4725, f. 2. 28 Ibid., ff. 2–4. 29 Synge, *Two affidavits*, pp 16, 19–20. 30 Leslie, *Ferns clergy*, p. 230. 31 Bruce Papers, NLI, D 27,151. 32 S.J. Connolly, *Religion, law and power: the making of Protestant Ireland* (Oxford 1992), p. 179.

From the reformation onwards unions, formal and informal, had been created between parishes where there were no Protestants at all with others containing a few; between those where grazing had removed large numbers of the population, and those where it might be possible to augment clerical income enough to support a clergyman, 'who knew not where to provide himself better'.[33] Many of these unions were strangely configured, with parishes separated by many miles and small fragments of one parish embedded within another.

Bishop Nicolson described the union of the parishes of Maghera and Killelagh as 'intermixed in great confusion'.[34] These unions, while logical, created problems with the requirement for the clergy to reside in his parish. In 1723, Archbishop Edward Synge reported from Galway that although ecclesiastical law laid an obligation on clergymen to reside, and he could deprive them of their livings if they did not, in three-quarters of the country there were no glebes, and those that existed were so small and inconvenient that it was impossible for the clergy to take up residence.[35] Failure to reside did not always attract sympathy. A radical writer in 1760 claimed that it was 'not unreasonable' for people to withhold their tithes if the minister did not reside. He had no sympathy with those ministers who said they could not serve because they had nowhere to live. Surely it was 'no distress' for a clergyman to live in a 'snug thatched house'. Excisemen, coast officers and surveyors sent from Dublin made no such complaint. If the clergy did not preach or administer the sacrament, 'to what end are they maintained?'[36] But the odds were against residence. Even in 1768, of forty-one Derry parishes, twenty-four had no glebe houses. In thirty-nine parishes in the diocese, either the rector or his curate or both resided. But one incumbent served a parish in Dublin, another lived out of the parish in Strabane and another, serving a country parish, was 'old and infirm' and for his health lived in Derry.[37] The size of unions often meant long hours of difficult and even dangerous travelling. Ministers encountered hazards while travelling: being bitten by wild animals, falling from horses and chaises and even drowning.[38]

---

33 Swift's observations, NLI, MS 4725, ff. 5–6. 34 Examples in the diocese of Elphin are the parish of Ballynakill, which had one section crossing the County Roscommon/County Galway boundary and the other 40 miles away in County Roscommon, and a small piece of the parish of Kilbryan was embedded within the neighbouring parish of Ardcarn. Map of the parishes of County Roscommon in Brian Mitchell, *A new genealogical atlas of Ireland* (Baltimore, 1986), p. 97; Bp W. Nicolson's observations on his visitation of Derry, 1718, NLI, MS 2668, f. 16. 35 [Abp] Edward Synge, *A brief account of the laws now in force in the kingdom of Ireland for encouraging the residence of the parochial clergy* ... (Dublin, 1723), pp 8, 13. 36 *The pedlar's letter to the bishops and clergy of Ireland* (Dublin, 1760), pp 13–15, 18–19. 37 Derry diocese 1768 parliamentary return. NLI, MS 2668. 38 The Revd Mr Gill was fatally bitten by a fox in 1733; William Harrison, rector of Strokestown, was drowned crossing a deep ford in November 1740. Three men died falling from their horses: William Crawford, rector of Erriglekeerogue in 1741; William Langton, dean of Clogher; and Master Supple. Lodge's obituaries taken from Robinson Library, Armagh Library, NLI, MS 2678, ff. 9, 10, 14.

Episcopal visitations often mentioned building or rebuilding churches to replace ruined or inconvenient buildings which, with their glebes, had been destroyed in the upheavals of the seventeenth century. Where practicable and where there were enough Protestants for a reasonably sized congregation, ruined churches were rebuilt and distant churches built in more convenient places. Many parishioners faced major difficulties in reaching a church at all. In 1718, Bishop William Nicolson found in Derry that parishioners were forgiven from attending in Termonamongan because of 'many rapid rivulets' running between their houses and the church, and Tamlaghtard parish was divided by 'a great bog' which made attendance impossible in the winter unless parishioners took a six mile detour. In his diocese, churches had to be rebuilt where the population, originally planted from England, had emigrated. In the seventeenth-century the diocese of Derry had had benefactions granted by both English gentry and city of London companies. Churches had been built to serve communities of English immigrants who, by the eighteenth-century, had long since departed. Faughvale church had been built by the Merchant Taylors' Company for an English colony, 'now decayed', at Macosquin. Errigal church in County Tyrone, where there had been an English plantation, again 'decayed', had been removed from the mountains to Garvaghey. A church had been on an island at Ballyneskirllin, but the plantation had now gone and was 'justly removed' by the Vintners' Company to Bellaghy.[39]

Episcopal and archepiscopal visitations also dealt with ministers who strayed from the path of righteousness in various ways. Desertoghil, County Derry, had presented a candidate 'in Bishop King's time' who had been rejected for 'whoredom &c'.[40] In the diocese of Ferns, clergy were censured in visitations as 'contumacious' for failing to repair the parish church, failing to put a wall around the church cemetery and for disregarding orders to reside in their parishes.[41] When Archbishop William King as metropolitan investigated Ferns and Leighlin he deprived some seven clergymen from their livings and censured thirty others. He also rejected those whom he regarded as unqualified.[42] Where churches were lacking, services were occasionally held in private houses, but conducting a marriage in a private house was illegal and ministers could be prosecuted.[43] Yet, many clergy were praised for being good preachers and 'very painfull' in their ministry.[44]

The few surviving visitations dealt with a wide variety of matters. The condition of the parish was uppermost, with reports on the size of congregations and the condition of churches financially and physically. A clergyman could be pro-

---

39 Bp W. Nicolson's visitation of the diocese of Derry, 1718, NLI, MS 2668, ff. 11, 14, 16, 17. **40** Ibid., f. 15.   **41** Samuel Thresher, curate of Graigue, and Philip Jones, vicar of Timahoe, were censured by Archbishop King. Visitation of the diocese of Leighlin, 1718, NLI, mic, p. 4294.   **42** Abp W. King to F. Annesley, 24 March 1713, TCD, MS 750/4/1, ff. 133–4.   **43** Visitation of the diocese of Meath, 1722, NLI, MS GO 199, f. 459.   **44** Mr William Sibthorpe, parish of Molengar, diocese of Meath. Visitations of some Church of Ireland dioceses, NLI, MS GO 199, f. 459.

nounced contumacious if he failed in his duty. Bishop Nicolson's visitation of Derry in 1718 included enquiries into the size of parishes, the presence of glebes and numbers of conforming parishioners in a part of Ireland with large numbers of both roman catholics and dissenters. His census also considered the furnishing of churches. He required many parishes to provide a cloth on the altars and a carpet in front, and to buy communion plate, bibles and prayer books.[45]

Clerical duties extended beyond conducting Sunday services and writing sermons. The cleric and his vestry were expected to maintain the altar and church plate and to keep a bible, a Book of Common Prayer and a book of homilies. In a union of parishes, the incumbent was expected to conduct a service in each of his parish churches in sequence, and it is not surprising that on occasion he would get muddled about dates and forget to come.[46] For a fee he married couples, baptised their children, churched women six weeks after they gave birth, and buried parishioners when they died. He attended the annual episcopal visitation at which he had to report on the condition of his church and graveyard, both of which he had to keep in good order. The clergy were expected not only to serve their Protestant congregation. They were also expected to strive to convert the Roman Catholic Irish. Successive enquiries from Dublin Castle and the Irish parliament asked the bishops to give numbers of roman catholics and their mass houses.[47] These enquiries would be passed to the parish clergy. Bishop Synge took them further by initiating a massive 'census' in 1749, listing the names, religion, families and households of his parishioners, collected through his clergy and their churchwardens.[48]

Clergymen were intimately bound up with the community, not only in pastoral care but also in dealing with the vestry. Vestries met with varying frequency, with an annual meeting (usually on Easter Monday or Tuesday) to elect parish officers and approve the outgoing churchwardens' accounts. Parishioners were expected to attend and vote. The incumbent was almost always present, but if not his curate took his place.[49] The main business of the vestry was to set the church rates and tithe payments on specific commodities, and to elect constables and overseers of the poor and parish surveyors who were in charge of the roads.[50] They dispensed food and fuel to the poor in times of hardship.[51] They discussed the con-

45 Bishop Nicolson's visitation of the diocese of Derry, 1718, NLI, MS 2668.   46 M.-L. Legg (ed.), *The diary of Nicholas Peacock, 1740–1751* (Dublin, 2005).   47 M.-L. Legg, *Census of the diocese of Elphin, 1749* (Dublin, 2004), pp. xi, xxv, xxviii.   48 Ibid., pp. xi–xii.   49 The minister of the parish of Mulrankin, Roger Vigors, who was the rector for 31 years, signed the minutes of the annual vestry every year from 1725 to 1734. Anthony French, curate of the Dysart Enos and Kilteal in Ferns, signed the minutes every year from 17 April 1759 to 27 March 1780. Vestry book of the parish of Mulrankin, RCBL, P.827.5.1; Vestry book of the parishes of Dysart Enos and Kilteal, RCBL, P.567.5.1.   50 T. Barnard, 'The eighteenth-century parish' in E. Fitzpatrick and R. Gillespie (eds), *The parish in medieval and early modern Ireland* (Dublin, 2005); Raymond Refaussé, *Church of Ireland records* (Dublin, 2000), pp 15–16.   51 During the years 1740–41 when extreme weather left many families in desperate need, clergymen were ordered to give parish relief, though the response by some clergymen was less than generous. David Dickson,

dition and repair of the church building, the bells, windows and altar and communion vessels to which occasionally the minister and patron of the church would
contribute.[52] They provided pickaxes, crowbars and wheelbarrows to mend the
roads.[53] On the cleric's relationship with his parishioners depended the successful
voting of the church rates and setting the tithe on which he was himself dependent, and this relationship could sometimes be stormy.

The Limerick farmer Nicholas Peacock was an official in the parish of
Kildimo, County Limerick in the 1740s, possibly an applotter and collector of the
parish cess. For him the duty to collect church rates may often have been onerous,
as in March 1741 he went to a local fair to find parishioners who still owed rates
from the previous year. He also put up advertisements at the church, stating the
newly set tithe.[54] Occasionally there were disputes about the level of tithes.
Peacock refers to a dispute in March 1749 which was resolved the next day, and in
Castlemartyr, County Cork, in 1752 the parishioners rejected the tithe applotment
of £5, but a week later they agreed it.[55]

Once a year, the bishop would hold a visitation. In large dioceses with difficult
topography the ministers went to the bishop to report on the condition of their
parishes rather than the bishop visiting them.[56] In his descriptions of his prepa-
rations for his visitations Synge shows that he viewed his clergy as important people, needing a level of hospitality he did not offer readily to his neighbours.
Between 1746 and 1752 Synge told his daughter of the annual upheavals caused
to his household by the descent of his clergy. In preparation he had to send to
Dublin for furniture, and get out china and glass from store. He was concerned
too about his cook's performance in cooking special dishes for the dinner for all
his clergy. His clergy usually stayed for two nights, and he abhorred 'all the clut-
ter which is the worst of it'.[57]

THE DIOCESE OF FERNS AND LEIGHLIN

Edward Synge was at Trinity College from 1706 to 1715. He took his B.A. in 1709,
and became a fellow and junior dean in 1710. In Dublin he held first the parish of
St Audoen, and was appointed a prebendary of St Patrick's in 1719. In 1730 he was
consecrated bishop of Clonfert, and the next year of Cloyne. In 1733 he moved to
Ferns and Leighlin and in 1740 was translated to Elphin.[58] It is his time in these
last two dioceses that I shall examine. One advantage of the diocese of Ferns and

Arctic Ireland: the extraordinary story of the Great Frost and forgotten famine of 1740–41 (Belfast,
1997), pp 35–43.   **52** Vestry book, Castlemartyr, 1751–1870, RCBL, P.607.5.1.   **53** Vestry minutes of the parish of Cloyne, County Cork, 1729, NA, M.6079.   **54** Legg (ed.), *Diary of
Nicholas Peacock*.   **55** Ibid., s.d. 5 and 12 May 1752; vestry book of Castlemartyr, 1751–1870,
RCBL, P.607.5.1.   **56** *Clergy-man's vade mecum*, p. 162.   **57** Legg (ed.), *Synge Letters*, p. 314.
58 Synge's full career is in Marie-Louise Legg, 'Edward Synge (1691–1762)' in *Oxford Dictionary
of National Biography* (Oxford, 2004).

Leighlin (the two dioceses had been united in 1600) was its relative proximity to Dublin. Against that was its size and spread across the counties of Wicklow, Wexford, Kilkenny, Queen's County and Carlow. It had a total of 216 parishes united into seventy-nine benefices. Of the former diocese of Leighlin, Edward Synge complained in 1737 that of eighty-two parishes, twenty-four were impropriate. In that of Ferns matters were worse: of its thirty-two churches and 134 parishes, sixty-one rectories were impropriate and in some parishes the clergy had only the small tithes; in others the impropriator gave only £2 a year to the incumbent. From his own family experience, Synge knew that dioceses near Cork and Dublin were easier to manage.[59] Writing in 1936 in his introduction to the succession lists for the Ferns and Leighlin clergy, the normally reticent James Leslie commented on its impropriations that 'the diocese of Ferns ... was probably the most badly treated in all Ireland'. This he attributed to the settlement of the Old English before the Reformation.[60] These families had bought up monasteries granted by the crown to laymen from the 1530s, together with their tithes. In Ferns, families like the Colcloughs pocketed the tithe income, and where they had the right of advowson they provided little or nothing for their candidates or for their curates.[61]

The other financial problem was the question of tithe agistment – the levying of tithes on land set to grazing. Strong farmers had taken advantage of the fine quality of the land to keep dry and barren cattle. They resisted the payment of tithes, arguing that as the land produced no harvest, the payment of tithes was unwarranted. This problem had agitated the Irish parliament from the beginning of the century. Edward Synge resisted these exemptions strongly. He responded that it was not he who needed the money but his clergy.[62] Edward Synge's battle over tithe agistment was considered by a committee of the Irish House of Commons in 1735. By then he had eight law suits against him. The committee immediately focussed, not on the legality of imposing a tithe on grazing land, but on the damage the imposition of tithes on grazing land might cause to the Protestant cause. Cases were cited of men who had emigrated or threatened to emigrate to America. It was said that by so 'driving many useful hands out of the Kingdom', support for the establishment and disagreements between the clergy and laity would give rise to popery and infidelity.[63]

59 William King made the same complaint in 1712, citing 99 parishes there with impropriate or appropriate tithes and only 32 parishes where tithe income supported the minister. Synge, *Two affidavits*, p.17; Abp W. King to F. Annesley, 7 June 1712, quoted in Connolly, *Religion, law and power*, p. 183. **60** Leslie, *Ferns clergy*, p. ix. **61** Anthony Colclough came to Ireland in 1540 with the lord deputy, Sir Anthony St Leger. He became constable of Ferns Castle and military governor of Wexford, and bought Old Ross Castle, Tintern Abbey and St Moleyns Abbey. Sir Henry Wallop, ancestor of John Wallop who became first earl of Portsmouth in 1743, was vice-treasurer and treasurer of war in Ireland in the late sixteenth century and bought large tracts of land in County Wexford, including the castle, manor and abbey of Enniscorthy. Burke, *Peerage* (1860) **62** Synge, *Two affidavits*, p. 6. **63** *Journal of the House of Commons (Ireland)*, vi, pp 658–73.

Unusually, in the Leighlin part of the diocese there was a strong political element amongst the clergy. The parish of Old Leighlin was one of the four 'bishops' boroughs', where an electorate of thirteen burgesses, all clergy, voted bishop's nominees into parliament free of expense.[64] There was no election in Old Leighlin when Synge was bishop, but later in the century a candidate was milked of money, not only for expenses, but also for a contribution to certified improvements.[65] Clergymen could also be politicians in their own right. In the borough of New Ross, William Harvey, the prebendary of Edermine and rector and vicar of the parishes of Mulrankin and Ardtroman from 1722 to 1737, became a burgess in Wexford in 1731 and, after resigning his parishes, mayor in 1753.[66]

The income from tithes figured in wills and marriage settlements and could become the subject of dispute.[67] The Colcloughs were both patrons and impropriators in Ferns and Leighlin and were tight-fisted with their tithe income.[68] The family held a grip on large parts of the diocese in the eighteenth century and in cases where they had the advowson, they appointed their relatives and friends. Worse, they could grow violent in defence of what they believed to be their rights. When Bishop Vigors in 1700 presented his own candidate to the parish of Owenduff, Caesar Colclough the elder dismissed him and collated his own chaplain. When the chaplain died, the bishop again collated his own candidate and again Caesar Colclough rejected him and placed his own candidate.[69] The Colclough family also owned the tithes of the four Wexford town churches. Their impropriations here were challenged in a case in 1746, when counsel against Colclough said, reasonably, that their claim would deprive the rector of these churches of all his tithes and leave him penniless. In response, Caesar Colclough's counsel claimed that they had been settled on Colclough's mother as part of her jointure. In 1740, Caesar Colclough detained tithes of fish due to the minister of the parish of St Mary's and St Patrick's, Wexford. Colclough's agent, Robert

64 The others were Armagh, Clogher and St Canice, Kilkenny. A.W.P. Malcomson, *Archbishop Charles Agar: churchmanship and politics in Ireland, 1760–1810* (Dublin, 2002), pp 176–7.   65 Ibid., p.180.   66 Edith Johnston-Liik, *History of the Irish parliament* (6 vols, Belfast, 2002), ii, p. 361; Leslie, *Ferns clergy*, p. xx.   67 Christoper Sherlock of Little Rath, County Kildare, left the tithes of three parishes in County Kildare to Maurice Eustace which were disputed by his cousin John Eustace. John Eustace to Maurice Eustace, 7 Nov. 1690, 28 Oct. 1691, 16 Jan. 1692, 12 Oct. 1692, 12 April 1693, 29 April 1693, Marsh's Library, MS Z3.2.6, ff 361–383.   68 It is not possible to be absolutely accurate in identifying rights of presentation and impropriations as Erck for the diocese of Ferns does not, as he does for Leighlin, give the patrons. Nor does Lewis in every case. J.C. Erck, *An account of the ecclesiastical establishment subsisting in Ireland; as also, an ecclesiastical register of the names of the dignitaries and parochial clergy* (Dublin,1830); Samuel Lewis, *A topographical dictionary of Ireland* (3 vols, Dublin,1837) The rectorial tithes of the parish of Owenduff were impropriate in the Colclough family and worth about £300. The Colclough family allowed the curate £32.   69 William King had a similar problem when he was bishop of Derry and had to spend £200 to buy peace in order to collate his own candidate in the parish of Donaghmore. Brief in the case of Bartholomew Vigors, bishop of Ferns, NLI, Colclough Papers, MS 26,481; Bp W. Nicolson, Observations 1718, ibid., MS 2668, f. 8.

Percival, prevented the collection of the tithe by Thomas Esmond, who was empowered to collect the fish, by threatening to 'break his head and knock out his brains'.[70] Some of the Colclough family had remained Roman Catholic, and perhaps those who had converted wanted to demonstrate their newly-found power.

The terrain of the country varied. The church at Aghold, diocese of Leighlin was 'very inconveniently situated in a bogg' and the parishioners could not attend in winter. A new church was built in 1722 with monies from the bishop, the provost of Trinity College, and local worthies.[71] In 1737, when it was decided that the church at Mulrankin was too small to accommodate the parishioners of the whole union, the chancel was demolished and rebuilt at the expense of 'several gentlemen and the consent of the late Revd Roger Vigors'. Money was also raised by building reserved pews for the Loftus family and the new rector, William Harvey.[72] The building of special pews was a mixed blessing, however. The wealthy laymen who spent money on pews and galleries often did so to the great inconvenience of other parishioners. The installation of Israel Mitchell's gallery at Stradbally, Queen's County meant that the pulpit had to be moved to the other side of the church.[73]

Vestry meetings were normally held in the parish church but occasionally had to make shift with rather unsuitable sites. In Kilcormac, diocese of Ferns, in 1738 the vestry met in 'the old walls' of the parish church and resolved to raise a penny rate to rebuild it. They still had no church in 1767, when the annual meeting was held in a parishioner's house. Later that year they were given a new and better site by the earl of Arran. In 1769, the vestry's meeting was in the new church.[74]

When he arrived in Ferns in 1733, Edward Synge had had little experience of selecting and presenting clergy. He had no opportunity to present candidates at Cloyne, being there too short a time. At Clonfert he presented only two candidates. One of them was Giles Eyre, a Trinity College contemporary and a relation by marriage through Synge's brother Nicholas. The other was an Englishman who would have been at Trinity College when Synge was junior dean.[75] Of the twenty men presented in Ferns between 1733 and his translation to Elphin in 1740, five had been his contemporaries at Trinity College, and of these four were local men from County Wicklow and County Wexford. Two men were his relations. A cousin, Richard Doherty, was appointed: first as curate of New Ross, diocese of Ferns, and in 1755 as prebendary of Kilmacullen and vicar of Drumcliffe and Taughnaugh, diocese of Elphin. On Doherty's death in 1760, Synge appointed his nephew Robert Curtis to the same prebendal stall and parishes.[76] Three

70 NLI, Colclough Papers. D 26,483.   71 Leslie, succession list of the diocese of Leighlin, NLI, MS 1772, p. 107.   72 Vestry book of Mulrankin, RCBL, P.827.5.1.   73 Vestry book of Stradbally, Queen's County, 19 Aug. 1723, RCBL, P.679.5.1.   74 Vestry book of Kilcormac, 3 Oct. 1738, RCBL, P21.5.1.   75 Giles Eyre was installed on 3 Nov. 1730 as prebendary of Drogta and rector and vicar of Clontuskert. Thomas Lancaster was collated vicar of Creagh in the same year. NLI, MS 2684, p. 449.   76 Doherty was distantly related to Edward Synge through a

others were from the locality and one was the son of a clergyman. Seven had no relationship, as far as we know, of any kind to Synge. Eleven members of the clergy of Ferns between 1733 and 1740 were sons of the clergy.

THE DIOCESE OF ELPHIN, 1740–1762

Edward Synge was translated to the diocese of Elphin in 1740 on the death of Bishop Robert Howard. The diocese had about the same income as that of Ferns and Leighlin. It had both advantages and disadvantages. In Synge's census of 1749 it had sixty parishes in three counties, and so was smaller.[77] County Roscommon was 'a very fine county and has most noble and rich pastures ... [with] a prodigious quantity of bullocks and sheep' and tithe agistment seems not to have been an issue.[78] But it was at least two days' journey from Dublin. Unlike the diocese of Ferns, travelling within the diocese was more difficult because communications were impeded by mountain ranges, rivers and bogs. It was not on the way to anywhere significant, except the port of Sligo. Clergy seem to have visited him at his palace at Elphin, rather than he going to visit them – at least those at a distance. He writes of going to Sligo town (almost the most distant part of his diocese) in 1747, but there is no record of his making the journey by 1752.[79]

There also seem to have been fewer difficulties in presenting candidates in Elphin, where the bishop presented to all parishes but one and the Crown presented the dean. Only in the parish of Kilglass did the bishop dispute the advowson with the King family, the impropriators.[80] Although there were many impropriations, it looks as though the impropriators may have behaved rather better towards the clergy than in Ferns. On coming into Elphin, Synge found he had to present seventeen men in the first four years. In all, between his arrival and his death twelve years later in 1762, he presented twenty-one men. Four were his contemporaries at Trinity College;[81] three were relations (including his brother Nicholas, who went on to be bishop of Killaloe in 1745); ten were from the locality; and three were the sons of clergy. Only four seem to have had no connection with Synge or with the area. He spread his net locally by appointing eight local men

Doherty/Synge marriage in the seventeenth century. Leslie, *Ferns clergy*, p. 230; Legg (ed.), *Synge letters*, pp xxxviii, 258, 296, 424. Robert Curtis (1729–?) was a son of Revd Robert Curtis, Synge's brother-in-law. Leslie, 'Elphin', p. 69; Legg (ed.), *Synge letters*, p. 18, n. 19.   77 Table 5.2, 'Some gross episcopal revenues', Connolly, *Religion, law and power*, p. 181.   78 James Kelly (ed.), *The letters of Lord Chief Baron Willes to Lord Warwick 1757–1762* (Aberystwyth, 1990), p. 96.   79 Legg (ed.), *Synge letters*, p. 53.   80 Erck, *An account*, pp 235–6.   81 These were William French, who entered TCD in 1708, took his BA in 1715 and became vicar of Ardcarn in 1743; George Blackburn, entered TCD in 1707, took his BA in 1711 and became vicar of Clooncraff and of Aughrim; William Digby, who entered TCD in 1712 and took a BA in 1716; Henry Cunningham, entered TCD in 1710, and graduated BA in 1714. He became archdeacon of Elphin in 1756. J.B. Leslie, 'Elphin biographical succession list', NLI, MS 5699.

to parishes and to the prebendal stalls.[82] William French, rector of French Park, was a younger son of the wealthy French family. He married well and became precentor of Elphin in 1752. Synge's cousin, Richard Doherty, was collated prebendary of Kilmacollum and vicar of Drumcliffe in 1755.[83] Six clergymen of Elphin were sons of clergymen. Bishop Hodson's Grammar School in the town of Elphin, founded around 1697, provided a living for the clerical headmaster and a nursery for many clerics. The income of the schoolmaster there was settled by a bequest of land in County Cavan whose rents in 1687 were valued at £20 a year.[84] The school educated six of the incumbents in the diocese between 1720 and 1760.

Like his father before him in Tuam, Synge was active in rebuilding and building churches. The church at Tibohine he had found to be 'decayed and ruinous' and in 1742 it was ordered to be built in a more convenient place and the churchyard to be enclosed. The land for the new church was granted by the major landowner at French Park, Arthur French. In 1747, Edward Synge intended to consecrate the church on Ascension Day, 28 May, but found that the churchyard was not yet completely enclosed, and some other things within the church had not been finished. It was eventually consecrated on 7 August that year.[85] In 1747 Synge also planned to build another new church 'near Mr Hawkes', whom he described to his daughter as 'so odd a man' that he expected trouble. Lewis Hawkes was vicar of Kilglass, where there was a dispute over the advowson, which may have accounted for the difficulties. The church there was built in 1752.[86] In the parish of Bumlin, the church was found to be ruinous and was ordered to be demolished. Thomas Mahon of Strokestown gave an acre of land to the bishop in 1754.[87] At the end of his life Synge was improving the cathedral and its surroundings.[88]

While we know a lot about the education and placement of the Protestant clergy during the eighteenth-century, we know almost nothing about their parochial ministry, their relationships with the parishioners and how their social status was perceived. Our lack of knowledge may just be due to the loss and destruction of archives. This article has focussed on two rural dioceses and has precluded work on the urban parishes of Dublin, Cork, Waterford and Galway. It may well be that these towns will yield up more information on what is an important and potentially fruitful subject.

---

82 Four of these were educated at Bishop Hodson's Grammar School: Edward Munns, born in Roscommon; William Digby; John Hickes; and Samuel Griffin, whose father had been the head teacher of the school. The other local men were William Glass from Athlone, Robert Phipps, born in Sligo, Richard Garrett, born in Athlone and Eubule Ormsby of Tubbervaddy. NLI, MS, 5699, pp 91, 109, 111–12, 207.   83 Ibid., pp 50, 131.   84 Michael Quane, 'Bishop Hodson's Grammar School, Elphin', *JRSAI*, 96 (1966), p. 160.   85 Order of Council, February 1742, in NLI, MS 5699, p. 225; Legg (ed.), *Synge letters*, pp 23, 30, 70.   86 Legg (ed.), *Synge letters*, pp 57, 61, 67, 453.   87 NLI, MS 5699.   88 Bp Edward Synge to Godfrey Wills, 10 Jan, 2 and 9 Feb, 8 and 15 March, 9 April, 5 Sep, 8 Nov 1760, 5 May, 14 July 1761, RCBL, MS 426/1–4, /6, /9, /10, /12, /14.

7

The clergy, 1780–1850

W.G. Neely

A visiting Church of England clergyman gave a very critical survey of his experience of the Church of Ireland:

> The parochial clergy are rather too well provided for in Ireland as their incomes almost always enable them to take up their abode in more amusing places than a country parish. As far as I can observe the clergy in general have a greater share of outward respect than their brethren in England because their revenues are greater, but I do not think them as lettered as clergymen, and I think they have even less spiritual influence over their flocks.

Too many were non-resident. In 1806, Bishop O'Beirne of Meath recorded forty-nine non-resident clergy in a total of ninety-two benefices.[1] Patrick Comerford in his survey of County Wexford found a rather better percentage but even there around a quarter of benefices were held by non-residents, although three clergymen living in Wexford may have had benefices close to the town.[2]

Much was done by curates, championed by Henry Grattan in the Irish parliament as the men who did the work. In a speech to the House of Commons in 1788, he called emotionally to his fellow MPs,

> See the curate. He rises at 6 for morning prayers, he leaves company at 6 for evening prayers. He baptizes, he marries, he churches, he buries. He follows with pious office his fellow ceatures from the cradle to the grave. For what immense income, what riches to reward his inestimable services. Do not depend upon the penury of the laity. Let his own order value his desserts, £50 a year. Fifty pounds for prayers, christening, for marrying, for church-

---

1 Akenson, *The Church of Ireland*, table 32.   2 P. Comerford, 'Church of Ireland clergy and the 1798 rising' in L. Swords (ed.), *Protestant, Catholic and dissenter: the clergy and 1798* (Dublin, 1997), p. 228.

ing. Fifty pounds so small an income in the opinion of the ecclesiastic sufficient for the duties of a clergyman. I think the curate has far too little blessed with full tenth. I think the Church would have abundantly too much.[3]

Grattan, in his eagerness to have the tithe reformed, was making an exaggerated case. Many curates were paid between £100 and £150. Some increased their incomes by acquiring minor additional posts or by teaching. Yet they were certainly not overpaid for doing the real work of the church. It was undoubtedly a time when those possessed of an ecclesiastical benefice were often well provided for. After 1750 the improvement in agricultural prices had improved the yield of tithes remarkably. Archbishop Brodrick, a keen reformer, comments on 'the clergy happily partaking in the general prosperity and increasing wealth'.[4]

In 1787, Bishop Woodward estimated the average annual income of the clergy in some dioceses. Top of the league was Raphoe with an average of £250, then Clogher with £187, Cloyne with £180, Cork and Ross at £150, and Dublin with £115. Lowest of all was Killala with £90. Woodward calculated that the average figure was £148 2s. 2½d.[5] The minimum stipend was set legally at £60, which in the nineteenth century was raised to £75. A great many of the clergy were pluralists with higher stipends. Altogether there were 2,436 parishes, of which 1,339 were in the bishop's gift. There were 282 crown livings and 344 under lay patronage. This was the figure arrived at by Daniel Beaufort.[6] The surveys commissioned by the Royal Dublin Society included excellent ones produced by some of the Church of Ireland clergy: Dubourdieu for Counties Antrim and Down, Townsend for Cork and Sampson on County Londonderry.[7]

Thanks to their social and economic standing, clergymen participated in public affairs. In addition to serving in their localities as justices of the peace, in the early 1780s some sympathized with the Volunteers and the patriotic movement for a free parliament. It was an exciting time, when clerical families delighted in the military displays. They appeared well satisfied with the earl of Charlemont's leadership but disturbed by the activities of the earl bishop of Derry, which seemed to threaten the social order. Few would have approved of his purple-clad cavalry and their triumphant entry into Dublin. All would have applauded the Volunteers' suppression of the White-Boys and their defence of the law. However, only two (Church of Ireland) clergymen were among the delegates at the Dublin

3 W.G. Neely, *The shaping of the church: a history of the Church of Ireland* (Dublin, 1994), p. 104.
4 Charles Brodrick to William Bennet, 9 Sep. 1802, NLI, MS 8892, quoted in Akenson, *The Church of Ireland*, p. 71.   5 R. Woodward, *The present state of the Church of Ireland* (Dublin, 1786), pp 41–7.   6 Akenson, *The Church of Ireland*, p. 330.   7 J. Dubourdieu, *Statistical survey of the county of Antrim* (Dublin, 1812); idem, *Statistical survey of the county of Down* (Dublin, 1802); H.Townsend, *A statistical survey of the county of Cork* (Dublin, 1810); G. Sampson, *The statistical survey of the County of Londonderry, Ireland* (Dublin, 1802).

conference, the Revd Mr Bruce from Carrickfergus and the Revd Mr Ryan from Carlow.[8]

Very different was the clerical attitude towards the United Irishmen. One clergyman went as far as becoming an officer in the Yeomanry, formed to oppose the United Irish. Dorothea Herbert, the daughter of a Church of Ireland rector, recorded in 1790:

> The rebellion now began to assume a most alarming appearance, not a night passed without nocturnal meetings and depredations and the public places were full of threats and proclamations. In many places open war was declared. In many more, all ranks and ages were enrolled in one side or the other.[9]

In County Wexford, as the rebellion developed in 1798, seventeen clergy were imprisoned by the rebels, and a clerical magistrate was pitch-capped. In all, five of the thirty-seven within the county were killed. When the rebels marched into Counties Kilkenny and Laois, many of the clergy dreaded a similar fate. The Revd Peter Roe sent regular letters to Dublin Castle, warning of conspiracies and plots, until years after Emmet's rebellion. Roe remained steadfast in his opposition to what he regarded as Roman conspiracy.[10] French invasion and the flight of the Kilkenny Yeomanry at the battle known as the Castlebar Races was another threat to Anglo-Irish security. Some clerical families, like that of the rector of Keady in County Armagh with a son killed at Waterloo, suffered as a consequence of the French wars. They never again enjoyed the sense of security that had prevailed in the 1780s. There is little evidence of clerical sympathy with those Protestants who joined the rebels. The Revd Henry Fulton, vicar of Nenagh, was arrested and later transported to Australia. He is the only Church of Ireland clergyman known to have been tried as a United Irish sympathizer.[11]

The clergy of the Church of Ireland, unlike their English counterparts, had an annual visitation by their bishop, who expected a report on their parishes to be presented. Also, in one year of every three, there was a visitation by the archbishop. In 1787, Euseby Cleaver claimed that 'the Church is not an inviting profession in Ireland, the clergy have many difficulties respecting their income and residence, even when times are not tumultuous'.[12] They were often not helped by the landed gentry, who resented paying tithes. Archbishop Brodrick claimed, 'not a gentleman out of twenty but is hostile to the tithe'.[13] Both Archbishop Robinson and Archbishop Agar bemoaned the attacks of the landowners on tithes. Such a situation increased the isolation of the clergy and encouraged the wealthier clergy to

8 Thomas McNevin, *History of the Volunteers* (Dublin, 1845).   9 *Retrospections of Dorothea Herbert* (2 vols, London, 1929–30), i, p. 272.   10 Samuel Madden, *Memoir of the Revd Peter Roe* (Dublin, 1842), pp 228–38.   11 William Hayes and Art Kavanagh, *The Tipperary gentry* (Dublin, 2003), p. 178.   12 A.P.W. Malcomson, *Archbishop Charles Agar* (Dublin, 2002), p. 190.   13 Ibid., p. 190.

absent themselves from their cures. At the same time, the disparities in clerical incomes were hard to justify. In 1808, it was calculated that 147 incumbents had an annual income of less than £100, 165 had an income between £100 and £200, 214 had an income between £200 and £500, and 116 commanded an income of more than £500. Perhaps Akenson overstated his case when he wrote of the clergy, 'the Church of Ireland was not simply a minority church, it was one surrounded by a sea of hatred', largely provoked by the requirement to pay tithes.[14] In comparison, the other major grievance, the privileged legal position of the established Church of Ireland, caused less trouble because the penal laws were rarely enforced in the later part of the eighteenth century.

After 1800, the Act of Union brought a series of reforms that moderated grievances. Akenson called the first three decades of the nineteenth century 'the era of graceful reform', but tithes remained as the root cause of hatred towards the clergy of the Church of Ireland. The popular press in Kilkenny attacked the clergy as black crows and sneeringly recorded the tenth potato, as the bishop's son, the Revd Hans Hamilton, was called by the local peasants. The violent protests of the Whiteboys made life difficult for the clergy. Dorothea Herbert spoke of a three-year war fought from 1780 by her father, the Revd Nicholas Herbert. He collected the tithe produce into his farmyard, while his aunt went in terror of the stacks being set on fire and of the rectory being burnt down around them. 'My father stood out each night, patrolling to see all was safe.'[15] The wagons sent out to collect the tithe crops were attacked frequently, and there were endless law suits. One hears of her mother sitting up all night with a candle and her book, to make sure all was safe. Like most clergymen, Herbert regarded the tithe as his legal due. Few took the attitude of a Tipperary rector, James Reid, who in 1737 had attacked the bishops in 'An essay on the simony and sacrilege of the Church of Ireland'. He called on parliament to take over the management of the wealth of the church. The Primate should be allowed an income of £1,500 p.a.; the three other archbishops, £1,200 each; the bishops, £1,000; and all rectors paid the same stipend. This would leave a surplus of £40,000 to be used to build glebe houses and schools. Reid prefigured Grattan's attitude.[16]

The Volunteers, the Kilkenny Rangers, restored law and order in their area and put an end to attacks on the clergy. A similar campaign in the diocese of Armagh was waged against the Oak-boys, who were suppressed through vigorous action led by the earl of Charlemont. Some of the peers and gentry had changed their view of the tithe and now sympathized with the clerical predicament. Increasing prosperity and horror at the violence of the Whiteboys had helped to bring about the altered attitude. The leading protestors in the provinces of Munster, Leinster and Connacht sprang from the prosperous farming communities rather than from the landless poor.

14 Akenson, *The Church of Ireland*, p. 66.   15 *Retrospections of Dorothea Herbert*, i, pp 22, 75–6.
16 Neely, *The shaping of the church*, p. 111.

An apparently anonymous 'Pastoral Annals' vividly described the attempt of a Donegal rector to collect his tithe, which he called 'this obnoxious assertion of a rightful claim'. He acknowledged that never more than half the tithe was paid. Idealistically he decided, like a fair number of rectors, to dispense with the proctor and negotiate his own tithe. He summoned his parishioners to meet and pay him. 'This announcement brought me into immediate and hostile collision with 1,800 persons – the lukewarm churchman, the rigidly stern Presbyterian bent on resistance, the wily papist, in those days a crouching slave.' The rector sat in vain with a hospitable bowl of whiskey before him to act as a sweetener whilst a huge crowd stood in sullen silence outside. Informed that he was not collecting money that day, they gladly came in to promise what they had no intention of paying. Twenty years on, he wrote 'to this very hour, the memory of that one short week affects me with abiding melancholy'.[17]

This was only one of many stories that were told. It was plain that something had to be done about tithes, the source of so much hatred. Grattan tried three times to introduce reform into the Irish parliament, but without success.[18] After Union in 1800, Castlereagh planned reform and Pitt hoped to achieve commutation by compensating the clergy with grants of land. Castlereagh believed that the existing system benefited no one. It brought the Church 'into odium without enriching its ministers'. He wanted to collect it in money payments only, but it was soon clear that there was little chance of such a parliamentary bill succeeding. In 1808, the campaign was taken over by Sir Henry Parnell, who proposed the abolition of tithes.[19] But, as often, the prevailing agricultural prosperity created little interest in reform. Only with a developing agricultural crisis after 1817 did reform acquire a new urgency in the farming community. A Tithe Bill was at last enacted in 1823. The clergy were left free to choose either composition or new lands. It was no real solution. By 1832, only half the parishes in Ireland had chosen the new system before the 'tithe war' intensified. The Roman Catholics grew more dissatisfied and, under the leadership of Bishop James Doyle of Kildare and Leighlin, demanded the total abolition of the tithe, complaining of the injustice of tithes being paid to some clergy in Meath, Ossory and in the ecclesiastical province of Cashel, who had no church building or Church of Ireland parishioners.

Before conditions deteriorated in the 1820s and 1830s, there were improvements in the lives of the clergy. Notable in this respect was the intensive campaign by the Board of First Fruits to build new churches and glebe houses. The Board benefited from regular parliamentary grants after 1786, at the rate of £5,000 p.a. £500 was granted to each church and £100 to each glebe. The rector had to pay to erect the house, the cost of which became a debt payable to him by his successor. In 1808 the parliamentary grant was increased to £10,000. Lord Liverpool's gov-

17 [J.S. Knox], *Pastoral annals* (London, 1840), pp 100–6.   18 Akenson, *The Church of Ireland*, p. 98.   19 Ibid., pp 101–3.

ernment was generous to the united Church of England and Ireland. As a result, by 1829, grants had been given for 550 glebe houses, 697 churches and the purchase of lands for 793 glebes. Earlier, in 1787, Beaufort had estimated that there were 2,436 benefices already better served than ever before. If, on the one hand, it seemed that the problems of the Church were being sorted out at last, on the other doubts were expressed about the effectiveness of the measures. A statute of 1808 gave bishops the power to enforce residence for nine months in each year. Under this act, Archbishop Agar obliged Nicholas Herbert to reside for three months in his parish of Knockgrafton, which he held in plurality.[20]

An Act of 1824 limited the power of bishops to grant dispensations and also empowered them to reduce clerical stipends if the residence requirement was not met. There is no doubt that during the first three decades of the nineteenth century, the clergy were gradually forced to take a new view of their profession and their responsibilities. Archbishop Stuart and his successor at Armagh, Lord John George Beresford, made it plain that there were professional duties and obligations that no clergyman could ignore. Along with others such as Agar and Brodrick, they laboured to improve the standing and lot of the clergy. If there was to be a fully resident clergy, then housing had to be provided. Agar told his diocese at a visitation in 1802 that only resident incumbents could set the appropriate spiritual and practical examples.

> It was the business of the beneficed pastor to pen his fold from the political world and recover the strayed sheep of his flock, to pour into the diseased mind the healing doctrines of religion and reconcile the poor and lowly to the inevitable inequalities of all human associations. He should have made himself familiarly acquainted with the condition of all his parishioners of every description and every sect.[21]

In 1806, there had been 1,253 clergy serving the church. By 1826, the number had increased to 1,977. By 1829, faculties granted by the archbishop of Armagh to hold two benefices had been reduced to one throughout all Ireland.[22]

Another important means of strengthening the administration of the Church was the re-introduction of rural deans in the eighteenth century. Bishop Berkeley of Cloyne had been the first to restore the system and when Charles Agar became archbishop of Cashel he set up rural deaneries throughout the archdiocese. In Armagh, Archbishop Robinson had investigated the possibility of doing the same, but it was left to his successor, Newcome, to introduce it. By 1820, sixteen of the twenty-two dioceses had rural deans. The office revolutionized the relationship between bishops and clergy by creating supervision and so ensuring that the epis-

20 *Retrospections of Dorothea Herbert*, i, pp. 171–2.   **21** Malcomson, *Agar*, p. 219.   **22** Akenson, *The Church of Ireland*, p. 130.

copal will was carried out regularly. In Ireland, inspection and supervision by archdeacons had largely lapsed. Under the Church Temporalities Act of 1833, the authority of archdeacons was restored. In consequence, the administration of the Church had become more professional, thanks to presence of archdeacons and rural deans as intermediaries between bishop and his clergy. No longer was the incumbent free to do largely as he pleased. Added to these innovations, the church commissioners became a new factor in clerical life.

The tithe issue had never been solved completely. During the 1820s, it reappeared in a form so bitter as to cause it to be named a 'war'. It brought misery and fear into many clerical homes. The passing of the 'great' reform bill in 1832, following the grant in 1829 of Catholic emancipation, ended any willingness on the part of the majority to put up with the grievance of tithes. Yet, the Church of Ireland clergy showed a new determination to use the very limited authority left to them. Some began to call in the police and the military to collect even minor arrears. No less than 31,624 writs to compel payment of tithes were issued between 1833 and 1835. Such actions served only to increase the sense of resentment. In many parishes, it proved impossible to collect the tithes, so depriving the rector of any income. Archbishop Beresford encouraged aggrieved incumbents to appeal for redress to the civil courts, but these suits further inflamed the situation.

Some clergymen behaved intemperately and provoked incidents that did their reputations little good. The reforming under-secretary for Ireland, Drummond, responded by forbidding the army to assist in the collection of tithes. There had been intimidation and violence from groups like the Whiteboys, Black-feet and Rockites. The prosperous farmlands in Kilkenny, Carlow, and the Queen's and King's Counties were particularly affected. The worst incident involved Dr Hans Hamilton, rector of Knocktopher in 1831. Following the example of his father, he had been charitable, but this generosity did not save him from attack. Several hundred peasants armed with hurly sticks assaulted him. A body of police was sent to protect him, but they too were attacked at Carrickshock and thirteen were killed. It was too much for Hamilton. He and his wife were smuggled to Kilkenny and then fled to England. He was a broken man, and died there in 1839.[23]

Serious trouble also occurred at Graiguenamanagh in County Kilkenny. There the absentee rector had never collected tithes from the parish priest. However, his officious curate demanded payment and a riot was the prelude to widespread violence.[24] In all, during 1832, there were 242 murders, 203 riots, 568 burnings and 723 attacks on houses. A Newtownberry in County Cork, there were no fewer than thirty-four murders. In the same year, an attempt to levy tithe on ten pigs led to the death of three peasants. While a pitched battle raged at the front of the cottage, Archdeacon Ryder broke in through a back window and collected the small sum

23 D. Bowen, *The Protestant crusade in Ireland, 1800–1870* (Dublin, 1978), p. 163. 24 Akenson, *The Church of Ireland*, p. 149.

1 Geoffrey Fyche, dean of St Patrick's, Dublin (died 1537)

2 Rowland Davies, successively dean of Ross and of Cork (died 1722)

3 Peter Drelincourt, dean of Armagh (died 1720), monument in St Patrick's Cathedral, Armagh by J.M. Rysbrack

4 Ardmore glebe house, County Armagh, *c.*1820

5 Derryloran glebe house, County Tyrone, originally of *c.*1709, remodelled *c.*1820

6 Killeeshill glebe house, County Tyrone, built, *c.*1807

7 Lissan glebe house, County Tyrone, built *c.*1807

8 Middletown glebe house, County Amagh, built, *c.*1812

9 W.C. Magee, bishop of Peterborough and archbishop of York, cartoon by 'Spy', *Vanity Fair*, 1869

10 Revd Samuel Hoops, rector of Kiltubrid

11 Ernest Lewis-Crosby, dean of Christ Church, Dublin, 1957

12 Crest of the Incorporated Society, 1733

PRIVATE EDUCATION.

A MARRIED Beneficed Clergyman of the Established Church wishes to procure Four PUPILS to prepare for College with his own sons. They will be treated with parental care and kindness, and in every respect as his own children.

Advertiser has had much experience in tuition, and resides in a beautiful and most healthful locality on the sea coast, within a short drive of Dublin. He can refer to several of the Fellows of College, and to many others of the highest respectability.

TERMS.—For Pupils under Twelve years of age, Sixty Guineas per annum; above Twelve years of age, Eighty Guineas per annum; to be paid Quarterly in advance.

No Midsummer Vacation.

Address "Rev. LL.D.," Office of the IRISH ECCLESIASTICAL GAZETTE, (148)

13 Advertisement for a school run by a clergyman, 1856

NOTICE.

THE
Protestant Inhabitants
OF
MAGHERADROLL
Are informed that, as their Undisguised Sentiments regarding the

NATIONAL SYSTEM
OF
EDUCATION

have been basely disregarded by those who called them forth, and, contrary to every principle of honour, having failed in their PUBLIC ATTEMPT at the introduction of

THAT SYSTEM,

have now, it appears, surreptitiously carried their point. THEY are requested to hold themselves in readiness to attend a Public Meeting, which shall be announced, as soon as certain DOCU-MENTS shall be prepared to be submitted to their considera-tion; and, if not to take further steps, to have the GRIEVANCE removed—at least, to publish their protest against IT, in the STRONGEST TERMS.

4th Jun 1836

Stuart & Gregg, Printers, Belfast.

14 Advertisement for a National School

15 Unveiling by Lord Cadogan of the statue of Lord Plunket, archbishop of Dublin, 1901

16 The first three Dublin University Fukein Missionaries

17 Gerald Dickson in camp, Manoharpur district, Chota Nagpur

that had caused these deaths. Bishop Doyle was violent in his denunciations, 'can Ireland, the poorest nation in Europe, support the most affluent and luxurious priesthood which inhabits the earth?' The whole province of Connacht became involved when a rector extorted the tithe on potatoes. It was apparently the first attempt to do so in that province, and it is hard to understand the foolishness of the rector. His bishop, Power le Poer Trench, made it clear that he did not support him.[25]

Archbishops Stuart and Brodrick saw that change had to come, as did Whately of Dublin and Beresford in Armagh. Whately believed that tithes should be made into a rent charge on the landlord. He also called for the abolition of the offensive cess. No Roman Catholic could accept that he or she should bear this charge for the expenses of the Church of Ireland. The consequence of withholding tithes was widespread poverty for many rectors. A fund of £12,000 was established in England and administered by Primate Beresford, who had himself given £2,400 and encouraged the Irish bishops to give a further £8,000. The wealthier incumbents of Armagh also subscribed to the fund – all in vain. The government was forced to act and agreed to pay £64,000 to the rectors who had lost their incomes. The sum was at first to be a loan, but had soon to be transformed into a gift and eventually became a fund of £1 million.

The government was slow to adopt the only realistic solution: the abolition of tithes. Opinion in parliament was deeply divided. A reform of the whole system of the Church of Ireland had become inevitable after Catholic Emancipation in 1829. Both Daniel O'Connell and Bishop Doyle were alarmed at the hostility towards all clergy, whether Roman Catholic or Protestant. The tithe dispute in Ireland was turning into a political issue on which governments rose or fell. The Church Temporalities Act of 1833 was an early response. Both primates – Whately with enthusiasm, Beresford, reluctantly – recognized that change must come. Disestablishment had entered the political agenda, but was as yet a profoundly offensive proposition to almost all the clergy of the Church of Ireland. At the parochial level, the Church was to all intents and purposes disestablished already. After the Church Temporalities Act of 1833, real power was exercised by the church commissioners and their civil servants. The commissioners commanded an income thanks to the transfer to them of the revenues of the sees that were suppressed when they fell vacant. After Beresford's tenure, the revenue of the archbishopric of Armagh would be reduced by £4,500 and immediately £4,160 was taken from the bishop of Derry's emoluments. Clergy with stipends of more than £300 had to pay a 5 per cent tax on their incomes. Those with incomes of £1,500 were to pay a 15 per cent levy. These arrangements were expected to yield £60,000 a year, which could be used to buy glebes where they were wanting, to subsidize house-building and enhance stipends. The commissioners were to pay for com-

---

25 Bowen, *Protestant crusade*, p. 168.

munion wine, cleaning and heating churches and for the washing of surplices and
linen. One concession was that the stipends of curates were to be deducted from
the taxable income of incumbents. The church after 1833 was to be run by civil
servants: it was a change that affected the life of every clergyman.

Friendly relationships between Church of Ireland clergy and Catholic priests
were still to be found in the early nineteenth century, but in some places there was
increasing tension and bitterness. Controversies such as those that had prevailed
in the early seventeenth century revived. Evangelicals were keen to make converts
and to attack Roman errors. This greater activism had been stimulated by the regular tours, almost every year, by the English Methodist, John Wesley. The first
clearly Evangelical rector was Thomas Tighe of Drumgooland in County Down,
who was appointed in 1778. Tighe had been educated at Cambridge, and had listened to Romaine and his evangelical fellowship. In 1805, Tighe's curate, Benjamin
Mathias, became a popular preacher in the Bethesda chapel in Dublin, where his
unlicensed preaching attracted Dubliners.[26] Students from Trinity College,
although forbidden to attend, listened, and shared many of his ideas. The approach
of the young at Trinity was also shaped by the regius professor of divinity, the
Revd Joseph Stringer, and the professor of Hebrew, the Revd Joseph Stopford,
who introduced considerable innovations in the training of those preparing for
ordination. Stopford stressed not only biblical studies, but pastoral care, and to the
latter end brought the students into schools and the Dublin charities. They were
encouraged to approach the ministry with pastoral earnestness. Greater care in the
preparation of ordinands was welcomed by Archbishop Beresford. The Primate
backed the efforts of Professor Henthorn Todd at Trinity College, Dublin, to
introduce examinations in a two-year course to precede ordination. Beresford
believed that the clergy must offer an example through their biblical knowledge,
pastoral dutifulness and acceptance of the theology of the church. He saw care-
lessness in administration as a betrayal of trust. In his own diocese, would-be clergy and the chaplains who examined them were furnished with an impressive
selection of books to be studied. Beresford left clergy in Armagh in no doubt that
theirs was a profession that required hard work and continuing care for parishioners. In addition, he urged incumbents to establish schools and oversee the quality of teaching within them.

One profoundly influenced by Stopford was the Revd Peter Roe, who was
appointed curate of St Mary's church in Kilkenny in 1800. Roe's rector was so
impressed that he resigned his living in 1805 on the understanding that Bishop
Hamilton would then appoint Roe to take the place. In 1801, Roe claimed to have
been converted to a new understanding of the ministry: 'I have reason to bless
God, that I have found the ways of religion ways of pleasantness, and though I was
always moral, yet until this year had I never known that I was far from God.'[27]

---

26 For Mathias, see J. Crawford, *The Church of Ireland in Victorian Dublin* (Dublin, 2005), pp
35–6.   27 Madden, *Peter Roe*, p. 27.

In 1798, Bishop O'Beirne of Ossory had invited his clergy to join him once monthly to study scripture. When O'Beirne left in that year, Roe succeeded in persuading twenty-four of his fellow clergy to join him in the first clerical society. The new bishop's son, Hans Hamilton, became the chief supporter of Roe. His father used the money he received as compensation for the abolition of the two parliamentary seats for the bishop's borough of St Canice in 1800 in an unusual fashion. He set up a health scheme. He appointed public health inspectors for the city of Kilkenny. The Revd Peter Roe, in charge of the main city parish, was appointed inspector for that parish and did much to improve living conditions. The innovative scheme seems to have lapsed when, in 1805, Hamilton moved on. His successor forbade Roe to hold his clerical meetings, but, despite the prohibition, they continued. Roe worked so hard that he saved time by taking his lunch of beer and cheese in the vestry. His ministry to the regiments of the city garrison was judged particularly successful. Roe was well-known to English evangelicals, met William Wilberforce and preached for John Newton. He ministered in Kilkenny for forty years.[28]

Another evangelical centre was established at Powerscourt in County Wicklow. The family of Lord Powerscourt followed the lead of the rector Robert Daly, a prominent evangelical. A brother of Lord Powerscourt became a noted preacher and anti-Roman controversialist. Lady Powerscourt eventually left the Church of Ireland and became a follower of the Revd Nelson Derby in the Brethren movement. Wives and daughters of prominent church members were active in many initiatives focussed on the parish, such as the establishment and running of Sunday schools.

New evangelical societies fostered their distinctive approach in many places. In 1818, the Irish Society was established to print tracts and bibles in Irish. In 1828, the Home Mission Society was founded to preach the gospel in Irish throughout the island. The Society was supported by leading evangelicals such as Joseph Singer, Robert Daly and Benjamin Mathias. In 1831, Edward Nangle began his mission to Achill Island. He opened schools and a dispensary. In order to protect his converts from persecution, he created a Protestant colony, similar to that already established by Lord Ventry on the Dingle peninsula. In 1849, Bishop Plunket confirmed 400 converts, though many emigrated from Achill during the famine, but in 1883 Nangle's successor still ministered to 208 parishioners even though forty-two had emigrated in that year.[29]

By 1849, the Irish Church Missions founded in London was a dominant force in the work of conversion. Some Irish peers with large estates supported them actively. Bishop Plunket encouraged them to work in Tuam, and Singer and Daly,

28 On Roe, see: W.G. Neely, *Kilkenny: an urban history, 1391–1843* (Belfast, 1989), pp 156, 231, 235, 237, 242, 251. 29 For the episode: I. Whelan, 'Edward Nangle and the Achill mission, 1834–52' in R. Gillespie and G. Moran (eds), *'A various country': essays in Mayo history* (Westport, 1987), pp 113–34.

both by then Irish bishops, backed them. The Revd Alexander Dallas was dedicated to the cause of this Society, but by the time of his death in 1869 it was clear that the second reformation had yet to come to pass in Ireland. Meanwhile relationships between the separate confessions had been embittered. The charge of 'souperism' had become a settled part of Irish folk lore in a country where hatred could characterize interdenominational dealings. 'Souperism' also became an element in the propaganda of the land war.[30] A partisan press fed the hostility with constant attacks on the clergy of the Church of Ireland. Akenson summed up the position of the evangelicals within the established church:

> There is no precise date on which the Church of Ireland became evangelical. Although the movement began in the eighteenth century and gathered force, it was not until the mid-nineteenth that the church could be safely described as predominantly evangelical and its was only after disestablishment that it became overwhelmingly so.[31]

Most evangelicals were rigid in their use of the Book of Common Prayer. Only extremists desired any change; most were content not to stress words capable of a high-church interpretation.

Not all who welcomed conversions from Catholicism were evangelicals. The Revd W.A. Fisher was a tractarian, landlord and rector of Crookhaven in County Cork. He was a converted Quaker. The region suffered terribly during the famine after 1846, and lost 5,000 of its population.[32] Fisher found himself the only clergyman in the district. There was no Roman Catholic priest left. Fisher, when he learnt that the ecclesiastical canon called on rectors to ring a bell daily for confessions, he decided to do so in order that people might know when to come. He sometimes spent the whole day hearing confessions. His church was crowded with converts, to the extent that he built a special church for them and two schools. He was so busy that he had to employ a curate. He welcomed rather than sought converts. His ability to preach in the Irish language gained him a larger audience. Two of the neighbouring incumbents died of famine fever. Wives and daughters of the clergy also gave their lives in attending the sick and starving. The Quakers discovered that the local rector was the sole person who could be trusted fairly to distribute the relief. The committees were praised unstintingly for their work.

Archbishop Trench gave encouragement to men like the landlord of Clifden in County Galway, who built a church and appointed an evangelical rector. He tried to be a just landlord, but he was ruined by the famine and had to sell his estate. Bishop Plunket ordained him in 1851 and appointed him rector so that he could

30 On the issue: D. Bowen, *Souperism: myth or reality* (Cork, 1970).   31 Akenson, *The Church of Ireland*, p. 132.   32 J.B. Carson, *Forty years in the Church of Ireland or the pastor, the parish and its people* (London, n.d.); P. Hickey, *Famine in West Cork* (Cork, 2002), pp 67–8, 145, 150, 162, 168, 208, 231, 236–8, 243–58, 352–3.

continue his work. At the time, that part of Mayo had only two small Church of Ireland parishes; by 1862, there were twenty-five. Clifden's regular congregation grew from twenty to 300 under Hyacinth D'Arcy.

The 1820s saw public debates between champions of the Roman Catholic and Church of Ireland positions. In 1824, Robert Daly, with the help of Edward Wingfield, organized a challenge to the Roman Catholics in Carlow, but such was the opposition that Daly and Wingfield had to flee over the wall of the backyard of the meeting place. Even more ambitious was a six-day debate in Dublin between the Revd Richard Pope and Father Tom Maguire in 1827. Both sides claimed victory, but little of permanence was achieved. Daniel O'Connell had taken the chair and served only to increase bitterness. Resentments worsened after Catholic emancipation. Church of Ireland clergy, faced with more assertive Roman Catholics, were often fearful and resentful.

Most clergymen were hostile to the teachings of the Church of Rome and contemptuous of priests trained at Maynooth. A minority became even more extreme in its outlook. Tresham Dames Gregg preached without charity and condemned everything Roman. Gregg, a Hebrew scholar, had a base as chaplain of St Nicholas within, in the city of Dublin. His intemperate language made him something of a hero among the still substantial Protestant working class in the area around Harold's Cross. With his prestige, Gregg founded the Protestant Operatives Association. In 1838, he joined Nangle in another challenge to Father Maguire. The result was that Gregg was imprisoned for a week as a disturber of the peace. Archbishop Whately was so outraged by Gregg's behaviour that in 1842 he revoked his licence to preach. But Gregg enjoyed popular backing. Thanks to the chaplaincy of an undissolved chantry he acquired a post for which he did not need archiepiscopal approval. Secure in this pulpit, he thundered forth to large congregations until he died in 1881. He was not exclusively populist. In 1853 he was awarded the degree of doctor of divinity by Trinity College. He successfully upheld his legal rights at disestablishment, but in later years was obsessed with obscure and partly unintelligible mysticism inspired by studying the Book of Revelation.[33] No less extreme was R.G. McGhee of Harold's Cross. He saw the new national schools as the work of the devil. As a result he was condemned by a distinguished convert from Rome, William Phelan, for saying he would rather see children doomed to hell by their attendance of the schools. Archdeacon Stopford of Armagh led an attack on McGhee's extreme opinions. In 1846, McGhee left Ireland to take up an appointment in an English parish.

Phelan was one of several converts from Roman Catholicism. He had been horrified by an allegation of a priest in Clonmel, that the admired schoolmaster, the Revd Richard Carey, was assuredly destined for hell as a heretic. Three boys from

---

33 Bowen, *Protestant crusade*, p. 109; Crawford, *The Church of Ireland in Victorian Dublin*, pp 24, 40, 56, 154, 157, 164.

the school – two brothers, Mortimer and Samuel O'Sullivan and Phelan – went on to Trinity College and then were ordained. Samuel O'Sullivan became chaplain to the Hibernian Military School in Dublin and was a bitter opponent of Roman Catholicism. Mortimer O'Sullivan and Phelan adopted a more moderate approach. Phelan, a considerable scholar and fellow of Trinity, quarrelled with the college authorities, but was given a curacy in Keady by Archbishop Beresford of Armagh, before being appointed to the parish of Killyman in 1827. Phelan wrote a history of the Church of Ireland, defending its claim to be the Catholic church in Ireland. Beresford thought so highly of him that he nominated him as a witness in the enquiry by the House of Lords committee into the state of the church. Mortimer O'Sullivan, an able preacher, was chosen by Beresford as his contact with the Orange Order. Such work belonged to the process which moved O'Sullivan towards a more extreme Protestant stance, influenced by a growing conviction that the Catholic clergy were adopting an extreme ultramontane position.

Dean Kirwan of Killala, like Bishop O'Beirne a convert, never denounced the teachings of Rome. Instead, he preferred to gain a reputation as the foremost charity preacher of his day. Fashionable Dublin flocked to hear him. He was rector of St Nicholas Without in Dublin and prebendary of Howth until the lord lieutenant, Cornwallis, gave him his deanery in 1800. In his sermons, it was said of Kirwan, 'the preacher's desk became the throne of light'. His aim was 'to fill the human breast with godlike forbearance, amity and love'. Indeed, Kirwan's comment on the history of religious strife and persecution was 'there is no species of history which a benevolent man or well-wisher to the human race reads with less pleasure or rather with more disgust than the ecclesiastical annals'. Kirwan was an example that shone in dark days when the pulpit was all too often dominated by Tresham Gregg and his type.

The strident and aggressive might command attention. Yet, others through their quieter labours excited at least local admiration. The intelligent and liberal-minded Elizabeth Grant, who came to live in County Wicklow, failed to see enough that was Christ-like in many of the clergy. Earlier she had complained about the Scottish clerics, 'but the Christian pastor, humble and gentle and considerate and self-sacrificing, occupied with the duties and filled with a charity of his master, had no representative as far as I could see among the dealers in old wares and rich dinners, old wines and bone china and massive plate'. She recognized the dangers for the clergy: 'one can be perpetually busy in the Lord's work, yet lose sight of the Lord'.[34] Yet there were those with quieter but durable achievements to their credit. William Sewell was one of the four founders of St Columba's College in Dublin.[35] St Columba's was a bold experiment, with its ideal of an Irish-speaking

34 Elizabeth Grant, *The highland lady in Ireland: journals, 1840–50*, ed. P. Pelly and A. Tod (Edinburgh, 1991)   35 The others were the earl of Dunraven, William Monsell, MP for Limerick, and James Henthorn Todd, professor of Hebrew at TCD. See below, p. 228.

clergy and landowners working for a nation united in sympathy. 'Through many vicissitudes and every sort of difficulty, St Columba's has carried on gallantly in its beautiful home, faithful to the ideas of its founders and sending out a steady stream of gentlemen for the service of Ireland.' The suspicion of evangelicals, the conversion to Rome of Dunraven and Monsell, and the resignation of the first warden were considerable blows. Nevertheless, St Columba's continued with sung services of morning and evening prayer and with the use of the Irish language and imbued the school with a religious ethos that persisted.[36]

A new sense of professionalism appeared from 1814 when Richard Graves, professor of divinity (at TCD) introduced a voluntary examination that could be taken with any obligation to pass by divinity students. It was a sign of new times. Attendance at lectures was required for two years instead of one. Some bishops, like John George Beresford, encouraged study and turned the examination of deacons and priests into real tests. Beresford drew up a list of books to be studied and on which his chaplains would examine candidates. Bishop John Law (in succession bishop of Clonfert, Killala and Elphin) urged clergy to share his conclusion that they ought to be useful agents of evangelization. 'Unable to make the peasants around me good Protestants, I ask to make them good Catholics, good citizens, good anything.'[37] Behind this lay the conviction that clergymen ought to be useful and ought to promote good in their communities. So Bishop Law encouraged priests to study the best available Roman Catholic books.

It is possible to cite other examples of the best and worst clergy. John Jebb as bishop of Limerick between 1823 and 1833 was regarded with respect, but his successor was an absentee. Bishop Hugh Hamilton saw the whole of Kilkenny as his responsibility. The evangelical Roe supported Hamilton in his efforts to improve the life of the town. When the bishop was compensated for the loss of the parliamentary seat of St Canice, he introduced a system of public health inspectors, Roe accepted one of the positions as an appropriate complement to being rector of St Mary's, Kilkenny. The scheme came to nothing because of Hamilton's early death in 1805. The bishop of Ossory from 1813 to 1841, Robert Fowler, did his best to destroy the clerical society founded by O'Beirne and promoted by Roe. Fowler owed his initial preferment to his father, the archbishop of Dublin. As rector of Sion Mills the younger Fowler had lived with his mistress. Despite setbacks, such as the flight to England of the younger Hans Hamilton (Bishop Hamilton's son) and Bishop Fowler's hostility, Roe continued the society until his death in 1845.

Men of probity and dedication could overcome a defective system. Lord John George Beresford was appointed archbishop of Armagh thanks to the political importance of his family. It is said that Beresford earned £800,000 as a bishop. Less remarked is the fact that he kept a separate banking account for his clerical income into which every penny was paid, with the rule that it must be spent before

36 Lionel James, *A forgotten genius: Sewell of St Columba's and Radley* (London, 1944), p. 120.
37 R. Wyse Jackson, *Scenes from Irish clerical life* (Limerick, 1941), p. 31.

the end of the year for the good of the church and clergy. Beresford was not unique. Power Le Poer Trench became a bishop thanks to his successful administration of the family estates. His whole life changed when he challenged his archdeacon at Emly, Digby, for preaching the necessity of conversion. Archdeacon Digby convinced him that this was the true doctrine of the church. As archbishop of Tuam, Trench's whole concern was to find evangelical clergy and appoint them to his western parishes. He established a boys' Sunday school and conducted bible study. On his translation to Tuam, Trench determined to appoint none but bible preachers to his parishes. He paid for additional curates in some parishes. It was left to his successor in Tuam, Thomas Plunket, to build on these foundations. The local Roman Catholic press wrote of 'thousands deserting the altars of their fathers'. John Jebb, although no evangelical, set an example in his sermons of preaching highly spiritual and moral doctrine. Other clergy demonstrated their usefulness by acting as magistrates in their localities. Near the end of the eighteenth century, no fewer than 300 clerics held this office: often they were the only active magistrates in the area.[38]

Many clergy involved themselves in agricultural improvements. Henry Maxwell, bishop of Meath, introduced English breeds of cattle. The Revd Thomas Percy, nephew of the bishop of Dromore, brought the true Berkshire breed of pigs into County Antrim. The Revd Daniel Beaufort popularized a patent drill in County Louth. Another country clergyman, William Richardson, also a fellow of Trinity, vigorously expounded the value of applying science, especially to the culture of different grasses.[39] Clerical members of the St George family subsidized improvements in the breeds of sheep by paying to import rams. The Revd George St George, while rector of Kilcooley, gave twenty guineas towards such imports. Jebb summed up the situation: 'a parish minister should possess an active, bustling disposition, with some turn for agricultural pursuits and much fondness for introducing habits of sobriety, industry, cleanliness and comfort among the lower orders'.[40]

The clergy in practising and encouraging improvements stood to benefit financially as the yield of tithes and glebe lands increased. Some of these improvements manifested themselves in new churches and glebe houses. Further aid came from the Board of First Fruits. Between 1786 and 1806, 210 churches were built and 209 glebes purchased. Yet, notwithstanding the activity, 34 per cent of the clergy were still returned as non-residents. Bit by bit, the situation improved, until a later observer could conclude, 'there is justice in the claim that good men laboured to keep the light of religion alive'. [41]

38 R.B. McDowell, *Ireland in the age of imperialism and revolution, 1760–1801* (Oxford, 1979), p. 169.   39 Ibid., pp 8–9.   40 Ibid., p. 170.   41 Wyse Jackson, *Scenes from Irish clerical life*, p. 32.

8

'An overriding providence': the life and ministry of Tresham Dames Gregg (1800–81)

John Crawford

Tresham Dames Gregg's strident anti-Catholicism, his championing of the Dublin Protestant working class in the late 1830s and 1840s during a period of political change and economic depression, and his insistence on a seamless link between the established church and the British state made him a household name in Dublin and throughout Ireland and Britain, during the nineteenth century.[1] Indeed as recently as 1932, the year of the Catholic Eucharistic Congress and the 1,500th anniversary of the arrival of St Patrick on the shores of Ireland, his anti-Catholic outlook was resurrected in the ultamontane and anti-Protestant *Catholic Bulletin*. The article on 'Greggism' was used as a bat to beat a Protestant archbishop of Dublin, John Alan Fitzgerald Gregg, who simply happened to share the same surname.[2] At the beginning of the twenty-first century we are at somewhat of a disadvantage as we are removed in time from the mentalities of ultra-Protestants like Tresham Dames Gregg and, for that matter, of his nineteenth century contemporaries of all shades of opinion. If we are to understand such militant evangelicals, it is necessary to take seriously their unswerving belief in an overriding providence of God in the daily events of human life and their intense preoccupation with biblical prophecy and the interpretation of 'the signs of the times', with detailed exegesis of texts and a search for 'truth' in the biblical books of Daniel and Revelation.[3] Gregg's passionate belief in the supernatural and in prophetic and mystical interpretations of the Bible and his preoccupation with 'the evils of popery' personified in the papacy, 'the antichrist', is an element found, to

---

1 Jacqueline Hill, 'The Protestant response to repeal: the case of the Dublin working class' in F.S.L. Lyons and R.A.J. Hawkins (eds), *Ireland under the Union: varieties of tension* (Oxford, 1980), pp 35–68; T.D. Gregg to Benjamin Disraeli, 1845–71, Bodleian Library, Oxford, Hughenden MS 129/3/B/xxi/9/326–49.   2 P.M. Lynch, 'Greggism' in *Catholic Bulletin*, xxii (January–December 1932), pp 568–71, 646–9; George Seaver, *John Allen Fitzgerald Gregg: archbishop* (London and Dublin, 1963), pp 191–2.   3 T.D. Gregg to Benjamin Disraeli, 24 March 1846, Hughenden MS 129/3.

some extent, in all ultra-Evangelicals of nineteenth-century Protestantism in Britain, Ireland and America. Evangelicalism and apocalyptic speculation went hand-in-hand. At the heart of such belief was that personal circumstances were to be borne patiently and cheerfully within the providence of God because the lonely battle against the antichrist of Rome was of cosmic significance.[4]

By the time Tresham Dames Gregg was born in Green Street, Dublin, on 11 August 1800,[5] the eldest son of Hugh Gregg (*c.*1775–1805) and Martha Dames (1780–1874), the Gregg family had roots in the city stretching back to at least the late seventeenth century. Hugh Gregg (*c.*1710–87) was 'an eminent peruke maker' living on High Street in St Audoen's parish and a member of the Guild of Barber-Surgeons, for many years representing the guild on the common council of Dublin Corporation.[6] His son, Tresham Gregg (1751–1809) was also a wig-maker, barber-surgeon and guild member until his election by the corporation as governor of Newgate prison, Green Street, in 1792, a position he held until his death in 1809. Gregg family tradition has it that during the 1798 rebellion he alerted the city authorities to imminent attacks by the rebels on Dublin castle and Newgate prison and arrested Lord Edward FitzGerald and took him into custody as he, with others, tried to scale the wall of the prison. Gregg, it is suggested, also had care of Robert Emmet in Newgate before his transfer to Kilmainham jail and execution in 1803 for his part in the abortive rebellion in that year.[7] Gregg's father, Hugh Gregg (1775–1805) died prematurely in Kilkenny 'after a long and painful illness' and, apart from his marriage to Martha Dames and the birth of two sons, nothing is known of his short life or, indeed, why he was in Kilkenny when he died. His widow, Martha, referred to as 'a women of singular energy and mental power',[8] remarried in 1816 to German-born Gregor von Feinaigle (1760–1819), an educationalist, mnemonist and a former Cistercian monk, who, after developing his educational theories on artificial memory at the Catholic Ampleforth School in

4 For the thinking of nineteenth century ultra-Evangelicals see Desmond Bowen, *The Protestant crusade in Ireland, 1800–70* (Dublin, 1978); John Wolffe, *The Protestant crusade in Great Britain, 1829–1860* (Oxford, 1991); Timothy C.F. Stunt, *From awakening to secession: radical evangelicals in Switzerland and Britain, 1815–35* (Edinburgh, 2000); Grayson Carter, *Anglican evangelicals: Protestant secessions from the Via Media, c.1800–1850* (Oxford, 2001).   5 Statutory declaration, Martha Feinaigle, 19 Sept.1829, in connection with Gregg's ordination to the priesthood, the archdiocese of York, Borthwick Institute, York, InstitAB/19/1821–31. Hugh Gregg and Martha Dames had a second son, Gilmore Dames Gregg who was a magistrate in Jamaica and died *c.*1880.   6 Guild of St Mary Magdalene; see Mary Clark and Raymond Refaussé (eds), *Directory of historic Dublin guilds* (Dublin, 1993), p.15; Hugh Gregg was son of Hugh Gregg and Mary Woodward who married in St Andrew's church, Dublin, 1706/7; he married Rose Tresham in St Audoen's church, Dublin, 1740.   7 J.T. Gilbert (ed.), *Calendar of ancient records of Dublin* (19 vols, Dublin, 1889–1944), xiv, p.147; xv, p.510; I am grateful to Colonel Tresham Dames Gregg, Penrith, Cumbria and Dr Henry Hutchings, Darlington, Co Durham, for the history and family tree of the Gregg family. Amazingly, the names 'Tresham Dames' have occurred in eight successive generations of the Gregg family since Gregg's birth in 1800.   8 Burial register, St Mary's parish, Kilkenny, 3 Dec. 1805; 'The late Madam von Feinaigle', in *Irish*

Yorkshire, came to Dublin in 1812.[9] He presented his theories to assemblies at the Rotunda and the Royal Dublin Society and was immediately encouraged (with financial support) to establish a number of Protestant schools in the city according to his educational principles, including a boarding school, the Feinaiglian Institution, at Aldborough House, opened in 1813, which he renamed 'the Luxembourg'. Feinaigle's system was not original but he had a recognised skill in presenting traditional methods of artificial memory as a rational way of remembering quantities of information.[10] Gregg's mother looked after the domestic arrangements at the Luxembourg, and Feinaigle opened a female school, with her help, at Clonliffe in 1815. Martha Feinaigle was later matron of the Rotunda Lying-in Hospital and lived with Gregg and his family at Sandymount, Dublin, to the ripe old age of ninety-four.[11]

Gregg was educated at the Luxembourg school and was taught first by his stepfather and, after his sudden death in 1819, by his successor as headmaster, the Revd John Hawksworth, a Congregationalist minister.[12] Here Gregg studied not only the Greek and Latin authors and logic but also had his first taste of mathematics and Hebrew which were to form an important basis for his often obscure writings in later life.[13] The school was in no way narrowly Protestant and offered a liberal education according to Feinaigle's system of artificial memory. Modern languages, drawing, history, elocution and geography formed part of the curriculum 'to habitually exercise the reasoning powers and thoroughly develop the intellectual faculties'. After the death of John Hawksworth in 1838 Gregg was appointed headmaster of the school and was blamed for its demise and closure a few years later. On taking up the headmastership of the school in 1838, Gregg uncompromisingly vowed that

Builder, xv (15 Sept. 1874), p. 77. **9** Marriage register, St Thomas's parish, Dublin, 3 July 1816; John Millard (ed.), *The new art of memory founded upon the principles of M. Gregor von Feinaigle to which is added some account of the principal systems of artificial memory* (3rd edn, London, 1813); A. Brian Laver, 'Gregor Feinaigle: mnemonist and educator' in *Journal of the History of Behavioural Sciences*, xv, no. 1 (Jan. 1979), pp 18–28. **10** *First half-yearly report of the committee of the Feinaiglian Institution* (Dublin, 1814), p. 6. **11** Michael Quane, 'The Feinaiglian Institution, Dublin' in *Dublin Historical Record*, xix (1963–4), pp 30–44 (I am grateful to the Revd Terence Richardson, Ampleforth Abbey, Yorkshire, for details of his research on Feinaigle); Alan Browne, *Masters, midwives and ladies-in-waiting: the Rotunda hospital, 1745–1995* (Dublin, 1995), p. 135. **12** Hawksworth, a minister of the Countess of Huntingdon's Connection, who established a congregation in Plunket Street, Dublin, in the early 1770s; he was headmaster of the Feinaiglian Institution, 1820–1838; Boyd S. Schlenther, *Queen of the Methodists: the countess of Huntingdon and the eighteenth-century crisis of faith and society* (Durham, 1997). **13** See, for example, *Suggestions as to the employment of a novum organum moralium, or thoughts on the attainment of demonstration and certainty in moral matters* (London, 1859); *The mystery of God finished in the final discovery of his counsels to mankind for the bringing in of the new dispensation* (London, 1861); *The way, the truth and the life: a series of discourses on scriptural subjects with an appendix on Christian philosophy* (London, 1861).

I'll make better Latin, Greek and Hebrew scholars than they can do at Eton
or Harrow, Westminster or Rugby, and their reading shall all be divine; they
shall learn these out of the Holy Bible while I am endeavouring in every
way to make their Latin, Greek and Hebrew convert their souls. My grand,
my chief, my principal business, shall be to convert souls and I know that in
that way I shall best promote their interests as scholars.[14]

He abandoned much of the liberal educational theory of his stepfather replacing
it with an outright Protestant and anti-Catholic bias which apparently did not
appeal to the school's middle class clientele. His replacement of the classical
authors with detailed study of the Bible in Hebrew, Greek and Latin was the
proverbial kiss of death to the school coupled with a decline in the north city where
it was located making it less appealing to the school's supporters. By 1846 the
school had become a military barracks.[15]

Gregg entered Trinity College, Dublin, in 1821 as a late entrant and may well
have delayed entrance to university to assist the teachers in the Luxembourg school
following his stepfather's death. Despite his liberal education at his stepfather's
school, his Dublin background meant that he was

imbued with very decided Protestant feelings and had been taught to regard
popery as an irrational and anti-scriptural system. The opportunities
afforded me from having spent much of my early years among Roman
Catholics … quite confirmed all the reasonings against popery that were
brought before me in the circle of my family and acquaintance.[16]

His experience of university life and the movement for Catholic emancipation
changed his viewpoint for a time as he 'read the newspapers and took an interest in
the opinions of public men'. He attended meetings of the Catholic Association and
developed a high regard for the abilities of Daniel O'Connell, a regard which
remained with him in later life despite O'Connell's differing political views on
church and state. However, it was during the same period, influenced as much by
his family background in the high church evangelical tradition of the Church of
Ireland, as by the vital religion he experienced in Trinity College,[17] he became
firmly convinced of 'the truth of the claims of the Church of Ireland to be the one,
holy, catholic and apostolic church of this land' established by law and, not unusually for the time, underwent an intense personal religious conversion:

14 *Irish Builder*, xvi (15 December 1875), pp 251–2.   15 Jacinta Prunty, *Dublin slums, 1800–
1925: a study of urban geography* (Dublin, 1998), chapter 8; Maurice Craig, *Dublin, 1660–1860*
(London, 1992), p. 233.   16 T.D. Gregg, *Free thoughts on Protestant matters* (Dublin, 1845), pp
152–7.   17 Joseph Leichty, 'Irish evangelicalism, Trinity College, Dublin and the mission of the
Church of Ireland at the end of the eighteenth century', unpublished PhD thesis, St Patrick's
College, Maynooth (1987).

> At length after various fruitless attempts to obtain legal justification, it occurred to me to try to be saved in the way I had so often heard but disregarded ... I pleaded the merits of a Saviour's death ... the depths of midnight darkness and miserable despondency were succeeded by a bright assurance of acceptance and the hope of full immortality. I had experienced the power of the Holy Spirit, a spiritual baptism; to be a true Christian a man must be born again.[18]

Thus Gregg's life of evangelical zeal, firmly set in the established Church of Ireland, began as he went the same night to his tutor, a Hebrew scholar, for counsel and advice.

By all accounts he excelled in his academic career in Trinity College and graduated in 1826 with university awards in Hebrew and mathematics. For two years he taught in Luxembourg school in Dublin and may well have been a teacher at a similar school established in about 1830 at Nore View, Kilkenny, where his father, Hugh Gregg, died in 1805, and where he was ordained deacon in the Church of Ireland by the bishop of Ossory, Robert Fowler, in 1828. By the end of 1829 he had left Ireland for England and was successively perpetual curate of Earlsheaton in the parish of Dewsbury, 1829–33, and curate-assistant of St George's parish, Sheffield, 1833–7, and ordained priest by the archbishop of York in 1830.[19] In seeking ordination at the hands of the archbishop he was in no way reluctant in telling him of his good ordering of his rural cure of Earlsheaton:

> I most humbly take the liberty of informing your Grace that since I have come here the congregation has considerably increased and, with the divine blessing, may continue to do so. That likewise I am stirring up the people to raise amongst them £200 as an augmentation to the estate (if I may call it so) of the church ... This sum laid out on the purchase of land yielding four per cent would, with the pew rents, make the living worth £76 per annum, a sum at least adequate to the support of a moderate person which, may it please your Grace, the present sum is not.[20]

It is not clear why he went to England. He may have been directed there through evangelical links between Kilkenny and Yorkshire. The Revd Peter Roe, the evangelical incumbent of St Mary's, Kilkenny, preached a number of times in Pannel parish church, Knaresborough in the late 1810s. Gregg married Sarah Pearson, daughter of Samuel Pearson of Pannel Hall, Knaresborough, in Christ Church,

---

18 Gregg, *Free thoughts*, pp 152–3.   19 W.J. Phelan, 'A forgotten Kilkenny school' in *Old Kilkenny Review*, x (1958), pp 27–30; ordination papers, Bp. Fowler of Ossory to Abp Vernon Harcourt of York, 18 Nov. 1829; Gregg's ordination as priest, 2 Feb. 1830, Borthwick Institute, York, InstitAB/19/1821–31.   20 T.D. Gregg to Abp Vernon Harcourt of York, 13 Jan. 1829, Borthwick Institute, York, InstAB/19/1821–31.

Harrogate, in 1832 and by whom he had seven children.[21] His experience of ministry in the growing slums and tenements of the industrial revolution in Leeds and Sheffield, and his observations on the Irish migrants working there, confirmed to him as an Irishman 'their ignorance and unthinking commitment to the superstitious tyranny of popery'. In Yorkshire he first entered into the public arena of the Roman controversy with public lectures which were later published, first in a local evangelical journal, the *Witness*, and later in a pamphlet and book in his own name. At this time he also republished a work by the seventeenth century scholar and philosopher, Joseph Mede, with his own commentary.[22]

On a visit to Dublin in early 1837, Gregg discovered that the trustees of Swift's Alley Free church were seeking the services of a chaplain and he applied for the position. He was appointed to begin work immediately on a salary of £100 per annum.[23] The chapel, located between Francis Street and Meath Street, in St Catherine's parish, had recently been purchased from the Baptists as a proprietary, or trustee, chapel by a number of evangelical Church of Ireland clergy and laymen, among them the dean of St Patrick's cathedral, Henry Dawson, the incumbent of St Catherine's parish, John Hastings, the minister of Trinity church, Gardiner Street, John Gregg, and Thomas 'Tract' Parnell, secretary of the evangelical Book and Tract Society. The chapel opened to serve the needs of the Protestant working class and, doubtless, to engage in proselytism among the majority Catholic population of the area.[24] The trustees of the chapel must have been well pleased with their new chaplain and Gregg, in turn, was developing his theology around the Roman controversy and becoming more certain of his motives for returning to Ireland and to his native city of Dublin:

> I felt extremely anxious to devote my labours to the service of Ireland. The exceedingly degraded condition which a vast number of poor Irish, who reside in England, are reduced to is very humbling and painful to the mind of an Irish clergyman resident in that country ... I was anxious to obtain a position in the Irish Church where I might be able to bring my energies to bear against the degrading system of Popery which is the true cause of the miseries of Ireland.[25]

21 Samuel Madden, *A memoir of the late Reverend Peter Roe* (Dublin, 1842), pp 279, 285, 292; marriage register, Christ Church , Harrogate, 21 Dec. 1832, Leeds District Archives; J.B. Leslie and W.J.R. Wallace, *Clergy of Dublin and Glendalough* (Belfast, 2001), pp 683–4.   22 T.D. Gregg, *Free thoughts on Protestant matter* (2nd edition, Dublin and London, 1847), pp 8–10; *The apostasy of the Roman Catholic church clearly demonstrated ... being a lecture delivered at Sheffield, Wakefield and Leeds by the Revd T.D. Gregg* (Sheffield, Wakefield and Leeds, 1835); *Mede's apostasy of the latter times with an introduction by the Revd T .D. Gregg* (Sheffield, 1836).   23 Trustee minutes, Swift's Alley Free church, 7 April 1837, RCBL, P345/5/1.   24 For the proprietary chapel movement in the Church of Ireland in Dublin see John Crawford, *The Church of Ireland in Victorian Dublin* (Dublin, 2005), pp 33–42, 178–80.   25 Gregg, *Free thoughts*, pp 8–9.

In a matter of months he had become well known in the city as an able controversial preacher with a significant following among the members of Protestant trade guilds, the freeman of the city, who were strong supporters of the orange institution. Though a contemporary speaks of him 'a very pious, ardent, good creature', in the Church of Ireland of the time more attention was paid to his ardour and it was not long until he was denounced by the Revd William de Burgh, among others, for describing the Catholic religion as idolatrous.[26]

Gregg himself considered his return to Dublin as auspicious, arriving as he did in the period following Catholic emancipation when Daniel O'Connell was renewing and strengthening his campaign for the repeal of the union and the reform of municipal politics then in the control of the Protestant minority. The late 1830s and early 1840s marked a period of economic depression in Dublin, especially in the textile industry traditionally associated with the Protestant artisan working class community in the city liberties, the parishes of St Catherine, St Luke and St Nicholas Without. Here Gregg threw in his lot with the Protestant working class and in 1841 founded the Dublin Protestant Operative Association to defend their rights against the repeal movement and the reform of municipal politics. The Association, under Gregg's leadership, stood out consistently against cooperation with Catholics for political ends with an uncompromising anti-Roman agenda.[27] All this went hand-in-hand with a heightened interest in apocalyptic prophecies and a revival in the 'no popery' cry which identified the papacy with the antichrist. In addition, the Napoleonic wars, and the social and economic upheavals which went with them, led to a bewilderment and anxiety among the artisan Protestants of Dublin which occasionally led to violent, but localised skirmishes with Catholics, often instigated by 'Gregg's lambs', the orange and trenchantly anti-Catholic residents of the men's home at Swift's Alley church.[28] Often Gregg required the protection of the police during his services in the church and when going about his business in the city and by this time he had already attracted a certain amount of public notoriety which he put down to his unswerving loyalty to divine providence and to the British church and state, a divine providence which led him to return to his native Dublin.[29] In 1838 he had a week-long public discussion on the religious and historical legitimacy of the established and Roman churches with a Catholic priest, Thomas Maguire, known in Catholic circles as 'Father Tom', parish priest of Ballinamore in County Leitrim, which attracted large crowds to the Round Room of the Rotunda who were willing to pay for the

26 William Arthur, *Life of Gideon Ouseley* (London and Toronto, 1876) pp 284–5; *Authenticated report of the discussion between the Revd T.D. Gregg and the Revd Thomas Maguire* (Dublin, 1839), p. xiii; William de Burgh, chaplain, Dublin Female Penitentiary, 1826–47; incumbent, St John's church, Sandymount, 1850–64. 27 T.D. Gregg, *Protestant ascendancy vindicated and national regeneration through the instrumentality of national religion urged* (Dublin, 1840); Gregg, *Free thoughts*, pp 33–5. 28 Hill, 'The Protestant response to repeal', pp 40–50. 29 Gregg, *Free thoughts*, pp 11–12.

privilege.[30] The debate ended in a stalemate, each side claiming victory over the other and correspondence continued between Gregg and Maguire and their respective supporters in the *Dublin Evening Post* and *Saunders' Newsletter* for the rest of the year.[31]

Some of his supporters in the Operative Association reported to him that a young Protestant girl, Ruth Hannah Wily, had been kidnapped and forced to enter a convent in George's Hill, Dublin, against her wishes. Gregg, with some of the girl's family and supporters, called to the convent on a mission of rescue but they were informed by the abbess that the girl was there of her own free will and had been accepted as a novice. This did not deter Gregg from referring to the convent as 'a house of witches' and part of 'the church of the devil'. A near riot ensued and the rumpus led to Gregg's arrest and his subsequent appearance in the police magistrate's court accused of a breach of the peace. In the ensuing court hearing, at which he appeared in his own defence, he refused to give the court an undertaking that he would enter into a £100 bond to keep the peace, describing one of the magistrates, Thomas Duffy, a Catholic, as 'an idolatrous judge', and ended up in the Richmond Bridewell for contempt of court until such time as his supporters persuaded him to accept that he had made his point and he, in turn, had accepted their offer to purge his contempt of court by paying the court bond.[32]

By this time he had clearly come to the notice, and, indeed, the censure of the archbishop of Dublin, Richard Whately, who had already refused, by default, to licence him as chaplain of Swift's Alley church, citing a defect in the church's original trust deed. In reality, Whately had an intense dislike for any form of Protestant extremism and he did all he could to exclude clergy like Gregg from his diocese. He had no sympathy with those who attacked the Roman Catholic religion and his perceived liberalism towards the church of Rome was the main reason for Whately's unpopularity, throughout his episcopate, with the evangelical constituency of the Church of Ireland in Dublin, especially among the artisan working class community of the city.[33] In early 1840 Gregg received an invitation from Hugh Prior, a personal friend and incumbent of Lucan in County Dublin to preach a controversial sermon in Lucan church. Significantly, Father Tom Maguire, Gregg's opponent in 'the great debate', had recently preached at the opening a a new Catholic church in Lucan. Whately, on hearing that Gregg was to preach in

---

30 For the career of the Revd Thomas Maguire see Prionnsíos Ó Duigneáin, *The priest and the Protestant woman: the trial of the Revd Thomas Maguire, P.P.*, Maynooth Studies in Local History (Dublin, 1997).   31 *Authenticated report of the discussion between the Revd T.D. Gregg and the Revd Thomas Maguire* (Dublin, 1839); Bowen, *The Protestant crusade in Ireland, 1800–70*, pp 106–9.   32 *An authentic report of the extraordinary case of the Revd T.D. Gregg, his committal to the Bridewell for refusing to give his recognizance and his speech before the magistrates with his letters to the Protestant public in vindication of himself* (Dublin, 1841).   33 Gregg, *Free thoughts*, pp 17–20; Crawford, *Church of Ireland*, pp 59–62; Donald H. Akenson, *A Protestant in purgatory: Richard Whately, archbishop of Dublin* (Hamden, 1981), pp 132–44.

such circumstances, immediately communicated with the churchwardens of Lucan parish inhibiting Gregg from preaching. Gregg was quite happy 'to submit to your Grace's pleasure' and did not preach. However, he immediately resigned his chaplaincy on the basis that the archbishop had, from the time of his appointment in 1837, left him 'in a position of irregularity without a licence to preach', and contended with the archbishop by letter on the issue but received no reply. The trustees of Swift's Alley church accepted his resignation and (obviously warned of their continued well-being as trustees by Whately) stated that 'because of the peculiar circumstances under which the resignation has taken place prevent the trustees from giving any opinion on the subject'.[34]

In a matter of months Gregg had found a new position in the church through his supporters among the Protestant artisan working class of the city. In May 1840 he was elected by the churchwardens and parishioners as chaplain, or chantry priest, of St Mary's chapel in the parish church of St Nicholas Within, a sinecure with an income of over £200, no church or chapel, and considered by the churchwardens and parishioners to be free from episcopal jurisdiction from the time of its foundation as a chantry in 1469.[35] The parish church (along with St Mary's chapel), in danger of imminent collapse, had been demolished by order of the ecclesiastical commissioners in 1836 and services were held in the school house in Patrick Street until the parish was united with that of St Audoen's in 1867.[36] Gregg's election to this sinecure was not without its difficulty as the archbishop put forward the Revd Richard Quaile Shannon as his candidate for the job. The election, held in the Tailors' Hall, Back Lane, returned 22 votes for Gregg and 39 for Shannon. It became clear to the churchwardens that nearly all those voting for Shannon were Catholics and they were of the view that only parishioners of St Nicholas Within who were members of the established church had the right to vote and, amidst heated exchanges, the meeting came to an abrupt end with one of the churchwardens, Luke Butler, declaring that he would take the matter to law. The case was heard in the court of the queen's bench in January 1841 when judgment was given in favour of the churchwardens and Gregg's election was confirmed. It was decided by the court that Catholics had no right to vote in the election, the revenue of the endowment had become 'protestant' at the reformation and could not be used for 'superstitious purposes', or be disposed of by those who adhered to the faith of the original donors.[37] Though the court proceedings

---

34 Gregg, *Free thoughts*, pp 8–25; *Christian Examiner and Church of Ireland Magazine*, 1 Feb. 1840, pp 59–62; trustee minutes, Swift's Alley Free church, 13 Jan. 1840, RCBL, P345/5/1. **35** Gregg, *Free thoughts*, pp 385–8; John Crawford, *Around the churches: the stories of the churches in the St Patrick's cathedral group of parishes* (Dublin, 1988), pp 46–9; for St Mary's chapel estate see *Fourth report of the commissioners of ecclesiastical revenue and patronage, Ireland*, H.C. 1837 (C500), xxi, pp 80–1; *Irish ecclesiastical directory for the year 1869* (Dublin, 1869), p. 122; St Nicholas Within, miscellaneous papers, Dublin diocesan registry, RCBL, D6/106. **36** *St Nicholas church, Dublin*, H.C. 1845 (C59), xliii; St Nicholas Within, Dublin diocesan registry, RCBL, D6/106; Crawford, *Around the churches*, pp 44–6. **37** M.J. Martyn, *The case of the Revd*

cost Gregg £200 (he appealed to the archbishop of Armagh for a refund but to not avail), it must have seemed a triumph for him and his supporters just at the moment when all seemed bleak for Dublin Protestants with the reform of city politics under the municipal reform act which would remove their power base on Dublin Corporation, change the political and religious makeup of that body and abolish the city guilds, traditionally Protestant.[38]

While there was nothing the archbishop could do to remove Gregg from his position as the elected chaplain in the parish of St Nicholas Within, he could refuse to allow him a licence to conduct services in his chaplaincy. Despite strenuous efforts by Gregg, and by the churchwardens and parishioners of St Nicholas Within, to establish his independence from episcopal control in what was seen as an ancient parish prerogative, in 1847 the diocesan consistorial court, before Joseph Radcliffe, the archbishop's vicar general, found in favour of the archbishop and in his judgement Radcliffe found, *inter alia,* that no acts were passed in Ireland to abolish chantries in parish churches and that the charter of 1469, under which the chantry and chaplain were appointed, endowed a chantry priest and at the reformation all duties of such priest ceased. It was only possible for Gregg to officiate as chaplain with the consent of Thomas Shore, the incumbent of the parish, and with the archbishop's licence.[39] In the 1840s and early 1850s the measure of Gregg's influence and the strength of his following is seen in the continued loyalty of the Dublin Protestant working class. A case in point is a committee set up in 1849 to raise funds to help defray Gregg's costs in the case brought against him by the archbishop of Dublin. Gregg refused to pay the costs himself and, to all intents and purposes, ignored the judgement of the court, using his title, 'chaplain of St Nicholas Within, Dublin', in his publications and preaching whenever opportunity arose.[40]

Following the reform of Dublin Corporation under the municipal reform act along with the abolition Protestant trade guilds, support for the Dublin Protestant Operative Association waned, as members threw in their lot with the Orange Institution. Gregg was not deterred and set about encouraging the better-off classes to join his crusade, especially in the wake of the Maynooth grant controversy of 1845. Gregg was deputed to attend an anti-Maynooth meeting in London on behalf of the Operative Association and out of this meeting the Dublin Protestant

Richard Q. Shannon v. the churchwardens of St Nicholas Within, Dublin (Dublin, 1841); St Nicholas Within, Dublin diocesan registry papers, RCBL, D6/106.   **38** Municipal reform act, 3 & 4 Victoria, c. 108 (10 Aug. 1840); Bowen, *The Protestant crusade in Ireland,* pp 108–10; Crawford, *The Church of Ireland in Victorian Dublin,* p. 154. Gregg was admitted as a freeman of the city 'by birth' in November 1837 (original certificate, in the possession of Col. Tresham Dames Gregg, Penrith, Cumbria).   **39** *Letter of the Revd Tresham D. Gregg to the churchwardens and parishioners of St Nicholas Within, Dublin* (Dublin, 1846); John H. Samuels (ed.), *A report of the arguments in counsel with the judgement of the court in the case of the office of the archbishop of Dublin against the Revd Tresham Dames Gregg in Michaelmas term, 1847* (Dublin, 1848), pp 90–2. **40** *The case of the archbishop of Dublin v. the Revd T.D. Gregg: address to the committee appointed to raise a fund to defray the expenses incurred in the case* (Dublin, 1849).

Association and Reformation Society was born, of which Gregg was one of the trustees. The membership was drawn from among Irish members of parliament and heavily representative of the burgeoning Dublin legal profession, as well as from among the evangelical clergy of the Church of Ireland. The object of the society was to establish a Protestant organization 'to watch the progress of public affairs and bear a scriptural testimony against whatever might be inconsistent with the principles of truth'.[41] Within a short few years the society, through Gregg's indefatigable work, had established links with the members of other reformation societies in Ireland and Britain, where Gregg was much in demand as a speaker and preacher. His contact with John Hope, the Edinburgh reformer and philanthropist, led to the publication by the Dublin society of a weekly newspaper, the *Sentinel*, of which Gregg was the editor. First published in Dublin (*c.*1850–3) and later in London (1853–6), during its short life its editor had much to say from a ultra-Evangelical viewpoint about the politics of the time, and especially the Crimean war, and when the paper ceased publication Gregg was left seriously in debt.[42] To alleviate his family's financial hardship he published a Hebrew grammar (as well a collection of his sermons) which was apparently a best seller for its time and went into three editions.[43] While Gregg shows a considerable scholarly expertise with Hebrew and its grammar and sets out his intention of simplifying it, he actually makes the whole thing more complicated.[44]

Just as Gregg had attracted the loyalty of the Dublin Protestant artisans in the 1840s, so he was similarly held in high esteem by the members of the Dublin Reformation Society. He was deputy grand chaplain of the Orange Institution of Ireland, 1854–69, with which the society had close links, and the members raised a fund to enable him to submit a dissertation for the degree of doctor of divinity of Trinity College, Dublin which he was awarded in 1853. His dissertation is a commentary, with the Hebrew text, on a passage from the Book of Daniel.[45] It is notable for a withdrawal from his earlier political concerns into millenarian and apocalyptic speculation which was to characterize his writings for the rest of his life and to leave him completely outside mainstream evangelical thought and remote from any possible preferment in the Church of Ireland. Indeed, within a few years he had developed a Hiberno-centric view of the Book of Revelation, believing that the battle of Armageddon would take place in Ireland and that 1866 would be 'the year of doom and of the beast number 666' and the final fall of the

41 S. Thewell, *Proceedings of the anti-Maynooth conference, 1845* (London, 1845); Hughenden MS 129/3. 42 Wolffe, *Protestant crusade in Great Britain*, pp 33–49, 138; D. Jamie, *John Hope: philanthropist and reformer* (Edinburgh, 1907). 43 *A methodization of Hebrew verbs, regular and irregular, on an original plan* (London, 1861); *Evangelical doctrine and apostolic order: sermons on the doctrines of the Church of England … and on its order and discipline* (3rd edn, London, 1861). 44 I am grateful to Canon David Crooks for his help on this point. 45 *The triumph of Christ and his truth: the perdition of antichrist and his idol: an oracle for the times … a dissertation preached before the University of Dublin … in two sermons preparatory to receiving the degree of doctor of divinity* (Dublin and London, 1853).

papacy, 'the abomination of desolation under the antichrist'.[46] In 1861 he purchased Tavistock chapel, a small proprietary chapel in the parish of St Pancras,
London (which put him in further debt) and, as disestablishment loomed on the
horizon, along with his eldest son, also Tresham, he visited New York twice in the
1860s to further expound his developing theories which now included the possibility of immortality, influenced as much by his mother's longevity as by the views
of John Asgill, an eccentric Irish Member of Parliament at the turn of the seventeenth and eighteenth centuries, whose writings he resurrected and republished in
America.[47]

Shortly before he died, he wrote to Pope Pius IX pointing out to him that,
'according to the numbers of his name', he would be the last pope to serve as
antichrist and took the opportunity of offering him 'perpetual life without transit
of the grave' and stood by what was for him now a veritable and eternal truth, no
one, not even the pope, would remove him from his position as chaplain of St
Nicholas Within, Dublin. Gregg died at Strand Road, Sandymount, Dublin, in the
company of his wife and family, on 28 October 1881 and his funeral, at Mount
Jerome Cemetery, attracted 'a large concourse of friends and supporters' including many Church of Ireland clergy, two of whom officiated at the service. The
Ecclesiastical Gazette commented, appropriately, that 'in his latter days [Dr Gregg]
was under the hallucination that he would corporeally live for ever and considered
himself the sole representative of the ancient Church of Ireland and he believed
that he would continue to be so till the end of time'.[48]

46 Gregg, *The mystery of God finished*, pp 450–7;   47 *The covenant of eternal life: an argument to
prove that death is not obligatory on Christians* (New York, 1875); *On the sacred law of 1866 conferring perpetual life with immunity from decay and disease* (Dublin and London, 1875); Martha
Feinaigle to T.D. Gregg, 22 July 1873 (original in possession of Col Tresham D. Gregg, Penrith,
Cumbria). On Asgill, see T. Barnard, *Irish Protestant ascents and descents, 1641–1770* (Dublin,
2004), pp 170–1; E.M. Johnston-Liik, *History of the Irish parliament, 1692–1800* (6 vols, Belfast,
2002), iii, pp 111–12.   48 *Ecclesiastical Gazette*, 5 Nov. 1881. Paul Connell, NUI Maynooth, is
engaged in doctoral research on 'The Protestant providential mind of Tresham Dames Gregg'
and I am grateful to him for his recent help.

9

The clergy and disestablishment

Richard Clarke

Within a generation of the arrival of disestablishment in their midst, the clergy of the Church of Ireland could look back with a degree of vanity, and perhaps even a little smugness, at that troubling and traumatic event.[1] Such is the healing power of hindsight. William Sherlock, a noted historian of the church and later archdeacon of Glendalough, could even think of disestablishment in terms of a spiritual resurrection for the Irish Church.

> Perhaps for the Church and for the people the bitterness of death is past. The Church of Ireland is at last freed from political trammels, and may disregard the supposed necessities of statesmen. And if the freedom was purchased by the sacrifice of earthly goods, neither the clergy nor her laity will complain of a tribulation that has bound them close in a common interest, and taught them to look wholly to the great Head of the Church for guidance, protection and strength.[2]

This did not mean that the Church of England had been forgiven for its actions of 1869. At the time of the visit of E.W. Benson, as archbishop of Canterbury, in 1896, the Revd J.H. Bernard (later to become dean of St Patrick's Cathedral Dublin and a future archbishop of Dublin and provost of Trinity College Dublin) could comment that the sense of having been abandoned by the Church of England still accounted 'in large measure for the emphasis that is, at times unduly, laid on the independence of the Irish Church'.[3] Robert Samuel Gregg, by now archbishop of Armagh, but at the time of disestablishment one of the rising stars

---

1 I have used the term 'clergy' throughout this essay to denote *clergy* as distinct from *bishops* and I have emphasised the role of the *clergy*, in this sense of the word. This is not to suggest that bishops and archbishops did not play a very major part in the stabilisation of the Church of Ireland following disestablishment, but rather because I believe that their role has been more than adequately dealt with in other studies.   2 William Sherlock, *Some account of St Brigid and of the see of Kildare, with its bishops* (Dublin, 1896), p. 38.   3 J.H. Bernard, *Archbishop Benson in Ireland* (London, 1896), p. 3.

among the clergy (and very prominent in the post-disestablishment synods of the Church of Ireland) could, even as late as 1895, question whether, although God had blessed the disestablished Church, the Church was 'supposed to owe her present health and activity to her foes, and to proclaim the goodness and wise foresight of those who wounded her and left her desolate?'[4] The independence of their church was indeed the very last thing sought by the clergy of the Church of Ireland in the uneasy years leading to disestablishment.

It may, at the outset, be noted that the Church of Ireland clergy were far from monochrome in churchmanship as they faced the prospect of disestablishment. The conventional wisdom that the churchmanship of the Church of Ireland was, at the time of disestablishment, predominantly evangelical is not a judgement to be seriously resisted. Indeed the history of the Church of Ireland in the earlier part of the nineteenth century can only be properly understood in the context of the rise of evangelicalism. In the context of disestablishment it should perhaps be emphasised that there were different thrusts within the evangelical mood of the Church, but it would seem that all were resistant to the severing of the institutional union of the Churches of England and Ireland. It should be added also that even the more liberal and high church of the clergy were influenced by evangelicalism and by a general hostility to Roman Catholicism.

There were, as has been suggested, different strands within evangelicalism which characterised much of the Church of Ireland of this time. There was, first, the style of evangelicalism which was based on the trustee chapels that were so much part of the Dublin church scene. This element provided the church with much of its leadership in the years leading up to disestablishment, men like Robert Daly and John Gregg who had by now become bishops, but also Achilles Daunt, incumbent of the Dublin trustee church of Saint Matthias at the time of disestablishment and later to be appointed to the deanery of Cork. There was also the proselytizing movement associated with the Irish Church Missions, which was waning by the 1860s, but which was very different in style, and was certainly more virulently anti-Roman Catholic. It was however less powerful in terms of leadership and influence for the wider Church. And we should further note the influence of revivalism, focused on the great Ulster Revival of 1859, which had particular impact on the northern part of the country but also in the cities, as far south as Cork. William Alexander, the bishop of Derry in the 1860s and later to become archbishop of Armagh, epitomised the high church strand of the Church of Ireland, but yet could say of the evangelical revival that it was 'wonderful and almost everywhere'.[5]

The impact of evangelicalism was profound, not only on energizing the laity of the church but also on giving them a theological self-confidence, the belief that they could indeed argue with the clergy on complex matters of doctrine, whether

---

4 *Journal of the General Synod*, 1895. 5 *Journal of the General Synod, 1905*, p. lxvii.

on baptismal regeneration, the nature of eucharistic 'presence', or on the essential efficacy of priestly absolution. A concomitant aspect of the trustee chapels and of the numerous societies for mission (whether 'mission' within the country or beyond its shores) was that financial generosity was required from the laity of the church, and this certainly equipped the Church of Ireland to face a disestablished status, where the church would soon become far more dependent on the open-handed giving of its lay members. It also gave the laity a subtle degree of control over the clergy (particularly the less senior clergy), who were, through the earlier part of the nineteenth century, losing some of their independence to those who were now, in effect, their paymasters. The ministers of trustee churches were, it should be remembered, appointed to all intents and purposes by the laity.

For all that the Church of Ireland might have presented an evangelical appearance to the country at large, a sizeable number of the Church of Ireland clergy would have considered themselves as 'liberals'. Some attention should now be given to this particular element among the clergy, as it was from here that much of the intellectual momentum of the church in the years surrounding disestablishment is to be found. Although liberalism is, in any age, intensely difficult to classify, it should be observed that the Irish form of ecclesiastical liberalism at this stage was directed principally towards ecclesiology and towards the doctrine of the sacraments. Its ecclesiology would have argued that although the Christian church was of divine creation, its authority was primarily *organisational* rather than for the transmission of any spiritual power.[6] In this way of thinking, ordination was principally the conferring of a legal requirement for ministry. Little was made of any ontological distinction between clergy and laity in sacramental functions, and there was certainly little or no sense of *episcope* as other than managerial. There should also be noted a definite wariness of any emphasis on the *transcendental* in doctrinal formulation. And there was what may only be described as a sheer revulsion at the *objectivity* predicated in any catholic sacramentalism. The Irish shape of Anglican liberalism added a distinctly 'illiberal' and virtually visceral attitude towards Roman Catholicism. It was also (and perhaps in consequence) less unsympathetic to Irish evangelicalism than might be expected, and frequent alliances were formed between liberal and evangelical clergy in the synods of the disestablished Church.

We might see the liberal mind of the Church of Ireland clergy at disestablishment as voiced most notably by Charles Parsons Reichel. A graduate of the University of Berlin, Reichel was of Moravian extraction. At one time a professor of Latin in Queen's College, Belfast (now Queen's University), he became incumbent of Mullingar in the diocese of Meath, and later archdeacon of the diocese. He became bishop of Meath in 1886. C.P. Reichel was a man of considerable irascibility but also of great eloquence. He was undeniably a capable scholar of the

6 The most colourful if partisan contemporary appraisal of the established church of Ireland and its clergy (including the theological complexion of the church) is to be found in James Godkin, *Ireland and her churches* (London, 1867).

patristic period, and had a particular interest in the theology of the orthodox churches.

Reichel's theology, which proved to be very influential in the synod debates of the 1870s, finds precise expression in a series of lectures on the Prayer Book, published in 1857.[7] Reichel presents the Anglican view of eucharistic presence in clearcut terms of *via media*. He attacked with passion the 'Romish and Zuinglian [sic]' theories of eucharistic presence as being equally misguided and equally rationalistic. The Church of Ireland, he argued, must be as distanced from attempting to explain the *mechanics* of a presence of the Body and Blood of Christ in the eucharist, as from denying the truth of a presence.[8] At this stage in his development (although he was later to change his mind on this), Reichel defended the formula for ordination in the Anglican ordinal, 'Whose sins thou dost forgive, they are forgiven'. He interpreted the terminology only in the sense of accommodating a re-admission to the visible Church after a previous excommunication. He also, in his theology of orders, gave a substantial importance to an equivalence of *priest* with *presbyter*.[9] During Reichel's incumbency in Mullingar, his relationships with the local Roman Catholics were so appalling that at one stage he required police protection against assault.[10] It should be added that Reichel's experiences of harassment were in no sense typical of Church of Ireland clergy in the country areas, but it perhaps serves to give some meaning to the emotional tone which his attacks on Roman Catholicism seemed to possess.

John Jellett was a liberal of very different temperament. He did not publish much, other than sermons. Belonging to an established family in the Irish ecclesiastical tradition, he was an academic, a mathematician, and a fellow of Trinity College Dublin. He was later to become its provost. As an effective contributor to the synods of the disestablished Church, Jellett always displayed an acute antagonism to anything theological which defied what he saw as empirical definition.

Far less combative than either Reichel or Jellett (and far more sympathetic to the higher church outlook), among the clergy of liberal viewpoint at disestablishment may be numbered John MacDonnell, dean of Cashel, and Robert Samuel Gregg, the son of Bishop John Gregg, the bishop of Cork and a doyen of trustee chapel evangelicalism. R.S. Gregg (of whom mention has already been made) was of a far broader outlook than his father. He was also politically shrewd, and represented the realistic and pragmatic frame of mind which was to gather momentum in the disestablished Church of Ireland. Gregg moved steadily up the ecclesiastical ladder as dean of Cork, bishop of Ossory, bishop of Cork (in succession to his father) and, for three years before his death in 1896, archbishop of Armagh.

A mathematician of world renown, in the fields of both algebra and conic geometry, although not yet known at the time of disestablishment as a theologian, George Salmon (later to become provost of Trinity College Dublin) found him-

7 C.P. Reichel, *Six lectures on the Book of Common Prayer* (Dublin, 1857). 8 Ibid., p. 2. 9 Ibid., p. 125. 10 See Henry E. Patton, *Fifty years of disestablishment* (Dublin, 1922), pp 140–6.

self, perhaps reluctantly, forced into a position of influence within the Church of Ireland. In the 1850s, he had written in the *Catholic Layman*, a periodical which sought to prove a *primitive* pedigree of Anglicanism. Salmon's later contributions to the life of the synod indicate that he was capable of forceful polemic in what was albeit a liberal rather than high church defence of the catholic foundations of the Church of Ireland.[11]

The liberal position, which requires a degree of theological knowledge to espouse coherently, was inevitably one with which few of the laity were explicitly connected although there were exceptions, notably Judge Robert Warren who later wrote one of the most incisive and penetrating books on the disestablishment of the Church and its aftermath.[12] To take a broad view of the appearance of the liberal tradition among the clergy, the distinctive feature to be noted is that it was not anti-evangelical to any degree. It was, as has been suggested, conspicuously anti-Roman Catholic, and it should not in this context at least be considered as possessing any sense of open-mindedness which might be anticipated by the title 'liberal'. A further point of divergence from English ecclesiastical liberalism of the period is that the Irish form was never greatly interested in contemporary biblical criticism or by current continental 'modernism'. So, for example, the 'Colenso affair', which featured significantly in the first Lambeth Conference of 1867, received little mention in the Irish church journals. Although the Irish bishops at the conference (influenced, no doubt by the generally conservative ambience) joined in condemning the ideas espoused by Colenso, the matter never touched any raw nerve of public opinion within the Church of Ireland.[13]

If we turn to what might be thought of as the high church element among the clergy, it must be said that much of the strength of this grouping was among the bishops. (This is a socio-ecclesiastical phenomenon of some interest, but one well outside the scope of this particular study.) The Irish high church possessed neither any particular sense of the aesthetic and visually ornate in the setting or performance of worship; nor is there much indication of the social missionary zeal of the London 'slum priest'. Nor did the Irish high church bear any great resemblance to the 'high and dry' atmosphere of an earlier high church strand in the English Church. And it should be noted that the high church in Irish church life at disestablishment was not in fact totally confined to the ranks of the bishops. Before disestablishment, the position of the Church of Ireland as the surviving catholic Church in the country had been defended vigorously at a church congress of the united Churches of England and Ireland held in Dublin in 1868[14] and also in a

---

11 An extremely useful study has been made of aspects of George Salmon's participation in Church of Ireland affairs by R.E.B. White in 'George Salmon and the Church of Ireland 1869–1871', unpublished BD thesis, Trinity College, Dublin (1978).   12 R.R. Warren, *The Church of Ireland since 1868* (Dublin, 1893).   13 A.M.G. Stephenson, *The First Lambeth Conference, 1867* (London, 1867), p. 270.   14 *Authorized Report of the Church Congress held at Dublin, 29, 30 Sept, 1, 2, 3 Oct. 1868* (Dublin, 1868).

series of essays published in the same year by 'Clergymen of the Established Church in Ireland'.[15] Of the clergy, the principal supporters of the high church tradition in the years leading to disestablishment were Alfred Lee and the Lord O'Neill (both from the northern part of Ireland), James Byrne – a protégé of Bishop Alexander – who was to become dean of Clonfert, and Canon Henry Jellett, an incumbent in the diocese of Cork and the brother (and frequent adversary) of the more broad-church John Jellett. The dean of the Chapel Royal, Hercules Dickinson, was among their number and was also a formidable debater, known as 'the witty Dean'. He appears to have exasperated a number of his admirers by occasional facetiousness, but his contributions to church life were always considered with interest.

In the following extract Alfred Lee best summed up high church anti-Romanism (and bitterness at English perfidy) which characterizes the high church movement in its Irish contours. Indeed these comments may be seen as characterizing the viewpoint of more than the high church of Irish clergy to the prospect of disestablishment.

> Let Englishmen once learn to recognise the true position which the Established Church holds in Ireland, as the old Catholic Church of the country; let them once see in her the one Institution which alone can successfully resist that advancing wave of Ultramontane audacity which threatens to surge up and overwhelm the land.[16]

Any rigid distinction between *high church* and *tractarian* in the context of the Church of Ireland at this stage in her history is difficult to maintain, but I would wish to include the figure of Richard Travers Smith in the former rather than the latter category. Any distinction may in fact largely be made on the basis of attitude to the English Church and hence to disestablishment. Within the high church, there was a primary concern to maintain the ecclesiological nature and doctrinal continuity of the Church of Ireland with its past rather than to regard the Church of England as the true basis for the *identity* of the Church of Ireland. The tractarians, for the most part, were also less open to compromise of any kind and their attachment to England ecclesiastically was less easily surrendered. There was in addition a determination on the part of the few tractarians in Ireland to deny the Church of Ireland the right to make *any* alterations – even those of a non-doctrinal nature – which might institutionalise the separation from the Church of England. There was also a hostility from the tractarian clergy to any significant lay involvement in the decision-making processes of the Church at national level. Such involvement was construed as Erastianism. There was also far greater sympathy to Anglo-Catholic developments in the Church of England. When one con-

---

15 'Clergymen of the Established Church in Ireland', *Essays on the Irish Church* (London, 1868).
16 Ibid.; A.T. Lee, 'Some account of the property and statistics of the Irish Church', p. 263.

siders that the birth of English tractarianism in 1833 was attributed to the interference of secular power in the affairs of the Irish Church (in the Irish Church
Temporalities Act), the distinction between Irish tractarianism and the Irish high
church becomes a little clearer.

To return to the figure of Richard Travers Smith, he was without doubt one of
the foremost scholars of the Church of Ireland. His particular area of interest, aca-
demically, was liturgy and patristics. At the time of disestablishment, he was curate
of Saint Stephen's parish, within the St Peter's corps of parishes in Dublin, a large
grouping of individual parishes under the statutory incumbency of the archdeaconry of Dublin. Smith had, due to a change in this archdeaconry, been disappointed in his hope of becoming the first incumbent of the newly built Saint
Bartholomew's parish in south Dublin, where Smith had been responsible for much
of the public fund-raising and which was opened for public worship in 1867.[17]

St Bartholomew's was to represent a more ornate form of worship than had
been known within the Church of Ireland hitherto, and from the day of its consecration, the church was inevitably to become the object of protestant suspicion.
Smith became incumbent of St Bartholomew's on the resignation of the first vicar,
Arthur Altham Dawson, in 1871. (Dawson returned to minister in England.) In
many respects, Dawson and Smith epitomize the distinction between tractarian
and high church. Smith spent the remainder of his ministry (until Christmas 1904)
as vicar of St Bartholomew's, and worked fully within the structures and constitution of the Church of Ireland to defend what he saw as the catholic position of
the Church of Ireland. His participation in the debates on liturgical revision – particularly those on the ordinal – was scholarly and well-argued. Although Smith
later became involved in ecclesiastical litigation concerning an ornamental cross in
St Bartholomew's church, he was not overly concerned with the outward aspects
of ceremonial. It was said of him after his death that, by his fidelity to the principles of the reformation, he had done more than most clergy to keep 'the waver-
ing from the attraction of Rome'.[18]

Turning to the tractarian tradition with the Church of Ireland in these years,
we would necessarily include the archbishop of Dublin, Richard Chenevix Trench,
within these ranks. Trench reluctantly involved himself – he could scarcely have
done otherwise – in the councils of the disestablished Church of Ireland. Others
of the Irish tractarian group would not follow his lead. William Lee (who was, like
Trench, a New Testament scholar) was appointed by his archbishop as archdeacon
of Dublin shortly after Trench's move to Dublin. He was one of the few Irish clergy of the period known in academic circles in England. Lee, who was also Archbishop King's lecturer in divinity in Trinity College Dublin, and therefore with
major responsibilities for the training of ordinands, refused to recognise the syn-

17 For an account of the foundation of St Bartholomew's Church, and of the ministries of
Smith and Dawson, see Kenneth Milne, *St Bartholomew's: a history of the Dublin parish* (Dublin,
1963), pp 6–46.   18 Cited in ibid., p. 19.

ods of the Church of Ireland after disestablishment. He had involved himself in the work of administrative reconstruction immediately after the act was passed, but he refused to accept the principle that the laity might act as an independent 'house' (with even an extremely limited power of veto) in the ecclesiastical legislature of the Church of Ireland. Thereafter he declined to be involved in the synodical work of the Church. Lee also maintained a close relationship with Pusey and Liddon and even sought at the time of disestablishment to build (with their support) a 'tractarian' church in Dublin which would be in communion with the Church of England. Arthur Dawson, the first incumbent of St Bartholomew's church had little influence on the events of revision as he was not a member of the general synod and, in any case, he left the Church of Ireland within two years of disestablishment. He did, however, involve himself in some controversy by producing a number of tracts. One in defence of private confession was used (by those who wished to remove the option for private auricular confession from the Book of Common Prayer) as evidence that the issue was indeed one of acute and pressing danger for the Church of Ireland.[19]

Equally resolved not to be tainted by the synodical machinery of the disestablished Church was the only other major representative of Irish tractarianism, William Maturin, incumbent of All Saints' Church, Grangegorman, also in the diocese of Dublin. From the time of his presentation to the parish of Grangegorman as perpetual curate on 1843, Maturin had made public worship in the church both more frequent and with an increased sacramental emphasis. A daily service was instituted from the beginning of his ministry and – almost unknown in the Church of Ireland at that time – there were two celebrations of the eucharist on Sundays and a further celebration on holy days. Tractarianism, as represented by Maturin, remained an object for the hostility of much of the membership of the Church of Ireland. But what also seems certain is that Maturin (unlike Lee) was widely respected even among those who could not accept his views, as an individual of intense sanctity and uprightness.[20]

Regardless of whether the clergy were ready or unready to work within the structures of a disestablished Church of Ireland, it is certain that few viewed the possibility of disestablishment with anything other than acute foreboding. The clergy, in company with the laity, saw themselves as engaged in a battle for the continued survival of the Church of Ireland. In short, when the question of disestablishment moved to the top of the parliamentary agenda as the first advance in Gladstone's famous 'mission to pacify Ireland', it was seen as a threat not only to privilege but to existence. Almost all Irish churchmen of influence worked energetically (although for the most part within the bounds of realism) against the destruction of the Irish Church establishment. The Irish bishops submitted to the

---

19 *Confession and Absolution* (Dublin, 1870).   **20** On Maturin and his curate, Henry Hogan, see R.G.F. Jenkins and G.O. Simms, *Pioneers and partners* (Dublin, 1985).

government draft proposals, in confidence, for further reform of the structures and finances of the Church of Ireland within the context of the establishment. But there was to be no deflecting of Gladstone from his fixed purpose. It was probably William Connor Magee, the dean of Cork, who was to become bishop of Peterborough shortly before disestablishment (and who later became archbishop of York) who expressed the mind of the Irish clergy most clearly; he had no doubts that disestablishment would leave the Church of Ireland extremely vulnerable, being in the position, as he put it in a colourful and oft-repeated phrase, 'of a garrison besieged by a hostile army, half regular, half savages'. Would Gladstone, Magee speculated, be strong enough 'to keep his savages from scalping us if we lay down our arms?'[21]

If it seems certain that the clergy shared for the most part this sense of outrage and pessimism at the prospects of disestablishment, there were exceptions. The most significant of these was the archdeacon of Meath (and incumbent of Kells) from the 1840s until the early 1870s, Edward Stopford. He presents a singular exception to the general rule. A son of the then bishop of Meath, the archdeacon was an able and vigorous individual who was certainly fitted to the responsibilities he was given. He was opposed to disestablishment on principle but, as a pragmatist and a realist, he could see what was bound to happen and in December 1868 (almost as soon as Gladstone had taken office), he wrote to the prime minister, offering his services as someone who knew the Irish scene and who would be able to give advice:

> Opposed as I am on principle to the disestablishment of the Church in Ireland, to which I can be no party; I yet desire now to reconcile those who agree with me on that question, to accept the inevitable and at once to withdraw the Church in Ireland from the arena of party conflict; by accepting a measure of disestablishment in this session of Parliament.
>
> I believe that by a measure wisely drawn in a liberal spirit this result could be obtained. I believe also that a measure improperly or unwisely drawn will throw us back on a traditional system of Church defence, which I have long disapproved and which I now wish to terminate.[22]

Stopford went on, it has to be said, to overstate his influence. He informed Gladstone that he had the confidence of many of the important and influential clergy and laity of the Church of Ireland. Gladstone, it would appear, was happy to have someone in Ireland who both seemed to know what he was talking about, and was not intent only with challenging his schemes. (We should recall that, for the most

---

21 J.C. MacDonnell, *Life and correspondence of W.C. Magee* (2 vols, London, 1896), i, p. 211. See also, chapter 10 below.   22 Bp E. Stopford to W.E. Gladstone, 22 Dec. 1868, BL, Add. MS 44,417, Gladstone Papers. Add. MS 44,417 (microfilm of British Library original at St Deiniol's Library, Hawarden).

part, the leadership of the Church of Ireland had refused to have any dealings with Gladstone other than to express their opposition to his plans.) In his reply to Stopford, Gladstone is cautious but also principled in making it clear that, although he will listen to Stopford's views, the two of them cannot have a totally confidential interchange of ideas if the archdeacon is to continue active and public opposition to disestablishment.[23]

The Gladstone Papers make it clear that Gladstone did keep regular contact with Stopford, even inviting him to Hawarden to discuss some of the issues. But two things should be borne in mind. The first is that although we can certainly see that Stopford made a contribution to Gladstone's thinking on the framing of the disestablishment bill, the prime minister was under relentless pressure from every interested party – the Church of Ireland bishops from one direction, the Roman Catholic hierarchy in Ireland from the opposite direction, the latter in alliance with the English non-conformists and with much of Gladstone's own Liberal Party, all of the latter group demanding that disestablishment would not be fudged in such a way as to be virtually meaningless. The disestablishment legislation was very much Gladstone's own work.

Stopford was, understandably, unable to make known publicly in the Church of Ireland just how involved he had been with Gladstone. In his history of the diocese of Meath published early in the twentieth century, John Healy was at pains to defend Stopford from the charge that he had been an ally of Gladstone.[24] He points out that Stopford had even seconded a motion at a public meeting in Navan, protesting at the disestablishment and disendowment of the Church of Ireland as 'destroying the religious character of the State, and alienating from the direct service of God property solemnly devoted to Him'.[25] This may all seem to have been a little disingenuous on the archdeacon's part, but we cannot seriously dispute that he was probably the one member of the Church of Ireland who had any influence on Gladstone. One of the aspects of the disestablishment legislation that unquestionably benefited the future Church of Ireland, and which Stopford had strenuously encouraged, was the option for what was called 'commutation'.[26] This was a system whereby clergy, who were entitled to a stipend for life from the state, could 'commutate' their expected income over the years of their life expectancy as a lump sum, and place this in the hands of the Representative Church Body, the trustee body for the disestablished Church of Ireland, to be used as *capital*, the interest on which could be used for the general payment of clergy in perpetuity. Stopford was an important (and almost solitary) influence in mitigating the effects of disestablishment legislation on the Church of Ireland. Gladstone recognised this, and in a letter from him to Stopford in April 1872 (the original of which is in

23 W.E. Gladstone to Bp E. Stopford, 24 Dec. 1868, BL, Add. MS 44,417, Gladstone Papers. Add. MS 44,417 (as above).   24 John Healy, *History of the diocese of Meath* (2 vols, Dublin 1908), ii, pp 198–200.   25 Ibid., ii, p. 199.   26 Bp E. Stopford to W.E. Gladstone, 6 Feb. 1869, BL, Add. MS 44,419, Gladstone Papers (as above).

the Representative Church Body Library in Dublin), he refers glowingly to Stopford's 'accurate, decisive and manly [*sic*] mind, of the working of which I had such valuable experience at the time of the Irish Church Bill'.[27]

But, if Stopford represents an interesting exception to the generality that the clergy of the Church of Ireland vehemently opposed disestablishment, the enactment of this disestablishment in 1869 revealed that there was no great unity when it came to envisaging what kind of church the Church of Ireland should now become. What is highly significant however is the willingness of the clergy to throw in their lot with the newly disestablished church, regardless of how divided they might be among themselves. To accept the offer of commutation meant, in effect, *trusting* the disestablished Church of Ireland, and *believing that it would survive*. Accepting commutation meant that the Church of Ireland would become the individual's paymaster rather than the government. The surrendering of annuities to the fledging independent church clearly gave the Church of Ireland a far greater chance of survival, by giving it some financial security. By 1872, well over 80 per cent of clergy had commutated. A year later, fewer than five hundred of well over five and a half thousand individuals (including non-clergy) who were eligible for government annuities had refused to commutate.[28] The clergy were, as a body, prepared to give the disestablished Church of Ireland their trust.

The period of time between the passing of the disestablishment bill and the bringing into force of disestablishment itself was a mere eighteen months. The range of doctrinal opinion and emphasis to be encountered among the clergy (as among the laity) represented an acute danger for the future of the Church of Ireland. Would it indeed be able to retain even a semblance either of visible unity or of ecclesiological continuity to the Church which it had been in the days of its establishment? The Church now had authority to do as it wished with the formal articulation of doctrine. It might use this power to turn the Church of Ireland into a Protestant sect. Alternatively it might make the decision to ensure that the disestablished Church of Ireland was, so far as was possible, indistinguishable from the established form.

As is well known, this decision was made over a period of several years, and was centred on the revision of the Book of Common Prayer. If the Prayer Book had been revised in a severely 'protestant' direction – for example, in expunging any idea of an objective regeneration at baptism, in 'clarifying' that there was no objective presence of Christ in the eucharist, or in removing from the formularies any belief that a statement of absolution by an ordained priest actually effected anything (and we should note all of these possibilities were on the agenda of those known as the 'revisionists') – the Church of Ireland would have lost its links both with the Church it had been, and also with its sister Anglican churches in England

27 W.E. Gladstone to Bp E. Stopford, 2 April 1872, Stopford Papers, RCBL. 28 Akenson, *The Church of Ireland*, p. 313.

and elsewhere. If, on the other hand, it made no concessions to the general tenor of evangelicalism, would it survive as a single entity?

A detailed account of the unfolding of these synodical debates on the Book of Common Prayer is well beyond the scope of this essay, but a number of salient points should be noted. The first is that, the Church of Ireland having devised a system whereby the clergy constituted a separate 'order' of synod which might veto doctrinal changes, much of the future of the church in terms of doctrine and unity was in the hands of the clergy. The church convention of 1870, which set up the systems for the government of the disestablished Church of Ireland, gave such power to the clergy. Any changes to the *status quo* relating to doctrine (and, indeed, any other matters where there was the demand for a vote by orders) required assent by both orders of the house of representatives, laity and clergy. The bishops constituted a separate house of general synod, but their power of veto was limited and circumscribed.

The bishops were most prominent in opposing alterations to the Book of Common Prayer, but many of those clergy to whom allusion has already been made fought on each side in the Prayer Book debates. For the most part, there was little enthusiasm from the clergy for a major revision of the baptismal service. When the proposal was made to the general synod for the removal from the Book of Common Prayer of the 'address' following the baptism of an infant, 'Seeing now, dearly beloved brethren, that this child is regenerate and grafted into the body of Christ's Church, let us give thanks…', the clergy defeated the proposal by a ratio of two to one against, although the laity had voted in favour.[29] One of the main figures in this debate was Reichel who argued heatedly against the proposal for change. We may capture something of the spirited flavour of the debates by observing an exchange between William Brooke, a prominent layman (and a distinguished lawyer), and Reichel. Arguing for an alteration in the baptismal service, Brooke told the synod that he was 'continually hearing cases of men, of earnest pious character who feel impelled by the Spirit of God to go forth and preach the Gospel …who were hindered in taking up the ministry of the Church of Ireland and England by reason of these very passages'.[30] His remarks drew a crushing rebuke from Reichel – 'If the Synod were always to consult the opinions of young men, whether they were unfledged Divinity students or young men heated from Merrion Hall [the Plymouth Brethren meeting hall in Dublin], he thought their legislation would be a very pitiful kind of proceeding'.[31]

As an indication of how complex the matter of clerical viewpoint on any issue might be, Reichel took a strongly 'revisionist' position when the discussion turned to the ordinal. He now argued strenuously for a removal of the words in the ordinal, where the priest being ordained is instructed by the ordaining bishop, 'Whose sins thou dost forgive, they are forgiven'. Reichel's main adversary was Richard

29 *Journal of the General Synod, 1873*, pp 220–1.   30 *Daily Express*, 2 May 1873.   31 Ibid.

Travers Smith.[32] Their discussion reveals considerable erudition on both sides. It
also demonstrates that there was an element of anti-Romanism lurking behind the
revisionist side. Reichel spearheaded the view that the movement away from the
primitive Church's practice of public confession was concomitant with a rise in the
tendencies to Romanist centralising. He charted a progression from a community
penitential discipline to the decree of the fourth Lateran Council of 1215 that private confession was obligatory, *ad salutem necessariam esse*.[33] But Reichel could
move to the more emotive arguments as well. The priest, he suggested might too
easily become 'the director of minds and conscience, and this influence might too
easily be abused, for purposes subversive, not merely of true religion, but for law
and order'.[34] But Smith was no insufficient foe. He also knew his patristics well
enough to be able to trade usable theological quotations with Reichel. So, with reference to Chrysostom's *De Sacerdotio* (Book 3),

> They who are in earthly authority have indeed power of binding but only
> the body, but this bond touches the soul itself and passes the heavens, and
> whatever priest do on earth, God confirms above.[35]

When matter came to synod the result was emphatic. Again, for all the divisions
within the ranks of the clergy, there was a consensus against radical change. When
the proposal to remove the words 'Whose sins thou dost forgive' from the ordinal
was put to the General Synod of 1873, whereas three-quarters of the laity voted in
favour of the change, two-thirds of the clergy voted against.[36] Although huge ideological divisions between the clergy and laity became apparent, the synodical system which had been introduced into the disestablished Church of Ireland ensured
that radical decisions would not be taken easily.

When it came to finding a solution to the problems of finding peace and internal consensus for the vulnerable church, it was one of the clergy (albeit an individual shortly to become a bishop) who found a path forwards. It is certainly to him
that the Church of Ireland owes its escape from self-destruction in the aftermath
of disestablishment. William Conyngham Plunket, the fourth Baron Plunket, had
no pretensions to learning but he did have what was more necessary, possessing (in
the words of his successor Reichel) 'an amiable character and tenacity of purpose'.[37] Born in 1828, Plunket was the grandson (on the paternal side) of the first
Baron Plunket, then lord chancellor of Ireland, and also (on his mother's side) of
Charles Kendal Bushe, lord chief justice of Ireland. He took a pass degree and was

32 Both Reichel and Smith resorted to pamphlets in the forwarding of their respective cases, e.g.,
C.P. Reichel, *Shall we alter the Ordinal?* (Dublin 1872); R.T. Smith, *We ought not to alter the Ordi-
nal* (Dublin, 1872).   33 C.P. Reichel, *The doctrine of Absolution* (Dublin, 1871), pp 36–7.   34
C.P. Reichel and A.A. Dawson, *A correspondence between the Rev C.P. Reichel, D.D. and the Rev
A.A. Dawson, M.A.* (Dublin 1871).   35 Smith, *We ought not to alter the Ordinal*, p. 52.   36 *Jour-
nal of the General Synod, 1873*, pp 236–8.

then ordained to become secretary to his uncle, Bishop Thomas Plunket, in Tuam
in the early 1860s. Plunket was revered by the evangelicals as a fellow traveller,
although he certainly displayed more liberal tendencies throughout his life. He also
had a very strong sense of the 'Irish-ness' of the Church of Ireland. Plunket was
also a natural diplomat and a seeker of peace, perhaps for peace at all costs. His
biographer underlined this Plaza Toro element in Plunket when he wrote of him
that 'when he took any uncompromisingly strict position as an extreme Low
Churchman, it was invariably on occasions when he was acting as representative of
that party, and ... would not lead them into a course of action which he knew they
would disapprove, however strongly he personally might hold more liberal views'.[38]
There were certainly far more rigorous theologians in the newly disestablished
church, but very few others who had more skill in the art of the possible.

   Although by 1873, it was realised on all sides that the antagonisms over doctrine
were seriously endangering the future the Church and thwarting progress in every
aspect of its life, it was Plunket who voiced these concerns unambiguously. He led
what was in effect a *demand* for consensus. In a pamphlet published in early 1874,
Moderate revision essential to Church unity, Plunket demonstrated his ability to artic-
ulate the central, pragmatic and generally 'common sense' mind of the Church of
Ireland:

> For my own part, I dread very much seeing moderate men drawn away on
> one side to an 'extreme right' that will persist to the end in conceding too lit-
> tle; and on the other to an 'extreme left' that will persist to the end in
> demanding too much. I believe that between these two extremes which I
> have described there is a 'right centre' and a 'left centre', consisting on the
> one hand of those who are willing to yield more, and on the other, of those
> who are willing to accept less than they themselves would personally desire;
> of those, in fact, who for the sake of unity and peace are prepared, at the cost
> of mutual sacrifices, to join in completing without delay a work of moderate
> revision, which will neither be frivolous or superficial, nor yet revolutionary
> or aggressive. It is my firm belief that amongst those who occupy this cen-
> tral position are to be found the great majority of Irish Churchmen, includ-
> ing the ablest and most influential of our clergy and laity.[39]

Although the nebulous idea of using rubrics as a solution to the problems of doctrinal division had been mooted, it was Plunket who produced a draft for a new
Preface to the Prayer Book to the 1874 Synod as the way forward. This contained
a multitude of declarations, far more elaborate, extensive and verbose than anything anyone else could ever have anticipated or dreamt up. Some basic drafting

---

37 Quoted in R.B. McDowell, *The Church of Ireland, 1869–1969* (Dublin, 1975), p. 96.   38 F.D.
How, *Archbishop Plunket* (London, 1900), p. 38.   39 W.C. Plunket, *Moderate revision essential to
church unity* (Dublin, 1874), p. 13.

was done by George Salmon, but the style was both too florid and the theology too loose to suggest major authorship by Salmon. The preface set out to do the impossible – to defend the revisionist argument, while at the same time explaining why virtually no revision was going to be done. The preface might unkindly be summarized as encouraging all and sundry to continue to believe whatever they already believed but not to upset others in the process. But it worked. Indeed the Church of Ireland public – certainly as characterised within the synod and in the popular press – was largely content with a series of vague assertions that the revisionist position was the most reasonable, but that no revision was going to happen. The final form of the preface in the 1878 Prayer Book even had the audacity to suggest, unblushingly, that the whole matter of revision had been approached calmly and carefully.[40]

On the revisionist wing, one of the foremost laymen might fulminate that the preface's defence of the Prayer Book 'was treating the revisionists as absolute fools'.[41] But Plunket nevertheless won the battle; the preface was passed by large majorities of both clergy and laity in the general synod. The day had been saved, but how would the clergy as a whole react?

The general synod of 1877 finalized the revision of the Prayer Book, and decreed that the new Book of Common Prayer would become the lawful liturgy of the Church on 30 June 1878, one year later. With little opposition, provision was made for any clergy who did not wish to recognize the Book or its new preface.[42] The new Prayer Book would however require assent in any ecclesiastical declaration and it therefore followed that no clergyman of the Church of Ireland could accept any preferment in the future, without recognizing himself as bound by the 1878 Prayer Book.

A mere handful of clergy took this opportunity to disassociate themselves from the disestablished Church of Ireland. A more useful statistical response to the general state of satisfaction of the clergy is provided by the replies to a questionnaire sent to every clergyman of the Church of Ireland by a 'Supply of Clergy Committee' in 1878.[43] The number of clergy in the Church dropped from a little over 2,000 in 1871 to just over 1,800 ten years later. In that time, however, the number of benefices had been reduced due to greater financial stringency, as the voluntarist nature of the disestablished Church took organisational effect. This questionnaire was completed by 516 clergy, little over a quarter of the total of those serving. When questioned about problems in attracting more clergy to the Church of Ireland, 149 expressed anxiety about the salaries, whereas 141 indicated resentment at the power of the laity. It seems reasonable to argue, therefore, that there was a certain residue of dissatisfaction among the clergy at the course of events since disestablishment, but that it could not be claimed that the Irish clergy were as a body

40 Printed in the 'current' Church of Ireland *Book of Common Prayer* (1926).   41 *Daily Express*, 4 May 1875.   42 *Journal of the General Synod, 1878*, p. 51.   43 These questionnaires are RCBL, MS A14.

greatly disaffected by the current situation. Even a high churchman such as Richard Travers Smith believed that his duty called him to remain with the Church of Ireland. A reflective appraisal from a high church standpoint appeared in the *Irish Church Society's Journal* later in 1877. It is an unsigned article but, to judge from the literary style, the author was very probably Smith himself who had acted as editor of the journal until the publication of this edition.

> We have a Church system, which if it has its very weak points, and be well calculated to give the laity large powers of obstruction and to inspire them even with the imagination that their powers and rights of obstruction are irresistible, yet, at all events, gives laymen that interest in the affairs of the Church which, were they well-instructed, would afford the richest promise of hearty working Churchmanship.[44]

He continued to throw down an open challenge:

> Which is more Catholic – an Irish priest celebrating at the north end without vestments but with the utmost reverence and frequency open to him, and spreading what he believes true as best he can among those to whom God has seemed to call him – or the same man in England, working amidst the glories of a Church system which the patient labour of others has developed?[45]

The Irish high church reception may thus be summarised as considerable relief that their position had not been made untenable, coupled with the conviction that their future lay in Ireland. Again, a far from friendly ambivalence to the Church of England remains apparent.

The final word may usefully be given to another of the Jellett dynasty, Morgan Jellett, an honorary secretary to the general synod, who in 1884 addressed a church congress in Carlisle on the topic, 'What can the Church of England learn from Scotland and Ireland in religious matters?'[46] Jellett went straight to the attack. When it is recalled that (although not a particularly vociferous member of synod) he had maintained an unwaveringly conservative stance during the revision debates, his verdict on the value of the Prayer Book revision was remarkably positive. As we would expect from almost any member of the Church of Ireland at that time, he blamed England for the problems which the Church of Ireland had been forced to face since the Reformation. The English Church had given the Church of Ireland its puritan bias, and furthermore had hampered the development of its identity by depriving it of convocation for over 150 years, so that the

---

44 *Irish Church Society's Journal*, iii (Nov 1877), pp 265–6.   45 Ibid., p. 272.   46 M.W. Jellett, *What can England learn from Scotland and Ireland in religious matters?* (London, n.d.).

Church had 'had to learn with great speed the need for mutual trust in discussing matters of mutual concern'.[47] Jellett went far further.

> I have no hesitation in saying that the discussions in the General Synod, carried on with ability and earnestness rarely excelled, had the greatest effect in promoting toleration and goodwill; and further, I would add, provided an education in Church principles, with the result that, at the close of the revision question for instance, the members of the Synod were much better churchmen than at the beginning.

Pointing out that, in addition to restoring many of her cathedrals and churches, the Church of Ireland had built forty-four churches since disestablishment, Jellett concluded with a parthian shot, noting 'an increased consciousness on the part of the laity that the Church rests on Divine, and not on political sanction'.[48] Resentment against the Church of England was being subtly superseded by a patent condescension.

47 Ibid., p. 3.   48 Ibid., p. 8.

10

William Connor Magee, the Church of England and the Church of Ireland

Alan Megahey

John Henry Bernard, dean of St Patrick's Cathedral in Dublin (and a future archbishop of Dublin), addressed members of the Anglo-Irish Church Society in the Jerusalem Chamber of Westminster Abbey in 1903 on 'the present position of the Irish Church'. He ended his survey of the church's history and contemporary situation with a definitive statement: 'We claim to be representatives of the ancient Church of our country; we have good historical proofs to furnish in support of our claim; our claim to the title "Church of Ireland" has been recognised by the law; we have maintained, through good and ill report, our witness for the catholic faith, against protestant dissent on the one hand and against Roman novelties of belief and practice on the other. Few as we are, we stand in Ireland at once for Catholicity and for freedom. That is our position. It is the same as yours. Whatever may be thought of our canons as to ritual and the like, we are the representatives of the Catholic Church in Ireland, as you and we understand Catholicity. And that is our highest title to the sympathy and friendship of the great Church of England.'[1]

Forty years earlier, William Connor Magee, rector of Enniskillen and soon to be dean of Cork, lamented the impending demise of Archbishop Whately of Dublin, whom he described as 'a link, and a strong one between us and England; and we shall feel the loss of him in the coming struggle'.[2] He felt that a strong personal link between the English and Irish churches would be of assistance during the expected battles regarding disestablishment and disendowment. Magee is perhaps a rather neglected figure in the Church of England and the Church of Ireland, yet he epitomises, in himself, the links between the two churches, and their contrasting experiences and developments. The connections between the established churches in England and Ireland had long been reinforced by the appoint-

---

1 J.H. Bernard, *The present position of the Irish Church* (London, 1904), p. 32.   2 W.C. Magee to J.C. MacDonnell, 14 Sept. 1863, in J.C. MacDonnell, *The life and correspondence of William Connor Magee* (2 vols, London, 1896), ii, 90 (henceforth cited as MacDonnell).

ment of Englishmen to Irish sees, particularly in the eighteenth century. From 1801 the connection was further reinforced by the uniting of the two churches as part of the Act of Union of the two kingdoms. With disestablishment that constitutional link was broken, which was why Bernard, and many others before and after, felt the need to educate their English brethren on the history, claims and practices of their sister church.

In 1868, Magee became bishop of Peterborough, 'the first Irishman since the Reformation who has ever held an English see', as he himself claimed.[3] In the past the Irish church had provided lucrative employment for Oxford and Cambridge men, and for scions of the English and Anglo-Irish aristocracy. Now the traffic was the other way, and the fact that Magee was the first Irishman to make the journey may seem, at first blush, surprising. His Irish church pedigree was impeccable. His grandfather had been archbishop of Dublin (1822–31). His father, John, was vicar of Drogheda (1830–9). Two of his uncles were incumbents in or near Dublin. Two of his aunts married clergymen, one of whom had the unusual task of performing the marriage of his nephew to his niece, when Magee married Anne, daughter of his uncle Thomas. Trinity College was enormously important to the Magee family. William's grandfather had been a professor there, and Donnellan Lecturer in 1795, as Magee himself was sixty-nine years later. Nothing gave Magee greater pleasure than to find, when he became archbishop of York, that the college library would house his bust alongside the one of his grandfather.[4] William Connor Magee's rise in the Irish church hierarchy, to become dean of Cork in 1864 and (in addition) dean of the Chapel Royal in Dublin in 1866, seems effortless, and would appear to presage his rising to fill the highest positions in the Irish church.

But Magee's career did not take that turn. In fact he spent thirty-six years of his working life in England, and only eleven in Ireland. Made deacon by Bishop Sumner in Chester in 1844, and then priested by Plunket of Tuam in 1845, he spent only two years as a curate – in his uncle's Dublin parish of St Thomas – before travelling to Spain to recuperate from illness. After a brief return to St Thomas's, he went to Bath where, in two different appointments, he was to spend the next eleven years of his life. There he made his name as a preacher, came to enjoy the ambience of the English church, and became a prebendary of Wells Cathedral. After his short spells as rector of Enniskillen (1860–64) and as dean of Cork (1864–68), he spent the rest of his life in England, as bishop of Peterborough (1868–91) and, for some months only, as archbishop of York. His life, and his observations on the Irish church when viewed from his episcopal seat in England, are reminders both of the common faith of these two parts of what was coming to be called the 'Anglican Communion', and of the wider scene of which the Church of Ireland was a part. While dean of Cork, Magee made one of his much-lauded

3 MacDonnell, i, 199. 4 MacDonnell, ii, 298–9.

appearances on an English platform, at the Church Congress in Bristol in 1864. He declared that there existed 'between the English and Irish Churches an enormous diversity', and that the 'theological, the social and the political surroundings of the Irish Church differ almost absolutely from those with which my English brethren are familiar at home'.[5] Magee made it his business to raise the profile of the Irish Church, as opposed to the Irish Establishment. He was always careful to make that distinction. The *Vanity Fair* cartoon depicting a man of striking ugliness but obvious presence, was captioned 'If eloquence could justify injustice, he would have saved the Irish Church'.[6] The 'injustice', as Magee saw it, was the fault of the political and not the religious 'establishment'. This ambivalence about the Irish 'establishment' is mirrored in his political stance; he was variously described as a 'Whig', a 'Tory', and a 'Conservative'. In truth, he was none of these things. He described himself as a 'moderate Liberal', and both distrusted and feared the 'Tory squirearchy' and the 'non-reforming and Orange ascendancy men'[7], but worried too about Gladstone's reliance upon 'Nonconformist and Revolutionary support'.[8] His geographical distance from Ireland, and his highly individual, almost apolitical stance, give his observations an enhanced interest and piquancy.

Magee was plunged into the debates over disestablishment as soon as he was consecrated bishop of Peterborough. His own feeling was that disestablishment and disendowment were inevitable, with room for negotiation only as regards the latter. His fears were summed up in a letter in 1869 to his good friend John MacDonnell, 'Your three rocks are coming over the surface already. (1) Liturgical revision, (2) Lay tyranny, and (3) Schism between north and south. Still I think you will weather them; but the second is your greatest danger.'[9] They were commonly held fears, and were prevalent in England. Lord Plunket tried to allay them when he addressed the Church Congress in 1875, a year before his elevation to the see of Meath. Plunket rejected any idea that liturgical revision was 'revolutionary or intolerant in its character',[10] and noted with scorn 'what strange misapprehensions were afloat respecting the supposed Presbyterian tendencies of the Irish Church'.[11] It was a spirited defence. But in fact Plunket was highlighting key divergences of practice between the Irish and English churches. As far as ritual was concerned, the two churches would go their separate ways. The Public Worship Regulation Act of 1874 had attempted to introduce more discipline in the English church, but to little effect. The Church of England in general saw widespread acceptance, over the subsequent century, of practices which most Anglicans in the 1870s would have regarded as 'Roman'. The use of eucharistic vestments, the eastward-facing position of the celebrant at holy communion, making the sign of the cross, mixing water with the wine before the consecration, using incense, and can-

5 Speech on 'Mutual relations of the Church in Ireland and England' in *Church Congress Report: Bristol 1864* (London, 1865), p. 142.   6 More properly, a chromolithograph, published 3 July 1869.   7 MacDonnell, i, 143.   8 MacDonnell, i, 232.   9 MacDonnell, i, 236.   10 *Church Congress Report: Stoke-on-Trent 1875* (London, 1876), p. 45.   11 Ibid., p. 42.

dles on the altar, were the classic 'signs' of high-churchmanship.[12] These practices became common, though by no means universal, in the hundred years after the parliamentary attempt to limit ritualism. Even Magee himself – always an outspoken opponent of 'Romish' ritual – came out in 1875 in support of the 'eastward position' when celebrating the eucharist.[13] Then two years later he declared his intention 'to wear a cope on all occasions when celebrating Holy Communion in our cathedral'.[14]

It must be remembered that there was also plenty of clamour in England for liturgical revision. The Prayer Book Revision Society had proposed a new book in 1873, which followed the Irish church's prohibitions in terms of ritual, but went even further in amending the communion service, substituting 'minister' for 'priest', and expunging all reference to saints' days, with their attendant collects and readings.[15] But in general, the English church was more and more widely adopting 'high church' practices. Magee saw himself holding the line between the 'puritans' and the 'Romanizers', though this did not prevent the former from using his assault on 'auricular confession' almost as a set text. It was quoted, and offered for sale in full, by the Protestant Defence Association of the Church of Ireland in 1890.[16] This lecture, and other anti-ritualist statements by Magee, are still offered for sale on evangelical websites. In the Irish church, the gradual spread of 'high church' practices did not happen. William Alexander, bishop of Derry (and later archbishop of Armagh), had something of a reputation for 'high church' tendencies, but he was able to tell his English brethren in 1901 that there was no risk of liturgical and ritual mayhem in Ireland, as '[W]e have got these three things: law which is able to enforce itself, indisputable canons, and Church courts of unquestionable authority'.[17] Nevertheless there were those, albeit few in number, who were unhappy with the 'somewhat Cistercian austerity' of the Irish Church, as Archbishop Gregg described it in 1928.[18] All Saints', Grangegorman, St Bartholomew's, Dublin, and later St George's in Belfast, even Trinity College Chapel, were regularly attacked as 'extreme'. In 1921, Gregg was alerted to the activities of the Revd W.C. Simpson, vicar of St Bartholomew's. He was an English 'anglo-catholic', who exhibited all the marks of high churchmanship in his ritual (except for the use of incense). The case dragged on for years, as did a similar one involving the Revd S.R.S. Colquhoun of St John's, Sandymount in the late 'thirties. The miscreants were admonished and fined.[19] In 1930 there was an

12 Kenneth Hylton-Smith, *High churchmanship in the Church of England* (Edinburgh, 1993), p. 273. 13 MacDonnell, ii, 21–2. 14 MacDonnell, ii, 82. 15 A.E. Peaston, *The Prayer Book revisions of the Victorian Evangelicals* (Dublin, 1963), pp 17 and 19. 16 *Facts showing the progress and present position of ritualism in Ireland* (Dublin, 1890), p. 21. 17 'Disestablishment and disendowment in Ireland: some of its gains' in *The Churchman*, no. 175 (April 1901), p. 343. 18 J.A.F. Gregg, 'The effects of disestablishment in Ireland' in *Review of the Churches*, v, no. 4 (Oct. 1928), p. 474. 19 Alan Megahey, *The Irish Protestant churches in the twentieth century* (London, 2000), pp 72–5.

attempt to bring in one small but significant change – to canon 36, which forbade the display of the cross on, over or behind the 'holy table'. Given the Simpson case, it was perhaps not an auspicious moment to do so. The somewhat unlikely mover was Bishop Day of Ossory (later primate for just three months in 1938). Day was 'particularly loyal to the canons of the Church of Ireland and scornful of any attempted evasion of their directions', but thought canon 36 'both unreasonable and unnecessary'.[20] Day's English education had been in low-church foundations (Oakham School and Ridley Hall, Cambridge), so he was no high churchman – just the person, therefore (along with Bishop Orr of Meath) to move the repeal of Canon 36. Gregg was in agreement, and although the resolution could not be accepted (for procedural reasons) in 1929, it was brought forward as a motion in the General Synod in 1930, passed resoundingly by the clergy, but rejected overwhelmingly by the laity. Not until 1964 was the canon changed, and other restrictive canons remained. R.P. McDermott, in an essay at the centenary of disestablishment, noted that the canons of 1871 had fastened permanently on the church 'the ceremonial preferences and prejudices of the average conservative mid-Victorian layman', and that although the prohibition of altar crosses had recently been repealed, 'this preposterous legislation remains in force, as the great majority of the laity have continued to desire that it should remain'.[21] Four years later, the canons were revisited, and some mild liberalisation was enacted.

The laity's vote in 1930, and McDermott's strictures, might seem to reinforce Magee's apprehensions about 'lay tyranny'. The laity had been given a significant role within the newly disestablished church, a century before such a development took place in England. There, the theory that the House of Commons was the platform for lay input held sway until the creation of the National Assembly of the Church of England in 1920, but even then, there was 'significant lack of participation by the laity in discussions and decisions on the church's doctrine and worship'.[22] Where they could wield real power was in parliament which retained (and retains) ultimate authority – and it was there that the Church's attempt to reform its prayer book foundered in 1927 and 1928. The Church of England had to wait until the passing of the Synodical Government Measure in 1969 before it could boast of significant lay participation in its decision making bodies at both national and diocesan level – a century after the Church of Ireland had committed itself to this course. The vesting of significant powers of influence and decision-making in the hands of the Irish laity was regarded with suspicion in England. In 1876, Lord Plunket had sought to allay English fears about 'the dangers that would attend any election of bishops or incumbents in which, according to the provisions of our new statutes, the laity were to be given a substantial voice'.[23] One counterbalance, men-

20 R.R. Hartford, *Godfrey Day: missionary, pastor and primate* (Dublin, 1940), pp 87–8.   21 R.P. MacDermott, 'The Church of Ireland since disestablishment' in *Theology*, lxxiii, no. 599 (May 1970), pp 209–10.   22 Kenneth Hylton-Smith, *The churches in England from Elizabeth I to Elizabeth II* (3 vols, London 1998), iii, 250.   23 *Church Congress Report: Stoke-on-Trent 1875*,

tioned by him and much trumpeted in later years, was the significant power of the Irish bishops. J.H. Bernard declared in 1924, that 'in no part of the Anglican Communion have the bishops more real authority than in the Church of Ireland'.[24] J.M. Harden, a canon of St Patrick's cathedral, quoted Bernard's statement in an article on the Church of Ireland in the following year, and commented: 'Some bishops even in England may be tempted to say, *O si sic omnes*'.[25] Certainly no English archbishop could have moved so decisively and authoritatively as Gregg in 1929. When some very small amendments to the prayer book were passed by Synod, he wrote to the clergy pointing out that 'the use of the Revised Prayer Book ... is of statutory obligation', and that 'the text of the old books must be changed with the pen into exact conformity with the text of the Authorized Book or new books must be obtained'.[26] This was a far cry from Magee's experience of 'the deliberate adoption of *distinctly* Roman doctrines, practices, rites, ceremonies, devotions and even phrases and turns of expression' by English clergy whom he saw demonstrating 'deliberate and insulting defiance not of the merely legal authority of bishops, but, as I personally know, of their earnest and paternal remonstrances and entreaties, far more frequently resorted to than we are given credit for'.[27]

The obituarist of Henry McAdoo noted that as archbishop of Dublin (1977–85) he had 'to hold together a diocese unique in Ireland, whose ecclesiastical breadth stretched from the Anglo-Catholicism of St John's, Sandymount, to the evangelicalism of St James's, Crinken (both trustee churches); he was probably never relaxed in either of them'.[28] In fact, McAdoo illustrates an aspect of how things had changed. He was, his obituarist comments, 'the last of the prince bishops', who among adults 'had an enormous understanding of his own position as a bishop, of the weight due to his office and responsibilities, and conscious of how he should be received'. By the end of the twentieth century, both in England and in Ireland, such institutional respect had dissolved. Alan Acheson relates how 'the House of Bishops continued to sit aloof from the House of Representatives' until in 1995 they were described by Canon Ricky Rountree as 'china dolls'; the following year they came down to the level of the clergy and laity.[29] Similar shifts in attitude in England were reflected in the abandonment of the 'My Lord' form of address, and indeed in calls to curb episcopal expenditure, or to reduce their stipends to the same level as those of incumbents.[30] Perhaps it was some compensation for Irish bishops that they could now wear pectoral crosses, and might even sport copes and mitres, without fear of reprisals. English bishops, who had been doing so for a century, had no such means of compensating for loss of status.

(London, 1876), p. 44. 24 J.H. Bernard, 'The Church of Ireland since disestablishment' in *Review of the Churches*, v, no. 1 (Jan. 1924), p. 70. 25 'The Church of Ireland to-day' in *Churchman*, xxxix, no. 4 (Oct. 1925), p. 297. 26 *Irish Churchman*, 10 Jan. 1929. 27 MacDonnnell, ii, 56: 1 Nov. 1876 28 *The Times*, 15 Dec. 1998 29 Alan Acheson, *A history of the Church of Ireland, 1691–1996* (Dublin, 1997), p. 247. 30 *Church Times*, 8 June 2001, 16 July 2004.

While at the General Synod of 1971 the laity finally concurred with the clergy in a mild liberalisation of the canons of the Church of Ireland, perhaps of even greater significance on that occasion were the debates initiated as a result of the tripartite discussions with the Presbyterians and Methodists. There was a 'widespread feeling that the laity should be given a real place in the spiritual life of the church – to share its ministry'.[31] This was to be a theme which would run through the discussions of churches throughout the Anglican communion in subsequent decades. The 1977 Lambeth Conference, rather surprisingly, debated (though did not endorse) lay presidency at the holy communion.[32] The 1988 conference spent much more time on discussing the role of the laity, declaring that 'we have come to a common concern that both the mission and maintenance of the Church in the future depend upon a radical commitment to the central role of the laity'.[33] It was becoming clear to the Church of Ireland and the Church of England that the laity must play a bigger role in 'mission and maintenance', for theological as well as for financial and practical reasons. Authority in the church would not be compromised by some sort of 'lay tyranny'; rather it would be compromised and misunderstood, as the dean of Raphoe noted in 1996, by 'those who would look backwards in history and seek to regain the authority (and power) of a past age'.[34]

Magee's third fear for the Irish Church was the danger of 'schism between north and south'. As rector of Enniskillen, he had experience for the first time of people 'who were much more of Orangemen than Churchmen', as his biographer puts it.[35] That alerted him to a social, political and economic climates very different from those he had known in Dublin and would experience in Cork. But he never pursued his thoughts on the 'northern question'. Although alarmed by the rise of Parnell, he saw the future in terms of 'Irish revolution first, and then an embittered struggle between the revolutionary and conservative forces in England and Scotland' leading to disestablishment in England: 'I give the Church of England two Parliaments to live through'.[36] He recorded no comments on what Roy Foster has called 'the powerful and integrated party machine ... developed by Ulster Unionism'[37], which helped bring about the 'schism between north and south' that Magee feared – though only in political terms. No schism developed within the church, but there were strains. It was a Belfast-based church newspaper which in 1909 mounted a virtual campaign to rectify what was seen as a Dublin- and southern-dominated Church. 'The vote of a Churchman living in an out-of-the-way part of Cashel, Killaloe, or Limerick is seven times as valuable as that of a Churchman in Belfast', the Revd J.B.A. Hughes pointed out to his

31 *Journal of the General Synod of the Church of Ireland 1971*, p. 171.   32 J.B. Simpson and E.M. Story, *Discerning God's will: the complete eyewitness report of the eleventh Lambeth conference* (Nashville, 1979), pp 156–7.   33 The Anglican Consultative Council, *The truth shall make you free: the Lambeth Conference 1988* (London, 1988), p. 49.   34 S.R. White, *Authority and Anglicanism* (London, 1996), p. 107.   35 MacDonnell, i, 85.   36 MacDonnell, ii, 217.   37 R.F. Foster, *Modern Ireland, 1600-1972* (London, 1988), p. 421.

colleagues at clergy meeting in Belfast.[38] 'The North does not get the representation it is entitled to', an editorial declared six months later, and complained that the 'monopolizing of St Patrick's [National Cathedral] by the Dublin clergy to this extent may be an abominable act of ecclesiastical selfishness'.[39] When, three years later, the Revd J.O. Hannay ('George A. Birmingham') spoke up in support of home rule at the general synod, his intervention – as the newspaper reported – was 'characterised by Archdeacon Pooler, a sturdy Northerner, as "a rodomontade of nonsense"'.[40] Although Church of Ireland clergy and laity were overwhelmingly opposed to home rule, strains between north and south developed during the war, notably over the Irish Convention which met in Dublin in 1917. Its report was deplored by Archbishop Crozier of Armagh.[41] Bishop D'Arcy of Down, who was to succeed Crozier in 1920, regarded it as 'the most convincing argument against home rule which has yet appeared', but the bishop of Killaloe praised it as a way forward.[42] Archbishop Bernard of Dublin also welcomed the possibility of 'a scheme of self-government for *all* Ireland'.[43]

The years of unrest and war which followed were difficult ones for the church in the south. Magee, in one of the gloomy prognostications which from time to time he conjured up, had lamented in 1869 (writing to his Irish soul mate) that 'bishops' lives in this country will not, I am convinced, average as long as landlords' in yours, which is a pity, as we are respectively the last of a race: neither bishop nor landlord being able to resist the process of republican natural selection to which they are now being subjected. I sometimes doubt whether revolution will not go further and faster here than with you'.[44] The bishops in England survived; the landlords of southern Ireland, already hard pressed by successive land acts, were under renewed threat, and it was a threat also to the finances of the church. Bishop Alexander of Derry lamented in 1901 that, with the contraction of the landed class, the 'danger is grave, perhaps alarming', though he clung onto the belief that 'no Church faithful to the truth, at peace with itself, and bearing the peaceable fruits of righteousness, will ever perish for lack of money'.[45] He was right, and the church survived the dark days of civil war and partition, though with dramatically depleted numbers: the Protestant population in the south contracted by 33.5 per cent between 1911 and 1926.[46] The picture in the north was different. The Revd James Hannay, whose father had been rector of Belfast, but who felt more at home in Dublin, noted in 1919 that Belfast and Dublin were 'very little more than a hundred miles apart, yet I suppose Manchester and Bombay are not more separated in spirit'.[47] But the headquarters of the church remained in Dublin, and almost every

---

38 *The Warden*, 26 March 1909.   39 Ibid., 29 Oct 1909.   40 Ibid., 26 April 1912.   41 Maurice Irvine, *Northern Ireland: faith and faction* (London, 1991), p. 206.   42 *Irish Churchman*, 2 May 1918.   43 Bernard's memorandum of 5 Dec. 1917, BL, Bernard Papers, Add. MS 52,781.   44 MacDonnell, i, 239: 23 Sept. 1869.   45 'Disestablishment and disendowment' in *The Churchman*, no. 175 (April 1901), pp 346–7.   46 Dennis Kennedy, *The widening gulf* (Belfast, 1998), p. 152.   47 G.A. Birmingham, *An Irishman looks at his world* (London, 1919), p. 264.

clergyman was trained in the southern capital. When Primate Gregg died in 1961 the Church's newspaper commented that 'the average man in the Six Counties thinks of Armagh as being a remote place and he suffers the disadvantage of never being able to experience close proximity to the General Synod and all the ecclesiastical hub-bub that makes the Primate of All Ireland a dominating figure in the life of the Church in Dublin', whereas 'many people in the North know little or nothing about the Archbishop of Armagh'.[48] But things were about to change.

A church report in 1967 underlined the anomalous situation: that nine southern dioceses with a population of 61,000 had 318 General Synod representatives, while the five northern dioceses, with a population of 343,000, had 330 representatives. Comparisons were drawn with the Church in Wales, which had more adherents and more clergy than its Irish counterpart. Yet the Church of Ireland had a total of 215 dignitaries (bishops, deans, archdeacons and canons), skewed again towards the south, while the Church in Wales had 91. The report, including a recommendation for a diocese of Belfast, was not implemented, but it was a sign of things to come.[49] The changing nature of Trinity College, Dublin, illustrates in microcosm a new age. In 1965 the college calendar finally dropped what had long been unenforced – the requirement that resident students attend chapel.[50] In 1970 the Roman Catholic Church's ban on its faithful attending Trinity was lifted.[51] Three years later, Archbishop Buchanan, having consulted his fellow bishops, stood in the college chapel to declare that it was no longer a Church of Ireland place of worship.[52] In 1978 the courses leading to the divinity testimonium were suspended, a non-denominational faculty of divinity was created, and the Church of Ireland's divinity hostel became the church's theological college in 1980.[53] In 1986 the new archbishop of Armagh, Robin Eames, became the first bishop (since Crozier in 1911) to step up to the primacy from a northern diocese, and the first whose *alma mater* was Queen's, Belfast, not Trinity, Dublin. And recognising demographic realities, Eames dared to suggest: 'Controversial it may be, but I could foresee a time when the primate should live in Belfast, with an assistant bishop in Armagh.'[54] The swing in focus away from Dublin was also symbolised by the general synod meeting in Belfast in 1986, and subsequently not only in Dublin and Belfast, but in Armagh and Cork. The 'schism between north and south' that Magee had foreseen failed to materialize when Ireland was partitioned, or when Éire became a republic outside the Commonwealth, or during the Northern Ireland 'troubles'. Some felt that the Drumcree standoff each July from 1995 threatened to undermine the unity of the church,[55] and certainly it was for

48 *Church of Ireland Gazette*, 12 May 1961.   49 *Administration 1967* (Dublin 1967), p. 123 and *passim*.   50 R.B. McDowell and D.A. Webb, *Trinity College, Dublin, 1592–1952* (Cambridge, 1982), p. 386.   51 Desmond Bowen, *History and the shaping of Irish Protestantism* (New York, 1983), p. 426.   52 'In Retrospect: Alan Alexander Buchanan' in *Search*, 17, no. 1 (Spring 1994), p. 38.   53 Alan Acheson, *A history of the Church of Ireland, 1691–1996* (Dublin, 1997), p. 241.   54 Alf McCreary, *Nobody's fool: the life of Archbishop Robin Eames* (London, 2004), p. 241.   55 *Irish*

Archbishop Eames 'a particularly heavy cross to bear'.[56] But it was not the main threat to the Church of Ireland as the twenty-first century dawned. Rather, like all churches in Europe, the problems of secularization and declining congregations seemed most menacing and intractable. For the Church of England those problems made Magee's gloomy presentiments about English disestablishment appear to be what he called, in a different context, 'wee bubbles upon the head of the cataract'.[57]

William Connor Magee represented, in his own person, the links between the sister churches in Ireland and England. Others followed, though not until well into the twentieth century. Among them were: Thomas Bloomer (Royal School, Dungannon and TCD), consecrated bishop of Carlisle in 1946; William Greer (St Columba's and TCD), bishop of Manchester, 1947; Gerald Colin (Mountjoy School and TCD), bishop suffragan of Grimsby, 1966; George Cassidy (Belfast High School and Queen's, Belfast), bishop of Southwell, 1999. All these had served in the Church of Ireland. There were other Irishmen who, though educated wholly or partly in Ireland, were ordained into the English Church: Henry Richmond, suffragan bishop of Repton, 1986; Roy Williamson, bishop of Bradford, 1984 and then Southwark, 1996; Wallace Benn, suffragan bishop of Lewes in 1997. They were but a small part of the diaspora. Of the almost 2000 priests who served in the dioceses of Connor and of Down and Dromore during the twentieth century, 311 (16 per cent) moved to England.[58] Other Irishmen made their impact on the English church outside the episcopal ranks. William Lefroy, dean of Norwich, was described on his death in 1909 as 'one of the best known Irishmen in the ministry of the English Church', who had been 'a leader of the evangelical party in England'.[59] Of very different churchmanship was Father Dolling, whose death in 1902 'was mourned as if he had been a reigning monarch or national hero'.[60] Born in Ireland, grandson of the Revd B.W. Dolling (for forty-six years precentor of Dromore), and a kinsman of Bishop Alexander, he was educated in England and became the model of an anglo-catholic slum priest. Another who achieved national celebrity was Geoffrey Anketell Studdert Kennedy, grandson of the dean of Clonfert. His father was an Irish priest who moved to England, where Geoffrey was born, though he went to Trinity College, Dublin. He came the best known chaplain in the first world war, when he acquired his nick-name, 'Woodbine Willie', and was the leading missioner of the Industrial Christian Fellowship before his untimely death in 1929. He shares with Magee the distinction of being one of the outstanding preachers of his day. But they were very different. Magee was undoubtedly 'an unsurpassed exponent of the art of persuasive

Times, 6 August 1998. **56** McCreary, *Nobody's fool*, p. 207. **57** Sermon entitled 'The miraculous stilling of the storm' in Grenville Kleiser (ed.), *The world's great sermons* (10 vols, London, 1909), vii, 26. **58** These statistics arrived at from examination of the entries in F. Rankin (ed.), *Clergy of Down and Dromore* (Belfast, 1996) and J.B. Leslie, *Clergy of Connor from Patrician times to the present day* (Belfast, 1993). **59** *The Warden*, 20 Aug 1909. **60** Bernard Palmer, *Reverend*

speaking',[61] but his sermons invariably spoke to the spiritual, religious and ethical needs of the individual. Kennedy, in the very different world that obtained just thirty or forty years later, 'translated religious terminology into the speech of the trenches and the market-place' and 'sounded the trumpet of social justice'.[62]

Thus did many Irishmen follow Magee across the sea, creating human links between the Churches of England and Ireland. There was far less movement the other way. One notable exception is Michael Dewar (Blundell's and Emmanuel, Cambridge) who espoused the Church of Ireland and the Orange Order with enthusiasm, and found in the homogeneity of the Irish Church something to be cherished. He tells the story 'of Archbishop E.W. Benson of Canterbury's visit to Armagh Cathedral, only a fortnight before his death in Hawarden parish church as Gladstone's guest. Bowing to his host the English Primate said: "The successor of St Augustine greets the successor of St Patrick", thus conceding one hundred and fifty years' seniority to the Irish Church'.[63] It is more likely that in fact Benson, having given Alexander the Aaronic blessing, kissed his archiepiscopal ring and said, 'I salute the ancient see of Armagh'.[64] That was significant enough. What Bernard called 'the ancient Church of our country' had an eloquent defender in Magee at the time of disestablishment, but he showed little interest in the Celtic period. His 'sketch of Irish Church history', written in answer to F.D. Maurice's article supporting disestablishment, begins not in the age of Patrick or Columba, but in the reign of Henry II. Magee explained that when the English king was granted by the (English) pope the task of 'civilizing' the Irish, 'he found there a Church already established and endowed – a Church which had been national, but which, even before his arrival, was becoming, like the rest of Christendom in that day, anti-national – owning the supremacy, to some extent at least, of the Pope, and likely to do so more and more'.[65] The rest of his argument dealt with the period of the reformation and afterwards. Similarly, in his famous speech to the Lords during the passage of the Irish Church Bill, there are no allusions to the Celtic church, and the argument's historical grounding was in recent events.[66] But during the decade after his death, the 'Irish renaissance' saw the burgeoning of a new interest in the nation's distant past, and in its distinctive language. It affected the Church of Ireland. Stained glass windows and altar frontals began to depict Irish symbolism.[67] In 1906 the holy communion was celebrated for the first time in Gaelic on

rebels: five Victorian clerics and their fight against authority (London, 1993), p. 195.   **61** R.P.C. Hanson, 'William Connor Magee' in *Hermathena*, cxxiv-cxxvii (1978–79), p. 47.   **62** Horton Davies, *Varieties of English preaching, 1900-1960* (London, 1963), pp. 112, 115.   **63** Michael Dewar, 'The Church of Ireland and its Prayer Book' in *Churchman*, 103, no. 2 (1989), p. 114. **64** Archbishop Alexander himself recalled the blessing and the kiss: see A.C. Benson, *The life of Edward White Benson*, (2 vols, London, 1899), ii, 772.   **65** 'The Irish Church Establishment: a reply to Professor Maurice' in *Contemporary Review*, vii (Jan-April 1868), p. 437.   **66** The speech is reproduced in *Speeches and addresses of the late W. C. Magee*, edited by Charles S. Magee (London, 1892), pp 1–31.   **67** Megahey, *The Irish Protestant churches*, p. 71.

St Patrick's day, 1906, in Christ Church Cathedral, the celebrant being J.O. Hannay.[68] The Irish Guild of the Church was founded in 1914 to celebrate and preserve 'what was best in Irish ecclesiastical traditions and customs'.[69] Its magazine, launched in 1919, contained articles in Irish and English, and disclaimed any notion that the Church of Ireland was 'an English Colonial Church'.[70] R.B. McDowell has said that in the middle of the nineteenth century, Irish churchmen were 'convinced that their church could claim to be the ancient church of Ireland, founded by St Patrick in the fifth century'.[71] In the twentieth century that conviction was given added content and colour, evident in particular in the writings and statements of Archbishops Bernard, Gregg, Day and Simms. Gregg was the enthusiastic president of the church committee formed to plan the celebrations for the 1,500th anniversary of St Patrick's arrival in Ireland, for he was, as his biographer comments, 'an enthusiast for Ireland's patron saint, but like the majority his enthusiasm was untempered by historical criticism'.[72] Godfrey Day, in his only presidential address (in 1938) at general synod, spoke with great pride of 'the Church of St Patrick, of St Columba and St Gall and St Canice ...'[73] George Otto Simms, elevated to the primacy in 1969, was 'by nature a contemplative and was so imbued with the Celtic Christian tradition that he delighted in spending hours in perusal of the text [of the Book of Kells]'.[74] All of this Celtic and Irish emphasis might have had the effect of creating greater distance between the Churches of Ireland and England, had it not been for another and related development, which was of world-wide significance.

The Revd Herbert O'Driscoll, brought up in Ireland but long a priest in Canada, noted that 'something extraordinary has happened since I left Ireland in 1954. For reasons that no one quite understands but many guess at, the story of Christian faith in Ireland ... has begun to impinge on the faith journeying of millions of people for whom the word Celtic has come to hold a remarkable fascination'.[75] A century after the English archbishop saluted the Irish primate, there was a growing enthusiasm for 'Celtic Christianity' throughout the British Isles and beyond. It seemed to resonate with modern sensibilities about the environment and about the need for peace and quiet, and it expressed in another way the recurrent Christian impulse to recapture the simplicities of the past. Some are dismissive. Gordon Mursell, in his magisterial survey of English spirituality, notes that this 'Celtic' enthusiasm 'may simply imply a longing to escape from the urbanized world of the twentieth century', and that there is little evidence that an emphasis on nature, or a predilection for solitude 'are any more "Celtic" than Anglo-Saxon

---

68 R.B.D. French, 'J.O. Hannay and the Gaelic League' in *Hermathena*, cii (Spring 1966), p. 45. 69 H.E. Patton, *Fifty years of disestablishment: a sketch* (Dublin, 1922), p. 287. 70 *Gaelic Churchman*, March 1919. 71 R.B. McDowell, *The Church of Ireland, 1869–1969* (London, 1975), p. 1. 72 George Seaver, *John Allen Fitzgerald Gregg, archbishop* (London, 1963), p. 188. 73 *Journal of the General Synod 1938*, p. lxxiv. 74 Lesley Whiteside, *George Otto Simms: a biography* (Gerrards Cross, 1990), p. 43. 75 Herbert O'Driscoll, *The road to Donaguile: a Celtic spir-*

or European'.[76] But there was no denying its popularity, even if, as one prayer book produced within this tradition admitted, the 'present revival of interest in things Celtic may eventually pass'.[77] For others, it is a vital way forward which in effect brings the various parts of the British Isles together, for it reminds us that when 'the Roman legions left, British stubbornness and then Irish imagination created the Celtic Churches to meet a new situation. To honour our Celtic past truly, we must work out, as they did, what it means to be the Church in the British Isles in our own time'.[78]

The church in the British Isles, and in the world-wide Anglican communion, owes much to the Irishmen who have served it in their native island and beyond. William Connor Magee was the Irishman who rose highest in the hierarchy of the Church of England. A century later, Robin Eames, archbishop of Armagh, was the first Irishman to rise to the highest levels of prestige and influence within the Anglican communion. In 1896 the archbishop of Canterbury had laid his hand on the archbishop of Armagh's head and had given him his blessing. In 2003, the archbishop of Armagh, in his capacity as senior primate of the Anglican communion, pronounced the blessing on the new archbishop of Canterbury at his enthronement. Rowan Williams, a Welshman, was the former primate of the Church in Wales. The last time such a 'Celtic' occasion had taken place at that level was in 1891 in York Minster, when William Alexander (soon to be Irish primate) had preached at the enthronement of his old friend, William Connor Magee, as primate of England. Those two occasions, separated by more than a century, are reminders of the ties that bound, and bind, the Church of Ireland and the Church of England.

itual journey (Boston, 2000), pp 103–4.   **76** Gordon Mursell, *English spirituality* (2 vols, London, 2001), ii, 249.   **77** *Celtic Night Prayer*, complied by members of the Northumbrian Community (London, 1996), p. vi.   **78** Fay Sampson, *Visions and voyages: the story of our Celtic heritage* (London, 1998), p. 162.

11

'We shall find a way through'[1]: the Church of Ireland, state prayers and liturgical realities

Daithí Ó Corráin

The unilateral decision by the first inter-party administration in 1948 to secede from the British Commonwealth and inaugurate a republic posed a challenge for the Church of Ireland. Despite disestablishment, the liturgy retained prayers for and references to the king and royal family. When Bunreacht na hÉireann was promulgated in 1937, the House of Bishops largely recommended that there be no change to the state prayers as the twenty-six counties remained within the Commonwealth.[2] But twelve years later, it was paradoxical that in a republic prayers would be offered for a foreign king. When the Republic of Ireland Act was signed into law in December 1948, the writer St John Ervine wondered: 'In law, all Episcopalians in Éire, like all other persons domiciled there, will be Republicans. Will the prayers for the King then be seditious?'[3] The order of public worship would have to reflect the changed constitutional position. But alteration of the state prayers required delicate handling. To some members of the Church of Ireland it opened the vista of two separate prayer books and perhaps a breach with fellow church members in Northern Ireland. To others it was an emotional and sentimental issue given the ties of blood, creed and culture with Britain and the Commonwealth. For still others, it represented an opportunity to pledge loyalty to the Southern state. The state prayers issue was by no means a crisis for the Church of Ireland, but it did represent something of a *crise de conscience*. This predicament

1 Abp John Gregg to Abp Geoffrey Fisher, 3 Jan. 1950, Lambeth Palace Archives, Fisher Papers, 72, f. 302. 2 'Report of proceedings of Standing Committee of the General Synod,' *Journal of General Synod* (henceforward *JGS*), pp 209–10. 3 St John Ervine to *The Times*, 23 Dec. 1948 [copy of letter], RCBL, Maude Papers, MS 262/1/2. Although John A. Costello stated that Éire had ceased to be a formal member of the Commonwealth in the Dáil on 28 July 1948, the Republic of Ireland bill was not introduced into the Dáil until 18 November 1948. It was signed by the President on 21 Decemeber and came into operation on Easter Monday 18 April 1949. For a discussion of the background to these developments, see Ian McCabe, *A diplomatic history of Ireland, 1948–49: the Republic, the Commonwealth and NATO* (Dublin, 1991).

exposed a generational divide among church members. It also revealed differing positions among the House of Bishops, clergy and laity and, until successfully resolved, appeared to threaten the unity of the Church of Ireland.

The clergy, having to serve a divided laity yet remain faithful to the guidance of the House of Bishops and the decisions of the General Synod, and by no means unanimous themselves, were in an invidious position. As we shall see, some were involved in the campaign to retain prayers for the king, but the majority followed the line of the House of Bishops. Throughout the controversy, the leadership of Archbishop John Allen Fitzgerald Gregg was pragmatic, unwavering and resolute. The implications for both the clergy and for the church as a whole were very clear to him. In his presidential address to the General Synod in May 1949, he acknowledged that 'the change which has come over the political scene ... causes the members of this Synod to acknowledge two diverse loyalties'.[4] However, he was emphatic that 'no change of political conditions will ever be allowed to mar the essential oneness of the Church of Ireland'.[5] Indeed Gregg's own career embodied the unity of the Church of Ireland across the political border. He served as archbishop of Dublin from 1920 until 1939 and Primate from 1939 until 1959. Less well known, however, is that he reluctantly but dutifully accepted translation from Dublin to Armagh. Professor Nicholas Mansergh recorded in his diary the view of Bishop John MacNeice of Cashel and Waterford (which the bishop expressed in writing to Gregg), that any refusal would be 'a great mistake chiefly because of [the] impression that the Church of Ireland was divided between North and South'.[6] Although two-thirds of the church's population resided in Northern Ireland, its administrative capital remained in Dublin. Furthermore, not only did the General Synod meet there annually but its ordinands were trained in Trinity College. For these reasons, Gregg and his brother bishops were keen to stress that any necessary change would be limited. In a letter to Lord Templemore, Bishop John Percy Phair of Ossory stressed that he and the House of Bishops felt that 'any alteration must be a minimum'.[7] In the meantime, Phair had instructed his clergy 'to continue to pray for the King until a definite direction has been given by the Church. You may rest assured that whatever is possible will be done to preserve our continuity.'[8] Archbishop Arthur Barton of Dublin also felt it prudent to play down any perceived threat to the unity of the Church of Ireland and urged that politics be kept out of discussions at the General Synod.[9]

A campaign for retention of the state prayers was initiated by Hugh Maude, a gentleman farmer from Clondalkin, who was both a member of the General Synod and of the Dublin, Glendalough and Kildare diocesan council. Maude, though

---

4 President's address, 10 May 1949, *JGS 1949*, p. lxxxiii.   5 Ibid.   6 'Diary entry Wednesday 14 Dec. 1938 (Dublin)' in Diana Mansergh (ed.), *Nationalism and independence: selected Irish papers by Nicholas Mansergh* (Cork, 1997), p. 133.   7 Bp J.P. Phair to Lord Templemore, 10 Dec. 1948, RCBL, Maude Papers MS 262/1/1/2/1.   8 Ibid.   9 Abp A. Barton to H. Maude, 20 April 1949, RCBL, Maude Papers, MS 262/1/1/2/28.

somewhat reluctant to go into print, was prompted to act by St John Ervine's letter. In a letter to the *Church of Ireland Gazette* on 14 January 1949, he stressed:

> Exceedingly important to us, members of the Church of Ireland, is the possibility of any alteration in the prayers for His Majesty the King and the Royal Family … The King binds us together as one great Christian family. It will be a bitter blow to a very large number in Southern Ireland if the State prayers are altered to preclude the King and the Royal Family.[10]

Maude revealed his motivation in a letter to David Wilson, dean of St Patrick's Cathedral in Dublin: 'There is a faction in this country belonging to our own great people, who have become lethargic. I am afraid defeatist too in their outlook towards their Church of Faith, their Country and their King.'[11] Having lost not only his brothers but the whole male side of his family in the service of the crown during or between the world wars, Maude was understandably aggrieved at the loss of prayers for the king.[12] He saw a stand on the state prayers issue as an ideal opportunity to rally Southern Protestants. The protracted debate which followed in the pages of the *Gazette* over the next two months revealed a generational and emotional divide among clergy and laity in terms of their response to the state prayers issue.

Maude was by no means without support. His efforts to retain the prayers were lauded in some quarters. For instance, one letter of encouragement felt he was 'making a great fight' and expressed the hope that his efforts would 'meet with complete success'.[13] Cecil Proctor, incumbent of Harold's Cross in Dublin, desired that prayers for the king would be continued because of the position he held in the Anglican Communion.[14] A.A. Luce, professor of moral philosophy and vice-provost of Trinity College, joined with Maude in trusting that the church authorities would 'not allow themselves to be stampeded into an orgy of liturgical regicide … for liturgical unity with our fellow Churchmen in the North is of first importance. If we are to remain one Church, we must retain the one Prayer Book.'[15]

10 H. Maude to editor of *Church of Ireland Gazette* (*CoIG*), 5 Jan. 1949 [copy of letter], RCBL, Maude Papers, MS 262/1/1/2/11; printed in *CoIG*, 14 Jan. 1949, vol. xciv, No. 3421, p. 10. A version was sent to the *Times* but does not appear to have been published.   11 H. Maude to Dean D. Wilson, 19 Jan. 1949 [draft of letter], RCBL, Maude Papers, MS 262/1/1/2/17.   12 H. Maude to Revd F. R. Alexander, 11 May 1949 [copy of letter], RCBL, Maude Papers, MS 262/1/1/3/65.   13 F. Moffett to H. Maude, 18 Jan. 1949, RCBL, Maude Papers, MS 262/1/1/2/16.   14 *CoIG*, 28 Jan. 1949, vol. xciv, No. 3423, p. 9. Born Sligo 1903; educated at The High School and Trinity College Dublin. Made a deacon in 1927; curate All Saints', Grangegorman 1927–30 and Christ Church, Leeson Park 1930–36; incumbent Harold's Cross 1936–63; missionary Colombo, Ceylon 1946–7. Prebendary of Dunlavin, St Patrick's Cathedral. 1962–3. Died 15 Dec. 1991. See J.B. Leslie and W.J.R. Wallace (ed.), *Clergy of Dublin and Glendalough* (Belfast, 2001), p. 991.   15 *CoIG*, 28 Jan. 1949, vol. xciv, No. 3423, p. 9. For Luce's biographical details see Leslie and Wallace, *Clergy of Dublin and Glendalough*, p. 839.

Luce did, however, acknowledge that south of the border public prayer for the king would be out of place and instead suggested a prayer amongst the occasional prayers. The alarming notion of a divided church was also touched on by T.F. Campbell, diocesan secretary of Armagh and incumbent of the Derrynoose Union. He hoped that 'both North and South we shall continue to pray for the rulers of both parts of our country, and not drive a wedge of partition into our Church of Ireland'.[16] A resolution by the Mulrankin, Rathmacknee and Kilturk Union in County Wexford sought to square this vexatious circle by suggesting that rather than pray geographically, the Church of Ireland should simply pray for 'all Christian kings, princes and rulers'.[17]

Younger members of the Church of Ireland, those born in the twentieth century or after the establishment of the state, tended to react differently to Maude's foray in the letter column. For instance, Frederick H. Garrett, curate of Rathkeale in County Limerick, felt it 'absurd' to pray for the king as the state prayers accorded him a 'position which he had not enjoyed since the passing of the 1937 constitution'. Garrett counselled that in this matter, 'facts and not sentiment must be the guide. And the hard facts are that the Twenty-Six Counties, whether one likes it or not, have become a Republic – a Republic outside the Commonwealth – in whose affairs King George VI has no say'.[18] One of the most discerning letters to comment on the generation gap came from the pen of R.F. Hipwell, rector of Castleventry in West Cork, who asked: 'is it unkind of me to remind Synodsmen that they are but mortal, and that south of the Border the number of people who feel absolutely no obligation of loyalty to the Crown is increasing yearly, while Unionism in the same area is decreasing proportionately?'[19] He believed that in another quarter century the political complexion of the Church of Ireland in the Republic would be very different and reminded synodsmen that they were 'legislating for posterity as well as for yourselves and your own political likes and dislikes'.[20] Some prominent younger members of the laity were also critical of Maude. For instance, David Webb, the respected Trinity College botanist, accused Maude of doing a disservice to the Anglican Communion by suggesting that it was somehow conterminous with the British empire and of refusing 'to face facts which, however unpalatable, remain facts'.[21] Hubert Butler felt that 'the Reformation is to-day more likely to be betrayed than saved by an indulgence in monarchic sentiment'.[22]

Archbishop Gregg summed up his divided constituency in a letter to Geoffrey Fisher, the archbishop of Canterbury:

> It is hard to find anything that suits the conditions in Éire. We have amongst our own people there ardent Republicans who have no wish to

---

16 *CoIG*, 11 Feb. 1949, vol. xciv, no. 3425, p. 9.   17 *CoIG*, 28 Apr. 1950, vol. xcv, no. 3488, p. 8. 18 *CoIG*, 28 Jan. 1949, vol. xciv, no. 3423, p. 9.   19 Ibid., 25 Feb. 1949, vol. xciv, no. 3428, p. 10. 20 Ibid.   21 Ibid., 28 Jan. 1949, vol. xciv, no. 3423, p. 9.   22 Ibid., 10 Feb. 1950, vol. xcv, no. 3477, p. 8.

hear the King's name – over against them being various of the British regime who will have the King, Republic or no Republic, and, as apart from these extremes, a central body of quiet worshippers who are ready to pray for all, without distinction who are in authority. We shall find a way through.[23]

In February 1949, Gregg made clear to Maude his belief that the matter had to be 'governed by the wishes of those who live in Éire. Change of some kind, I think, there must be'.[24] As he latter expressed it at the General Synod in May, 'For in our prayers, above all, there must be reality … sad as I am sure the hearts of many will be, we must obey the call of our Christian duty, even if it wounds our sentiment'.[25] The Primate's realism was shared by many of the laity. For instance, Sir Cecil King-Harmon, while sympathetic to Maude's position, nonetheless felt that 'we must have regard to the facts as they *are* and not as we would wish them to be. The essential fact is that we are now a Republic whether we like it or not.'[26] Though 'sorely against the grain' with King-Harmon, he argued that precisely because many felt strongly on the issue, 'political controversy should not be introduced in our form of *Public* Worship. We can always pray for the King in private.'[27] Many clergymen occupied this middle ground. Ernest Bateman, rector of Booterstown, Dublin since 1933, was a typical example. Though saddened to see Ireland leave the Commonwealth, he was nonetheless willing pragmatically to accept a republic. 'As a form of government I dislike it, but I intend to be loyal to it, and I hope that, when the Synod comes to deal with Forms of Prayer to be used within the new Republic, they will not force upon me a divided loyalty.'[28]

Bateman's comment captures the clash that the state prayers could potentially provoke between loyalty to the constitution of the state and obedience to principle. At the Clogher diocesan synod in September 1949, Bishop Tyner drew attention to this conundrum. He outlined the necessity for some alteration of the state prayers, but realised that it would be 'manifestly insincere to suggest that a legislative Act of either Church or State could transform treasured and deep rooted convictions'.[29] He added that 'as a Church they had an age-long tradition of loyalty to the Constitution under which they were governed, and in this spirit they should render due respect and service'.[30] This was the line pursued by the House of Bishops which was anxious to take the onus of responsibility off the shoulders of individual clergymen, until new prayers could be authorized.

23 Abp J. Gregg to Abp G. Fisher, 3 Jan. 1950, Lambeth Palace Archives, Fisher Papers, 72, f. 302.   24 Abp J. Gregg to H. Maude, 4 Feb. 1949, RCBL, Maude Papers, MS 262/1/1/2/26. 25 President's address, 10 May 1949, *JGS 1949*, pp. lxxxiii-iv.   26 Cecil S. King-Harmon to H. Maude, 7 May 1949, RCBL, Maude Papers, MS 262/1/1/3/56, King-Harmon's emphasis. 27 Ibid., King-Harmon's emphasis.   28 *CoIG*, 28 Jan. 1949, vol. xciv, No. 3423, p. 10.   29 *Impartial Reporter*, 6 Oct. 1949.   30 Ibid.

At a meeting on 5 April 1949, just under two weeks before the Republic of Ireland Act was due to come into operation, the Standing Committee of the General Synod appointed a sub-committee to draft the necessary resolution on which to found a bill to make temporary provision for state prayers in churches outside Northern Ireland.[31] This consisted of Archbishops Gregg and Barton and their legal advisers, R.G. Leonard and E.C. Micks. A bill in the names of James McCann, bishop of Meath and future Primate, and Leonard was proposed at the 1949 General Synod. This was unsuccessfully opposed by Frank FitzGibbon and Maude.[32] On the second reading Bishop McCann appealed to those present, 'if you do not pass this bill, I simply ask you what are we going to do?'[33] The bill to cover the interim period until permanent arrangements were made at the General Synod in 1950 was duly passed. Outside Northern Ireland, the formula 'O Lord guide and defend our Rulers' was to be used instead of 'O Lord, save the King' in morning and evening prayer.[34] The Prayer for the King and Commonwealth was to be replaced by 'Almighty God, who rulest over the nations ... Grant to thy servants, The President of this State and The Governor of Northern Ireland, and to all in authority, wisdom and strength to know and do thy will.'[35]

This neither satisfied Maude nor deterred him from further agitation. He was not alone. A resolution by members of the Loyal Orange Institution of Ireland in Donegal, which protested against the proposed changes to the Prayer Book and argued that the bishops' decision was too hasty, was sent to the bishop of Raphoe.[36] Ernest H.C. Lewis-Crosby, dean of Christ Church in Dublin since 1938, was one of Maude's closest allies.[37] Both men were critical of an editorial in the *Irish Times* in mid-May which advocated 'the cultivation of a totally new outlook' by Irish Protestants.[38] The editorial understood but did 'not necessarily share the feelings of the older generation of Irish Protestants, who have a long and not dishonourable tradition of loyalty to the British Crown'. But, it continued,

> Facts, however, must be faced. This part of Ireland is now completely separated from Great Britain and the Commonwealth; and Protestants, as well as Roman Catholics, must be prepared to draw the inevitable conclusions ... Henceforward, Irish Protestants in the South must make up their minds that they can have only one political allegiance; they must be unconditionally loyal to the Republic. Their children will continue to enjoy all the advantages of British citizenship in the United Kingdom and throughout

---

31 'Report of proceedings of Standing Committee of the General Synod for period ended 31 March 1950,' *JGS 1950*, p. 151.   32 'First day's proceedings, Tues 10 May 1949,' *JGS 1949*, pp xci–xcii; *Irish Times*, 11 May 1949.   33 *Irish Times*, 11 May 1949.   34 'Resolutions adopted by the General Synod,' *JGS 1949*, p. cxxxvii.   35 Ibid.   36 *Irish Times*, 5 May 1949.   37 For his biographical details, see Leslie and Wallace, *Clergy of Dublin and Glendalough*, p. 824.   38 *Irish Times*, 14 May 1949.

the Commonwealth; but they must not expose themselves to the taunt that they are in the State while not of it.[39]

Dean Lewis-Crosby responded with a letter to the editor which underlined that 'common prayers required unity and concord'.[40] In a letter of support to Lewis-Crosby, Maude believed the *Irish Times* never stood up firmly for Protestants and maintained that 'there are yet a vast number here and overseas, of our church people in all walks of life who are bewildered ... fearful that if a firm stand is not made that we have shown a weakness'.[41] Cecil Proctor, too, felt the *Irish Times* seemed to be 'facilitating in every way those who write in favour of the Republic. I have knowledge that letters on the other side have not been published – I mean letters simply emphasising our British connections, not necessarily anti-Nationalist in sentiment.'[42] In determined mood, Lewis-Crosby floated the suggestion that those not satisfied with the form proposed by the House of Bishops 'consult together and decide on the line of future action' lest the General Synod be corralled into acceptance of the bishops' solution without an alternative set of recommendations.[43] Maude agreed, but was anxious that from the outset 'the clergy – especially the senior men, such as yourself – must not appear to the public to be, shall I say disloyal, to the bishops'.[44] Lewis-Crosby offered Christ Church Chapter House as the venue for a gathering of concerned clergy and laity on 16 June.[45]

Following this meeting in the Chapter House, the details of which are not recorded in Maude's papers, Maude wrote to Archbishop Gregg. He felt compelled to inform the Primate frankly that many members of the Church were willing to oppose the continuation of the interim prayers and omissions. The letter asked the House of Bishops 'to consider seriously authorising a prayer, in the interim period between the Synods, for the King's welfare, apart from the Commonwealth Prayer, which is not a direct and personal appeal to God for the King's welfare'.[46] It was suggested that this be an occasional prayer to be uttered at 'the discretion of the clergy', which 'would temporarily help many Protestants, who are, to-day, wounded and offended'.[47] The letter closed with the request that there be either an authorised prayer for the king or that all state prayers be omitted.

Gregg's reply was pragmatic and somewhat legalistic. He put it to Maude that an unusual situation existed because 'there was no provision for meeting the case of

39 Ibid.   40 *Irish Times*, 16 May 1949.   41 H. Maude to Dean E.H. Lewis-Crosby, 16 May 1949 [copy of letter]; RCBL, Maude Papers, MS 262/1/1/3/69.   42 C. Proctor to H. Maude, 24 May 1949, RCBL, Maude Papers, MS 262/1/1/3/74.   43 E.H. Lewis-Crosby to H. Maude, 18 May 1949, RCBL, Maude Papers, MS 262/1/1/3/72.   44 H. Maude to E.H. Lewis-Crosby, 19 May 1949 [copy of letter]; RCBL, Maude Papers, MS 262/1/1/3/72.   45 E.H.Lewis-Crosby to H. Maude, 3 June 1949, RCBL, Maude Papers, MS 262/1/1/3/79.   46 H. Maude to Abp J. Gregg, 17 Jun. 1949 [copy of letter], RCBL, Maude Papers, MS 262/1/1/3/94.   47 Ibid.

there being *no* King. Accordingly, the only thing they could do was to come to the Synod and ask it to *cut the knot*.'[48] Furthermore, he reiterated the fact that removing discretion from individual clergy was the rationale behind the interim prayers and that the 1949 Synod 'acted with a full and complete knowledge of the situation, and could have rejected the prayers offered if it had wished, but it accepted them, and settled the matter for the next twelve months'.[49] Gregg's final sentence was a blunt reminder that 'the Church's governing body has spoken, and the Bishops – who asked it to speak – must obey'.[50] Maude regarded the Primate's response as 'an acknowledgement of weakness' and resolved to canvass the opinion of every rector in Southern Ireland in the early autumn to get the true picture.[51] Joseph Riversdale Colthurst, retired incumbent of Calary, Glendalough, County Wicklow and another staunch supporter of Maude, thought that the Primate was

> losing his grip. The leading motif in his mind and the archbishops seems to be to try to placate one section of our Church, at the expense of the other – an intrusion of politics into our forms of worship of a most deplorable kind. How the R.Cs must chuckle if they have any inkling of what is going on.[52]

Cecil Proctor was 'greatly disappointed' at Gregg's approach. He constructively suggested to Maude that direct opposition might not be as effective as a series of amendments.[53]

This line of action was actively pursued by Maude and his allies who tried to boost the Church of Ireland community's awareness of their position. In September 1949, Colthurst proposed a resolution at the East Glendalough Clerical Society in favour of a prayer for the welfare of the king and royal family. He intended to forward a copy to the joint secretary of the General Synod.[54] In the name of the members of Fingal Clerical Society, Dean Lewis-Crosby sought sanction for prayers for the king and Commonwealth, because 'it would be a mistake to quench the desire of those who worship in our churches to offer prayers in public worship for their brethren in Northern Ireland, Great Britain and the British Commonwealth and the rulers thereof'.[55] Maude highlighted the issue in a speech at the joint diocesan synod of Dublin, Glendalough and Kildare on 26 October 1949. He stressed the 'long-unbreakable ties with the Commonwealth of Nations

---

48 Abp J. Gregg to H. Maude, 22 Jun. 1949, RCBL, Maude Papers, MS 262/1/1/3/98. Gregg's emphasis. **49** Ibid. **50** Ibid. **51** H. Maude to Rita Ingram (Maude's secretary), 29 Jun. 1949 [copy of letter], RCBL, Maude Papers, MS 262/1/1/4/101. **52** J. R. Colthurst to H. Maude ('confidential'), 30 Jul. 1949, RCBL, Maude Papers, MS 262/1/1/4/120. **53** C. Proctor to H. Maude, 6 July 1949, RCBL, Maude Papers, MS 262/1/1/4/104. **54** J.R. Colthurst to H. Maude, 24 Sept. 1949, RCBL, Maude Papers, MS 262/1/1/4/124. **55** E.H. Lewis-Crosby to H. Maude with copy of proposed amendments to the archbishops' prayers, 4 Oct. 1949, RCBL, Maude Papers, MS 262/1/1/4/130.

and with its Head', but made clear that he did not pray for the king 'as the King of this part of the country, nor do we translate any of these prayers into a political petition'.[56] Nonetheless, he continued,

> it does offend and wound the spirit deeply to hear and find that the King's name has been left out of the services and prayers of this Church in the South ... We may be divided in our views on the best for our country with regard to politics. Let us be united in devout prayer for all men, especially for those who carry the heaviest responsibilities in a difficult and changing world.[57]

Furthermore, Maude raised a motion, seconded by Captain T.F. McKeever, 'That this House desires to record its disapproval of the existing temporary State Prayers'. In his speech, McKeever suggested that abolition of the existing state prayers would drive a wedge between northern and southern members of the Church of Ireland.[58] Had it been put to a vote, this resolution threatened to divide the joint diocesan synod. As president of the diocesan synod, Archbishop Barton was unwilling to countenance a division on a motion which may have introduced political feelings and accordingly requested that it be withdrawn.[59] Having made his protest, which one supporter described as 'calm and level-headed', Maude acceded to this.[60] Archbishop Barton privately admitted his gratitude for Maude's discretion and commented that he would have been 'almost equally distressed at its being passed or rejected'.[61]

The decision of the Standing Committee of the General Synod to appoint a sub-committee to report on the state prayers, on 18 October 1949, was something of a victory for Maude's coalition.[62] It allowed that faction at least the prospect of influencing what would come before the General Synod in 1950. Frank FitzGibbon felt 'we have gained something most important'.[63] Colthurst put it to Maude in military language: 'while we have hitherto been engaged in long-range bombing, we shall now be engaged in hand to hand fighting, having successfully breached the wall of the citadel!'[64] The twelve-member subcommittee included Archbishops Gregg and Barton; the bishops of Meath, Ossory, and Derry and

56 Copy H. Maude's speech to the joint diocesan synod of Dublin, Glendalough and Kildare in Dublin, 26 Oct. 1949, RCBL, Maude Papers, Miscellaneous. 57 Ibid. 58 *Irish Times*, 27 Oct. 1949. 59 *Belfast News-Letter*, 27 Oct. 1949. 60 J.R. Colthurst to H. Maude, 28 Oct. 1949, RCBL, Maude Papers, MS 262/1/1/4/142. 61 Abp A. Barton to H. Maude, 31 Oct. 1949 [copy of letter], RCBL, Maude Papers, MS 262/1/1/4/149. 62 John Briggs (Assistant Sec. of the General Synod) to Abp Gregg, 21 Oct. 1949 (RCBL, General Synod 2/16, General Synod Standing Committee, Sub-Committee on State Prayers). 63 Frank FitzGibbon to H. Maude, 24 Oct. 1949, RCBL, Maude Papers, MS 262/1/1/4/136. 64 J.R. Colthurst to H. Maude, 24 Oct. 1949 [copy of letter], RCBL, Maude Papers, MS 262/1/1/4/137.

Raphoe; J.E.L. Oulton, Regius professor of divinity at Trinity College; Senator
W.B. Stanford; Canon J.P. Shortt; Archdeacon William Webb of Glendalough;
Lord Farnham; F. FitzGibbon, KC; and R.G. Leonard, KC.[65] Maude felt that with
the exception of his associate Frank FitzGibbon, a synodsman since 1932, and the
bishop of Derry, the committee had been filled by Gregg with those opposed to
retention of the state prayers.[66] Archbishop Barton claimed that the nomination of
the committee was left solely to Gregg.[67] Maude was co-opted as a member on the
death of Archdeacon Webb on 26 December 1949.

Gregg enquired of Bishop Basil Roberts, secretary of the Society for the
Propagation of the Gospel in Foreign Parts, if an analogy existed elsewhere in the
Anglican communion. Roberts in turn sought the advice of the archbishop of
Canterbury.[68] Archbishop Geoffrey Fisher was unsure how chaplains abroad
prayed for the government of the country concerned. In his view

> Armagh must make up his mind whether he wants one prayer for the whole
> of Ireland or two – one for N. Ireland and one for S. Ireland. If the former,
> our State prayer would have to be a good bit adapted to fit both the King
> and the Government of Éire. I should have thought that much his best
> course was to keep all our prayers about the King, the Empire and the
> Commonwealth and the Royal Family for N. Ireland and to have a separate
> prayer or prayers for use in S. Ireland.[69]

So it proved.

The result of the sub-committee's efforts was contained in a bill brought before
the General Synod in 1950. The House of Bishops has not made the deliberations
of the Standing Committee and its sub-committees public. However, a letter
among Maude's papers reveals that it was Robert McNeill Boyd, bishop of Derry
and Raphoe since 1945 and a chaplain to the forces awarded the Military Cross
during the First World War, who defused protest over the prayer for the king outside Northern Ireland.[70] He ingeniously proposed the addition of the words 'in
whose Dominions we are not counted as aliens', which he regarded as 'a reasonable ground why any citizen might pray for the King without imputing disloyalty
to his own State'.[71] He sought, in confidence, Maude's views on this before sub-

---

65 'Report of proceedings of Standing Committee of the General Synod,' *JGS 1950*, p. 152.
66 H. Maude to Frank FitzGibbon, 10 Nov. 1949 [copy of letter], RCBL, Maude Papers, MS
262/1/1/5/156.   67 Abp A. Barton to John Briggs, 24 Oct. 1949, RCBL, General Synod
2/16, General Synod Standing Committee, Sub-Committee on State Prayers.   68 Basil C.
Roberts (secretary of The Society for the Propagation of the Gospel in Foreign Parts) to Revd
H. M. Waddens, 20 Dec 1949, Lambeth Palace Archives, Fisher Papers, 72, f. 299.   69 Abp G.
Fisher to Revd B. C. Roberts, 29 Dec. 1949, Lambeth Palace Archives, Fisher Papers, 72, f. 300.
70 For Boyd's biographical details, see F.W. Fawcett and D.W.T. Crooks, *Clergy of Derry and
Raphoe* (Belfast, 1999), p. 190.   71 Bp R.M. Boyd to H. Maude, 3 Dec. 1949, RCBL, Maude
Papers, MS 262/1/1/5/178.

mitting it to the sub-committee as 'an expression of what those who still find the pull of the older connection would wish to express in worship, having regard to the changed conditions'.[72] It met Maude's objections.[73] The amended prayer for King George VI thus read:

> Almighty God, the fountain of all goodness, we humbly beseech thee to behold they servant, King GEORGE the Sixth, in whose dominions we are not accounted strangers. Endue him with thy Holy Spirit; enrich him with thy heavenly grace; prosper him with all happiness and bring him to thine everlasting kingdom; through Jesus Christ our Lord.[74]

The dilemma posed by prayers which contained references to the king, such as Morning Prayer, was solved by the simple expedient of enclosing such references in square brackets prefixed with the letters *N. I.* Similarly, any words enclosed in square brackets prefixed with the letters *R. I.* were to be used in the Republic only.[75] The *Gazette* quipped that the solution was not unlike algebra with the insertion and removal of brackets![76] In the Republic, a prayer for the President and all in authority would be read:

> Almighty God, who rulest over the nation of the world ... Grant to The President of this State and to all in authority, wisdom and strength to know and do thy will. Fill them with the love of truth and righteousness, and made them ever mindful of their calling to serve thy people faithfully to thy honour and glory; through Jesus Christ our Lord.[77]

Analogous minor amendments were made in the order for prayers of thanksgiving, communion and catechism. Thus only *one* Book of Common Prayer would be required by the Church of Ireland, an outcome which pleased all concerned. Thanking Maude, Boyd felt those attached 'to the older loyalties have much for which to be thankful with regard to the outcome of the sub-committee's efforts. For a minority [on the sub-committee] we achieved as much as we could expect, and that without too much tension.'[78] Maude intimated to Colthurst that he was 'amused' and 'shocked' that 'those who were extreme in their views at the beginning are now pretending that they always wanted a prayer for the King'.[79]

For the Church of Ireland population in the Republic, the state prayers issue was also a turning point in terms of party-political allegiance. Those who had supported Fine Gael in the February 1948 election, because the party was regarded as

---

72 Ibid.   **73** H. Maude to Bp R.M. Boyd, 6 Dec. 1949 [copy of letter], RCBL, Maude Papers, MS 262/1/1/5/179.   **74** *JGS 1950*, p. xcv.   **75** *JGS 1950*, pp xcii–xciii.   **76** *CoIG*, 19 May 1950, vol. xcv, no. 3491, p. 7.   **77** *JGS 1950*, p. xciii.   **78** Bp R.M. Boyd to H. Maude, 10 March 1950, RCBL, Maude Papers, MS 262/1/1/5/193.   **79** H. Maude to J.R. Colthurst, 24 May 1950 [copy of letter], RCBL, Maude Papers, MS 262/1/1/5/211.

dependable on constitutional issues, were shocked when John A. Costello seceded from the Commonwealth. Bishop John Percy Phair found it hard 'to understand why this measure has been introduced, especially since we were told expressly that no such change was contemplated. It has given a shock to many who like myself supported the ruling party at the election. Who is one to trust these days?'[80] Another clergyman felt that the 'Government was guilty of a breach of promise in the action they have taken,' a point also made by W.B. Stanford in his memoirs.[81] In a letter to the *Irish Times*, Cecil Proctor wondered if a single T.D. or Senator could be found 'to voice the feelings of the pro-Commonwealth community?'[82] A week later William Sheldon, an active member of the Church of Ireland and independent T.D. for Donegal East, answered the call. He bitterly criticised the government in the Dáil:

> To argue, that by going further apart we are getting nearer together, is an insult to the intelligence of those who have been repeatedly assured that Fine Gael desired association with the Commonwealth … it should be recognised that there is a minority which believes that this nation could find full expression for its national outlook and at the same time remain within the comity of nations called the Commonwealth of Nations.[83]

Sheldon articulated a belief among the Church of Ireland population in the South that membership of the British Commonwealth posed no threat to Irish independence and should not have been abandoned. This was reinforced by India's subsequent example of remaining within the Commonwealth as a republic. As Lord Rugby (Sir John Maffey), the first UK representative to Ireland, later expressed it, Costello 'brought about a position in which all the bridges went down between Éire and the Commonwealth'.[84] Confidence in Fine Gael had been previously undermined by a diplomatically unprecedented telegram to the pope, 'desiring to repose at the feet of your Holiness the assurance of our loyalty and of our devotion to your

80 Bp J.P. Phair to Lord Templemore, 10 Dec. 1948, RCBL, Maude Papers, MS 262/1/1/2/1.
81 Edward F. Grant to H. Maude ('private'), n. d., RCBL, Maude Papers, MS 262/1/1/2/39;
W.B. Stanford, *Stanford: Regius professor of Greek, 1940–80, Trinity College, Dublin: memoirs* (Dublin, 2001), p. 124.   82 C. Proctor to *Irish Times*, 16 Nov. 1948 [copy of letter], reprinted in W.C.G. Proctor, *A Dublin theological scrapbook* (Dublin, 1973), p. 41.   83 Dáil Debates (hereafter DD), 113, cols. 442–3, 24 Nov. 1948. Born Derry 1907; educated Foyle College and Queen's University, Belfast, where he read mathematics and science. First elected in 1943 for Donegal East as member of Clann na Talmhan, he switched to the Farmer's Party in 1944 but from 1948 was returned as an Independent. He did not stand in 1961 when Donegal was split into two 3-seater constituencies – North-East and South-West. Former chairman of Dáil Public Accounts Committee, the joint committee on Statutory Instruments and the Inter-Parliamentary Union, he retired from politics in 1973. He served as honorary secretary to the General Synod at different periods. He died on 1 November 1999.   84 Lord Rugby to Éamon de Valera, 18 May 1957, University College Dublin Archives, de Valera Papers, P105/2940.

August Person'.[85] In a letter to the *Irish Times*, Victor Griffin, then a curate in Derry, protested that the government of a state, which professed to be democratic and republican, should not on election to office 'set about publicising their subservience to a foreign pontiff or to any religious leader'.[86] Allied to the Mother and Child *débâcle*, the upshot of Fine Gael's actions was a reappraisal of Church of Ireland political opinion, in some quarters, in favour of Fianna Fáil, which was seen as 'less supine in the face of ecclesiastical pressure'.[87] One such critic was Cecil Proctor who, in a letter to the *Irish Times*, wrote 'we have not got the same confidence as we once had in the Fine Gael party, where changes in the Constitution are concerned'.[88]

As might be expected, the successful resolution of the state prayers issue did not extinguish a residual loyalty to the crown. When King George VI died on 6 February 1952, the Standing Committee sent a letter of sympathy signed by Gregg, with studied correctness, 'on behalf of the Standing Committee of the General Synod of the Church of Ireland.'[89] However, such sympathy was not simply confined to members of the Church of Ireland. President Seán T. Ó Ceallaigh felt the death of the king 'caused an extraordinary outburst of feeling everywhere. Even in Ireland, one could sense the depth of the sympathy that arose spontaneously.'[90] As international courtesy dictated, both the Taoiseach and the President sent letters of sympathy to Churchill and Princess (now Queen) Elizabeth respectively.[91] On the day of the king's death, de Valera requested that flags be flown at half-mast on all state civil buildings and a week later he made a dignified statement in the Dáil, tendering on behalf of the Irish people 'a neighbourly understanding and a neighbourly sympathy'.[92] The government was represented at the funeral by Frank Aiken, minister for external affairs, and F. H. Boland, the Irish ambassador in London. A memorial service, one of a number which took place in the state, was held in St Patrick's Cathedral on 15 February, at which the President was represented by Colonel Ronald Mew and the government by Erskine Childers.[93]

The state prayers controversy could be regarded as a collision between inveterate sentiment and emotionalism on the one hand and a necessary response to an

85 Cited in Dermot Keogh, 'The role of the Catholic Church in the Republic of Ireland 1922–1995' in *Building trust in Ireland: studies commissioned by the Forum for Peace and Reconciliation* (Belfast, 1996), p. 130.   86 Victor Griffin, *Mark of protest: an autobiography* (Dublin, 1993), p. 82.   87 Kenneth Milne, 'Brave New World' in Stephen R. White (ed.), *A time to build* (Dublin, 1999), p. 21.   88 C. Proctor to *Irish Times*, 11 Mar. 1954 [copy of letter], reprinted in Proctor, *A Dublin theological scrapbook*, p. 52.   89 'Report of proceedings of Standing Committee of the General Synod,' *JGS 1952*, p. 92.   90 Seán T. Ó Ceallaigh to Shane Leslie, 25 Feb. 1952, NLI, Shane Leslie Papers, MS 22,848.   91 É. de Valera to W.S. Churchill, 6 Feb. 1952 [copy of telegram]; S.T. Ó Ceallaigh to Princess Elizabeth, 6 Feb. 1952 [copy of letter], NA, Department of the Taoiseach (hereafter DT) S 15256A.   92 Minute by D. Ó Suilleabháin, 6 Feb. 1952, minute of 7 Feb. 1952, NA, DT S 15256A; DD, 129, col. 410, 13 Feb. 1952.   93 William Cecil de Pauley, dean of St Patrick's Cathedral, to É. de Valera, 10 Feb. 1952; President's secretary to Maurice Moynihan (secretary to government), 11 Feb. 1952; M. Moynihan to W.C. de Pauley, 12 Feb. 1952 [copy of letter], NA, DT S 15256A.

altered constitutional position on the other. However, when viewed against the backdrop of an all-Ireland church, the majority of which resided north of the border, it takes on a somewhat different colour. The British Commonwealth was regarded as a bond which further linked northern and southern members of the church. This tie was suddenly and unexpectedly broken. However, any suggestion that this might weaken the unity of the Church of Ireland across the political border was deeply repugnant to Archbishop Gregg. The press of circumstances demanded a reshaping of the state prayers lest the Church of Ireland's allegiance to the Republic be called into doubt. For proponents of the retention of prayers for the king, such as Hugh Maude and Dean Lewis-Crosby, the matter was a heated one. But Gregg and the House of Bishops resisted any reflex response. By such judicious handling, the issue was defused in a manner which both reaffirmed the Church's unshakeable ties of creed and its loyalty to the states in which it operated. Thus, preaching in All Saints' Church, Blackrock, County Dublin, on 10 February 1952, the Revd Harry Dobbs could claim his faithful were loyal citizens of the Republic but also that

> loyalty to the sovereign was in our blood…It is an imperishable thing, and we older people are not ashamed of our faithfulness…especially to the King…[we] who were bound to him by invisible ties which no political revolutions could sever, grieve for his passing as deeply as do his own subjects.[94]

Gregg and the Church of Ireland had 'found a way through'.

---

94 Copy sermon preached in All Saints' Church, Blackrock on 10 Feb. 1952, RCBL, Crawford Papers, MS 402/6.

12

The clergy and the schools

Kenneth Milne

Many traditional perceptions of the Reformation in Ireland under Henry VIII have undergone substantial revision in recent decades, but two stand virtually unchallenged: that Henry's proposals for parish schools were concerned with promoting English law and culture rather than religion, and that this ambitious scheme largely failed. Writing in 1837, three hundred years later, Sir Thomas Wyse, the leading Catholic educationist of his day, commented on the fact that the whole Henrician system[1] 'was confided to the hands of the clergy', there being no alternative: they were the only men of education in the parish.[2] But it was a law on paper only! Wyse had already, in 1835, proposed (unsuccessfully) legislation to refine the National School system introduced four years previously. He claimed that the Tudor statute had its roots in traditional church policy stretching back to the middle ages, and had in particular Scottish ancestry. But the laws in Ireland had results that were very different from those in Scotland, for in Ireland: 'the schools were English – the people Irish: the schools became Protestant – the people remained Catholic'.[3]

In fact, this Tudor legislation, making no specific reference to the teaching of religion, was similar in purpose to fourteenth-century laws seeking to pre-empt the Gaelicization of the colonists, and Sir Henry Cowley, writing to Thomas Cromwell, said as much when he averred that 'many of the old statutes of Kilkenny are good to be put in execution'.[4] King Henry's legislation did, nonetheless, involve the clergy in the educational process of the state by requiring every archbishop and bishop, 'and every other having authority and power to give order of priesthood, deacon and subdeacon' to demand of ordinands that they would do their utmost not only 'to learn the English tongue and use English order and fashion', but also to provide in the parish 'a school for to learn English'. The statute

---

1 'An act for the English order, habit and language', 28 Henry VIII, c. 15. 2 Thomas Wyse, 'Education in the United Kingdom: its progress and prospects' in *Central Society of Education*, i (London, 1837), pp 27–64, at pp 47–50. 3 *Hansard's parliamentary debates*, 3rd ser., xxvii, cols 1209, 1216 (19 May 1835). 4 State Papers, Henry VIII, ii (part iii), p. 449.

laid down a scale of fines and other penalties to which defaulting bishops and priests were liable, and there is a little evidence that in Henry's latter years inquisitions were held, in the diocese of Armagh at least, in an attempt to detect defaulters, and that fines were levied.[5] But the legislation omitted to make any provision for the payment of the masters.

In attempting to assess the extent to which local performance matched government intentions from Tudor times onwards, we frequently have recourse to the several official investigations into educational provision that took place from the late eighteenth century, and at this point it may be helpful to digress slightly to say something about these enquiries. The first such body was appointed in 1788 (reporting in 1791) and was in large measure the result of the zeal for educational reform displayed by Thomas Orde, chief secretary from 1784 to 1787. Its remit was to report on the funding and condition of schools of both public and private endowment.[6] Some years later, another enquiry was instituted, commissioners (generally referred to as 'the board of education'), being appointed to report on the condition of all schools in Ireland. It sat from 1806 to 1812, producing fourteen reports in all, its membership including the archbishops of Armagh and Dublin and the dean of St Patrick's, illustrating an aspect of clerical participation in matters educational that is sometimes overlooked: committee service. This was especially notable in the case of Archbishop Charles Brodrick of Cashel, who sat on the board as coadjutor for the ailing archbishop of Dublin and found himself a signatory to its fourteenth and final report.[7] Yet another investigatory body was set up in 1824, again because the chief secretary, now Lord Stanley, gave priority to educational matters and in particular to the need to address the grievances about schools that were persistently brought to the attention of government by the Catholic hierarchy. In 1825 the commissioners produced a report that was, as we shall see, hard-hitting and highly influential.[8]

The parliamentary commission that reported in 1791 found no evidence whatever to suggest that many, if, indeed, any schools resulted from the Henrician legislation of 1537,[9] while the board of education, whose findings on the parish schools were first published in 1809,[10] recorded that in 1552 the lord chancellor, Cusack, had complained to Northumberland, president of the council in England, that laws to enforce the English language were inefficacious and that so deficient in the use of English were some of the clergy of the Church of Ireland that the law allowed them to officiate in Latin.[11]

---

5 H.A. Jefferies, *Priests and prelates of Armagh in the age of reformations, 1518–1558* (Dublin, 1997), pp 144–5, n. 5.   6 D.H. Akenson, *The Irish education experiment: the national system of education in the nineteenth century* (London and Toronto, 1970), p. 69.   7 Kenneth Milne, 'Principle or pragmatism: Archbishop Brodrick and church education policy' in *As by law established*, pp 187–94.   8 Akenson, *Irish education experiment*, pp 94–8.   9 'Report of commissioners of Irish education enquiry' in *Evidence taken before her Majesty's commissioners into the state of the endowed schools in Ireland, 1857–8* (2336), xxii, pt 2, pp 342–5.   10 *Eleventh report of the commissioners of the board of education, Ireland: parish schools*, H.C. 1821 (743), xi, p. 2.   11 Ibid.

A further attempt at school provision was made under Elizabeth by 'An act for the erection of free schools' of 1570.[12] Henceforth (in theory) there was to be a free (grammar) school in every diocese, and the schoolmaster was to be an Englishman, 'or of the English birth of this realm of Ireland'. The archbishops of Armagh and Dublin, and the bishops of Meath and Kildare, were to appoint these masters in their respective dioceses, and elsewhere the appointments were to be made by the lord deputy. The bishops and clergy were to bear the cost of the master's salary and of erecting and maintaining school-houses. As with the parish school legislation, this too was more honoured in the breach than in the observance. Indeed its passage through the Irish parliament had not been easy, and provides an early example of how differing opinions among the leading figures in church and state could delay measures that needed urgent attention if they were to be effective. In the event, the bill 'was refused' in the parliamentary session of 1569, only reaching the statute book the following year.[13] Once enacted, however, it required enforcement, which was lacking, even though prominent figures such as Lord Chancellor Weston regarded state-controlled education as a *sine qua non* for the preservation of English rule and 'religious conquest',[14] and Adam Loftus, archbishop of Armagh and subsequently of Dublin, not one of its original sponsors, petitioned the crown in 1578 that steps be taken for the execution of the statutes for erecting schools 'recently made'. The response was favourable (even if little seems to have been done).[15]

The commission that reported in 1791 could find no trace of any such free grammar schools, even in diocesan registers, which is not to say that some had not existed previously, which we know to have been the case. But the comments of observers towards the end of Elizabeth's reign, however extravagantly expressed, testify to a high incidence of poorly-educated clergy, who would scarcely have been equipped to discharge the obligations imposed on them by the act, even had they been so disposed, and, more to the point, adequately funded. Edmund Spenser, through his interlocutor 'Irenius', expressed the need for 'one petty schoolhouse, adjoining unto the parish church to be the more in view',[16] drawing an unflattering contrast between the popish clergy who braved every danger to travel to Ireland, and the complacent clerics of the established church, reluctant to be drawn from their 'warm nests and sweet lovers' sides' to work in God's harvest. Yet, Spenser conceded, even had they done their duty, it would have availed them little, for, while there were laws to make provision for such public institutions, they

---

12 12 Eliz., c.2.   13 *Cal. SP, Ireland, 1509–1573*, p. 400.   14 Helga Hammerstein, 'Aspects of the continental education of Irish students in the reign of Queen Elizabeth' in T.D.Williams (ed.), *Historical studies VIII: papers read before the Irish Conference of Historians, Dublin, 27–30 May 1969* (Dublin, 1971), p. 137; *Cal. SP, Ireland, 1509–73*, p. 428.   15 J. Morrin (ed.), *Calendar of the patent and close rolls of chancery in Ireland: 18th to 45th of Queen Elizabeth*, ii, 25.   16 Edmund Spenser, *A view of the state of Ireland (1596)*, ed. W.L. Renwick (London, 1934), p. 204.

were not executed.[17] William Saxey, who seems to have been a somewhat choleric chief justice, writing to Viscount Cranborne in 1604, referred to the poor quality of Irish bishops, the egregious Myler McGrath among them, who retained many benefices to themselves, the parishioners being more likely to encounter a tithe-proctor than an incumbent.[18] Though Saxey may have been a somewhat hostile witness, the bishop of Cork having complained that he treated him (the bishop) 'no better than if I were his horseboy'.[19] A free school had indeed been founded in that diocese, like those erected by Lancaster and Long (Loftus's successors in Armagh), and Brady of Meath.[20] Robert Gafney, taught school in Kilkenny, without stipend, and was a convert highly suspect in the eyes of Loftus, but vouched for by Robert Garvey, one of the ecclesiastical commissioners set up to improve the state of the church in about 1576.[21]

Abundant evidence points to failure to implement the law where both parish and free diocesan schools were concerned. In 1552, as we have seen, the lord chancellor, Cusack, a keen reformer, was complaining about this and a commission issued to Loftus and others in 1593 'to put in force as far as concerns the clergy the act of 28 Henry VIII, for the English order, habit and language' says as much.[22] Considering the difficulties presented by any attempt to implement the schools' policy in the accessible dioceses of the Pale, it is small wonder that little could be achieved in those regions where the organisation and resources of the church were minimal.[23] The failure to provide a site for a diocesan school in the diocese of Limerick was attributed to 'the ordinary [bishop] and others of the clergy' failing to meet their financial obligations under the act.[24] A newly-appointed bishop, Thornburgh, appealed to the privy council in London 1594 to instruct the mayor and aldermen of Galway to bring their wives and children to church to hear his sermons, so much had the leading citizens of that place repudiated the Reformation.[25] Understandably, the power to appoint masters given to the lord deputy in most dioceses was resented by the clergy, who believed that the patronage ought to be theirs, and that he who pays the piper should call the tune – a source of discontent that had, in part, accounted for the bill's delayed passage through parliament.[26] Nor should we lose sight of the difficulties posed by the unstable state of the country, complicated by the lingering disruption following the Kildare rebellion.[27]

17 Ibid., pp 208–9. 18 Ibid. 19 *Cal. SP, Ireland, 1599–1600*, p. 225. 20 Brendan Bradshaw, 'Sword, word and strategy in the Reformation in Ireland' in *HJ*, xxi (1978), p. 486. This article describes the tensions existing between some of the reformers. 21 W.M. Brady (ed.), *State papers concerning the Irish church in the time of Queen Elizabeth* (London, 1868), pp 32–6. 22 *The Irish fiants of the Tudor sovereigns* (4 vols, Dublin, 1994), iii, 1593. 23 Aidan Clarke, 'Varieties of uniformity in the first century of the Church of Ireland' in D. Wood and W.J. Sheils (eds), *The churches, Ireland and the Irish* (London, 1989), p. 115. 24 Morrin, *Patent and close rolls*, p. 42. 25 Brendan Bradshaw, 'The Reformation in the cities of Cork, Limerick and Galway, 1534–1603' in J. Bradley (ed.), *Settlement and society in medieval Ireland: studies presented to F.X. Martin, O.S.A.* (Kilkenny, 1988), p. 463. 26 Richard Mant, *History of the Church of Ireland* (2 vols, London 1840), i, p. 289. 27 Steven G. Ellis, 'The Kildare rebellion and the early Henri-

However, an isolated reference to recognition of the law relating to clerical duties in this regard occurs in the chapter acts of St Patrick's Cathedral, Dublin, when a newly installed archdeacon of Glendalough (whose jurisdiction included much of County Wicklow, one of the most unsettled parts of Ireland) was reminded of his obligation to teach or cause to be taught 'an English school' within the archdeaconry 'as law requires'.[28] The Church of Ireland had also to contend with the successful and popular schools that continued to be run by Catholics, Peter White's legendary school in Kilkenny being a case in point. According to Helga Hammerstein, the only comparable Protestant school opened in Tudor Ireland was that created by James Fullerton and James Hamilton in Great Ship Street, Dublin, attended by James Ussher.[29] How unrealistic highly-placed ecclesiastics could be is evident from Archbishop Loftus's claim, when arguing against the suppression of St Patrick's and its transformation into an educational institution, that 'I might say schools are provided for, in every county here'.[30]

The early years of the seventeenth century saw the introduction of a new scheme for schools in the context of the Ulster Plantation. Though limited in scope, and getting off to a very uncertain start, the royal free schools resulted in the foundation of some institutions that endure to the present time. As with earlier government-sponsored initiatives in education, the primary concern in Ulster was with civilizing the native Irish and forestalling the lapse of settlers into Irishry, and as before, the clergy figured in the plan. James I intended that in each of the confiscated counties, Armagh, Cavan, Coleraine [Londonderry], Donegal, Fermanagh and Tyrone, a free school should be established. The project was slow to get under way, so much so that in 1612 the king ordered that all the lands earmarked for schools should be conveyed to the appropriate bishop, who would designate the school site.[31] Not all instantly complied, but some schools eventually appeared. Charles I, to move the process forward, granted to the archbishop of Armagh and his successors large tracts in several Ulster counties, including profitable land and bog in County Armagh itself worth £662 os. 7d. per annum, a not inconsiderable sum.[32] Charles created further 'royal' schools in Banagher (King's County) and Carysfort (County Wicklow), but few of these Stuart foundations gained plaudits from the 1791 commissioners. While warm in their praises for Armagh, elsewhere they uncovered a high incidence of alienation of property and inadequate management. The masters were generally (though not invariably) in holy orders, and in many cases the incumbent of the parish appointed a substitute to conduct the school and paid little attention to it himself. Where the rector retained the mastership, there might be

cian Reformation' in *HJ*, xix (1976), pp 807–30.   **28** RCBL, C2/1/3/9, f. 33v.   **29** Hammerstein, 'Aspects', p. 140.   **30** Brady, *State papers*, p. 95.   **31** James VI and I to Sir Arthur Chichester, 30 Jan. 1612, in *Cal. SP, Ireland, 1611–1614*, pp 467–8. Part of the text (together with the king's orders of 1623) is to be found in Áine Hyland and Kenneth Milne (eds), *Irish educational documents I : a selection of extracts relating to the history of Irish education from the earliest times to 1922* (Dublin, 1987), pp 42–4.   **32** *1791 Report*, p. 345.

no pupils (the case in Banagher),[33] whereas the incumbent of Carysfort had franchised out the school to an 'obscure man' to whom the profits of the school accrued, in return for an annual payment to the rector of £10.[34] A sorry tale of unsuitable appointments and mismanagement of assets was also the case in Cavan,[35] while the good intentions of the London companies to discharge their educational obligations in Coleraine seem to have been dogged by confusion.[36] A school was founded, but the mayor, commonalty and citizens petitioned the London commissioners to the effect that the 700 acres originally set aside for its endowment had not been used. While a school did undoubtedly exist, there was a mystery as to the fate of its endowments, so that it could not be 'free' as originally intended. The manner in which endowments were mismanaged, indeed misappropriated, led the 1791 education commissioners to declare that, 'this traffic in great charitable foundations, which might be rendered so highly useful to the community is too shameful to need any comment', and they proposed radical remedies, not least the reduction in the, to their mind, inordinate salaries that the proprietors of the schools were awarding themselves.[37] Generations were to pass before adequate regulation of educational endowments came about.[38] Remedies were indeed applied, if gradually, to the ordering of royal as of other foundations, culminating in major reforms in the endowed schools in the late- nineteenth century.

What distinguished the royal schools from earlier state initiatives in popular and grammar school education was the fact that from the outset they were provided with endowments, and when these were properly administered, the schools prospered, so that some of them survive today, in both jurisdictions of Ireland. Another legacy from the Stuarts, the Hospital and Free School of King Charles the Second, in Dublin ('The King's Hospital'), was established by royal charter in 1671 at the prompting of Dublin Corporation, and from its inception until the late-twentieth century was headed by clergy of the Church of Ireland. The schools founded under the trust established by Erasmus Smith, a Cromwellian layman, provided under a charter of 1669 for grammar as well as elementary schools, and the headships, and indeed other teaching positions, in the grammar schools were from the outset held by clergy.[39]

By the beginning of the eighteenth century, state policy had turned from the prescriptive to the proscriptive. What was now at stake was not the survival of English language and custom, but the Protestant constitution and the hegemony of those who benefited under it. Parliament was once again to attempt to use educational statutes to further state policy in general. Laws were passed prohibiting Catholics from school-teaching, and making it unlawful for Catholic families to

---

33 *1791 Report*, p. 346. 34 Ibid. 35 Philip O'Connell, *The schools and scholars of Breifne* (Dublin, 1942), chapters iv and v. 36 See T.W. Moody, *The Londonderry plantation, 1609–41: the city of London and the plantation of Ulster* (Belfast, 1939), pp 172, 198, 205. 37 *1791 Report*, p. 346. 38 See p. 224 below. 39 W.J.R. Wallace, *Faithful to our trust: a history of the Erasmus Smith Trust and the High School, Dublin* (Dublin, 2004).

send their sons abroad for education,[40] but to very limited effect. The Catholic schoolmaster continued, sometimes clandestinely, as often as not quite openly, to 'teach school' often in the primitive accommodation known as the 'hedge school'. The better-off Catholic families employed tutors, frequently priests, to teach their young, prior, in many instances, to sending them to the continental colleges, whatever the risks, where they were prepared for ordination. For their part, the clergy of the established church tended the children of their own community (and frequently others) through the parochial charity schools, in some cases developed from parish schools and indistinguishable from them, and which became prominent features in the early eighteenth century.[41]

When Michael Sadleir, the influential English educationist, wrote in 1897 that 'national education in Ireland began when the Irish parliament established parish schools', he was rather stretching the point.[42] Yet some continuity, of purpose, if not of achievement, can be discerned in the successive attempts over generations, at times official, more often voluntary, to provide 'popular' education. The clergy of the established church were deeply involved in them all, and in none more so than in the charity schools. The change in name, if not in nature, was neatly encapsulated by the commissioners of the board of education, who, in their eleventh report, voiced the opinion that parish schools as originally conceived were no longer needed for their original purpose – the introduction and defence of the English language – nor could they any longer discharge the purpose that they were 'converted' to – the advancement of the Protestant religion.[43] Indeed the commissioners went so far as to recommend that consideration be given to dropping the clerical oath requiring incumbents to set up such schools.[44] However, that obligation was valued by men such as Archbishop Brodrick of Cashel, who, though a signatory to the board's final report which proposed a new system of elementary education, and harbouring few illusions as to the effectiveness of the bulk of parish schools, believed, as did the Primate (Archbishop Stuart), that without the oath clerical superintendence of schools would decline even further.[45]

The Revd Edward Nicholson, himself the founder of one of the earliest charity schools, Primrose Grange in County Sligo, pointed out in 1714 that there were many such, and enumerated several that owed their foundation to clergy (such as himself), a bishop (Archbishop Vesey of Tuam) and a number of distinguished laity. Indeed, the surge of interest in charity schools, taken up in Ireland mainly through Irish adherents (such as Nicholson himself) to the Society for Promoting Christian Knowledge in England, was gathering momentum and led to the formation of a Society for Advancing Charity Schools in Ireland.[46] We can trace their

---

40 7 Will.III, c.4.   41 Kenneth Milne, *The Irish charter schools, 1730–1830* (Dublin, 1997), pp 17–18.   42 [M.E.Sadleir], *Special reports on educational subjects 1896–7* (London, 1897), pp 211–57, at p. 211.   43 *Eleventh report*, pp 273 ff.   44 Ibid.   45 Milne, 'Principle or pragmatism: Archbishop Brodrick and church education policy' in *As by law established*, pp 187–203, at p. 190.   46 Edward Nicholson, *A method of charity schools, recommended, for giving both a religious educa-*

growing number, supported by subscription, in the Society's regular reports, and by the 1730s they existed in their hundreds and were to be found in every county.[47] They were, it has been argued by David Hayton,[48] symptoms of an early eighteenth-century 'second reformation', concerned with religion and manners. And, while by no stretch of the imagination as universal as the Henrician parish schools were intended to be, the parochial charity schools were the nearest that the parish clergy had yet come to fulfilling local needs. Some of the schools, given a broader curriculum and Lancastrian pedagogy by the Kildare Place Society from 1811, and financial resources by the state from 1831 (if they had come into the National School system), were to be the forerunners of the country-wide National Schools that came into being in 1831.[49]

Before turning to changes in state policy, two other voluntary initiatives need to be considered. They – the 'Association for Promoting Christian Knowledge', founded in 1792, and the 'Sunday School Society for Ireland', established in 1809 – would engage the energies of the established church and its clergy in the generations that preceded the introduction of the National Schools. Neither body, though still active, is today associated in the public mind with the running of schools, and yet, in pre-National School days, they provided or supported elementary education for thousands of children in hundreds of schools, and played a not insignificant part in promoting the cause of literacy in Ireland.

Thoughtful members of the established church feared for its future influence in society, not only because of the vitality of popery and dissent, but also from weaknesses within. They believed infirmity of faith and weakness of moral fibre to be omnipresent and requiring to be combated. The Association for Discountenancing Vice and Promoting the Practice of Virtue and Religion, the title by which the body was originally known, had such a purpose, and its strictures were directed as much at the well-to-do as at the poor. Preaching in aid of the association two years after its foundation, the Revd Richard Graves identified as 'the distinguishing character of this age and country ... that of levity and indifference to religion, and by consequence a relaxation of moral principle, which allows men to pursue self-gratification and self-interest ...'[50] The association was founded in 1792 by three Dublin clergy and the prominent evangelical bookseller William Watson, at whose premises in Capel Street the early meetings were held.[51] The keystone of its work was, from the start, the publication and distribution of bibles, prayer-books and tracts, and these were issued in very considerable numbers. The association also held catechetical examinations in Dublin and other centres, the candidates

tion, and a way of livelihood to the poor children in Ireland (Dublin, 1712), p. 33.   **47** A list of schools founded 1695–1733 is to be found in D. Hayton, 'Did Protestantism fail in eighteenth-century Ireland? Charity schools and the enterprise of religious and social reformation, *c.*1690–1730', in *As by law established*, pp 166–86, at pp 183–6.   **48** Ibid., p. 167.   **49** See p. 225 below.   **50** Kenneth Milne, 'APCK: the early decades', in *Search: a Church of Ireland Journal*, xv (Winter, 1992), pp 69–70.   **51** Ibid.

being selected by the parish clergy from children attending their schools and whose proficiency in the scriptures and formularies of the church rendered them eligible to compete for premiums. Prizes were awarded not simply for 'quickness of recollection and exactness of recitation', but also, very significantly, for comprehension. One of the final acts of the Irish parliament that went out of existence in 1800 was the granting of incorporation to the association, which from 1801 received parliamentary aid (from Westminster) amounting to £300 per annum. The association's most conspicuous initiative following incorporation was the grant-aiding of schools, and it was convinced that the education of the young was, contrary to the view held by some sections of public opinion at the time, of benefit to society, in that it 'inculcated habits of obedience, the exercising of patience and perseverance in unpleasant tasks'.[52]

Surveys of existing educational provision were conducted, and, satisfied that such provision was seriously deficient, the association formulated an education scheme in 1803. The returns made by the parochial clergy for the survey indicated that less than one third of children 'fit for school' were receiving any education, and that most of those who did were attending hedge schools, frequently run by itinerant and unsatisfactory masters and mistresses.[53] From the northern clergy in particular came expressions of fear of 'atheistical and deistical' doctrines that were being propagated in such schools – doubtless part of the lingering influence of the French revolutionary ideas that were so prevalent in much of the north. The association presented a plan to government proposing financial support for the establishment of schools and support for schoolmasters. Parliament raised its annual grant to £1,000, to supplement the association's income from subscriptions and the sale of publications. By 1805 there had been thirteen applications for school grants and ten for masters' salaries. By 1824 pupils numbered 15,922 (two thirds of whom were Protestants). The Revd William Lee, curate of Newport, County Tipperary, a scrupulous inspector of schools, wrote approvingly of the state of those APCK-supported schools visited by him in 1819–20.[54] However, the political climate of the times was unhelpful to such voluntary endeavours, and as the 1825 commissioners were to conjecture, the association's work could 'hardly be expected to inspire the Roman Catholics or Presbyterians with confidence, being under the immediate superintendence of the clergy of the established church, the doctrines of which they have always consistently and avowedly taught to all who would consent to learn them'.[55] Nonetheless, the provision of support for schools remained a major activity of the APCK for a little longer, until, like other similar bodies, it fell victim to changed government policy whereby in the early 1830s funding was withdrawn from such confessional bodies in favour of the newly-created National Schools.

---

52 Ibid. 53 Ibid. The Irish education enquiry found 7,600 'pay schools' under lay Catholic teachers (*Irish education enquiry*). 54 Ibid. 55 Ibid.

The Sunday School Society for Ireland in like manner attempted to fill the gap in elementary schooling, and can similarly claim a place in the genealogy whence the National Schools descended, and likewise its schools were superseded by them. The existence of Sunday Schools in Dublin and parts of Ulster is recorded in the late eighteenth century,[56] and the Society was founded in 1809 and owed as much to lay (Quaker in particular) initiative as it did to the clergy of the established church. However, in the nature of things, the spread of the Society's work depended to a large extent on clerical goodwill. Like the members of APCK, those who espoused the cause of Sunday Schools were acutely aware that Satan found work for idle hands to do, and that Sunday was the day when the children of the poor were most likely to be idle. What better, then, than to provide such children on that very day with the opportunity for education denied them on working days? While not itself managing schools, the subscriptions collected by the Society went towards aiding clergy, employers and landlords who sponsored schools. 1,640 foundations were aided by the Society in 1824, catering for 157,184 children.

Among the leaders of the established church in the eighteenth century, some took seriously what they believed to be their duty to the Catholic poor, and were not content with policies of prohibition. Henry Maule, successively bishop of Cloyne, Dromore and Meath, was encouraged by the successful spreading of charity schools in England under the auspices of the Society for Promoting Christian Knowledge, and saw enormous possibilities for undertaking similar work in Ireland, among the Catholic poor in particular. He found a powerful sympathiser in Hugh Boulter, as archbishop of Armagh from 1724 to 1742 the most powerful ecclesiastical figure in Ireland. Also, as one of the lords justices, Boulter carried considerable political weight. Boulter and Maule between them were instrumental in creating the Incorporated Society for Promoting English Protestant Schools in Ireland, whose institutions, commonly called 'charter schools' after the royal instrument of George II that brought them into being, presented the clergy with a fresh opportunity for educational involvement.

The charter schools were established so that 'the children of the Popish and other poor natives' could be instructed in the English tongue and the formularies of the established church of Ireland. Boys and girls were boarded (when possible in schools remote from their families) and prepared for work in farming, the linen trade, and domestic service, following which they were apprenticed to Protestant masters. Funding came from crown and parliament and well-wishers in Britain and Ireland. The involvement of the clergy was manifested in three ways: as founders and patrons, as members of local supervisory committees and, most directly of all, as catechists. The number of schools founded in the course of the Society's first century of existence never exceeded seventy, including four 'nurs-

56 H.R. Clayton, 'Societies formed to educate the poor of Ireland in the late eighteenth and early nineteenth centuries', unpublished PhD thesis, Trinity College, Dublin (1980), pp 68–9.

eries', feeder establishments for the very young. But such scandalous mismanagement was uncovered, even by well-disposed investigators, that the charter schools became in Irish folk memory of equal notoriety with Dotheboys Hall in Yorkshire, immortalised by Dickens.

The founders of the schools tended to be drawn, as was envisaged from the start, from the landlord class, to whom great advantages would accrue as a pool of well-trained Protestant artisans, farm labourers and domestic servants was created. There were, however, some clerical sponsors, such as the primate himself, Bishop Maule and Bishop Pococke of Ossory. Clergy served on the local committees that were set up to provide supervision of the individual schools, and often, it would seem, they were seriously negligent in discharging their duties. It was, nonetheless, to the catechists that the society looked to maintain standards, and frequently looked in vain. Had the rules of the society been strictly enforced, then the temptations that led poorly-recompensed masters and mistresses to exploit the children by over-working and under-feeding them, might have been at least somewhat reduced. But all too often the catechists were deceived, even self-deceived, and again and again the society in Dublin had reason to question catechists' reports. Some clergy took their responsibilities seriously. An outstanding champion of the charter schools was the Revd Elias Thackeray, whose school in Dundalk received his closest attention, and who was to devise a scheme for training teachers.[57] Likewise, the Revd Mr Jones came up with a scheme for a seminary at Kildimo, County Limerick, which would train parish clerks and schoolmasters (often the same people). The Revd Dr Ward, catechist of Farra school, near Mullingar, visited frequently and filed comprehensive and accurate reports on the school.[58] Such paragons apart, the catechists were far from assiduous in their duties, and the *coup de grace* was dealt the system by the damning report on the charter schools made by the Irish education inquiry that reported to parliament in 1825–6.[59] A picture of deprivation, cruelty and squalor was unveiled,[60] extending to corruption at head office in Dublin. One commissioner, giving evidence, attributed much that was wrong to the negligence of local committees, who depended for their information on the catechists (whose efficiency was 'very various indeed'), leading them in many instances to espouse the cause of the master.[61]

In the light of the revelations of the 1825 report, there was no prospect that government would look to the charter schools to provide that system of national elementary education towards which it was moving. Nor did other educational enterprises in which the established church had a part commend themselves more favourably. D.H. Akenson wrote that such was the plethora of reports on the Church of Ireland from one commission or another in the nineteenth-century, that parliament was as well informed about the operation of the Irish church as it was

---

57 Milne, *Charter schools*, pp 105–6.   58 Ibid., p. 114.   59 *First report of the commissioners of Irish education inquiry*, H.C. 1825 (400), xii.   60 Milne, *Charter schools*, p. 269.   61 Ibid., p. 271.

about any institution in the whole empire, and much of this scrutiny was directed at educational institutions in which the church was involved.[62] The commissioners' report of 1791, the series of reports to parliament from what was called 'the board of education', spanning the years 1808–12, and the fruits of the education enquiry that reported from 1825–7, all presented a picture of a ramshackle system of educational provision in which the established church was heavily implicated, at a time when government was under pressure to provide an education for the Irish poor that was acceptable to the Roman Catholic hierarchy, which government ministers were keen to propitiate at a time when it was clear, both in Dublin and London, that the Roman Catholic bishops, ever protesting their loyalty and their grievances, were potentially a more effective ally in rendering Ireland peaceful and loyal than the bishops of the Church of Ireland were in a position to be. Elements within the established church fought every inch to preserve what they considered to be its prerogatives. Nowhere was this more evident than in episcopal criticism of the proposals for setting up National Schools (which came to be the preferred state option) and in church reaction to them when eventually they came into being.

In October 1831 the chief secretary, Edward Stanley (later earl of Derby), wrote to the duke of Leinster informing him of the government's intention 'to constitute a board for the superintendence of a system of national education in Ireland' and inviting him to be its president.[63] Members of the board (three Church of Ireland, two Presbyterian and two Roman Catholic), included the powerful figure of Archbishop Whately of Dublin, who fervently believed in the project to the extent that not only did he serve assiduously as a commissioner, frequently chairing meetings, but also prepared text books for use in the schools that in his, though not everyone else's, view conformed with the national commissioners' principles governing the teaching of the curriculum.[64] 'The Stanley letter' is regarded as the foundation document of the National School system, setting out the principles on which this new departure was to be founded, a key one being that it would 'unite in one system children of different creeds'. In a sense, as a system, it did so, but not, as things turned out, under one roof. The Church of Ireland, having survived the shock of losing its monopoly of state-provided education (something that to many seemed a natural prerogative of the 'national church'), turned its attention to the curriculum, and, in common with the other two larger churches on the island, set about re-shaping both the principles and practices of the new Commissioners of National Education to meet their ecclesiastical demands. In time, a denominational system evolved, but not before there had been many battles with the commissioners, and initially, an effort by influential figures within the Church of Ireland to provide a rival to the National Commissioners in the shape of the Church Education Society, in whose schools the children of the Church of Ireland would be required

62 Akenson, *The Church of Ireland*, p. 164.   63 Hyland and Milne (eds), *Documents*, i, 98.   64 Akenson, *Irish education experiment*, pp 132, 242.

to attend catechetical lessons. Competition certainly provided a fresh incentive to rouse the clergy to a state of activity in the promotion of schools such as they had never evinced before.

The Church Education Society held its first Annual General Meeting on Thursday 23 April 1839 in the 'Rotundo' of the Lying-in Hospital in Dublin, having had to select this venue at a very late stage when the Examination Hall in Trinity College, originally promised them, mysteriously became unavailable.[65] Whether or not Archbishop Whately of Dublin, a strong supporter of the National Schools, had a hand in this cannot be stated for certain, but clearly prominent figures such as he who disapproved of the Church Education Society, will have been in the minds of the members of that body when they made it clear 'that the speakers who have undertaken to advocate the cause of the Society, although they may doubtless feel it necessary to express their conscientious dissent from the principles of the National Board, will do so upon purely religious grounds'.[66] Similarly, there is evidence in the papers of Archbishop Beresford of Armagh (who petitioned government, unsuccessfully, for government aid for the society), that there were dioceses where support for the National Schools rendered a clergyman unacceptable for appointment.[67] Supported by funds raised centrally and by diocesan education societies, the Church Education Society's achievements peaked in the early 1850s, when 120,202 pupils were enrolled in its 1,885 schools.[68] By then, the Society had designated St Peter's schools in Dublin as its 'model school' and taken over from the Kildare Place Society its teacher-training establishment.[69] However, the seemingly inexorable growth of the national school system, the ravages made on the assets of the established church by disestablishment and disendowment in the 1870s, and, as ruefully admitted in the society's Annual Report for 1887, the fact that 'young clergy do not see things as they were seen in 1839',[70] all contributed to its decline, and it abandoned its policy of school provision and left the field to the National Schools, which, anyway, were by this time all but denominational in fact if not in theory.

This chapter has been largely devoted to a survey of clerical involvement in education at elementary, or what we would now call, primary level. Understandably, since the provision of basic literacy for the masses was a major challenge, the needs of those seeking a post-primary, or grammar school, education could be addressed on a much smaller scale and were hardly regarded as a fit sphere of state activity. There were individual clerical schoolmasters who made a major contribution to the education of many prominent figures of church and state, such as Dr Ball, who at his school of St Michael-le-Pole, in Ship Street,

65 *First annual report of the Church Education Society for Ireland with an appendix, and a list of subscribers* (Dublin, 1840), pp 5–6. 66 Ibid. 67 Beresford correspondence, PRONI, D6/64/A/501, for an example. 68 *Church Education Society Report*, 1851. 69 S.M. Parkes, *Kildare Place: the history of the Church of Ireland Training College, 1811–1969* (Dublin, 1984), pp 38–40. 70 *Church Education Society Report 1888*, p. 8.

Dublin, prepared many men for university, the eminent lawyer and politician, Sir Jonah Barrington among them.[71] Charles William Benson headed the famous Rathmines School from 1859 to 1899 and his distinguished *alumni* were many.[72] Archbishop Power le Poer Trench owed his early schooling to 'Mr Ralph', whose academy at Castlebar was, according to the archbishop's biographer, 'of great repute'.[73] Indeed a perusal of the clerical succession lists makes abundantly clear the part that the individual clerical schoolmaster played until well into the nineteenth century.[74]

The line to be drawn between schools that were private enterprises and those of corporate foundation is not as clear as might be expected. It was by no means unusual for endowed institutions to be privatized, a fate that befell several royal schools from time to time, as investigations revealed. However, the pages that follow are devoted to those institutions that were intended to have been corporate, whatever their vicissitudes, into which category fell the diocesan and at least some of the royal schools planned by the Stuarts.[75] Prestigious foundations such as Kilkenny College, Swift's *alma mater*, had medieval roots, and by definition were under clerical auspices, given that the clergy were (along with the lawyers) the educated class. In the years following the dramatic disclosures of serious malpractices relating to the charter schools of the Incorporated Society, that body underwent a transformation, turning from elementary schools (largely intended for Catholic children) to grammar schools (for Protestant pupils), where, again, the clergy featured almost exclusively among the headmasters. The society itself, though its constitution was recast in the late nineteenth century, was conducted (and, for that matter, continues to be conducted) by a governing body comprising bishops, clergy and laity. In Ulster, the royal schools continued their long history, and in the north, though not exclusively so, they were joined in the nineteenth century by academies under Presbyterian, Methodist and Quaker auspices. The Presbyterians of the north were particularly interested in securing sound Presbyterian education, and they continued to send candidates for the ministry abroad (chiefly to Scotland).[76] Another early foundation was Midleton College, County Cork, founded by Elizabeth Villiers, countess of Orkney, and whose governors and early headmas-

---

71 Jonah Barrington, *Personal sketches of his own times* (3 vols., 1827–32), i, 57.   72 J.B. Leslie and W.R.J. Wallace, *Clergy of Dublin and Glendalough: biographical succession lists* (Belfast, 2001), *sub. nom.* Benson, C.W. The succession lists, whether printed, or in typescript in RCBL provide abundant evidence of the part played by individual schoolmasters.   73 Sirr, *A memoir*, p. 4.   74 See many clerical biographies in, for example, Fred Rankin (ed.),*Clergy of Down and Dromore* (Belfast, 1996) and Leslie and Wallace (ed.), *Clergy of Dublin and Glendalough*. Both editors give credit to Canon J.B. Leslie, many of his succession lists are in print, though some remain only in typescript in RCBL. Entries relating to Ireland in the *New Oxford Dictionary of National Biography* likewise show how great was the contribution of the clerical schoolmaster.   75 Much about the affairs of the royal schools in the nineteenth century is to be gleaned from the correspondence of Primate Beresford (PRONI, DIO4/8/1–35).   76 T.W. Moody and J.C. Beckett, *Queen's, Belfast 1845–1949: the history of a university* (2 vols., London, 1959), i, pp xli–xlii.

ters were members of the clergy.[77] Already, however, accountability on an unprecedented scale was being required, beginning with the Educational Endowments (Ireland) Act of 1885, which established a permanent regulatory body to oversee educational endowments, draft schemes, and even to alter the conditions attaching to endowments in the interests of enhanced performance in the schools.[78]

While the clergy maintained a high profile in grammar schools well into the twentieth century, particularly where ownership and governance were concerned, a much higher degree of supervision was introduced and state intervention increased as the Intermediate Commissioners, and then the government ministries, came to play the major part in financing secondary education.

A very particular manifestation of clerical involvement in education has been that of the cathedral choir schools. Those connected with the two Dublin cathedrals claim origins in the fifteenth century. While records for the early years of their existence are sketchy, we know that in 1431 Archbishop Richard Talbot instituted and endowed at St Patrick's a college of six minor canons and six choristers to ensure that there was a permanent provision for polyphonic choral arrangements.[79] The choir school served as the diocesan school for at least part of the eighteenth century. Until the nineteenth century choristers were indentured apprentices, the master of song contracting to feed, clothe, house and maintain his charges as well as training them in music.[80] A typical entry in the chapter minutes records a payment of £11 16s. 4d., being one third of the cost of 'supplying the choir boys with bedding'.[81] A similar model for the education and boarding of choristers obtained at Christ Church, where in 1480 Thomas Benet, a merchant whose father was to be mayor of Dublin, granted an endowment to sustain four choristers and in 1493 they formed the nucleus of the cathedral choir school founded by David Winchester, prior of the Augustinian canons who provided the cathedral chapter.[82] The boys, or rather their parents, entered into a form of indenture whereby the choristers were apprenticed to the cathedral, receiving not only a musical training but also board and lodging (which in due course was replaced by a maintenance allowance to parents). Similarly, the boy choristers at St Patrick's Cathedral, Armagh, were indentured apprentices.[83] A former master at St Patrick's, Dublin, Charles Crowe, bequeathed a sum to support a diocesan school in Cloyne, which by 1729 was known as 'Crowe's foundation', and another endowment provided for instructing 'the charity boys' in singing at the cathedral services.[84] Archbishop Charles Agar of Cashel made provision for 'singing boys' at his cathedral there (largely out of his own resources), build-

---

77 Trevor West, *Midleton College, 1696–1966: a tercentenary history* (Cork, 1966), pp 10–11.   78 48 & 49 Vict., c.78.   79 Rex Cathcart, *'An help for school boys': the choir and grammar schools 1431–1991* (Dublin, 1991), p. 1.   80 Ibid., p. 2.   81 RCBL, Chapter act books of St Patrick's Cathedral, C2/1/3/10, p. 103 (17 Mar. 1798).   82 Barra Boydell, *A history of music at Christ Church Cathedral, Dublin* (London, 2004), pp 25–7.   83 PRONI, Beresford correspondence, DIO 4/37/5/4.   84 W.H. Grindle, *Irish cathedral music: a history of music at the cathedrals of the Church of Ireland* (Belfast, 1989), p. 53.

ing a house appropriated to the vicar choral 'who has the care of the six choir children'. Boys were lodged locally, taught to sing and play the harpsichord, and
instructed in reading, writing and arithmetic.[85] A force to be reckoned with in the
counsels of the Incorporated Society as a member of its powerful committee of fifteen, Archbishop Agar persuaded the society to admit only boys to the charter
school at Cashel so that 'if duly qualified', they might be 'instructed in music and
introduced to the choir', and the girls already in the school were despatched to the
school at Newport.[86]

Two distinctive nineteenth-century initiatives in Dublin owed much to clerical encouragement. St Columba's College (1843), originating in County Meath,
was the creation of a group of clergymen imbued with the principles of the Oxford
Movement and 'opposed equally to Rome and to extreme Protestantism'. The
most eminent among them was James Henthorn Todd, Celtic scholar and president of the Royal Irish Academy. From the outset they hoped to use the Irish language to commend the doctrines of the established church of Ireland (as
evangelicals had attempted to do) to boys in an academic setting redolent of the
kind of English boarding school with which several of the founders were familiar.[87]
Two decades later, Archbishop Richard Chenevix Trench of Dublin put his full
weight behind the plans of Mrs Anne Jellicoe for advances in the provision of education for women that resulted in the foundation of Alexandra College, in Dublin
The archbishop encouraged her to develop her original modest proposals for a
school for governesses into a much more ambitious project along the lines of
Queen's College, London, with which he had been closely involved before coming
to Ireland, and which would provide girls with higher education and equip them
for entry to the university careers that the newly-founded Royal University of Ireland (but not yet Trinity College) had opened up to them.[88]

Given the fact that, except for a very few schools indeed, the National School
system became denominational in all but name, it was hardly surprising that the
teacher training colleges that were created to serve the schools were likewise church-
related. From the time that it was formally taken under Church of Ireland auspices
in 1884 until 1977, the training college in Kildare Place, Dublin, was to be headed
by clergymen: Canon H. Kingsmill Moore (1884–1927); Canon E.C. Hodges
(1927–43), subsequently bishop of Limerick; Revd G.O. Simms (1943–51), later
archbishop of Dublin, then archbishop of Armagh; and Canon Robert J. Ross
(1951–77).

With the partitioning of Ireland in 1922, the education systems north and south
diverged. Paradoxically, the largely nineteenth-century British structures persisted for much longer in the Irish Free State, later the Republic of Ireland, than they

---

85 A.P.W. Malcomson, *Archbishop Charles Agar: churchmanship and politics in Ireland, 1760–1810*
Dublin, 2002), pp 318–19.   86 Milne, *Charter schools*, p. 139.   87 G.K. White, *A history of St
Columba's College* (Dublin, 1980).   88 A.V. O'Connor and S.M. Parkes, *Gladly learn and glad-
ly teach: a history of Alexandra College and School, Dublin, 1866–1966* (Dublin [1984]).

did in Northern Ireland, where major re-casting of the system occurred almost as soon as the north was granted a degree of political autonomy, to be followed by further remodelling in 1947, which owed much to the English and Welsh changes introduced in Britain by the Education Act of 1944. There were no changes in the role of the clergy in the south, where there was little innovation in education, either curricular or managerial, until the 1960s. Apart, that is from the major upheaval caused by the introduction of the Irish language to the system in a dominant position, and the setting up of an alternative post-primary system of vocational (in reality, until recent decades, technical) schools which were under local government control, and in which the rights of entry by clergy for the purposes of denominational religious education were secured.[89] It was to the advantage of the Protestant community in the Free State that their children attended schools consistent in ethos with their homes, yet within the state system, providing them as it were with a congenial ark to carry them through the somewhat perilous waters of political and cultural change.

A majority of schools under Protestant management in Northern Ireland was transferred to local education authorities (later education and library boards), the churches retaining a role at both school and county levels through their transferors' representatives, frequently clergy, who served on boards of management and on the local education authority itself. Northern clergy also continued to have access to pupils of their own religious denomination for the purposes of religious education (the basic RE programme being an agreed syllabus). In the Republic, a major change in the National (primary) Schools was the replacement in the 1970s of the single school manager (almost inevitably the local rector) by a representative board of management, the membership of which was largely in church hands, and, of considerable significance, Church of Ireland schools remain under the patronage of the bishop, who is custodian of the religious ethos of the schools in his diocese. The management structures of secondary (grammar) schools in the Republic are in process of being made more representative of parent and teacher interests, but this does not necessarily entail any diminution of clerical participation. However, the demands on the clergy made by management duties, especially at primary level, are considerable and, given the growing complexity of a fast-changing educational system in the Republic, these demands are set to increase.

Looking to the future, a new factor in clerical involvement with schools is coming into play with the growing number of teachers, men and women, who are being ordained to the auxiliary (non-stipendiary) ministry of the Church of Ireland. Previously, as we have seen, many clergy exercised whole or part of their ministry in school management or school teaching. Now the reverse also is happening, as teachers respond to the call to ordained ministry and bring with them

89 Vocational Education Act, 1930.

the skills previously obtained in the educational sphere. This should prove to be of considerable value to the church, particularly where religious education is concerned, for the classroom may well provide clergy, north and south, with greater opportunity than the parish affords, for introducing the school-going population to the satisfaction to be gained from theological and biblical studies.

13

Scholars and antiquarians: the clergy and learning, 1600–2000

Toby Barnard

Clerics of the Church of Ireland wielded their pens in a variety of causes, many of them topical and controversial. A few immersed themselves in scholarly matters. Four broad themes can be identified in this scholarship. A first concern was with issues common to pastors in all the Christian churches: to explore, understand, refine, expound and defend Christianity. The writers tackled theology and history as recorded in the bible and the subsequent chronicles of Christians' tribulations and triumphs. A second sphere of activity was peculiar to Protestants: to record and promote their own brands of theology, ecclesiology and history. A third preoccupation was unique to the Protestants in Ireland. They justified their own distinctive theological stance, embodied in the articles of 1615, and recollected their sufferings. Irish Protestants constructed a long pedigree for themselves, into which Patrick and other early Christian missionaries were fitted. Such claims to a venerable past, together with questioning of them, stimulated further enquiries. Accordingly, the literary and physical remains of early Ireland were examined minutely and (in time) greater care was taken to preserve them. It was, for example, a bishop of the Church of Ireland, Henry Jones, more famed as a fighter than as a bibliophile, who ensured the survival of the Book of Kells, by having it deposited at Trinity College in Dublin while he was vice-chancellor there during the 1650s.[1]

The first three overlapping spheres – Christian annals and exegesis; Protestant theology and history; the distinctive story and stance of Irish Protestantism – arose naturally from the calling of Church of Ireland clergymen. A fourth area of interest resembled the enquiries of others of reasonable education, comfortable means, standing and some leisure, such as doctors, lawyers, office-holders and even landed gentry. Both in town and country, they diverted themselves by observing and describing what they saw around them. With their families and neighbours, they

---

1 W. O'Sullivan, 'The donor of the Book of Kells', *IHS*, xi (1958–9), pp 5–7.

read, made music, acted in plays, formed collections, sketched and noted the local flora, fauna, antiquities and curiosities. Matters such as topography, philology, astronomy and music looked unrepentantly secular. Yet, even in these investigations, shared with lay-people, the clergy were thought to bring a special approach inseparable from their spiritual functions. Interest in the profane might originate in the wish better to understand creation and venerate the creator. One clerical enquirer in the mid-eighteenth century, Richard Barton, curate of Lurgan, contended that, 'knowledge is the handmaid of religion, and closely attendant on it...The phenomena of the natural world ... is the handywork of God'. Accordingly, it was a fitting study for a clergyman like Barton.[2] Successive surveys of the topography of Ireland, the prelude to a more thorough exploitation of natural resources (in some of which Barton was involved), accorded with the belief that the resources themselves – and the duty to use them profitably – were God-given.

In 1730, Robert Howard, bishop of the Connacht diocese of Elphin, regretted that, 'letters and study are very uncommon things in country parsons'. Although he tried to change the situation, not least by providing improving books in his own residence at Elphin, he had still to admit that when marooned there during the summer, 'I want the opportunities of conversation, speculations about many points, new sights, &c – these would be infinitely more agreeable to me than a bare unentertaining superiority and constantly lying open to the talk and business and idleness of all sorts of people'.[3] Howard's was a complaint frequently repeated, especially by the inquisitive who felt exiled and isolated away from (and sometimes even in) Dublin. A critic of supposed clerical indolence lamented in the 1840s, 'it is a sad thing to think how our clergy have neglected to gather round the church the associations of antiquity', so that much evidence of the earlier Christian churches in Ireland had been destroyed.[4] Some of the internal exiles managed to overcome the practical and psychological obstacles and turn rural retirement into an opportunity for scholarly enquiries. Two principal types of activity will be considered below: that which scrutinized the religious, civil and natural histories of Ireland, physical and personal reminders of which abounded; and that which related less obviously to the clerics' immediate environments, such as the heavens, the Book of Enoch or cuneiform inscriptions from Egypt.

II

In the seventeenth century, two factors earned the Church of Ireland a high reputation for scholarship. The first came from the vigour of a fledgling church vulnerable to Catholic attacks. Arguments used in England and Scotland to demonstrate

2 R. Barton, *Lectures in natural philosophy* (Dublin, 1751), pp xvi, 95, 111–12.   3 Bp R. Howard to H. Howard, 29 July 1730, 28 Aug. 1730, NLI, PC 227.   4 M. Ferguson, *Life of the Right Rev. William Reeves, D.D.* (Dublin and London, 1893), p. 18.

the divine truths professed by Protestants were given a specific Irish twist. The eagerness of Protestants in Ireland to demonstrate impeccable credentials as true heirs of the original disciples made them cherish connections with the first adherents of Christianity on the island. One result was a fierce contest between Catholics and Protestants over the ownership of St Patrick.[5] The Protestant position was expounded most learnedly in the early seventeenth century by James Ussher, successively bishop of Meath and archbishop of Armagh. He wrote at a time of acute tension between the distinct confessional communities, and, with all his erudition, was a Protestant partisan.[6] Concurrently, a desire to convert the Catholic majority, and to counter the increasing assertiveness and successes of its clergy, prompted a few Protestants to study the Irish language. The motives resembled those of Catholic missionaries outside Europe who learnt and used the vernaculars as part of a strategy that was calculated to bring about their end. Despite the negative intentions, the resulting scholarship fostered understanding of Gaelic Ireland and the preservation of its language.[7]

A second factor which brought scholarly vitality to the seventeenth-century Church of Ireland was its close congruence with the Church of England. This showed in the frequency with which those of English (and Scottish and Welsh) birth were installed in Irish dignitaries. The practice was not much liked in Ireland, but it did invigorate clerical scholarship. William Bedell, an enthusiast for the Irish language as a tool of evangelization, had come – ironically – from England.[8] Later in the century, and indeed into the nineteenth, the same currents of patronage floated such notable scholars as Jeremy Taylor, Narcissus Marsh, Robert Huntington, William Nicolson, Francis Hutchinson, Richard Pococke, Thomas Percy, Richard Mant and Richard Whately into Irish waters. In this way, the British colonization of Ireland, and specifically of the Church of Ireland, strengthened the connections of the island not just with British but with international scholarship. Many of the enquiries had topical and ideological purposes. Yet, the quest to untie knotty problems in manuscripts and texts sometimes transcended confessional differences. In the early seventeenth century, for example, Archbishop Ussher happily corresponded with Catholic scholars, although his ultimate objective was to refute their theological system.[9]

5 B. Cunningham and R. Gillespie, '"The most versatile of saints": the cult of St Patrick in the seventeenth century', *Archivium Hibernicum*, xlix (1995), pp 82–104; J. McCafferty, 'St Patrick for the Church of Ireland', *Bullán*, 3 (1997–9), pp 87–101; B. McCormack, *Perceptions of St Patrick in the eighteenth century* (Dublin, 2000).   6 J. Ussher, *A discourse of the religion anciently professed by the Irish and British* (London, 1631). Cf. Alan Ford, 'James Ussher and the creation of an Irish Protestant identity' in B. Bradshaw and P. Roberts (eds), *British consciousness and identity: the making of Britain, 1533–1707* (Cambridge, 1998), pp 185–212.   7 T.C. Barnard, 'Protestants and the Irish language, c.1675–1725', *JEH*, 44 (1993), pp 243–72, reprinted in T.C. Barnard, *Irish Protestant ascents and descents* (Dublin, 2004), pp 179–207.   8 T. McCaughey, *Dr Bedell and Mr King: the making of the Irish Bible* (Dublin, 2001).   9 W. O'Sullivan, 'Correspondence of David Rothe and James Ussher', *Collectanea Hibernica*, 36–7 (1994–5), pp 7–49.

Ussher cast his intense gaze back to the centuries before the Anglo-Normans arrived. Some of his colleagues focussed on the more recent experiences of the Protestants in Ireland. By the end of the seventeenth century, local history furnished ample matter for reflection, rebuke and rejoicing. In particular, the sufferings and deliverances of the 1640s and (to a lesser degree) between 1689 and 1691 were kept green in Protestant minds. Clergymen, regarding themselves as special targets of Catholic violence during those episodes, made sure that the backslidings, martyrdoms and endurance of the Protestants of Ireland were known to audiences within and outside the island. In the main, the clerical memorialization took the forms of scarifying descriptions of atrocities and annual sermons, a few of which were given permanent life by being printed.[10] Larger scale ruminations on the events were composed mostly by laymen. However, William King, at the time ministering in Dublin, published what proved to be the most influential account of the Catholic threat to Protestant Ireland in James II's reign. A second clerical historian of the Williamite deliverance, George Story, an Englishman, was rewarded with the deanery of Limerick. Neither King's nor Story's clerical saga – opportunistic and propagandist, even journalistic – constituted scholarship of the kind practised by Ussher.[11]

William King, consecrated bishop of Derry in 1691 and translated to the archbishopric of Dublin in 1703, personified the increasing intellectual brio of clergy in the Church of Ireland after 1660. Many had been born in Ireland and educated in the well-conducted and dynamic Trinity College in Dublin. King belonged to this group, which took command of bishoprics in the 1680s and 1690s. Its activities embraced politics, ecclesiastical administration and reform and more disinterested scholarship. Moreover, in any account of what Church of Ireland clerics contributed to scholarship, their distinctive achievements are hard to disentangle from those of the propertied, leisured and privileged – from the mid-seventeenth to the early nineteenth century, a predominantly Protestant group. In many instances, the concerns of laypeople and churchmen overlapped.

It was widely thought that knowledge could be extended best by cooperation, both institutional and voluntary, rather than through individual exertion. This belief produced initiatives in the 1650s and 1680s. Throughout the seventeenth century – and indeed into the twentieth – correspondence imposed a structure on otherwise desultory investigations. It also encouraged a feeling of shared and useful endeavour. Archbishop Ussher believed this. At the same time, some within Ireland, Ussher among them, hooked up with other, transnational networks.[12]

10 T.C. Barnard, 'The uses of 23 October 1641 and Irish Protestant celebrations', *English Historical Review*, cvi (1991), pp 889–920, reprinted in *Irish Protestant ascents and descents*, pp 111–42.   11 W. King, *The state of the Protestants of Ireland under the late King James's government* (London, 1691); G. Story, *An impartial history of the wars of Ireland* (London, 1693); G. Story, *A continuation of the impartial history of the wars of Ireland* (London, 1693).   12 E.A. Boran, 'An early friendship network of James Ussher, archbishop of Armagh, 1626–1656' in H.

Among the most notable in the mid-seventeenth century was that centred on Samuel Hartlib, a Protestant refugee driven from central Europe by Catholic aggression. Hartlib's programme – in parts, millenarian and utopian, but also renovative, innovative and useful – appealed to several brought to Ireland in the aftermath of English reconquest in 1649. All except one of Hartlib's followers in Cromwellian Ireland were laymen.[13] The exception was a cleric recently lifted into the chair of mathematics at Trinity College, but previously beneficed in the provinces.[14] Several Church of Ireland bishops had earlier endorsed Hartlib's plans since they accorded well with long-standing ambitions to turn Ireland into a prosperous, peaceful and Protestant country.[15] However, political turmoil prevented these enterprising bishops from translating aspirations into actuality.

Central to Hartlib's vision was collaboration in order to collect, collate and spread information. Only in Dublin did a concentration of the leisured and literate offer a receptive environment. The group enjoyed a fitful existence in the 1650s. Nevertheless, its approach survived and would revive and be modified during the 1680s, thanks to enthusiasts in Trinity College, supplemented by interested office-holders and land-owners. This coterie, the Dublin Philosophical Society, if more sizeable than the Irish circle of Hartlib's friends, in the end also foundered. It had lasted longer and had achieved more in collecting information about the terrain, antiquities and resources of Ireland county by county. But little appeared in print and the direct impact on public policy or social and economic improvement seemed negligible.[16] The work would have to be re-started in the 1730s: again by enthusiasts connected with Trinity College and frequently in the capital. As in the Dublin Philosophical Society, so with the successor bodies of the eighteenth century – first, the Dublin Society, then the Physico-Historical Society, Hibernian Antiquarian Society and Royal Irish Academy – Church of Ireland clergy were present, but not usually pre-eminent. Four of the Philosophical Society's original fourteen members in 1683 were or soon would be in holy orders. When the Society was resurrected in 1693, the clerical contingent had increased to fifteen in a gathering that now numbered forty-nine.[17] Bishops lent tone if they could be advertised as members. Already in 1693, seven of the fifteen were and another three would become bishops.[18] In Dublin regularly for the sittings of the House of

Hammerstein-Robinson (ed.), *European universities in the age of reformation and counter reformation* (Dublin, 1998), pp 116–34.   13 T.C. Barnard, *Cromwellian Ireland* (Oxford, 1975), pp 213–48; T.C. Barnard, 'The Hartlib circle and the origins of the Dublin Philosophical Society', *IHS*, xix (1974), pp 56–71.   14 T.C. Barnard, 'Miles Symner and the new learning in seventeenth-century Ireland', *JRSAI*, cii (1972), pp 129–42.   15 E.A. Boran, "Propagating religion and endeavouring the reformation of the whole world. The Hartlib circle in the mid-seventeenth century' in V. Carey and U. Lötz-Heumann (eds), *Taking sides? Colonial and confessional mentalities in early modern Ireland. Essays in honour of Karl S. Bottigheimer* (Dublin, 2003), pp 165–84.   16 The fundamental study is K.T. Hoppen, *The common scientist in the seventeenth century. A study of the Dublin Philosophical Society, 1683–1708* (London, 1970).   17 Hoppen, *The Dublin Philosophical Society*, pp 204–5, 235.   18 These figures assume that 'Mr Carre' is Charles Carr,

Lords, they did attend meetings. Some, indeed, sympathized with and had long striven to advance investigations into the natural, civil and ecclesiastical histories of Ireland.

A similar pattern can be observed in the later organizations. Success depended on having an impressive and fashionable list of members. Accordingly bishops were conspicuous among the founder members of the Dublin Society in 1733.[19] By 1744, a second, complementary organization, the Physico-Historical Society, had been created. Of fifteen members present at a meeting on 14 April 1744, seven were clergymen. They included three bishops, a dean, an archdeacon and a fellow of Trinity College. Moreover, of ten members deputed to drum up recruits for the society in their localities, six were clerics.[20] It was, furthermore, two clerical members who prepared an account of the society that was published in a bid to rekindle interest.[21] A list of members of the society published in 1745 revealed that almost a third – seventy-two – were clergymen. They were exclusively Protestant and overwhelmingly, if not entirely, members of the Church of Ireland. Ten bishops had joined, but what is notable is the number of cathedral and parish incumbents. Signing up to the society was not, sadly, any guarantee of sustained enthusiasm. The business of the society was largely forwarded by a small band of devotees. They tended to be resident in or near Dublin. In this more restricted group clerics still featured, but not so strikingly. Henry Maule, bishop of Meath and another indefatigable exponent of material and moral improvement, sometimes took the chair at meetings. So, on occasion, did John Wynne, a prebendary and precentor of St Patrick's and keeper of the nearby Marsh's Library, Francis Corbett, dean of St Patrick's from 1747, Kane Perceval, another prebendary of St Patrick's, and Dean Charles Massy from Limerick. The Revd Brabazon Disney, a fellow of Trinity, acted as secretary of the society for Connacht.[22]

III

The genesis of the Dublin Philosophical Society in 1683 owed much to a stronger taste for scholarly enquiries within Trinity College. From the 1650s, a succession of erudite provosts or fellows – Winter, Symner, Dodwell, Lingard, Huntington and Marsh – trained pupils, a minority of whom developed similar interests. Not all entered the church. One, the inspiration behind the Philosophical Society, William Molyneux, after travelling outside Ireland, practised at the bar. However, others, such as Anthony Dopping, William King, Edward Synge, Samuel Foley, St

the future bishop of Killaloe.   19 H.F. Berry, *A history of the Royal Dublin Society* (London, 1915), pp 24–7.   20 Minute Book, Physico-Historical Society, RIA, Ms 24 E 28, s.d. 14 April 1744.   21 Ibid., s.d. 15 April 1745; [K. Perceval and P. Read], *An account of the rise and progress of the Physico-Historical Society* ([Dublin, 1745]).   22 Minute Book, Physico-Historical Society, RIA, Ms 24 E 28, passim.

George Ashe and William Palliser, were ordained and, after fellowships or Dublin incumbencies, were elevated to the episcopate. In advance of and parallel to the study of the natural world undertaken by the members of the Society, a group within the college discussed theology.[23] Unravelling problems was felt to involve close study of the best texts, the acquisition of which for either the college library or personal collections justified the sometimes obsessive and aggressive bibliomania of the enquirers. The quest also inspired the preparation of new editions of sacred texts, and to this end information about, transcriptions of, or (best of all) the purchase of manuscripts.

Curiosity about what unknown documents could be found in the non-Christian worlds went hand in hand with the evangelization of those places. A notable encourager of the plunder was Narcissus Marsh, provost of Trinity between 1679 and 1682, then successively bishop of Ferns and Leighlin, archbishop of Dublin and of Armagh.[24] Marsh helped to foster an atmosphere in Trinity in which scholarship, and the collection of documents that might further it, were prized. It went alongside his support for the practical objectives of the infant Dublin Philosophical Society, encouragement of the study of the Irish language – and through it of its earliest written forms – and his concrete effort to improve standards of clerical (and lay) learning with the establishment of a public library near the Dublin archiepiscopal palace of St Sepulchre, known later as Marsh's Library.[25]

If the Jesuits and other Catholic orders pioneered investigation of the languages and cultures of the Orient, Protestants arrived in the baggage of commercial ventures in the Levant. Two who became bishops in Ireland at the end of the seventeenth century – Edward Smyth (bishop of Down and Connor) and Robert Huntington (bishop of Raphoe) – had served as chaplains in Smyrna and Aleppo. They had been encouraged to acquire, almost indiscriminately, manuscripts and books that might elucidate the earlier cultures of those places. St George Ashe, another Dublin alumnus and briefly its provost, did not travel so far east. However, he put a spell in Vienna as secretary to the English ambassador to good use. He had manuscripts there and in Augsburg and Nuremburg copied, and corresponded with scholars in Russia and Italy. The results were sent back to his acquaintances in Ireland.[26]

---

23 St G. Ashe to H. Dodwell, 18 Dec. 1684, 31 March 1685, 23 June 1685, Bodleian, MS Eng. Lett. C. 29, ff. 2, 4, 6b.   24 C. Wakefield, 'Archbishop Marsh's oriental collections in the Bodleian Library' and W. Horbury, 'Christian Hebraism in the mirror of Marsh's collection' in M. McCarthy and A. Simmons (eds), *The making of Archbishop Marsh's Library: learning, politics and religion in Ireland, 1650–1750* (Dublin, 2004), pp 76–84, 256–79.   25 For Marsh's character and achievements: T.C. Barnard, *Irish protestant ascents and descents* (Dublin, 2004), pp 143–207; R. Gillespie (ed.), *Scholar bishop: the recollections and diary of Narcissus Marsh, 1638–1696* (Cork, 2003), pp 1–13; McCarthy and Simmons (eds), *The making of Archbishop Marsh's Library*, pp 11–31, 85–98.   26 Barnard, *Making the grand figure*, p. 319; T.C. Barnard, 'Collecting in eighteenth-century Ireland', *Irish Architectural and Decorative Studies*, vi (2003), pp 141–2.

This flame that burnt brightly in Trinity throughout the seventeenth guttered low in the eighteenth, as the college's concern veered away from underpinning and advertising the truths of a particular brand of Christianity to maintaining and championing a political and social system rooted in confessional discrimination: what would later become known as the Church of Ireland ascendancy. Trinity College remained important in the scholarly formation of the clergy. Its provosts and fellows, even when in holy orders, generally showed greater concern with secular affairs and their own personal advancement. Yet, literary and scholarly activity was not unknown among the senior members of the college. The Revd Patrick Delany, famed as the most popular tutor of the second and third decades of the century, published prolifically. Many of the sermons and addresses printed in several volumes had been delivered originally in the college chapel or the two Dublin cathedrals where he held dignities. One collection treated – rather bathetically – 'various very important and interesting subjects'. They extended from charity and theft through the observation of Lent to the support of clerical widows and orphans in the diocese of Dublin. Even so, he feared that the topics might be thought 'trite'.[27] His writings exemplified the trend away from the voluminous scholarship of the previous century.

The intellectual atmosphere created by clerical dons valued suavity and reasonableness. Delany preached on social duties; he reflected on polygamy, in order to free Christianity from the aspersion that it discouraged population increase.[28] He examined Revelation with candour in an attempt to check the licentiousness and unbelief of the age. His life of King David, dedicated to the lord lieutenant of the day, afforded an example of how divine providence might smile on a public figure 'in the upright and conscientious discharge of his duty'.[29] He thought that the uncritical zeal for mathematical reasoning had infected divinity. Worse still, 'that cold, dry, didactic way' was carried into pulpits by preachers. At the same time, worshippers went to church, 'not to serve God, to be instructed, to confess their sins, to repent, and be reclaimed, but merely as they go to the great assemblies to be entertained'.[30]

Delany actively backed the Incorporated Society which promoted Protestant schooling as a means to change 'a nation overrun with sloth and superstition'. He criticized English maladroitness in stunting Irish manufactures.[31] Yet, he did not join the Physico-Historical society. His feelings may have resembled those of his

27 P. Delany, *Eighteen discourses and dissertations upon various very important and interesting subjects* (London, 1766).   28 'Phileleutherus Dublinensis' [P. Delany], *Reflections upon polygamy*, 2nd edn (London, 1739).   29 P. Delany, *An historical account of the life and reign of David, King of Israel* (3 vols, Dublin, 1743), i, p. vi.   30 P. Delany, *The present state of learning, religion, and infidelity in Great-Britain* (London, 1732), pp 6–8, 28. Cf. R. Gillespie, 'The reformed preacher: Irish Protestant preaching, 1660–1700' in R. Gillespie and A.J. Fletcher (eds), *Irish preaching, 700–1700* (Dublin, 2001), pp 127–43.   31 P. Delany, *A sermon preach'd before the Society corresponding with the Incorporated Society in Dublin ... March 13th, 1743/4* (London, 1744), p. 17.

contemporary at Trinity, George Berkeley, from 1734 bishop of Cloyne, who declared that 'I wish them [the Physico-Historical Society] well but do not care to list myself among them'.[32] Delany did belong to the Dublin Society in its earliest phase – between 1733 and 1740 – but even then did not use it as a vehicle for his pet projects. Berkeley, probably because remote in Cloyne, abstained from the Dublin Society. (He seldom came to Dublin even for the parliamentary sessions.) Instead, he pursued his own personal campaign of aesthetic and cultural reformation in his locality, to the efficacy of which even Charles Smith attested in his history of Cork published under the auspices of the Physico-Historical Society.[33]

Delany's most durable contribution, other than to act as the foil for his opinionated wife, was to preserve and publicize the music of Carolan. This belonged to a thread within the clergy that ensured the recording of varieties of Irish traditional music. Delany's contemporary, the Dublin curate, Matthew Pilkington (like Delany overshadowed by a more voluble wife) made an outstanding contribution. Pilkington also pioneered the systematic study of the history of painting.[34] Others interested in music included clerical members of the Philosophical Society, notably Marsh and Ashe, and (in the eighteenth century) the Revd Charles Bunworth, rector of Buttevant, and the Revd Charles Baldwin.[35] A taste for music may have arisen from the need for diversion in remote rural rectories and from the requirements of orderly worship. However, in a few cases, such as Pilkington and Delany, it was an aspect of the wide-ranging curiosity about the antiquities and customs of the island. The same curiosity was later shown by the Revd Edward Ledwich and, in the second half of the nineteenth century, by James Goodman, rector of Abbeystrewery (Skibbereen) in West Cork. Goodman proved a notable collector of traditional music, especially in Kerry and Cork. Thanks to him, much that otherwise would have been lost was saved. In addition, his linguistic facility secured his appointment as professor of Irish in Trinity College. In an arrangement to be envied by other frustrated scholarly parsons, Goodman was allowed to divide his year between his living and the university.[36]

32 A.A. Luce and T.E. Jessop (eds), *The works of George Berkeley, bishop of Cloyne* (9 vols, London, 1948–57), viii, pp 285–6; cf. D. Dickson, *Old world colony: south Munster, 1630–1830* (Cork, 2005), p. 552, n. 11.   33 C. Smith, *The ancient and present state of the county and city of Cork* (2 vols, 2nd edn, Dublin, 1774), i, p. 139.   34 B. Bryant, 'Matthew Pilkington and *The Gentleman's and Connoisseur's Dictionary of Painters*: a landmark in art history' in A. Laing (ed.), *Clerics and connoisseurs: the Rev. Matthew Pilkington, the Cobbe family and the fortunes of an Irish art collection through three centuries* (London, 2001), pp 51–62; H. White, *The Keeper's Recital: music and cultural history in Ireland, 1770–1970* (Cork, 1998), pp 15–20.   35 Will of Revd C. Baldwin, 1747, NLI, Ainsworth reports on private collections, no. 51; Barnard, *Making the Grand Figure*, p. 359; Hoppen, *The common scientist*, p. 33; D. Ó Catháin, 'Revd Charles Bunworth of Buttevant: patron of harpers and poets', *JCHAS*, 102 (1997), pp 111–18.   36 J. Byrne, 'Canon Goodman', unpublished M.A. dissertation, NUI, Cork (2004); J. Bryne, 'Canon Goodman', *Journal of the Skibbereen and District Historical Society*, i (2005), pp 53–95; J. Coleman, 'Seven Cork clerical writers', *JCHAS*, ix (1903), pp 153–5; H. Shields (ed.), *Tunes of the Munster pipers: Irish traditional music from the James Goodman manuscripts*, i (Dublin, 1998).

IV

One of the two architects of the Dublin Society was the Revd Samuel Madden, a well-to-do squarson with a substantial estate at Manor Waterhouse in County Fermanagh. It tended to be those of the same kind – William Perceval, dean of Emly, his son, the Revd Kane Perceval, other Dublin clergy like John Wynne and John Lyon, and later William Henry, rector of Urney – who devoted greatest energy to the cause of improvement through the society and its shorter-lived companion, the Physico-Historical Society. In outlook and activism the clergy seemed to differ little from their colleagues in the professions and government service. In preparing descriptions of the several counties, considerable dependence had been put on local clergymen, either themselves to supply the information or to organize others to do so.[37] Among those who responded were the Revd William Henry, the Revd John Richardson and the Revd Richard Barton. All were ardent improvers, seeing the causes of spiritual enlightenment, economic betterment and cultural advance as intertwined. Richardson, rector at Belturbet, already had a long commitment to Protestant evangelization in the Irish language, and now wrote about County Cavan.[38] In 1744, the Physico-Historical Society asked that the bishops and clergy should recommend its work to those in their jurisdictions.[39] It can be assumed that they did so, and often set an example by becoming members themselves. Nevertheless, the initial enthusiasm evaporated rapidly, and by the mid-1750s the society had foundered. A few of the intended county histories – for Cork, Down, Dublin, Kerry and Waterford – were published. They had been composed by the laymen, Walter Harris and Charles Smith. Topographical accounts by Barton, the curate of Lurgan, were also printed.[40] The majority of those by the Revd William Henry had to wait much longer to be published, and then only in part.[41]

Those interested in useful and scholarly investigations contented themselves for the moment with the better-grounded Dublin Society. Henry, for example, used it as a platform for some of his improving projects. The Revd John Wynne, having served long as a secretary, was rewarded with a gold medal in 1760.[42] In 1773, the

---

37 Physico-Historical Society Papers, Archbishop Robinson Library, Armagh, list of those to whom sent, 18 May 1739.   38 Ibid., accounts of Co. Cavan, 12 July 1739, 5 April 1740; Barnard, *Irish Protestant ascents and descents*, pp 189–96, 202–4; E. Magennis, ' "A land of milk and honey": the Physico-Historical Society, improvement and the surveys of mid-eighteenth-century Ireland', *PRIA*, 102, C (2002), pp 199–217.   39 Minute Book, Physico-Historical Society, RIA, MS 24 E 28, s.d. 14 April 1744.   40 R. Barton, *A dialogue concerning some things of importance to Ireland; particularly to the County of Ardmagh* (Dublin, 1751); idem, *Lectures in natural philosophy* (Dublin, 1751); idem, *Some remarks, towards a full description of Upper and Lower Lough Lene, near Killarney* (Dublin, 1751).   41 W. Henry, *An account of Lough Lheichs in the county of Cavan* ([Dublin], 1736); C.S. King (ed.), *Henry's Upper Lough Erne in 1739* (Dublin, 1892); Magennis, ' "A land of milk and honey" ', pp 209, 215–16.   42 Minute book, 1758–1761, s.d. 9, 16 and 30 March 1758, 20 April 1758, 23 and 30 Nov. 1758, 12 and 19 April 1759, 8 Nov.

society, like its forbears, appealed to Church of Ireland incumbents for information about their parishes through which a national survey could be accomplished.⁴³ Others pursued their researches within alternative institutional frameworks or privately. Two eighteenth-century clergymen illustrate contrasted strategies. The Reverend John Lyon, if remembered at all, is known as the keeper of Jonathan Swift in his final, distressing years. A different tribute was offered by William Monck Mason in 1819. 'There is no one', Monck Mason suggested, 'to whom the Irish antiquarian is more indebted; to his diligence we chiefly owe the preservation of whatever remains of the ecclesiastical antiquities of Dublin.'⁴⁴ Monck Mason himself acquired some of Lyon's collections relating to Dublin and its environs.⁴⁵ Recent scholars share Monck Mason's high opinion. 'The very accurate and intelligent' Lyon, although he published nothing, re-arranged and catalogued the archives of the two Dublin cathedrals and of Trinity College.⁴⁶ By doing so, Lyon helped to ensure the preservation and later use of the documents. In part, his motives were utilitarian. Leases, surveys and charters were needed to ensure that the institutions could collect their rents, repel competitors and uphold rights and privileges.⁴⁷ Struggles with rivals had already inspired King, as archbishop of Dublin, to have important documents copied.⁴⁸ Their orderly re-arrangement by Lyon was welcomed by the chapters of the cathedrals and board of the college.⁴⁹ The arbitrariness with which he dismembered earlier arrangements of documents to fit his own principles may displease later archivists, but they concede how much the accessibility and even the survival of the manuscripts owe to him.⁵⁰ However, Lyon's concern extended beyond utility into antiquarian and indeed patriotic interests. He apostrophized the chapter of Christ Church: 'the idea of your ancestors was to hide away in safety the charters and muniments belonging to this most ancient and august metropolitan church, yours indeed was to examine and free

---

1759, 24 April 1760, 1 May 1760, 13 Nov. 1760, 18 Dec. 1760, 16 April 1761, 28 May 1761, RDS. For Wynne: Cotton, *Fasti*, ii, pp 112–13, 138, 143, 178.   **43** J.C. (ed.), 'Mallow district in 1775', *JCHAS*, xxi (1915), p. 17.   **44** W.M. Mason, *Hibernia antiqua et hodierna, being a topographical account of Ireland* (Dublin, 1819), pp 65, note n, lxiii.   **45** They are now NLI, MSS 100–105. **46** Catalogue of books, records and leases of the dean and chapter of St Patrick's, Dublin, RCB, C.2.1.26.1; Catalogue, TCD, MS MUN/Lib/1/53; cf. W. Harris (ed.), *The whole works of Sir James Ware concerning Ireland revised and improved* (3 vols, Dublin, 1739), i, sig. a2.   **47** See, for example, two guard books with their contents listed by Lyon: RCB, C.2.1.22/1 and 2.   **48** Abp W. King to Revd E. Synge, 27 Feb. 1704[5] and 17 March 1704[5], RCBL, C.2.1.22/46, nos 81 and 85; account books of Abp W. King, TCD MSS, 752/2, f.193; 752/3, ff. 97, 141v; Bp J. Evans to Abp W. Wake, 23 Dec. 1720, Christ Church, Oxford, Wake MS 13, f. 215.   **49** Rev. F. Corbet to J. Lyon, 23 June 1747, 22 Nov. 1749 and undated, RCBL, C.2.1.22/46.   **50** R. Gillespie, 'The archives of Christ Church cathedral, Dublin', *Irish Archives. Journal of the Irish Society of Archives*, 5 (1998), pp 3–12; W. O'Sullivan, 'Introduction to the collections' in M.L. Colker, *Trinity College Dublin. Descriptive catalogue of the medieval and renaissance Latin manuscripts* (Aldershot, 1991), pp 28–9; W. O'Sullivan, 'The eighteenth-century rebinding of the manuscripts', *Long Room*, i (1970), pp 19–28.

them from the forgetful injuries of time…In your judgement, unless I am deceived, it is indeed shameful to be learned in ecclesiastical things relating to foreign people but ignorant of one's own.'[51]

Why Lyon developed his fascination with history and how he then acquired the principles and skills on which his labours were based mystify. Education at Trinity College presumably helped him to the linguistic, if not the palaeographical, techniques. Upbringing (seemingly in relatively humble circumstances) and education in Dublin evidently kindled curiosity about his venerable surroundings. By the 1730s, when he first showed a leaning towards archival work, he may have been responding to impulses already apparent among the capitular clergy in the capital. During the decade, there was a palpable stirring of interest in the histories of the two cathedrals, as well as of other ancient ecclesiastical foundations. In 1738, the chapter of St Patrick paid Lyon ten guineas for his 'collections illustrating the history of St Patrick's'. The gratuity encouraged him to continue and improve researches started by a more idiosyncratic enquirer, Isaac Butler. In 1740 Lyon was formally connected to St Patrick's by appointment to a minor canonry.[52] Meanwhile, he was discovering important documents in private hands. He was drawn into the collaborative efforts of the Physico-Historical Society, serving on its large committee in 1744, and being elected to its council in 1747. These appointments suggested enthusiasm for the work of the society and his availability thanks to living in Dublin.[53]

Lyon, despite his methodical labours in the archives, published nothing under his own name. A successor in similar mode was the Revd William Lodge, the first librarian of Archbishop Robinson's library in Armagh. Lodge was the sole surviving child of John Lodge, a notable antiquary of Ireland and compiler of a voluminous Irish peerage. Thanks to the younger Lodge's appointment some of his father's collections and notes came to the Armagh library. Later, more were acquired from a grandson, the Revd William Robinson Lodge, rector of Killybegs. The two clerical Lodges did not match John Lodge's researches, but they did continue the concern of their forbear that unique documents should be preserved. Furthermore, thanks to their links with Armagh, they steered elements of Lodge's collections into the custody of the Church of Ireland.[54] The Revd William Lodge

51 M. Sheehy, 'The Registrum Novum', *Reportorium Novum*, iii (1963–4), pp 249–50.   52 Chapter Act Book, St Patrick's Cathedral, Dublin, 1720–63, s.d. 9 May 1735, 11 Jan. 1737[8], 17 March 1740[1], 15 May 1741, 17 March 1742[3]; RCBL, C.2.1.3.8; Proctors' accounts, St Patrick's, 1718–35, s.d. 9 May 1735; 1735–55, s.d. 14 Jan. 1737[8], 4 June 1741, 17 March 1742[3], ibid., C 2.1.10 (1 and 2); H.J. Lawlor, *The Fasti of St Patrick's, Dublin* (Dundalk, 1930), pp 140, 146, 166, 204; H. Williams (ed.), *The correspondence of Jonathan Swift* (5 vols, Oxford, 1963–1965), iv, p. 534; v, p. 275.   53 Minutes of the Physico-Historical Society, s.d. 7 May 1744, 4 March 1744[5], 16 Feb. 1746[7], 6 March 1748[9], RIA, MS 24 E 28; Mason, *Hibernia antiqua et hodierna*, p. 85, note g; [K. Perceval and P. Read], *An account of the rise and progress of the Physico-Historical Society* [Dublin, 1745].   54 J. Lodge to Lord Perceval, 23 Dec. 1742, BL, Add. MS 47,013B, ff. 108–9; J. Dean, *Catalogue of manuscripts in the public library of Armagh* (Dun-

also displayed another interest common among eighteenth-century clergymen. He enumerated the population of the city of Armagh. Lodge went beyond the information required by periodic parliamentary enquiries, to conduct a detailed census of the structure, confession and occupations of households. As such it has proved a treasure trove for later demographers.[55] Other clerics made similar surveys: Edward Synge, when bishop of Elphin in 1749; James Mockler of Mallow; Daniel Beaufort at Navan; James Whitelaw (in 1798) in Dublin; and, perhaps most comprehensively, Horatio Townsend in County Cork.[56] As with Lodge, so with Beaufort and Townsend, this activity was merely one facet of an inventive and inquisitive personality. In particular, the versatile Beaufort contributed importantly to the mapping and description of Ireland.[57]

V

Enquiries into the Irish past had come within the purview of the Dublin Society and its predecessors. Yet, given the society's emphasis on the topical and useful, antiquarians sought an alternative forum. In 1772, thirty members of the Dublin Society formed a committee to enquire into the antiquities of Ireland. Of them, nine were Church of Ireland clergymen. They were soon joined by Thomas Percy, the learned bishop of Dromore. Not all were active, but the Revd Thomas Leland, from Trinity College, acted as secretary, the Revd Peter Chaigneau, as treasurer and librarian, and others such as the bishops of Cloyne and Cork, Dean Richard Woodward, Dean Thomas Barnard of Derry and Dr Stewart, forwarded the project. The Society thought that the clergy, together with country gentlemen, would have a special role in the endeavours of the committee, since they would be asked to answer detailed questions 'respecting the antiquities of their respective parishes'. The group, seeking to transcend sectarian differences, invited Charles O'Conor of Belanagare, John Carpenter, the Catholic archbishop of Dublin, and Thomas

---

dalk, 1928); W. Reeves, 'Memoir of the Rev. William Lodge, LL.D', *Ulster Journal of Archaeology*, new series, i (1894–5), pp 87–90.   55 L.A. Clarkson, 'Household and family structure in Armagh city, 1770', *Local Population Studies*, 20 (1978), pp 14–31; L.A. Clarkson, 'Armagh, 1770: portrait of an urban community' in D. Harkness and M. O'Dowd (eds), *The town in Ireland*, Historical Studies XIII (Belfast, 1981), pp 81–102; B.F. Gurrin, 'The Union of Navan in 1766', *Ríocht na Midhe*, xiv (2003), pp 144–67; M.L. Legg (ed.), *The census of Elphin, 1749* (Dublin, 2004).   56 J.C. (ed.), 'Mallow district in 1775', pp 17–29; J. Whitelaw, *An essay on the population of Dublin* (Dublin, 1805); T. Graham, 'Whitelaw's 1798 census of Dublin' in *History Ireland*, ii/3 (1994), pp 10–15.   57 J.H. Andrews, *Shapes of Ireland maps and their makers, 1564–1839* (Dublin, 1997), pp 214–47; C.C. Ellison, *The hopeful traveller: the life and times of Daniel Augustus Beaufort, LL.D. 1739–1821* (Kilkenny, 1987); C.C. Ellison (ed.), 'Materials for the Dublin Society agricultural survey of County Louth, compiled by Dr D.A. Beaufort', *Journal of the County Louth Archaeological and Historical Society*, xviii (1973–6), pp 121–31, 167–94, 304–9.

Hussey, future bishop of Waterford, to join.[58] In practice, the historical activities could hardly be divorced from clerical involvement in the contested politics of the day. Woodward, a member of the select committee, would emerge in 1787, by then bishop of Cloyne, as the foremost defender of the privileges of the established church. Others, such as Barnard, Leland, Edward Ledwich and Thomas Campbell, if less strident in enunciating the notion of a Church of Ireland ascendancy, nevertheless sought through their historical writings to shore up the endangered Church.

Diehards were not satisfied with the achievements of the committee. Accordingly, in 1779, a few devotees established the Hibernian Antiquarian Society, in which one Church of Ireland cleric, Edward Ledwich, was conspicuous. But, thanks to Ledwich's combativeness, this society quickly dissolved in acrimony.[59] In its place the Royal Irish Academy was founded in 1785. As with the earlier organizations, so with the Academy, clergymen were recruited, but did not dominate its proceedings. Its original Antiquities Committee had six recorded members, of whom four were Church of Ireland clergymen: William Hamilton, Lefanu, Daniel Beaufort and Bishop Barnard.[60]

Throughout the eighteenth century and into the nineteenth, scholars argued over who had first colonized Ireland – the Milesians, Phoenicians, Scythians – and whether they had arrived from Spain or northern Europe. Champions of the Church of Ireland wished also to demonstrate origins of Christianity independent of any mission despatched from Rome and so to claim the founders of Christian Ireland, notably Patrick, as their own.[61] A number of clergy entered the lists. Thomas Barnard, dean of Derry and future bishop of Killaloe and Limerick, sought to synthesize the ideas of others in essays published in the *Transactions* of the Royal Irish Academy in 1787.[62] More aggressive was a second cleric, Edward Ledwich, the veteran of the short-lived Hibernian Antiquarian Society.[63] Beneficed at Aghaboe in Queen's County, Ledwich represented himself as a country parson distant from Dublin, with its libraries and congenial groups of enquirers. This complaint of being 'buried in an obscure corner' and being encumbered with a family would be echoed by successors into the twentieth century. Ledwich even contemplated exchanging his living at Aghaboe for a poorly paid curacy closer to the capital.[64] However, he managed to compensate for his comparative isolation by

58 Minutes, select standing committee for antiquities, Dublin Society, 1772–3, RIA, MS 24 E 7. 59 RIA, MS 24 E 7; W. Love, 'The Hibernian Antiquarian Society', *Studies*, 51 (1962), pp 419–31; Magennis, '"A land of milk and honey"', pp 199–217. 60 RIA, Minutes of Antiquities Committee, i, 1785–1830, p. 34. 61 C. O'Halloran, *Golden age and barbarous nations: antiquarian debate and cultural politics in Ireland, c.1750–1800* (Cork, 2004), pp 8–9. 62 Minutes, select standing committee for antiquities, Dublin Society, 1772–3, RIA, MS 24 E 7, p. 114. 63 An earlier Reverend Dr Edward Ledwich was active in the Physico-Historical Society. He was to suggest candidates for membership of the Society from Kildare and King's County. Minutes of the Physico-Historical Society, s.d. 14 April 1744, RIA, MS 24 E 28. 64 E. Ledwich to W.B. Conyngham?, 13 April 1779, NLI, MS 1415/126; same to J.C. Walker, [May 1789], TCD, MS

frequent purchases of books and correspondence with the like-minded.[65] Led-wich's book-buying suggested healthy finances, as did his thoughts in 1789 of tak-ing a tenancy of a central Dublin house, requiring an entry fine of 300 guineas and a yearly rent of £65. From the mid-1790s, he was able to spend part of each year in Dublin.[66] Moreover, before he settled in Queen's County, he had seen North America as an army chaplain and been beneficed in Wiltshire.[67]

In 1779, the bishop of Ossory, William Newcombe, alleged that, apart from Ledwich, only two other clergy around Dublin bothered with antiquarian mat-ters.[68] Ledwich was no retiring violet. He had plunged into The Hibernian Anti-quarian Society and brought about its quick disintegration.[69] Without institutional backing, he published his discoveries and speculations: first in *Archaeologia*, the journal of the London Society of Antiquaries, but then under his own auspices. The links beyond Ireland with societies in London and Scotland gave him a wider perspective. Certainly, he expressed his indebtedness to the recent writings on Scotland, particularly those of and stimulated by Sir John Sinclair. Through sta-tistical accounts of the Scottish shires, Sinclair aimed to speed agricultural improvements. Ledwich was moved to write, as some in Scotland had been, to refute the daily misrepresentations of 'ignorant itinerants'.[70] Of Ledwich's publi-cations, the most notable were *Antiquities of Ireland*[71] and an account of his own parish in Queen's County.[72] Like Lyon before him, Ledwich was influenced by the atmosphere of the moment, conducive to antiquarian observation and speculation. In one particular, he echoed Lyon. Ledwich suggested that the recently established Royal Irish Academy publish the most important manuscripts, such as the 'Crede Mihi', Archbishop Allen's register, and 'the Black Book', from Christ Church in Dublin: manuscripts that Lyon had helped to save.[73] Publication had to wait until the twentieth century and occurred under the auspices of a different body.

In the years since Lyon started in the 1730s, theories multiplied: about the ori-gins of the Irish language and peoples and the purposes of features like round tow-ers and raths. Investigations of notable sites had been undertaken; the results – sometimes in the shape of sketches and engravings – were published. Concur-rently intellectual and artistic fashions had changed, bringing greater appreciation

1461/3, f. 147; E. Ledwich, 'Some observations on the ancient laws and records of Ireland', BL, Egerton MS 212, f. 48.   **65** M. Nevin, 'Joseph Cooper Walker, 1761–1810', *JRSAI*, 126 (1996), pp 152–66; 127 (1997), pp 34–51.   **66** E. Ledwich to H.T. Clements, 14 March 1789, [March 1790], TCD, MS 1461/3, ff. 127, 205; same to J.C. Walker, [May 1789], 21 Nov. 1796, 7 July 1799, ibid., MS 1461/3, f. 147v; 1461/4, ff. 32, 103; M. Hewson, 'Edward Ledwich's gift', *Long Room*, 30 (1985), p. 30.   **67** O'Halloran, *Golden ages and barbarous nations*, p. 66.   **68** Bp W. Newcombe to W.B. Conyngham?, 13 March 1779, NLI, MS 1415/159–60. The two were Arch-dall and Mahon.   **69** Love, 'The Hibernian Antiquarian Society', pp 419–31.   **70** *A statistical account of the parish of Aghaboe, in the Queen's County, Ireland* (Dublin, 1796), p. iv.   **71** Dublin, 1790.   **72** E. Ledwich to W.B. Conyngham?, 1 May 1779, NLI, MS 1415/129–30; same to ?J.C. Walker, 20 Sep. 1786, TCD, MS 1461/2, f. 153v.   **73** E. Ledwich to ?J.C. Walker, 21 May 1787, TCD, MS 1461/2, f. 233v.

of the picturesque, primitive and ruined. Ledwich seems to have been touched by these currents. He portrayed his times as 'an age of most prying curiosity'. A more explicit statement about his own responses spoke of his 'very great love of such monuments' as were depicted in 'drawings of very ancient ruins, and buildings not quite ruinous'.[74] Yet, in his enthusiasm for historical objects, he may have surrendered to other impulses. A wish to divert himself in the tedious intervals between seasonal rural frenzy, when he had to oversee the harvest, collect his tithes and participate in the county assizes, was one. Ledwich conscientiously discharged his parochial responsibilities. He was to the fore in promoting manufactures – notably of textiles – to alleviate the prevalent poverty.[75] He applauded others who joined the endeavour, especially Dr Charles Coote, the dean of Kilfenora. Dean Coote acted as agent of his absent kinsman, the earl of Mountrath. Coote gave benefactions towards establishing an Irish cotton manufactory and to create funds on which industrious tradesmen in Maryborough and Mountrath could draw.[76]

Ledwich was combative. Belief in England and Protestantism as the main sources of Irish improvement, common to his predecessors among Hartlib's friends or the Physico-Historical Society, ran through the account of his parish of Aghaboe. He also revealed topical concerns: the absenteeism of the principal proprietors of the district and the resulting dearth of substantial houses. Yet Ledwich wished to exonerate Ireland from the strictures of 'shallow observers and uninformed travellers'. So he contended that even 'common Irish cabins' with their wretched exteriors sometimes concealed commodious interiors. Furthermore, he stated that his own parish was free of the land-jobbers who, elsewhere in the island, proved 'such pests of society' and prevented the emergence of substantial yeomanry. He drew a comforting picture of cottiers well able to subsist thanks to their own and their wives' and children's labour, especially in the textile industries. His reassurances were accompanied by seemingly plausible figures of earnings and outgoings.[77]

Ledwich's interest in the antiquities around him might be strong, but he was hardly consistent in his attitude towards scholarship. He rejected topics such as the history of gardening or the Irish wolf-hound ('a rather barren subject') that might appeal to a wider and more frivolous readership.[78] Although not indifferent to possible financial gain, Ledwich admitted that he had enough money not to need any extra that might come from publications. Instead, he confessed that 'my ruling passion is to leave some memory of my existence'.[79] To this end, he vowed to avoid

---

74 E. Ledwich to ?J.C. Walker, 6 Aug. 1785, 26 June 1786, 22 July 1786, TCD, MS 1461/2, ff. 46, 124v, 138. 75 E. Ledwich to J.C. Walker, 30 July 1785, 28 Jan. 1786, 8 July 1786, TCD, MS 1461/2, ff. 44, 79v, 130; J. O'Hanlon and E. O'Leary, *History of The Queen's County* (2 vols, Dublin, 1907), i, pp 172–3. 76 Ledwich, *Antiquities*, p. v. 77 Ledwich, *Aghaboe*, passim, especially pp 51–63. 78 E. Ledwich to H.T. Clements, 19 and 23 May 1788, [24 Feb. 1789], 5 March 1789, TCD, MS 1461/3, ff. 59, 63, 118, 123v. 79 E. Ledwich to J.C. Walker, undated, ?Jan. 1794, TCD, MS 1461/3, f. 274.

'the dry uninteresting…style' of the pioneering English antiquarian, William Camden, and was tempted into 'those historiettes and anecdotes which enliven and divert both writer and reader'.[80] Yet, he proposed a reprint of two pioneering works from seventeenth-century Ireland: Boate's and Molyneux's natural histories. He thought that 'the old trash … is not unpleasant as it shows the beginning and dawning of that science in this isle'.[81] He also applauded Spenser's and Sir John Davies's writings on Ireland and deplored the 'extraneous trash' added to the work of another seventeenth-century antiquary, Sir James Ware, by Walter Harris in a later edition. Yet, on another occasion, he had to concede that he could add little to Harris's edition of Ware's works.[82]

Praise of Spenser and Davies, prime apologists for English settlement in Ireland, betrayed Ledwich's partisanship. The same trait underlay his brusque dismissals of writers more sympathetic to the ancient and Catholic Irish. He gleefully derided 'the galled papist' and 'scribbling popish friars'.[83] Nor did his contemporaries, John Curry, Charles O'Conor and Sylvester O'Halloran, escape his contempt for 'the pompous but puerile fictions and assertions of national antiquaries'.[84] Ledwich contended that the Catholics' writings were preoccupied with 'their lost estates and the want of success in their numerous rebellions to recover them', and therefore distorted. Ledwich voiced assumptions common to privileged members of the Church of England, especially when their privileges were attacked openly during the 1780s.[85] But earlier Protestant chroniclers of Ireland were also criticized. The Revd Anthony Raymond, rector of Trim during the 1720s, was praised for his ability to read 'the common Irish', but dismissed for composing 'a great deal on the fabulous history of Ireland without throwing one ray of light on the subject'.[86]

Ledwich, sometimes mischievous and intemperate, courted controversy. He spiced up his treatment of St Patrick, knowing it 'would make a noise and I hope will be the means of promoting a sale'.[87] In offering his iconoclastic conclusions about St Patrick – that no such historical figure existed – he confessed, 'I am unsainting St Patrick fast', and added with relish, ''twill be fine sport'. Later, when

80 E. Ledwich to H.T. Clements, 24 Dec. 1787, TCD, MS 1461/1, f. 20. 81 E. Ledwich to ?J.C. Walker, 21 May 1787, TCD, MS 1461/2, f. 233v. 82 BL, Egerton MS 212, ff. 41v, 42, 44v-45, 48–49v; E. Ledwich to H.T. Clements, undated [1790], TCD, MS 1461/3, ff. 200–0v. 83 E. Ledwich to ?J.C. Walker, 25 Feb. 1786, 13 May 1786, 19 June 1786, 7 April 1787, 20 Nov. 1786; same to unknown, [Nov. 1787], same to H. T. Clements, 13 July 1788, TCD, MSs. 1461/2, ff. 95v, 107v, 120v, 162v, 225, 286; 1461/3, f. 70. 84 E. Ledwich to ?J.C. Walker, 25 Feb. 1786, 13 May 1786, 19 June 1786, 7 April 1787, 20 Nov. 1786; same to unknown, [Nov. 1787], same to H. T. Clements, 13 July 1788, TCD, MSs. 1461/2, ff. 95v, 107v, 120v, 162v, 225, 286; 1461/3, f. 70. 85 E. Ledwich to ?J.C. Walker, 7 March 1787, TCD, MS 1461/2, f. 202. 86 E. Ledwich to ?J.C. Walker, 29 April 1786, 13 May 1786, 19 June 1786, 13 March 1787, 5 Sept. 1796, TCD, MSs. 1461/2, ff. 103, 107v, 120v, 209–9v; 1461/4, f. 27. On Raymond, see A. Harrison, *The dean's friend: Anthony Raymond, 1675–1726, Jonathan Swift and the Irish language* (Dublin, 1999). 87 E. Ledwich to H.T. Clements, undated [1789], TCD, MS 1461/3, f. 108.

his interests turned to Homer, he had the same doubts about the Greek poet's existence as he had had about Patrick.[88] He justified his trenchant manner by arguing
that 'strong language' was necessary to state his 'truths'.[89] It also attracted attention and sold his publications. His very waywardness and misapprehensions
aroused interest and thereby stimulated others.

VI

Ledwich acknowledged his indebtedness to earlier scholars. Yet, there was a tendency for each generation to believe it had constructed better methods of enquiry
and analysis and to belittle much that had gone before. The channels through
which antiquarianism passed were often subterranean. In the mid-eighteenth century, the Revd Richard Barton mentioned several otherwise obscure clerics who
shared his tastes. The Revd Mr Carroll, living near Lough Neagh, 'has a curious
disposition to search into nature's works, consistently with his clerical employment'. Carroll occupied himself usefully in 'religion and husbandry'.[90] The Revd
James Hackett, 'a gentleman of letters and taste', was reported to be writing a history of Armagh and finishing another of Egypt.[91] The Revd John Payne was
praised for his 'ingenuity', particularly in the understanding of gem stones.[92] Soon
Payne earned wider renown by publishing a volume of designs for houses, characterized by convenience and economy.[93] He designed a glebe house at Trim for the
Revd Adam Lyndon, and some of his interest may have arisen from the need to
assist clergymen, like himself or Lyndon, anxious to erect or improve houses in
their parishes.[94] Beaufort also sketched architectural schemes, including one for the
church at Collon in County Louth, which was built.

Individual incumbents might strive within their livings to enquire into the past
and improve present conditions. In order to reduce their sense of isolation, they
backed the various collaborative undertakings, so that, at least through correspondence, they might feel themselves to be part of a larger group. Barton had contended that the clergy could appropriately interest themselves in such enterprises
because they were an extension of their spiritual duties. However, sharper incentives to do so probably came from earlier education which equipped them to
enquire and speculate and from the leisure that they enjoyed. In most cases, cler-

---

88 E. Ledwich to H.T. Clements, [1789] and 15 March 1790, TCD, MS 1461/3, ff. 108, 128;
same to J.C. Walker, 15 Oct. 1796, ibid., MS 1461/4, f.29. 89 Ledwich, *Antiquities*, p. iv. 90
Barton, *Lectures in natural philosophy*, pp 95, 99. 91 Barton, *A dialogue concerning some things of
importance to Ireland*, p. 18, note *. 92 Barton, *Lectures in natural philosophy*, p. 176. 93 J.
Payne, *Twelve designs for country houses* (Dublin, 1757). 94 C. Casey, 'Books and builders: a bib-
liographical approach to Irish eighteenth-century architecture', unpublished PhD thesis, TCD,
2 vols (1991), i, pp 22–3, 166–77; M. Craig, *Classic Irish houses of the middle size* (London, 1976),
pp 39–48.

gymen commanded lower incomes than the country and urban squires active in the Dublin Society, and may have been on an economic and social par with figures like the apothecary, Charles Smith, who drove the Physico-Historical Society. Even so, in their benefices, clerics tended to provide a focus sometimes complementary to that of the squire in his mansion but frequently as an alternative to the absent or unconcerned landlords. It was natural, then, that curiosities and information should be vouchsafed by the locals to interested incumbents. It was, for example, the Revd James Moore, master of the free school in Cavan, who acquired an unusual horn: this he duly despatched to the Physico-Historical Society in Dublin.[95] When Smith prepared a second edition of his history of Cork, he could add information about curiosities supplied by local clergymen: Marmaduke Cox and a Mr Gore, near Assolas.[96] In the same county, the Revd James Hingston built up a library of nearly 2,500 titles, easily surpassing the collections of lay neighbours.[97]

The groups and projects in which Ledwich was involved, albeit rather tangentially at times, continued and multiplied in the nineteenth century. Many preoccupations persisted, as did the propensity of collaborators and colleagues to fall out. Clergy of the established church remained well-placed to engage in the enquiries. As university graduates, they commanded some of the necessary linguistic and analytical skills, and enjoyed leisure and standing. The results were displayed strikingly in the Revd Edward Hincks. For forty-one years rector of Killyleagh in County Down, Hincks won an enduring reputation as a pioneer in the decipherment of cuneiform script and Egyptian hieroglyphics. Hincks's achievements were the more impressive since he was never able to visit Egypt or Assyria. His interests were probably fostered by his father who moved from Cork, where he had kept a school and been employed by the Royal Cork Institution, to Belfast. There he taught Hebrew in the Academical Institute. The family had Presbyterian antecedents, but the younger Hincks proceeded in 1803 to Trinity College Dublin, where he secured a fellowship, was ordained, and then moved to the college living of Ardtrea. He exhibited considerable intellectual and literary versatility, publishing a long poem on Bonaparte at the moment of Napoleon's exile and recording astronomical observations. He settled not altogether contentedly into the routines of a country parson, yet discharged his duties punctiliously. One parishioner, the future Lady Dufferin, sensed that the drudgery was not congenial: 'of course he should not have been confined to a little country parish, but should have been in the society of other learned men, and have had complete leisure for his investigations, in the atmosphere of some great university'.[98] Absent-mindedness caused

95 RIA, MS 24 E 28, Minute book, Physico-Historical Society, s.d. 15 May 1744.   96 Smith, *Cork*, i, pp 409, 411.   97 RCBL, MS 521.3; T.C. Barnard, 'A clerical library in County Cork', forthcoming; W.M. Brady, *Clerical and parochial records of Cork, Cloyne and Ross* (3 vols, Dublin, 1864–5), ii, p. 189.   98 E.F. Davidson (ed.), *Edward Hincks: a selection from his correspondence* (Oxford and London, 1933), p. 22.

further difficulties. Failing to exchange his surplice for a black gown, he mounted the pulpit in order to preach only to find, when he disrobed in the vestry, that his academic hood had been ritually torn up as a protest against his supposed high church practices. Hincks schemed to have himself removed to a location – perhaps the British Museum – closer to his interests. It was to no avail: he lacked effective patrons and had to watch while less distinguished contemporaries prospered and (in the case of Sir Henry Rawlinson) made unacknowledged use of his researches.[99]

The idea of bringing texts in oriental languages to bear on the problems of the scriptures, in the seventeenth century a spur to Marsh and Huntington, inspired Hincks. Similar skills were commanded by Richard Laurence, archbishop of Cashel between 1822 and 1838. Laurence, before his appointment to Cashel, was regius professor of Hebrew in Oxford. He translated three apocryphal books from Ethiopian.[1] In addition, he published documents relating to predestinarian beliefs persecuted by Mary I's government and to the early reformed church in Saxony in the 1530s.[2] He also ventured into controversies with rigid Calvinists and opponents of infant baptism. Laurence, although of English birth, once removed to Ireland, emphasized his vestigial Irish links through his wife (she had died before he was elevated to Cashel). Moreover, the archbishop's brother, French Laurence, had been close to Edmund Burke, 'the great ornament and pride of Ireland', and who, 'boasting by maternal descent of Irish blood, eminently possessed in promptitude of feeling, warmth of affection and frankness of disposition, an Irish heart'.[3]

The archbishop assisted scholarship in another way. In 1823, he brought his son-in-law, Henry Cotton, from England to serve as his domestic chaplain. Soon Cotton was advanced into the archdeaconry of Cashel. In time, the archdeacon repaid some of his obligations by editing and publishing the early poems of the Laurence brothers.[4] Cotton might seem merely another beneficiary of nepotism, but the Church of Ireland also gained. Cotton had previously served as a sublibrarian in Oxford's Bodleian Library. Once in Ireland, he transferred his scholarly skills, and in time compiled and published the most comprehensive listing of

---

99 A. Crookshank and D. Webb, *Paintings and sculptures in Trinity College Dublin* (Dublin, 1990), p. 71.   1 *The ascension of Isaiah the prophet*, translated by R. Laurence (Oxford, 1819); R. Laurence, *The Book of Enoch the prophet: an apocryphal production, supposed to have been lost for ages* (Oxford, 1821); R. Laurence, *Ascensio Isaiae vatis* (Oxford, 1819); R. Laurence, *Primi Ezrae libri ... versio Aethiopica ... Latine Angliceque reddita* (Oxford, 1820).   2 R. Laurence, *Authentic documents relative to the predestinarian controversy, which took place among those who were imprisoned for their adherence to the doctrines of the reformation by Queen Mary* (Oxford, 1819); idem, *Extracts from a formulary for the visitation of the Saxon churches* (Oxford, 1838); idem, *The visitation of the Saxon reformed church in 1527 and 1529*, ed. H. Cotton (Dublin, 1839).   3 H. Cotton, *Poetical remains of French Laurence, D.C.L., M.P. and Richard Laurence, D.C.L., archbishop of Cashel* (Dublin, 1872), p. 113; R. Laurence, *A charge delivered to the clergy of the dioceses of Cashel and Emly a the primary visitation, in September, 1822* (Dublin, 1822), dedication.   4 Cotton, *Poetical remains.*

Church of Ireland clergy. Others, such as James Hingston in Cloyne, had already listed the bishops and clergy of their dioceses, but Cotton's *Fasti* embraced the entire Church of Ireland. Researches of this kind were not innocent of confessional partisanship. They served as another device to demonstrate the antiquity of the Church through an unbroken succession of clergy reaching back into the centuries before the reformation. First the threat and then the actuality of disestablishment may have strengthened the wish to proclaim a venerable ancestry.[5]

Archbishop Laurence's scholarship was more a product of his years in Oxford than in Munster. Cotton's statement that his father-in-law had learnt Ethiopian only after he arrived in Ireland cannot be correct, since the translation of Enoch had been published before Laurence's departure from Oxford.[6] Laurence, although of 'retired habits' from youth, did not neglect his episcopal duties. The same could be said of Mant and Whately. The former did eventually direct his busy pen towards the church in which he had been consecrated a bishop; the latter schemed, but schemed in vain, to improve the education offered by Dublin University. Indeed, his projects included an unsuccessful campaign to establish a theological seminary for the Church of Ireland.[7]

Richard Mant, equally facile as poet, hymn-writer and Anglican apologist, was consecrated bishop of Killaloe and Kilfenora in 1820 and translated to Down, Connor and Dromore in 1823. Quickly, he turned his attention to local matters. He appealed to the detailed history of the Church of England since the reformation to rebut the notion that observing church festivals was 'popish'. One tangible result of his episcopate, under the auspices of the Church Accommodation Society, was the building of new places of worship.[8] A second was his *History of the Church of Ireland from the Reformation to Revolution*.[9] Conceived as a riposte to the recently published account of the Presbyterian church in Ireland by J.S. Reid, Mant's *History* was avowedly partisan. Nevertheless, it made use of primary materials, including the unpublished manuscripts of Archbishop King, to construct an effective narrative where none had existed previously.

Richard Whately, like Mant, had been nurtured in an Oxford University emerging from the seemingly placid Augustan era. There Whately's writings on logic were essential reading for undergraduates. His eccentricity was noticed even in an institution in which oddity, whether assumed or unconscious, abounded. Head of a hall, for a time he had John Henry Newman as his deputy. In Oxford, he was

5 For Cotton's papers: RCBL, MSS 42 and 117. H. Cotton, *Fasti Ecclesiae Hibernicae* (6 vols, Dublin, 1845–78); J.S.C. and J.R. Garstin, 'Archdeacon Cotton', *The Irish Book Lover*, 2 (1910), pp 1–4. 6 Cotton, *Poetical remains*, p. 114. 7 J. Crawford, *The Church of Ireland in Victorian Dublin* (Dublin, 2004), pp 61, 93–4, 112–13. 8 R. Mant, *A charge delivered to the clergy of the diocese of Killaloe, at the primary visitation, Thursday, August the third, 1820* (Dublin, 1820); R. Mant, *Feriae Anniversaraiae. observance of the church's holy-days no symptom of popery* (2 vols, Dublin, 1847); W-B. Mant, *Memoirs of the Right Reverend Richard Mant, D.D.* (Dublin, 1857); Akenson, *Church of Ireland*, p. 161. 9 2 vols (1840). Cf. Mant, *Memoirs of Mant*, pp 390–2.

elected to the chair of political economy. Then, in 1831, the British prime minister uprooted him to make him archbishop of Dublin. Reluctantly, he accepted 'a call to the helm of a crazy ship in a storm'. In Ireland, Whately continued to write and publish, but mainly confessional polemic. Never entirely at ease among the clergy of the Church of Ireland, he aroused some of the same animosity that had earlier been directed against other English-born prelates, from John Bramhall to Thomas Lindsay and George Stone. As well as his educational campaigns, Whately repudiated the cosy arrangements of predecessors when he distributed the considerable patronage in his gift as archbishop. The greater vigilance may have been weakened by Whately's poor judgements of character. For many tastes, he was not fervent enough in battling against Catholicism (earlier he had supported Catholic emancipation), and was felt to be lukewarm in his backing of the proselytizing Irish Church Missions.[10]

The imported clergy can be contrasted with the locals. Hincks has already been mentioned. Less remote from topical issues was another home-grown product, Caesar Otway. Having served as a country parson, Otway moved to Dublin in 1836 as assistant chaplain of the Magdalen chapel in Leeson Street. He appreciated and exploited the potential of the popular press to convey evangelical messages, and was involved with George Petrie in the creation of the *Dublin Penny Journal*.[11] He cashed in on the growing taste for apparently authentic descriptions of provincial Ireland. He used the genre, which soon would be popularized by the Halls and Thackeray, to give a new twist to the familiar advocacy of material and spiritual improvements, and the crediting of both to English and Scottish settlement and to Protestantism. He decried landlords who, for electoral advantages, favoured Catholic tenants and alleged that their selfishness had transformed Ireland into 'one wide expanse of populous pauperism'.[12]

Another venerable tradition was represented by the Reverend Horatio Townsend. He wrote extensively about agricultural conditions in the south-west early in the nineteenth century. Less aggressively partisan than Otway, he subscribed to many of the familiar tenets of improvers, still connecting economic backwardness with catholicism. Some of Townsend's observations were addressed

---

10 Akenson, *Church of Ireland*, pp 166, 202–3, 208; D.H. Akenson, *A Protestant in purgatory: Richard Whately, archbishop of Dublin* (Hamden, Conn., 1981); R. Clarke, *Richard Whately: the unharmonious blacksmith* (Dublin, 2002); Crawford, *The Church of Ireland in Victorian Dublin*, pp 61, 93–4, 112–13; B. Hilton, *The age of atonement: the influence of evangelicalism on social and economic thought, 1785–1865* (Oxford, 1988), pp 46–55, 201–2; S. Rashid, 'Richard Whately and Christian political economy at Oxford and Dublin', *Journal of the History of Ideas*, 38 (1977), pp 147–55; S. Rashid, 'Richard Whately and the struggle for rational Christianity in the mid-nineteenth century', *Historical Magazine of the Protestant Episcopal Church*, 47 (1978), pp 293–311; J.M. Goldstrom, 'Richard Whately and political economy in schoolbooks, 1833–80', *IHS*, 15 (1966–7), pp 131–46.   11 J. Leerssen, *Remembrance and imagination: patterns in the historical and literary representation of Ireland in the nineteenth century* (Cork, 1996), pp 114–15, 117.   12 C. Otway, *Sketches in Ireland* (Dublin, 1827), pp 140, 147, 267–9.

to, and published by, the Dublin Society.[13] Between 1840 and 1860, Archdeacon Arthur Rowan of Ardfert compiled a history of Kerry, based on original documents in the Public Records in Dublin and elsewhere. He passed his interests and skills to a daughter.[14]

Traditional, too, was the scholarly focus of the Irish-born cleric who rose high in the hierarchy in the nineteenth century and whose erudition excited the greatest admiration. William Reeves, a Trinity graduate, was ordained in 1838, and soon beneficed in the north of Ireland. The enormous volume of Reeves's publications was matched by their quality. Early Christian Ireland was his forte.[15] He combined minute knowledge of the written sources and intimacy with the physical remains and topography. In 1847, he published an exhaustive investigation of *The ecclesiastical antiquities of Down, Connor and Dromore*. Three years later his edition of the Acts of Archbishop Colton provided a similar survey of the bishopric of Derry.[16] Of even wider significance was his edition of Adamnan's *Life of St Columba*, in which he deployed his vast knowledge of the early Irish Christian church.[17] Concurrently, he delved into the origins and significance of townlands. Preferred to the vicarage of Lusk in County Dublin in 1857, he was more conveniently placed to continue his researches. Even better was his appointment in 1861 to be librarian of Archbishop Robinson's library at Armagh. Until 1865, he combined the Armagh post with his County Dublin incumbency. Nepotism benefited Cotton; pluralism, Reeves. If Armagh offered a congenial setting for Reeves's work, the library gained materially from his attention and eventual donations. It was he who bought for Armagh a remnant of Lodge's papers from the latter's grandson, the rector of Killybegs. In addition, Reeves was active in preserving ancient monuments in his neighbourhood: most notably, while at Lusk, the round tower and (later) Emain Macha, the fort at Navan near Armagh.[18] In a precocious display of ecumenism, the Skye terrier of the parish priest at Lusk adopted Reeves. So devoted was 'Carlo', the dog, that the priest allowed him to migrate north with Reeves. Whately, too, inspired canine affection: his dog, 'Jet', padded behind his hearse. Reeves was passed over for the professorship of ecclesiastical history and the librarianship of Trinity College, Dublin (twice in the case of the first post). However, he served as dean of Armagh from 1875 to 1886, and as bishop of Down, Connor and Dro-

13 Brady, *Clerical records*, i, p. 292; H. Townsend, *An essay on the agriculture in the county of Cork* (Cork, 1803); idem, *A discourse addressed to the Farming Society of the County of Cork* (Cork, 1805); idem, *Observations on the Catholic claims* (Dublin, 1812); idem, *A statistical survey of the county of Cork* (Dublin, 1810); idem, *A view of the agricultural state of Ireland* (Cork, 1815).   14 A.M. Rowan to Cartwright, 19 Nov. 1898, TNA, HMC, 1/242; Mealys, Castlecomer, sale December 2004, lot 466. Archdeacon Rowan published *Lake lore: or an antiquarian guide to some of the ruins and recollections of Killarney* (Dublin, 1853).   15 J.R. Garstin in Ferguson, *Reeves*, pp 196–210.   16 Irish Archaeological Society (Dublin, 1850).   17 1857.   18 Ferguson, *Reeves*, p. 175; J. Thompson, 'William Reeves and the medieval texts and manuscripts at Armagh', *Peritia*, 10 (1996), pp 363–80; D.R.M. Weatherup, 'The Armagh Public Library, 1771–1971', *Irish Booklore*, 2 (1976), pp 268–99.

more from 1886 until his death in 1892.[19] He was seventy-one when consecrated as a bishop (no notion of a retiring age then), and his continuing commitment to scholarship was shown with his election as president of the Royal Irish Academy.

VII

Disestablishment turned the Church of Ireland into an institution manned almost exclusively by those born and raised in Ireland. Even before that, it was affected by the legal relief and greater visibility accorded to the Catholic church, culminating in emancipation in 1829. As Catholics emerged from the shadows, priests began to join formally in the collective endeavours. As has been shown, earlier Protestant scholars sought help from learned Catholic clerics. When Ledwich was active, the scholarly societies had been keen to recruit members of the Catholic hierarchy such as the successive archbishops of Dublin, Carpenter and Troy.[20] Cooperation between the confessions characterized the earliest societies established in the provinces during the mid-nineteenth century. In many districts, Catholics quickly eclipsed the Church of Ireland clergy: another reflection of the superiority in numbers enjoyed by the former. The Kilkenny Archaeological Society owed much to James Graves, a Church of Ireland clergyman of the diocese of Ossory from 1846 until 1886. Half the committee of a dozen for the society were in holy orders, including one Catholic.[21] On occasion, names were intended to give lustre to learned societies. Some titular vice-presidents or committee-men took little or no part in the business, as had been the case earlier with the Dublin Society and Physico-Historical Society. Nevertheless, at Kilkenny – as elsewhere – the clergy chaired meetings, read papers and published their contributions. Graves himself contributed notably through his history (in conjunction with Prim) of St Canice's Cathedral, for which Graves supplied the measured drawings. Reeves had assisted, too: by reading Graves's and Prim's proofs.[22]

When the *Ulster Journal of Archaeology* was first published between 1853 and 1862 as a northern riposte to the Kilkenny group, three Church of Ireland ministers – Reeves, Canon A. Hume and Revd George Hill – were active, alongside the Catholic James O'Laverty and several laymen. When the society was revived in the 1890s, only the Revd Charles Scott, rector of St Paul's Belfast, appeared in the company of a dozen 'conductors'.[23] In Cork, between 1835 and 1876, three clerics presided over the Cuvierian Society. Two belonged to the Church of Ireland; one

---

19 In general, Ferguson, *Life of Reeves*.   20 E. Ledwich to ?J.C. Walker, 11 June 1785, TCD, MS 1461/2, f. 38v; D. Murray, *Romanticism, nationalism and Irish antiquarian societies, 1840–1880* (Maynooth, 2000).   21 *Journal of the Kilkenny and South-East of Ireland Archaeological Society*, new series, i (1856–7), p. 6.   22 J. Graves and J.G.A. Prim, *The history, architecture and antiquities of the cathedral church of St Canice, Kilkenny* (Dublin, 1857), pp vi–vii.   23 *Ulster Journal of Archaeology*, 1st series, i (1853), p. 7; 2nd series, i (1894), pp [1–2]

was a Catholic. The group eschewed possible polemics by decreeing that 'no subject either political or religious shall be introduced'.[24] This resembled the spirit in which Reeves had argued that historical enquiries 'afford a natural ground on which Irishmen of all creeds and shades of opinion may meet on a common platform'.[25] The Cuvierian Society was succeeded by the Cork Historical and Archaeological Society. The moving spirit of the latter was Canon Richard Sheehan, a Catholic. Sheehan's appointment as bishop of Waterford and Lismore in 1892, shortly after the formation of the Cork group, threatened it with instant dissolution. That fate was averted when Sheehan agreed to remain as chairman until a successor could be found. The new bishop soon breathed life into a second project: the Waterford and south-east of Ireland Archaeological Society.[26] At early meetings in Cork, members congratulated themselves on the eirenical spirit in which potentially contentious topics were treated. Church of Ireland clergymen offered papers, including some on their clerical predecessors, such as Bishop Berkeley and Dean Edward Worth, and on ecclesiastical relics. One clerical contributor, William Whitelegge, was a veteran of the Cuvierian Society, over which he had presided between 1871 and 1872.[27] Canon Courtenay Moore, the rector of Mitchelstown, skilled in the several genres, even wrote on Robert Samuel Gregg, a member of the society and recently translated from the bishopric of Cork to the primatial see of Armagh.[28] However, showing the confessional balance sought by the society, Moore's tribute to Gregg was followed by fulsome obituaries of the Catholic bishop of Cloyne and the abbot of Mount Melleray, both, like Gregg, members of the Society. Canon Moore also wrote on inanimate objects such as the Galtee Mountains and Mitchelstown Caves.[29] Yet, just as the commanding presences in the Cuvierian Society had been laymen, such as Richard Caulfield, so in the early years of its successor it was Robert Day, an ardent collector and polymath, whose writings dominated the journal.

The establishment of a similar society and journal in County Kildare owed much to the support of the duke of Leinster and the wide-ranging interests of his kinsman, Lord Walter Fitzgerald. The initiatives were supported by the dean and archdeacon of Kildare, together with one of the canons of the cathedral and the catholic bishop. When officers were first chosen, Michael Comerford, co-adjutor bishop of Kildare, was vice-president (the president was the duke). Half the council of six were clergy: Archdeacon de Burgh, Canon W. Sherlock and the Jesuit historian, Denis Murphy.[30] In Louth, where the county archaeological society was

---

24 J.E. Rockley, 'The Cork Cuvierian Society reconsidered', *JCHAS*, 108 (2003), pp 119, 129. 25 Ferguson, *Reeves*, p. 59. 26 'The history of the society', *JCHAS*, i (1892), p. 3; 'Proceedings of the society', ibid., i (1892), p. 21; P. Holohan, 'The Cork Historical and Archaeological Society: foundation and consolidation, 1891–1943', ibid., 86 (1991), pp 19–21; 'Late Most Rev. Dr. Richard A. Sheehan', ibid., xxi (1915), pp 153–5. 27 Rockley, 'The Cork Cuvierian Society reconsidered', p. 129. 28 'His Grace the Most Rev. Robert Samuel Gregg, D.D.', *JCHAS*, iii (1894), pp 12–14. 29 *JCHAS*, iii (1894), pp 1–5. 30 *Journal of the County Kildare Archaeological Society*, i (1891–95), p. 1.

founded in 1904, only Catholic clergy were to be found among the original officers: one of the four vice-presidents and three of the ten-man council. This was still the situation in 1907.[31] Galway was similarly lacking in clerical antiquarians from the Church of Ireland. Its county historical society, established in 1900, had the Catholic bishop of Clonfert, John Healy, as vice-president and two Catholic parish priests on the committee of five.[32] The absence of the Church of Ireland from the activists of several societies reflected small numbers of Protestants in many districts and preoccupation with other matters. Further, it reminds that, notwithstanding the distinguished contributions of a few, the bulk of the clergy – like the laity – contented themselves with less taxing relaxations. Reeves, dismayed by the apparent intellectual torpor, wished 'to tell my brother parsons what is going on, and what treats they lose as long as they forget the history of poor Erin'.[33]

Scholars such as Reeves were never more than a small minority among the Irish bishops; the same was true of the proportions among the cathedral and parish clergy. Indeed, it is striking that scholars of the calibre of Lyon, Ledwich, Hincks, Graves, Lawlor, Seymour and Leslie found themselves beached either in parochial cures or in cathedral canonries. Those beneficed in Dublin, such as Lyon and Lawlor, enjoyed easier access to the libraries and archives. Clerics at a greater distance frequently repined at the obstacles in the way of their continuing with scholarship, and worked unsuccessfully for a remove to a more convenient cure. Scattered talents were drawn together when it was decided to construct a history of the Church of Ireland, timed to coincide with the Eucharistic Congress of the Roman Catholic Church at Dublin in 1932.[34] Underlying the three volumes edited by Alison Phillips were competitive and propagandist intentions. There were fears that the project, by being published by Oxford University Press rather than by an Irish house (Tempest at Dundalgan was the obvious alternative), would identify the Church of Ireland with England rather than the emergent Ireland.[35] Leading scholars within the church, ordained and lay, were sounded out. Several were too aged or indolent to complete their chapters, so that a disproportionate share fell to the active and conscientious, among whom St John D Seymour was notable.

Seymour, beneficed in County Tipperary, had already acquired an enviable reputation, moving rapidly from the conventional pietistic homage to his diocese – Emly and Cashel – through publishing its succession lists, inventories of the older church plate and (eventually) a full history. Later he catalogued the manuscripts in the Cashel diocesan library.[36] Earlier, he served as a vice-president of his local North Munster Archaeological Society. Soon he branched into investigations of Anglo-Norman writing in Ireland, an innovative survey of witchcraft in Ireland

31 *Journal of the County Louth Archaeological Society*, i/1 (1904), p. 72; i/4 (1907), p. 118.   32 *Journal of the Galway Archaeological and Historical Society*, i (1900).   33 Ferguson, *Reeves*, p. 67.   34 St J.D. Seymour to W.A. Phillips, 20 Oct. [?1930], 27 Feb. [1931], RCB, MS 60/323, 340.   35 J.B. Leslie to W.A. Phillips, 5 May 1930, RCBL, MS 60/171.   36 RCBL, D.9, 1.9/3.

and – his most durable contribution to Irish historical scholarship – a full analysis of the ecclesiastical systems between 1647 and 1661 when the episcopalian order in Ireland was superseded by experimentation on English and Scottish models. Seymour, despite his distance from Dublin, worked through the surviving official records of the Commonwealth and Cromwellian Protectorate in Ireland. The value of his thorough and judicious analysis was further enhanced when most of the documents which he had used were destroyed in the Four Courts in 1922. Seymour, like Ledwich, schemed for a remove closer to Dublin and its libraries. Election to the Royal Irish Academy in 1922 showed his high reputation, and gave him reasons to continue to visit the capital. It was in the Academy's *Proceedings* that several of his papers on medieval literature in Ireland were published. Planning the *History of the Church of Ireland* brought further opportunities to come to Dublin. In common with the other contributors, Seymour was paid for his chapters. The rate – £1 for each page – may have encouraged prolixity. Certainly it was a welcome supplement to his and others' stipends.[37] After the *History* was published in 1933, Seymour, although remaining archdeacon of Cashel until 1950, fell silent.[38]

More traditional interests were manifested by some of Seymour's contemporaries. He had started with clerical succession lists, but soon moved on. J.B. Leslie, although he wrote a history of the parish, Kilsaran, of which he became incumbent, otherwise contented himself with the compilation of the clerical biographies.[39] Equally limited were the activities of W.H. Rennison, whose focus remained the clergy and their parishes in the united dioceses of Lismore and Waterford, and of C.A. Webster, who confined himself to Cork and Ross.[40] The memorialization of their predecessors was a valuable act, but lacked the sense of the larger contexts with which Seymour enhanced his works. Country incumbents, like Seymour and Webster, pursued their researches with difficulty. Their concern with remote periods belonged to a venerable tradition and need not be interpreted as a retreat from the strife of their day. Occasionally those called from their scholarly studies to present-day realities, notably the patrician scholar, R.P.C. Hanson, consecrated bishop of Clogher in 1970, preferred to return to the academy in 1973 rather than remain longer in a troubled station.

Notwithstanding the erosion of standing, income and leisure for most ministers of the Church of Ireland by the middle and later decades of the twentieth century, scholarship did not entirely vanish. At one level, the clergy continued to con-

---

37 Same to same, 10 Sep. 1930, 'Wednesday', ibid., MS 60/322, 343.   38 T. Barnard, 'St J.D. Seymour, 1880–1950' in *Search: a Church of Ireland Journal*, 26/1 (2003), pp 30–3.   39 J.B. Leslie, *History of Kilsaran union of parishes in the county of Louth* (Dundalk, 1908).   40 St J.D. Seymour to W.H. Rennison, undated [before 1920], RCBL, MS 40/11/27; P.G. Lee, 'The Reverend William Henry Rennison, B.A.', *JCHAS*, xxxiii (1928), pp 51–2; W.H. Rennison, *Succession list of the bishops, cathedral and parochial clergy of the dioceses of Waterford and Lismore* (Waterford, [1920]); C.A. Webster, *The diocese of Ross: its bishops, clergy and parishes* (Cork, 1936). Some of Rennison's papers are in RCBL, MS 40.

tribute to their local historical societies. Robert Wyse Jackson, bishop successively of Limerick and Meath, with his writings on silver and glass, serves as an example of the persistence of such tastes. The North Munster Antiquarian Society was one beneficiary; another was the literary and current-affairs journal, *The Bell*. F.R. Bolton, originally from England, investigated the Caroline tradition of high churchmanship in its Irish manifestations. He moved to Ireland three years before his study was published, and was appointed dean of Leighlin.[41] Interests that overlapped with Bolton's were evident in an Irish-born clerical scholar prominent during this period, H.R.McAdoo, archbishop of Dublin between 1977 and 1985. He, too, wrote about the theology and ecclesiology of the Caroline church, in England as well as in Ireland. His investigations reverted to Jeremy Taylor, bishop of Down and Connor after Charles II's return.[42] McAdoo's immersion in the theology of the eucharist enabled him not just to write a history of it, but to put it to use through his long service on the Anglican-Roman Catholic International Commission between 1967 and 1981.[43]

Trinity College Dublin, at least until 1970, served not only as a seminary for would-be clergy but retained a Church of Ireland ethos. As such it offered sanctuary to a few Irish Protestant scholars in holy orders. One veteran was the Revd A.A. Luce, first professor of moral and mental science (1934–49) and subsequently vice-provost (1946–52). Luce's labours as editor and biographer of the eighteenth-century bishop of Cloyne, George Berkeley, increased knowledge and understanding of perhaps the most formidable intellect ever to grace the Church of Ireland episcopate. George Otto Simms (archbishop of Armagh from 1969 to 1980) served as chaplain (dean of residence) of the college between 1939 and 1952. Even after his elevation to the episcopate, he regularly lectured and wrote on the Book of Kells and other early illuminated manuscripts from Christian Ireland.[44] Like McAdoo, Simms preserved a tradition in which the leaders of the Church of Ireland possessed a strong sense of its long and sometimes tortuous history: a sense helped by their facility in the Irish language. The tradition, fortunately, survives both on the bench of bishops and in the parochial ministry.

41 F.R. Bolton, *The Caroline tradition of the Church of Ireland* (London, 1958), p. xvi. 42 H.R. McAdoo, *The structure of Caroline moral theology* (London, 1949); idem, *The spirit of Anglicanism* (London, 1962); idem, *The Eucharistic theology of Jeremy Taylor today* (?London, 1989); idem, *Jeremy Taylor Anglican theologian* (Keady, 1997). 43 H.R. McAdoo [and K. Stevenson], *The mystery of the eucharist in the Anglican tradition* (1995); K. Milne, 'Henry McAdoo', *Oxford DNB*; K. Stevenson, 'The Most Rev Henry McAdoo', *The Independent*, 12 Dec. 1998. 44 K. Milne, 'The Most Rev George Simms', *The Independent*, 21 Nov. 1991.

14

Irish clergy abroad

W.J. Marshall

May the Church of St Patrick, of St Columba, and St Gall and St Canice, of George Berkeley, of Robert and Louisa Stewart, of George Pilkington, of George Alfred Lefroy, of John George Frederick Hearn, of Frances Hassard and Marie Hayes, and hundreds of other men and women, less well known perhaps, but of equal faith and devotion – may our ancient Church of Ireland ever be true to her glorious ancestry, and may she ever realize that her supreme purpose, for which she was founded by her Saviour Christ, is to preach His Gospel to all mankind.[1]

Godfrey Day was primate of the Church of Ireland for only six months in 1938 and the words quoted above occur in the sole presidential address that he was able to give to the general synod. Day was himself a member of the Cambridge Mission to Delhi and it is significant that he links the Church of Ireland missionary outreach in modern times with the inspiration of its Celtic past. Noteworthy also is his inclusion of men and women, laity and clergy, in his list. Though our subject is Irish clergy overseas, we need to bear in mind the laymen and women who were their fellow-workers in the world church.

The early Irish Church was noted for its exports of clergy, ascetics, wandering scholars and emigrants of various kinds. They were very numerous. James Kenney writes, 'the Irish emigrants of the early middle ages were those religious men and women, pilgrims, hermits, missionaries, whose names are found associated with every country, almost every country-side, of western Europe'.[2] Some of them may have gone even further. St Brendan the Navigator and St Cormac the Voyager were such famous travellers that their exploits were highly embroidered by legend. Yet behind the legends there is probably some historical truth, and St Brendan in

---

1 *Church of Ireland Journal of the General Synod 1938*, pp lxxiv–v. 2 James F. Kenney, *The sources for the early history of Ireland, I: ecclesiastical* (New York, 1929), p. 487.

particular may well have reached the North-American continent in the sixth century. But it is the devotion of the Irish monks to learning, particularly their study of the scriptures, that is perhaps their most outstanding long-term contribution.

Why did these early Irish monks and clerics travel so much? The ascetic spirit in Celtic monasticism was undoubtedly a factor. To leave one's native land and suffer exile was the supreme renunciation. Whatever the main reason for their going 'on pilgrimage for Christ', it is an undoubted fact that they were energetic missionaries, teachers and preachers.

One of the greatest and most famous of the early Irish missionaries is St Columbanus, who preached and founded monasteries in France (Gaul), Switzerland and northern Italy.[3] His career shows that the Irish abroad were not always welcome. Columbanus followed Irish customs on such matters as the date of Easter and monastic rules. He and his companions were often in conflict with the local bishops and were not slow to rebuke kings. Later, Celtic customs were abandoned in favour of Roman usage but tension and opposition remained. Gough Meissner writes, 'these wandering Irish clergy were a continual source of trouble to the ecclesiastical authorities, and legislation was continually passed against them'.[4] It would be quite wrong to idealise the missionaries from the early Irish church, though in their quarrels they were sometimes in the right, and they were an inspiration for later generations of Irish clergy abroad, among whom we shall discover some of the same characteristics.

THE SEVENTEENTH AND EIGHTEENTH CENTURIES

To some extent, Ireland came under English rule in the twelfth century and was more thoroughly conquered under the Tudors in the sixteenth century when the Church of Ireland became Protestant (though it only won over a small minority of the population). It was staffed by many English and some Scottish clergy as well as by Irish graduates from the newly founded Trinity College near Dublin. From the seventeenth century, some Irish clergy of the reformed church went abroad as chaplains in the expanding British empire, chiefly at first in north America and India.

Thirteen British colonies were founded on the east coast of the north American continent. Among the Anglican ministers who worked there we have definite evidence from the seventeenth century of an Irish connection in Francis Le Jau, a Huguenot, born in France, who graduated from Trinity College, Dublin, and who was at work in the Leeward Islands in 1693. He later became a missionary of the Society for the Propagation of the Gospel (SPG) in South Carolina in 1706.[5]

---

3 For a convenient account of his life and writings see Tomás Ó Fiáich, *Columbanus in his own words* (Dublin, 1974).   4 Phillips, *Church of Ireland*, i, p. 346.   5 Daniel O'Connor and others, *Three centuries of mission: the United Society for the Propagation of the Gospel 1701–2000* (London, 2000), p. 28.

The foundation of SPG in 1701 gave an impetus to the church's work overseas and to some extent modified its dependence on the state. An Irish branch of the society was founded in 1714. Even before that, some Irish clergy had enrolled in the society as missionaries, including one, William Cordiner, who was appointed to Maryland in 1707. However, he did not reach America, because the ship on which he was travelling, the *Chester* man-of-war, was captured by the French. He was imprisoned in France, where he ministered to his fellow prisoners.[6]

Cordiner's experience is a vivid reminder of the hazards of travel in the eighteenth century. Apart from the perils arising from the wars with France, the voyage across the Atlantic in a cramped sailing ship was long, uncomfortable and often dangerous. Until the consecration of Samuel Seabury in Scotland in 1784, there was no Anglican bishop in America. Accordingly, anyone on that side of the Atlantic seeking Anglican orders had to make the double journey to Britain. Daniel O'Connor states, 'one-fifth of those who attempted the double crossing from America for ordination during the eighteenth century were lost at sea'.[7]

One who successfully made the double voyage was Laurence Coughlan. He had been an Irish immigrant in Newfoundland, where his people in Harbour Grace and Carboneer asked the SPG in 1767 to appoint him as their minister. He crossed the Atlantic to be ordained. He noted that one-fifth of his parish were Irish and that many of them, 'all Papists', came to church when he preached in Irish. He hoped that in time some might come to see 'the errors of Popery'.[8]

The most famous Irish cleric who went to America in the eighteenth century was George Berkeley. Berkeley's eminence as a philosopher tends to overshadow his other great achievements, but his American enterprise is important in a number of ways, though his main aim of establishing a college in Bermuda was unsuccessful. When he was dean of Derry he sailed for America with his newly married wife in September 1728, and after a long, stormy voyage, which included a stop in Virginia, he reached Rhode Island on 23 January 1729.[9] His project was carefully thought-out and prepared. In a letter of 1723 he set out his aims and plans:

> He will spend the rest of his days in the island of Bermuda. He will build a college there for the education of the sons of English planters and of the native Indians in religion and useful learning. They will come from the mainland of America, and will stay in the island till they are of M.A. standing; they will return to their own people fitted to be missionaries.[10]

6 H. Vere White, *Children of St Columba* (Dublin, 1914), p. 61.   7 O'Connor, *Three centuries of mission*, p. 29.   8 White, *Children of St Columba*, p. 62.   9 A full account of Berkeley's Bermuda project and stay in America is given in A.A. Luce, *The life of George Berkeley* (London, 1949), chapters vii, viii and ix.   10 Ibid., p. 97.

To finance the project he had collected £3,400 in private subscriptions by 1725. Parliament voted £20,000 for the work, but, as is the way of politicians, specified no time when the sum was to be paid. Berkeley and his family waited in Rhode Island as letters passed slowly between him and London but no money came.

> Gibson, the Bishop of London, approached Sir Robert Walpole about it, and received the explicit reply, "If you put this question to me as a Minister, I must and can assure you that the money shall most undoubtedly be paid as soon as suits with public convenience; but if you ask me as a friend whether Dean Berkeley should continue in America, expecting the payment of £20,000, I advise him by all means to return home to Europe and to give up his present expectations".[11]

Berkeley regretfully took this advice and returned to Ireland without having set foot in Bermuda. His great project did not succeed – neither the first nor the last failure in the history of missions. It is generally agreed that it was impracticable, since Bermuda is 600 miles from the mainland. Yet Berkeley's emphasis on the importance of education as a constituent of missionary work is in the tradition of the Celtic monastic schools and has been followed by missions generally up to the present time. He gave to Yale University most of the books he had brought to America, and also the proceeds from the sale of the house and farm he had bought there. His name was given to the Berkeley Divinity School, Newhaven, and to Berkeley University in California.

During the two years and eight months he spent in America, Berkeley preached regularly in Trinity Church, Newport, Rhode Island, and visited the surrounding countryside where he met and learnt about the state of the American Indians. The material he gathered formed the basis of the SPG anniversary sermon which he delivered on his return. In this he described the sorry state of the Indians, and castigated the English planters for their behaviour towards them.[12]

One of the clergy Berkeley met in America was a fellow Irishman, James McSparran, who was born in Dungiven, County Londonderry, graduated from Glasgow University, became a Congregationalist minister in Boston, Massachusetts, and returned to Britain to be ordained an Anglican priest. He went back to America 'to take charge of the Narragansett mission in 1721, and he was minister of St. Paul's Church there for nearly thirty-seven years, dying in 1757.'[13] He was known as 'the apostle of Narragansett', an area of Rhode Island state now called Washington district.

An Irishman noted for the development of the Anglican Communion was Charles Inglis (1733/4–1816), the first Anglican bishop in the British colonies.

---

11 Ibid., p.142.   12 Raymond W. Houghton, David Berman, Maureen T. Lapan, *Images of Berkeley* (Dublin, 1986), p. 67. A fuller summary is given in White, *Children of St Columba*, pp 25–6.   13 Luce, *Life of Berkeley*, p. 122.

(Samuel Seabury was consecrated before Inglis for the church in the newly independent United States of America.) Son of the rector of Glencolumcille, Inglis went to America as a layman to teach in Pennsylvania. He had to go to England to be ordained by the bishop of London and on his return he served for a time in Pennsylvania and then became curate of St Paul's Church, New York. He became rector in the middle of the American War of Independence, having as curate refused to omit the prayers for the king and the royal family when Washington captured New York. After the war he moved to Nova Scotia along with large numbers of loyalists, including many Mohawk Indians who remained loyal British subjects. Inglis was consecrated the first bishop of Nova Scotia by the archbishop of Canterbury in Lambeth Palace chapel on 12 August 1787. He arrived in Halifax on 15 October and ordained his nephew, Archibald, four days later, 'the first Anglican ordination on Canadian soil'.[14] His letters patent gave him jurisdiction over all British North America and he was an indefatigable traveller (presumably by boat, foot and horse), visiting most of it, except that he did not manage to reach Newfoundland. He was energetic in having churches built and founding schools, including one in Windsor with his nephew Archibald as head. He laid the foundation stone of a university in Windsor in 1790 on promise of a royal charter, which eventually arrived in 1802.

Daniel O'Connor in his history of the SPG, referring to the eighteenth century, states, 'the majority of missionaries were from among the excessive numbers of poorer clergy with little or no expectation of ever escaping from the poverty at the bottom of the Church's essentially class-determined structure'.[15] This is as likely to be true of Ireland as it was of England. In both countries there were probably more clergy seeking ordination than there were places for them. However, that does not necessarily impugn the sincerity or heroism of those who crossed the Atlantic in the SPG's first hundred years.

The other main area where priests from the Church of Ireland worked in the seventeenth and eighteenth centuries was India. The East India Company was founded in 1600 and provided chaplains for its 'factors' (merchants and officials). M.E. Gibbs in her history of the Anglican Church in India states that the chaplains of the eighteenth century 'were probably a fair cross-section of the English churchmen of their day'.[16] There were some who, like many Company officials, engaged in private trading (a temptation also to chaplains and missionaries in North America). One such was John Evans who 'was dismissed in 1690, "having betaken himself so entirely to merchandizing".'[17] This did not stop him from being appointed bishop of Bangor in 1706 and translated to Meath in 1716!

A more welcome Irish connection is found in the case of Richard Hall Kerr, one of the evangelical chaplains of the East India Company appointed at a time when

---

14 Philip Carrington, *The Anglican Church in Canada* (Toronto, 1963), p. 46.   15 O'Connor, *Three centuries of mission*, pp 28–9.   16 M.E. Gibbs, *The Anglican Church in India* (Delhi, 1972), p. 9.   17 Ibid., p. 9.

some of the directors were prominent evangelical laymen. After graduation from Trinity College, Dublin, he was ordained deacon by the bishop of Sodor and Man in 1789 and went to Bombay in 1790 to superintend a school.[18] Two years later he taught in Madras and was appointed military chaplain there, with some misgivings as he was only in deacon's orders. After some years, due to the objections of another chaplain, he applied for leave, made the long voyage home by sailing ship round South Africa, was ordained priest and returned to India in 1803. A fellow-chaplain described him as 'a strenuous preacher of repentance, going forth in the spirit of John the Baptist to prepare the way for greater things than he was permitted himself to see accomplished'.[19] He died, aged forty-one, in 1808, worn out by his labours.

THE NINETEENTH CENTURY

In the nineteenth century there was a great flowering of church and mission work overseas, in which most European churches took part. The nineteenth century was also the imperial age. The expansion of the British Empire, particularly in Africa, meant that many Irishmen (of most denominations) served abroad as colonial administrators, soldiers, chaplains and missionaries. They also served in countries outside the empire such as China and Japan. Limitations of space require a very selective treatment of the Church of Ireland clerical contribution. It will be considered under countries or areas.

Canada

Irish Anglicans, lay and clerical, continued to settle in the United States after independence as the American frontier expanded westwards. For example, Bishop McIlvane of Ohio attracted many to his diocese.[20] Yet Anglicans from Ireland tended to concentrate on Canada rather than the United States. F.D. Creighton states, 'by the 1840s there was an Irish-born population of 134,000 in Ontario alone, the majority of whom were Protestant, and of these the majority were likely to have been Church of Ireland'.[21] No doubt many Irish-born clergy served as their pastors. From Charles Inglis onwards, large numbers of Church of Ireland clergy have gone to Canada, a process which has continued to the present day. Missionary societies had a major role at the beginning and during the period of westward expansion, but the church

18 Ibid., pp 41–3. See also S.J. McNally, *The chaplains of the East India Company*, entry under 'KERR, Richard Hall'. I am indebted to Mr Tim Thomas of the British Library, Oriental and India Office Collections, Reference Enquiries, for access to this resource. 19 Gibbs, *Anglican Church in India*, p. 42. 20 Alan Acheson, *A history of the Church of Ireland, 1691–1996* (Dublin, 1997), p. 184. 21 F.D. Creighton, 'Against the tide: an examination of Church of Ireland migration in the eighteenth and nineteenth centuries', unpublished MSSc dissertation, p. 43. I am grateful to Dr Patrick Fitzgerald of the Centre for Migration Studies, Ulster American Folk Park, for drawing my attention to this and other relevant material.

became self-supporting and in time sent missionaries to other countries. The Church Missionary Society (CMS) was founded in 1799 as one of the manifestations of the eighteenth-century evangelical revival. An Irish auxiliary, the Hibernian Church Missionary Society, now CMSIreland, came into being in 1814. CMS sent many missionaries to Canada in the nineteenth century both to care for, or re-evangelise, the settlers, and preach the gospel to the original inhabitants of Canada.

SPG also continued to receive support in money and personnel from Ireland. One of the SPG missionaries, Travers Lewis, is important in the development of the Anglican Communion as he was the main mover among the Canadian bishops in persuading the archbishop of Canterbury to call the first Lambeth Conference in 1867. Lewis was ordained for the curacy of Newtownbutler, County Fermanagh. In Canada he was a travelling missionary at Hawkesbury on the Ottawa River, later became rector of Brockville, Ontario,[22] and was consecrated first bishop of the newly-formed diocese of Ontario in 1861 at the early age of thirty-six. Lewis died in 1901 after forty years' service as bishop. He saw Canada develop as a self-governing church in the Anglican Communion and presided over the church's first general synod in 1893.

An older contemporary of Lewis, who also hailed from Ireland, was Benjamin Cronyn. He came to Canada in 1832 and worked in London, Ontario. He was often in conflict his bishop, John Strahan of Toronto, for example, over the foundation of Trinity College in Toronto. When the diocese of Toronto was divided, Cronyn became bishop of the new diocese of Huron. He was very successful in recruiting young men in Ireland for his diocese. The Bible class in Dublin run by the renowned evangelical preacher, Charles Fleury, provided a good supply.

One of the most colourful priests from Ireland who served the church in Canada was Henry Irwin, popularly known as 'Father Pat'.[23] He fulfilled the Irish stereotype (which many from Ireland do not) – a keen horseman, good company, a bit wild, extravagant in his behaviour and generosity. His father was incumbent of Newtownmountkennedy in County Wicklow and two of his brothers also served the church overseas, in the West Indies and the United States, and in South Africa, respectively. After graduating from Oxford and theological training and curacy in England, Irwin went to Canada in 1885 where he served in the diocese of New Westminster, British Columbia. He entered with zest into the life of the miners, prospectors and railway workers on the Canadian Pacific Railway, sharing their dangers and hardships, travelling great distances on horseback among widely scattered camps. 'Father Pat', as he was known from curacy days, describes himself on his camping journeys as 'a dirty, travelled-looking individual, a poor imitation of a parson, sitting on one side of a log fire; a tin plate with his bacon and beans on it, and his tinney of tea; bread just cooked on the fire in a dirty pan'.[24]

22 Carrington, *Anglican Church in Canada*, p. 129.   23 See Mrs Jerome Mercier, *Father Pat, a hero of the Far West* (Gloucester, 1909). I am grateful to Canon Robert Jennings, former rector of Newtownkennedy, for lending this and other relevant works.   24 Quoted from his letters,

In 1890 Irwin married the daughter of a naval superintendent and ministered for a time in Vancouver. Tragedy struck with the arrival of a stillborn baby and the death of the mother three days later. Irwin never fully recovered from the blow. He again threw himself into pioneering work in a mission district among the mining camps, with a reckless ascetic zeal like that of the early Celtic monks. His bishop eventually persuaded him to set out for Ireland to rest and build up his strength. He took the train across Canada but for some unaccountable reason he left it some miles from Montreal, in the depths of the Canadian winter. A farmer found him struggling along a frozen trail and brought him by sleigh to Notre Dame Hospital in Montreal. The nuns gave him every possible care, but he died on 13 January 1902, aged forty-three, and his body was brought back to Vancouver where he was buried beside his wife and child.

India

Both CMS and SPG were active in India in the nineteenth century. J.H. Hodgins gives the names of all Irish missionaries working under CMS between 1814 and 1994 and the largest number of ordained missionaries in any one country was in India, followed closely by China. Its first missionary there from Ireland was a Corkman, Robert Vincent Reynolds, who was accepted in India by CMS in 1829. He went to Burdwan and Gorakhpur as a layman and was ordained by the bishop of Calcutta. CMS missionaries from the Church of Ireland were well spread over the Indian subcontinent, from Madras and Bangalore in the south to the Punjab in the north. Many were teachers as well as priests, like J.H. Gray, principal of the CMS theological college in Madras. He had some students from the Syrian Orthodox Church, which was in India at least from the fourth century and whose members believe it to have been founded by St Thomas the apostle. Other clerical missionaries were medical doctors, like Robert Elliott from Donoughmore, County Tyrone, who ministered among the Santals in Taljhari, and, after a period back in Ireland as rector of Altedesert in Armagh diocese, went to work in a hospital in Gaza in Palestine.

Perhaps the most remarkable of the Irish CMS missionary priests in India was James Long, who worked there from 1840 to 1872.[25] Though he received some training at the CMS college at Islington, he was largely self-taught. He was called, with some exaggeration, 'an Irish Mezzofanti', after the eighteenth-century Italian cardinal who was reputed to be fluent in fifty-one languages. Long, however, was undoubtedly a good linguist. He had a strong social conscience and when he was in Tharkapur, south of Calcutta, he championed the Bengali workers against the injustices of European planters. He was commissioned to translate a Bengali play which showed the planters in a bad light. As a result he was accused of libel, fined 1000 rupees and sentenced to a month's imprisonment. A wealthy Bengali paid the fine, and Long's time in jail earned him great influence with Indians.

Mercier, *Father Pat*, p. 55.   25 J. Hodgins, *Sister Island: a history of the CMS in Ireland, 1814–1994* (Dunmurry, 1994), pp 96–7.

SPG had some work in India in the eighteenth century but it greatly expanded in the nineteenth with a large number of missionaries throughout the sub-continent, including many Irish. The Dublin University Mission to Chota Nagpur was founded under the auspices of SPG in 1891, one of the three university missions to India founded in the nineteenth century, the others being the Cambridge Mission to Delhi (1877) and the Oxford Mission to Calcutta (1880). The Lefroy mentioned by Godfrey Day was a foundation member of the Cambridge Brotherhood and came from County Down. These university missions were an expression of the great missionary enthusiasm which inspired many young people in the late nineteenth century, reminiscent of the 'pilgrimage for Christ' zeal of the Celtic monks. Those who had the privilege of a university education felt a passion to share with others 'the heritage they so richly enjoyed', the tradition of 'true religion and sound learning', and what were then considered the superior benefits of European civilisation. They were probably also imbued with a youthful spirit of adventure, and may have realised that they would likely find more responsible posts on the mission field than in their home countries.

A meeting of three Trinity College graduates in the curate's lodging in Dromore, County Down, in July 1890 was the beginning of the Dublin University Mission to Chota Nagpur.[26] The trio decided to offer themselves to SPG as a brotherhood to work anywhere in the world. They would receive no salary but only a living allowance and they would remain unmarried while members of the brotherhood. About the same time SPG received an appeal for missionaries from the first bishop of the newly-formed diocese of Chota Nagpur. The offer was the answer to the appeal. A brotherhood of five men, and a nurse, Frances Hassard (also mentioned by Godfrey Day), sailed for India in December 1891, arriving in Calcutta by January 1892. The bishop assigned them the district of Hazaribagh in the north of the diocese. As soon as they were sufficiently fluent in Hindi, they preached in the bazaar in Hazaribagh and in the surrounding areas. Even before that, Kenneth Kennedy, medical doctor as well priest, and Frances Hassard began treating the sick who came to them. By the end of the century the Mission had founded St Columba's Hospital, St Columba's High School for boys and St Columba's College, as well as several primary schools and some dispensaries in the district. Another priest-doctor was J.G.F. Hearn who became head of the mission in 1900 but was invalided home in 1911 suffering from tuberculosis from which he died. Hearnganj, the Christian village on the outskirts of Hazaribagh, commemorates his name.

Throughout the nineteenth century, chaplains ministered to the British residents in India – officials of the East India Company and, after the Mutiny, of the British *raj*. The British and Indian armies (the latter with mainly European officers) had their chaplains. The Irish were prominent among the British rulers of

26 K.W.S. Kennedy, *Fifty years in Chota Nagpur* (Dublin, 1939), p. 9.

India at all levels from junior members of the army and Indian Civil Service to the post of viceroy.[27] Many clergy from the Church of Ireland served as establishment chaplains right up to Indian independence in 1947. In the nineteenth and even early-twentieth centuries most of them and most missionaries would have accepted without question the rightness of British rule in India. Without any sense of irony they regarded it as bearing the white man's burden in the country which was the brightest jewel in the imperial crown.[28]

China

While it was natural for Anglican missionary societies to concentrate on the vast and growing British empire, they by no means neglected other regions, especially the world's most populous nation, China. CMS was first there, followed by SPG. The Irish CMS missionary, Robert Stewart, inspired the foundation of the Dublin University Fukien Mission in 1885, part of the same wave of missionary enthusiasm we noted in the beginnings of its younger sister, the Chota Nagpur Mission. The first to join was J. Stratford Collins, curate of Parsonstown (Birr). A photograph in the mission's history shows him in Chinese dress along with two colleagues in dark suits and clerical collars.[29] His identification with local culture, unusual among Victorian missionaries, stood him in good stead when he went to Kienning in Fukien province. It was a violently anti-western place and on one occasion Collins walked through a riot 'unmolested through wearing, as his custom was, Chinese garb'.[30]

Anti-western feeling, caused largely by the opium wars, rather than specifically anti-Christian feeling, was widespread until the Boxer Rising in 1900. Robert Stewart, the man who inspired the foundation of the Fukien Mission and became its head, was martyred by a fanatical anti-foreign group, along with his wife, one of their five children, an Irish nurse and six lady missionaries, in 1895. 'Four of the five orphaned children ... became missionaries.'[31]

The Fukien Mission, like that in Chota Nagpur, gave great importance to education. Stewart founded primary schools and a college in Fuchow, one of the great examination centres of the Chinese empire. Out of it developed Trinity College Fuchow, as it was named in 1912 under another Irish priest and educationalist, William Pakenham-Walsh (whose younger brother, Herbert, joined the Chota Nagpur Mission).

---

27 See Keith Jeffrey (ed.), 'An Irish empire?' Aspects of Ireland and the British Empire (Manchester, 1996), chapter 3; and Narinder Kapur, The Irish Raj: illustrated stories about Irish in India and Indians in Ireland (Antrim, 1997).   28 Kennedy, in spite of his great love of India and Indians, was remarkably unsympathetic to Indian nationalism and uncritical of British rule. See his Fifty years in Chota Nagpur, pp 62–3.   29 R.M Gwynn, E.M. Norton and B.W. Simpson, 'T.C.D.' in China: a history of the Dublin University Fukien Mission, 1885–1935 (Dublin, 1936), photo opposite p.11.   30 Ibid., p. 22.   31 Hodgins, Sister Island, p.142.

West Africa

During the nineteenth century Europeans penetrated to most parts of the African continent. CMS sent missionaries to Africa soon after its foundation, though its greatest numbers went there towards the end of the century. H.J. Allcock from Cork was sent to Fournah Bay College (founded by the CMS in 1827) in Sierra Leone as vice-principal and soon became its principal. He described the course of studies undertaken by the African students as, the Bible in its original languages, 'together with standard theological works as are usually read by our Divinity students at home, including Butler's *Analogy* and Whately's *Logic*'.[32] Allcock had to return home after four years due to his wife's ill health. Another Irishman in Sierra Leone, Richard Kinahan from Belfast, caught blackwater fever and died after eighteen months.[33] West Africa for much of the nineteenth century was accurately described as the white man's grave. It was even more the white woman's grave, as many wives of settlers and missionaries succumbed to the fierce climate without modern medicine.

Sierra Leone had been founded as a country for freed African slaves, and one of Allcock's first students was Samuel Adjai Crowther (c.1809–91), the former slave who became the first African to be consecrated an Anglican bishop. It is interesting to note that Crowther ordained Thomas Phillips, a lay businessman from Dublin, as priest, the first European to be ordained by an African bishop in modern times. The CMS had established a mission in eastern Nigeria led by Bishop Crowther, and Phillips was sent by the society as a 'personal friend and counsellor to the bishop'. However, Philips resigned after nine months; 'his view of the situation did not tally with the Committee's'.[34] Reading between the lines, it would seem that the mission headquarters in London wanted greater control over Bishop Crowther and the work in Nigeria than Phillips thought was right.

East Africa

It was later in the century that Anglican Christianity penetrated to east Africa, chiefly through CMS missionaries. Mission work spread inland from Mombasa. In 1876 CMS missionaries began work in Uganda and Irish people, men and women, lay and ordained, were among them almost from the start. Under the Kabaka, Mwanga, Christians were persecuted and many became martyrs. An Irish layman, George Pilkington from County Westmeath, Bible translator and evangelist, met his death when he accompanied Baganda soldiers under British command as an interpreter and was shot in a skirmish on the Sudanese border.

Among the early ordained missionaries in east Africa was Henry Cole from Thurles. He went to Tanganyika (now Tanzania) as an agriculturist in 1879. After his first tour he was trained at the CMS Islington College and ordained. He then worked in Tanganyika for about twenty-seven years.[35] Another ordained missionary was Philip O'Flaherty who went to Uganda after an eventful career. Born in a

32 Ibid., p. 15.   33 Ibid., p. 16.   34 Ibid., p. 20.   35 Ibid., p. 51.

Roman Catholic family in County Mayo, he went to an Irish-medium school, became a Presbyterian, was a soldier in the Crimean war, served as a lay missionary of the Free Church of Scotland in Turkey, was ordained and served curacies in the Church of England and was then accepted by CMS for Uganda.[36]

South Africa

The first Anglican priests in South Africa were chaplains to the colonists. Of those who were missionaries as distinct from chaplains, one of the first was an Irishman, William Wright, who founded a school for coloured people just outside Capetown in 1821. Wright, along with members of the London Missionary Society (LMS), opposed the policies of the governor, Somerset, and eventually had to leave the colony.[37]

It was in South Africa that the struggles of the Anglican churches in the British colonies to free themselves from state control were perhaps most acute. Robert Gray became the first bishop of Capetown in 1848, and, with the help of others, made the church in South Africa into a self-governing province of the Anglican Communion, but not without much conflict and litigation in subsequent years. A prolonged dispute arose in the diocese of Grahamstown. The dean, Frederick Williams, an Irishman, did not like his new bishop, Nathaniel Merriman, and refused to recognise his jurisdiction over the cathedral. He claimed that his cathedral was founded by the Church of England and not under the authority of the Church of the Province of South Africa (CPSA). The diocesan court suspended the dean, who ignored the sentence, and the case went to the privy council in England. The whole unedifying and tedious dispute only ended with the deaths of the bishop in 1882 and the dean in 1885.[38]

Another Irish priest who had a dispute with his bishop was John Darragh. The cause was quite different – provision for a mission church for the new shanty towns around Johannesburg. Darragh was 'vigorous, intelligent and able', but ran the mission into debt. The bishop of Pretoria, Henry Bousfield, did not share his vision for the church in the new, urban South Africa.[39]

These disputes are reminiscent of the quarrels which the Irish monks like Columbanus had with their bishops in Europe during the early centuries. But while larger-than-life characters like Williams and Darragh make the most interesting stories, they are not typical of the often humdrum work of Irish and other missionaries. In South Africa as well as other places they often plodded on with a patient, conscientious, unspectacular ministry.

36 Ibid., p. 57.   37 Peter Hinchliff, *The Anglican Church in South Africa* (London, 1963), pp 19–21.   38 Ibid., pp 122–8. Williams was succeeded by another, very different, Irishman, Davis Croghan, who fully supported the constitution of the CPSA. See also, Patrick Comerford, 'Bishop Ricards and Dean Croghan: the contrasting tale of two Wexford missionaries in South Africa', *Journal of the Wexford Historical Society*, 18 (2000–2001), pp 21–44.   39 Hinchcliff, *Anglican Church in South Africa*, pp 158–62.

Australia

Captain Cook sailed into Botany Bay in 1770, hoisted the British flag and claimed the continent for Great Britain. The first use England made of her new possession was to send convicts there. One of the convicts in the first group to arrive was a Church of Ireland minister, Henry Fulton, accompanied by his wife and child as free settlers. He was a political prisoner, suspected of support for the 1798 uprising. He received a conditional pardon on arrival (later made absolute) and ministered in different places in the colony.[40]

Fulton may have been more acceptable to the convicts, as himself formerly one of them, than the other chaplains. Free settlers and government officials formed part of the Australian community from the start and in time other settlements were formed outside New South Wales. Anglican clergy and laity exercised a ministry in the new colonies as best as they could. William Grant Broughton was appointed first bishop of Australia in 1836 with his headquarters in Sydney, and other dioceses were later formed. The second bishop of Sydney, Frederic Barker, was an ardent evangelical and had worked for a time with the Church Home Mission in Ireland. Like Bishop Cronyn in Canada, Barker recruited several Irish clergy to his diocese.[41] CMS and SPG contributed men and money for church work in Australia. SPG had provided Bishop Barker with 'a grant of £300 per year to provide for a travelling and organizing priest beyond the borders of the diocese'. The bishop appointed one of his Irish recruits, Edward Synge, to the post. 'Setting out on foot in 1855, he made a tour of 3,500 miles. His plan was to remain a week or more in each district and hold services wherever he could. He would then call a meeting of the principal settlers, form a committee and raise subscriptions for the support of a priest in the future. He continued this work for ten years, until the whole area which now forms the diocese of Goulburn was organized.'[42]

Care for the settlers was a big task for the church, but the early chaplains and the missionaries also made some attempt to evangelise the aboriginal inhabitants of the continent, however ill-equipped they were to relate to their culture. An SPG missionary from Ireland, George King, went to Western Australia and opened a school in 1842 for aboriginal children, a number of whom he baptized in St John's Church, Fremantle.[43] The whole story of the church's relations with the Australian aboriginals is a sorry and complex one, and including great injustices inflicted by white people and continuing programmes of reparation and reconciliation in the twentieth century.[44]

---

40 Acheson, *Church of Ireland*, pp 91–2. See also pp 184–7 for other Irish clergy who served in Australasia.   41 Stephen Judd and Kenneth Cable, *Sydney Anglicans* (Sydney, 1987), p. 80.   42 H.E. King, *Australia* (London, 1935), p. 39.   43 Ibid., p. 21.   44 For a balanced account see John Harris, 'Anglicanism and indigenous peoples' in Bruce Kaye (ed.), *Anglicanism in Australia: a history* (Melbourne, 2002).

Anglican expansion in the nineteenth century took place in many other parts of the world, including the Near and Middle East, North and Central Africa, Ceylon (Sri Lanka), Japan, South America, New Zealand and Oceania. In addition to SPG and CMS, other missionary societies were founded in the nineteenth century, such as the Colonial and Continental Church Society (now the Intercontinental Church Society), the South American Missionary Society (SAMS), the Missions to Seamen (now the Mission to Seafarers), the Universities Mission to Central Africa (now merged with SPG to form USPG) and the Mission to Lepers (interdenominational, now the Leprosy Mission). Ministers from the Church of Ireland served in all or most of these places and societies during the nineteenth century.

Large numbers of Irish clergy went abroad as chaplains to the armed forces. It would be impossible to identify all of them; chance references occur in many sources. For example, the maternal grandfather of C.S. Lewis, Thomas Hamilton, was a Royal Navy chaplain with the Baltic squadron during the Crimean war and also served in an Anglican church in Rome before returning to Ireland where he became first rector of St Mark's, Dundela, Belfast.[45]

Broadly speaking, the nineteenth century was a time when Europeans dominated most of the world, confident in what they considered their superior civilisation and convinced of the truth of their religion. At best, they were anxious to share their riches with the rest of the world. At worst, they thought other races inferior and assumed a right to rule over them. Missionaries and chaplains abroad, including Irish clergy, were, on the whole, high-minded, self-sacrificing and paternalistic in their attitudes. They could also be guilty of racism and arrogance.

THE TWENTIETH CENTURY

A good case could be made for regarding the end of the 1914–18 war as the start of the twentieth century. From then on the colonies of the European nations gradually achieved independence, more quickly after World War II. The churches planted by missionaries and settlers by degrees became self-governing, often before their countries became politically independent. At the same time, more and more nationals were ordained and became church leaders. Attitudes to other religions changed. Christians sought dialogue and points of contact with them rather than simply trying to refute them. Attempts were made to express the gospel through the art, music and thought forms of the countries where it was proclaimed instead of the western forms of the first missionaries. Sometimes foreign missionaries were more eager to introduce indigenous customs to the church than the national Christians themselves. Cooperation between different denominations was probably always greater on the mission field than in Europe and the younger churches were the pioneers of the twentieth-century ecumenical movement.

45 Roger Lancelyn Green and Walter Hooper, *C.S. Lewis* (London, 2002), p. xix.

Rather than survey the activities of Irish clergy abroad everywhere in the twentieth century, I shall concentrate on one man's work. Gerald Dickson (1882–1975) was a pioneer missionary in the diocese of Chota Nagpur, Bihar, India, from 1910 to 1939. There is no published account of his career, but typewritten copies of extracts from his diaries give a picture of mission work in a changing period.[46]

Gerald Dickson was born in Queenstown (Cobh), County Cork, but grew up in Fahan, County Donegal, where his father became rector. After schooling in Foyle College, Derry, and St Columba's College, Dublin, he graduated from Trinity College, Dublin. He was ordained and served two curacies in England, where he had gone to theological college. Having offered to serve under SPG, he received six month's medical training, which proved very useful later. He sailed from Tilbury Docks, London, and reached Calcutta in November 1910 after a twenty-five days' voyage via the Suez canal. During a short stay with the Oxford Mission to Calcutta, he witnessed the baptism of a Brahmin convert by total immersion, a practice he usually adopted for the many baptisms he celebrated in Chota Nagpur.

Dickson was able to travel by train to Ranchi, the diocesan centre of Chota Nagpur. The bishop, Foss Westcott, assigned him to the Singhbhum district in the south of the diocese and introduced him to the area by going with him, another missionary and servants on an extended camping tour, travelling on foot and by bicycle and having to ford several rivers. Dickson was stationed first at Chakradharpur, on the Bengal and Nagpur Railway, where he learnt Hindi, the most widely spoken language in north India. Manoharpur, a village on the railway near the confluence of the Koel and Koina rivers, was chosen as a base from which he would work as district missionary. By June 1914 he had had a school and bungalow built and made Manoharpur his permanent residence. Like many an enthusiastic young missionary eager to become fully part of the local community, he at first had his main meal each day with the masters and boys, only to go down with dysentery and have to spend six weeks in the railway hospital.

The people of Manoharpur district mostly belong to the Munda tribe, whose ancestral religion is animism and language Mundari. Dickson buckled down to learn it and confides to his diary, 'I keep on at my Mundari trying to memorise (say) thirty words a day. But I note that my attempts to speak are usually greeted with laughter'. This has probably been the experience of most people trying to learn a new language in its native place.

The Great War broke out the year Dickson began to live in Manoharpur, which led to the German Lutheran missionaries being interned. Bishop Westcott undertook the care of the Lutheran church during the war and returned it intact afterwards. The Lutheran parishes were mostly in the charge of Indian pastors; Anglican missionaries had responsibility for oversight of schools and grants. Dickson added Lutheran stations to the places he visited.

---

46 A copy entitled 'Foundation stones in Manoharpur' is in RCBL.

After the war, the development of Manoharpur proceeded. The boys' school expanded and from time to time pupils would ask for baptism. Medical work and a girls' school were started by two Anglican nuns of the St Denys sisters, who already had a house at Itki in the diocese. A large church in Manoharpur, named after St Augustine of Hippo, was consecrated by Westcott, who had left the diocese to become metropolitan. It must have been an impressive ceremony with procession, candles and incense, and the metropolitan in cope and mitre. Dickson took the lead in introducing ceremonial to the diocese, so as to proclaim the gospel by appeal to all the senses and to give an active role in worship to as many people as possible.

Dickson spent much of his time on camping tours, usually accompanied by Indian padres and catechists and sometimes by the diocesan bishop. The camping tours were to care for and encourage the village congregations and to preach the gospel to all. This was done with the help of magic lantern slides. Dickson wrote, 'I never tire of showing Hole's pictures of the life of Christ on the lantern.' Large numbers became Christian. That period was a time of mass movements towards Christianity, chiefly among the tribal and scheduled (lower) caste peoples of India, and a commission on mass movements visited Manoharpur district in 1931. Dickson is realistic enough to note cases of lapsed Christians, even whole villages, due to poor shepherding, alcohol or other causes.

The diary has many descriptions of river baptisms. One in 1927 captures the scene well. The bishop at the time was Kenneth Kennedy, a founder member of the Dublin University Mission to Chota Nagpur who later moved to the southern, Mundari-speaking, areas of the diocese.

> The next day we got to Urming at 10.00. There 104 candidates for baptism had arrived from the villages of Kareda and Urming. 100 were passed as ready for their baptism. This took place in the river, Padre Dayal and I administering the rite … It was touching to see the way in which the little tots of four and five years old came fearlessly into the water to be baptised. Not soon will the people forget the sermon which the Bishop preached after the baptism under a tree, in his beloved Mundari.

Touring in Manoharpur district meant long journeys by foot or bicycle, with unbridged rivers to cross. If the river was shallow enough it could be forded. Otherwise a dugout boat called a *donga* was used. When the *donga* was overcrowded passengers had to stand up, which made it top-heavy, sometimes leading to tragedy. An English missionary, Roy Glossop, in the neighbouring Munda district of Kamdara, was drowned when a *donga* capsized, as were also his bearer's young wife and her niece, whom he had tried to save. Dickson preached in Mundari at the memorial service.

When sickness was prevalent, especially before the nuns started their medical work, Dickson went round the villages with medicines. He records dosing forty-five people in one heathen village. He commented, 'it sometimes strikes me that we approach (outwardly) to our Lord's ministry in this, rather than in any other way'.

Not all his patients were seriously ill. One Sunday evening a man came to him with a cut eye and covered in blood. The man had been to church that morning and was part of a brawl in the village afterwards. Dickson wryly noted, 'I had preached about living in "love" in the morning; so much for sermons!' He often had reason to exercise his sense of humour and proportion. In India church doors and windows are kept wide open because of the heat and all sorts of creatures can come in. One day when Dickson was preaching, a large Hanuman monkey came into church. 'Of course I lost the attention of the congregation and I hastened to finish my sermon. The Hanuman came right up to the chancel steps, and seemed to lift up his hand in blessing when I did.'

Much of Gerald Dickson's career in India could be paralleled by the experience of nineteenth-century missionaries in many parts of the world. But there are also indications of new attitudes and the growth of Indian responsibility in the church. At a district council meeting in 1926, he noted that lay members realised they had real voting power and sometimes outvoted his opinion. India was still under British rule when he left in 1939 but the Anglican church there had become a self-governing province of the Anglican Communion as the Church of India, Burma and Ceylon. When Kennedy resigned as bishop in 1936, a new bishop was chosen according to the constitution of the independent church. (Dickson refused to be nominated as a candidate, though he had charge of the diocese as commissary during the interregnum.) Compared with the nineteenth century, his diary shows more friendly relations with Lutherans and Roman Catholics. Dickson came to appreciate some of the good elements in Hinduism and other religions. He could describe Diwali as the 'prettiest and least harmful of all the Hindu feasts', and he walked through Manoharpur with his schoolboys to see the multitudes of lights.

After he left India Gerald Dickson got married and became rector of Fahan where he had grown up and where his father had been rector. He retired at the age of 82 in 1965. Since the parish was united with others he was allowed to stay on in Fahan rectory. He died in 1975.[47]

In the twentieth century the Church of Ireland continued to supply ministers to the Anglican churches in English-speaking countries such as the U.S.A., Canada and Australia, and also as chaplains to the armed forces. J. Patterson Smyth, vicar of St Ann's, Dublin, a well-known author in his time, was one of the many Irish priests who went to Canada, where he became rector of St George's, Montreal. Thomas C. Hammond went to Australia after his time as superintendent of the Irish Church Missions. He was principal of Moore College, Sydney, now and for

---

47 I am indebted to Gerald Dickson's son, Professor David Dickson, for details of his father's life before and after his time in India.

a long time a centre of conservative evangelical scholarship.[48] Herbert O'Driscoll, author and lecturer, was ordained for the curacy of Monkstown, Dublin diocese, spent most of his ministry in Canada and was also head of the College of Preachers in the United States.

The influence and number of foreign missionaries in most of the younger churches of the Anglican Communion probably reached a peak in the years just before the 1914–18 war. However, large numbers of missionaries, including Irish clergy, continued to work in several countries up to the middle decades of the twentieth century. This was particularly true of East Africa. Walter H. Good from Cork was a priest and teacher in Mombasa, 1921–5, and three of his four children became missionaries. His son, Stanley, also worked in Kenya, chiefly in theological college teaching, and lived through the dangerous times of the Mau-Mau rising in the 1950s. He helped establish an East African Diploma in Theology with colleges in Uganda, Tanganyika (now Tanzania) and the Sudan as well as well as Kenya. Alan Lindsay from County Antrim was also a theological teacher, in Burundi. His wife Catherine, the daughter of Walter Good, was a medical doctor.[49]

Some conservative members thought CMS was becoming too liberal regarding the Bible, so they founded a new society in 1922, the Bible Churchmen's Missionary Society (BCMS, later called Crosslinks). BCMS and Crosslinks have widespread support in Ireland, both in funds and personnel. A number of Irish clergy have served with BCMS/Crosslinks in parts of Africa, South America and other countries. Brian Herd went as a missionary to Uganda in 1961 and was bishop of Karamoja for one year (1976–7) during the cruel regime of Idi Amin. All twenty-nine dioceses of Uganda now have African nationals as bishops.

From the 1920s onwards more and more native clergy were ordained in the younger Anglican churches and in time became church leaders. Expatriate missionaries continued to work alongside their indigenous fellow-workers and in a number of places still do. This happened when Anglican churches became self-governing and when (usually later) their countries became politically independent. Ideally, though often not in practice, the withdrawal of foreign missionaries took place 'sideways' rather than 'upwards'. That is, it was not appropriate that the top posts in the church should be retained by foreigners till the end. Rather, the ideal was that foreign missionaries would remain at all levels in decreasing numbers, often serving under nationals. The Irish CMS missionary, Anthony Blacker Elliott, was consecrated assistant bishop to the first Indian to become an Anglican bishop, Azariah of Dornakal.[50] Specialised posts like those of theological college teachers were often held by westerners. The Irish theologian, Anthony Hanson, was a lecturer in Bangalore Theological College in India between 1947 and 1959. In an

---

48 Hammond's career is described in Warren Nelson, *T.C. Hammond: Irish Christian, his life and legacy in Ireland and Australia* (Edinburgh, 1994). 49 Hodgins, *Sister Island*, pp 53–4. 50 Ibid., p. 102.

autonomous Anglican church, nationals and expatriates are both eligible for appointment to all posts. When the bishop of Delhi, Arabindo Nath Mukerjee, was appointed metropolitan in 1950, his successor was Fred Willis, then head of the Chota Nagpur Mission, 'the last of several noteworthy Irish bishops in the C.I.P.B.C. [Church of India, Pakistan, Burma and Ceylon]'.[51]

Sometimes political changes entailed a sudden exodus of foreign missionaries. The best-known example is the communist take-over of China in 1949. All members of the Fukien Mission had to leave China. Many of them served in neighbouring and more distant countries, and the name of the mission was changed to 'the Dublin University Far Eastern Mission (DUFEM)'. It supported missionaries in Singapore, Malaysia, Japan, India and Uganda. In Japan in 1940 the Nippon Sei Ko Kwai (Japan Holy Catholic Church, the name of the Anglican church there) decided it was better that all foreign missionaries should leave. Gordon Walsh, born in Fahan, County Donegal, was bishop of Hokkaido and commented that independence for the Japanese church 'had happened too suddenly and in too aggressive a manner'.[52] After the 1939–45 war missionaries returned, including some from Ireland, but from then on all the bishops of the Nippon Sei Ko Kwai were Japanese.

The change in India was much more gradual, but in 1966 the Indian government ruled that all non-Indians in paid work required a residence permit, renewable annually. Foreign missionaries already in India were generally allowed to stay, but no new missionaries were given entry permits unless it could be proved that there was no qualified Indian available for their work. There are very few expatriates now serving in the Indian church. The work formerly done by the Dublin University Mission to Chota Nagpur, for example, is now entirely in the hands of Indians.

The wheel has turned full circle from the missions of the early Irish monks in continental Europe to the Church of Ireland today. Ministers of the Church of Ireland still go to serve in other countries. CMSI, for instance, at present supports John McCammon in Kenya and Keith Scott in Zambia. USPG missionary Noel Scott has been working in Zimbabwe for the past thirty-six years and was arrested for organising a prayer vigil relating to justice issues in 2002. Now retired but active and living in Zimbabwe, he is still subject to harassment, with others, for his stand on human rights.[53] But significant of the changing mission scene is the presence of Anglican priests from other countries now working in the Church of Ireland. Jerome Munyangaju from Tanzania is rector of Killyleagh, Down diocese. François-Xavier Murenzi from Rwanda was ordained in Ireland and served as bishop's curate of Athy, Glendalough diocese, for four months until his tragic death as a result of a car crash. Ministers from countries such as the USA, Canada and New Zealand hold posts in the Church of Ireland. The Porvoo Agreement

51 Gibbs, *Anglican Church in Ireland*, p. 391.   52 Hodgins, *Sister Island*, p. 153.   53 *Church of Ireland Gazette*, 26 March 2004, p. 16.

of 1992, which established full communion with the Nordic and Baltic Lutheran churches, enables inter-change of clergy. A Lutheran priest from Sweden, Mari-anne Witting, was introduced as bishop's curate of the Donagh Group and Ematris Group of parishes in Clogher diocese on 11 December, 2003. In a post-Christen-dom world, the church everywhere is in a missionary situation (even if this is not always recognised). To use the word 'missionary' solely for one who goes to minis-ter in a distant, non-Christian land is no longer appropriate. The Church Mission-ary Society is now called the Church Mission Society, keeping the same initials, and its workers are known as mission partners. All mission societies see themselves as assisting the world church in its world mission. In this task we may expect the Church of Ireland to continue sending its priests to other countries, and increas-ingly to receive personnel from other countries to assist in its mission in Ireland.

Index